THE WORKING ALLIANCE

Recent titles in the

Wiley Series on Personality Processes

Irving B. Weiner, *Editor*
University of South Florida

The Working Alliance

Theory, Research, and Practice

Edited by

Adam O. Horvath

Leslie S. Greenberg

A WILEY-INTERSCIENCE PUBLICATION

JOHN WILEY & SONS, INC.

New York • Chichester • Brisbane • Toronto • Singapore

Library of Congress Cataloging in Publication Data:

The Working alliance : theory, research, and practice / edited by Adam
  O. Horvath, Leslie S. Greenberg.
     p.   cm. — (Wiley series on personality processes)
  Includes bibliographical references and index.
  ISBN 0-471-54640-2 (alk. paper)
  1. Therapeutic alliance. I. Horvath, Adam O., 1941-
II. Greenberg, Leslie S. III. Series.
  [DNLM: 1. Psychotherapy—methods. 2. Research—methods. WM 420
W9258 1994]
  RC489.T66W65   1994
  616.89'14—dc20
                                       93-21150

Printed in the United States of America

10 9 8 7 6 5 4 3 2 1

To the memory of Edward Bordin: His lifelong pursuit of a deeper understanding of the causes and remedies for human suffering has been an inspiration.

Contributors

Jon G. Allen, PhD
Staff Psychologist
The Menninger Clinic
Topeka, Kansas

Edward S. Bordin, PhD
Emeritus Professor of Psychology
(deceased)
University of Michigan
Ann Arbor, Michigan

Donald B. Colson, PhD
Director of Psychology
C.F. Menninger Memorial Hospital
The Menninger Clinic
Topeka, Kansas

Lolayfaye Coyne, PhD
Director, Statistical Laboratory
Research Department
The Menninger Clinic
Topeka, Kansas

Siebolt H. Frieswyk, PhD
Director, Psychotherapy Training
Karl Menninger School of
Psychiatry
The Menninger Clinic
Topeka, Kansas

Glen O. Gabbard, MD
Vice-President, Adult Services
The Menninger Clinic, and
Director, C.F. Menninger Memorial
Hospital
Topeka, Kansas

Louise Gaston, PhD
Assistant Professor
Department of Psychiatry
McGill University
Montreal, Quebec, Canada

Marvin R. Goldfried, PhD
Professor of Psychology
State University of New York at
Stony Brook
Stony Brook, New York

Leslie S. Greenberg, PhD
Professor of Psychology
York University
North York, Ontario, Canada

William P. Henry, PhD
Assistant Professor of Psychology
University of Utah
Salt Lake City, Utah

Adam O. Horvath, EdD
Associate Professor
Counselling Psychology Program
Simon Fraser University
Burnaby, B.C., Canada

Leonard Horwitz, PhD
Training and Supervising Analyst
Topeka Institute for Psychoanalysis
The Menninger Clinic
Topeka, Kansas

Lester Luborsky, PhD
Professor of Psychology in Psychiatry
University of Pennsylvania
Philadelphia, Pennsylvania

Charles R. Marmar, MD
Associate Professor of Clinical
    Psychiatry
University of California, San
    Francisco
San Francisco, California

J. Christopher Muran, PhD
Program Director, Brief
    Psychotherapy Research Program
Beth Israel Medical Center
New York, New York

Gavin E. Newsom, MSW
Director of Social Work
The Menninger Clinic
Topeka, Kansas

William M. Pinsof, PhD
President
The Family Institute
Professor
School of Education and Social
    Policy
Northwestern University
Evanston, Illinois

Patrick J. Raue, MA
Doctoral Candidate in Psychology
State University of New York at
    Stony Brook
Stony Brook, New York

Jeremy D. Safran, PhD
Professor and Director, Clinical
    Psychology
Graduate Faculty of Political and
    Social Science
The New School for Social
    Research
New York, New York

Lisa Wallner Samstag, MA
Program Coordinator, Brief
    Psychotherapy Research Program
Beth Israel Medical Center
New York, New York

Hans H. Strupp, PhD
Professor of Psychology
Vanderbilt University
Nashville, Tennessee

J. C. Watson, PhD
Assistant Professor of Psychology
University of Windsor
Windsor, Ontario, Canada

Series Preface

This series of books is addressed to behavioral scientists interested in the nature of human personality. Its scope should prove pertinent to personality theorists and researchers as well as to clinicians concerned with applying an understanding of personality processes to the amelioration of emotional difficulties in living. To this end, the series provides a scholarly integration of theoretical formulations, empirical data, and practical recommendations.

Six major aspects of studying and learning about human personality can be designated: personality theory, personality structure and dynamics, personality development, personality assessment, personality change, and personality adjustment. In exploring these aspects of personality, the books in the series discuss a number of distinct but related subject areas: the nature and implications of various theories of personality; personality characteristics that account for consistencies and variations in human behavior; the emergence of personality processes in children and adolescents; the use of interviewing and testing procedures to evaluate individual differences in personality; efforts to modify personality styles through psychotherapy, counseling, behavior therapy, and other methods of influence; and patterns of abnormal personality functioning that impair individual competence.

IRVING B. WEINER

University of South Florida
Tampa, Florida

Contents

Introduction

ADAM O. HORVATH and LESLIE S. GREENBERG

Psychotherapy research has now entered its fifth active decade. In general, the evidence has supported the value of psychotherapy: Patients who are treated show significantly more improvements than those in control conditions. It also seems evident that, with a few exceptions, different therapies produce comparable therapeutic gains (Luborsky, Singer, & Luborsky, 1975; Smith & Glass, 1977; Stiles, Shapiro, & Elliot, 1986). These research results, however, also suggest that different therapies produce comparable outcomes despite differences in premises, different assumptions about the etiology of human dysfunction, and different techniques. These findings raise fundamental questions about which elements of therapy are responsible for positive change. With the realization that change may be achieved through such apparently diverse treatments, attention has shifted to the relationship between client and therapist, a common factor to all forms of treatment.

The alliance was the first concept put forward to capture the special role of the relationship between healer and client (Freud, 1913). The earliest versions of this model, which focused on positive transference and predicted that in a successful alliance clients would identify the therapist with benevolent figures in their past, have been gradually expanded and revised over the years within the psychodynamic framework (Greenson, 1965; Zetzel, 1956). Approximately 20 years ago, the construct was further reworked in light of the possibility that the alliance was a common relationship variable across *all forms of therapy* (Bordin, 1975; Luborsky, 1976).

At the core of the current formulation of the alliance is the notion of *collaboration.* The concept focuses on the importance of the client and therapist forming a partnership against the common foe of the client's debilitating pain. This collaborative relationship not only provides the client with a safe environment to explore the self, but the process of developing this kind of relationship may also capture the client's key relational issues, past and present. Thus, through development and maintenance of the alliance, the therapist can simultaneously attend to the content of the client's relational difficulties and foster a process conducive to client change. A

1

unique feature of the alliance concept is that it integrates the relational and technical aspects of treatment into an overarching model of the therapeutic working alliance. From the perspective of the client's change process, it seems unlikely that there are actually two distinct mechanisms (a technique element and a relationship component); it is more probable that these factors are interdependent and catalytic to each other. The emphasis on these two features—the *interactive* nature of the relationship and the *integration* of the technical and relational aspects—sets the alliance apart from other relationship constructs.

Over the past 20 years, the alliance has been one of the key relationship concepts investigated by researchers. Current findings suggest that the quality of the working alliance in the initial stages of treatment is predictive of a significant proportion of the final outcome variance. The magnitude of this relation was estimated by Horvath and Symonds (1991): A meta-analysis of the results of 24 studies published between 1975 and 1991 yielded an average effect size of $r = .26$. Some conservative assumptions used in this analysis make it possible that the true magnitude of this relation is somewhat greater; the link between early alliance and therapy impact might be as high as .32 (see Chapter 11).

At first glance, the absolute magnitude of this value may not seem large. However, when the impact of the alliance is compared with other relationship factors whose relation to outcome has been estimated, the alliance appears to be a robust variable (Garfield & Bergin, 1986; Mitchell, Bozart, & Krauft, 1977). Also, in evaluating the true significance of the alliance, we need to take into account that its development is impacted by pretherapy variables. For example, several authors in this volume report that both client and therapist factors influence the formation of alliance. It is also likely that these pretherapy variables, to some degree, are directly responsible for the determination of the outcome. Moreover, as noted previously, the alliance is not construed as a factor that is curative in and of itself, but rather as an interactive element that is synergetic with the therapeutic tasks used. Thus it is unrealistic to expect a dramatic effect size when the alliance and outcome relation is measured independent of other variables. We believe that ultimately a more accurate estimate of the true significance of alliance in therapy will emerge as more sophisticated research designs estimate the unique weight associated with pretherapy, alliance, and specific technical factors simultaneously. In this light, it appears that the alliance is currently the best model of the in-therapy *pantheoretical process variable.*

The evidence of the strong link between alliance and outcome appears to come mostly from measures taken early in treatment. This appeals to common sense; failure to engage with the therapist, inability to agree on what needs to be done, or lack of development of trust within the first three sessions will probably lead to disengagement from therapy. It seems likely that the client approaches the initial sessions with hope, expectation of speedy relief, and some anxiety. If the beginning of a collaborative relationship is not developed expeditiously, hope may turn to pessimism. If the therapist seems to ignore the client's expectations of immediate relief from discomfort rather than realistically renegotiating them, the client's anxiety will be heightened. The failure to develop a collaborative stance may also signal that the client has externalized the locus of change and expects it to originate from the environment or from the therapist rather than from within. This unrealistic expectation implies that the therapist and the client have not established a workable framework for therapy, and poor outcome is likely.

Although positive alliance development does not have to take place *immediately* at the commencement of therapy, it appears that the development of a "good enough" alliance is necessary before the therapeutic work can succeed. It seems reasonable to think of alliance development in the first phase of therapy as a series of windows of opportunity, decreasing in size with each session. The foundation for collaborative work entails adjustments in both the client's and therapist's procedural expectations and goals. The longer the participants find themselves apart on these issues, the more difficult it becomes to develop a collaborative framework. Thus, by the third to fifth session, the quality of the alliance is becoming increasingly reflective of the potential of future success.

Empirical investigation of the later stages of the alliance have revealed interesting and complex patterns of development, decay, and renewal. Once workable levels of alliance have been developed, the relationship component of the therapeutic journey may become a roller coaster. The in-therapy relationship may mirror the relational issues of the client (and possibly the therapist), and the task of resolving the alliance issues can become isomorphic with the client's struggle to change pathogenic habits of thinking and feeling. The therapist's ability to meet these challenges directly and to move with the client's experiences rather than to redirect or deflect them appears to influence the quality of the therapy process and outcome.

We believe that this midstage of the alliance is the most challenging area in need of both conceptual and clinical clarification. Whereas Bordin (see Chapter 1) and a number of other researchers (e.g., Luborsky, Chapter 2; Pinsof, Chapter 8; Safran, Chapter 9) propose that the alliance rupture and repair cycle captures the core of the client's difficulties making the work on the alliance central to the work of therapy itself, others (e.g., Raue & Goldfried, Chapter 6; Watson & Greenberg, Chapter 7) do not feel that the rupture and repair cycles necessarily recapitulate the client's core issues. At a more basic level, these differences reflect the different theoretical emphases on the role of past relational paradigms in the therapy process. The cognitive-behavioral and experiential theorists emphasize the here-and-now relationship between the client and therapist, whereas others are more impressed with the influence of past relational experiences on subsequent encounters and give greater weight to the potentially recursive nature of the client's relationship patterns. Also, some ruptures may relate to and recapitulate past issues, and other misalignments or misunderstandings may relate specifically to here-and-now issues. Although both positions imply that tears in the alliance need the therapist's urgent attention, different technical strategies would be indicated depending on what these alliance crises actually represent. Current research cannot conclusively resolve these questions. More work is needed to examine alliance processes in midtherapy and discover the relation of the content of ruptures to both the client's early object relations and current interpersonal patterns.

Relatively little work has been done on the alliance in the last stages of therapy. Part of the reason for this may be the lack of interest in predictor variables near termination. Nonetheless, it seems quite possible that the quality of the relationship at this point may have important implications for the long-term effectiveness of the therapy. It seems likely that, for lasting stability of gains, the responsibility for the accomplishments in therapy needs to be at least partly "owned" by the client. If the attribution for change is vested in the therapist, the lack of belief in self-efficacy makes relapse more likely. On the other hand, in situations where the client who feels that "I had to do it all by myself" the patient may still be in a fragile position. A good alliance at termination may reflect a realistic view not only of the relationship but also the therapy process itself. Investigation of alliance during its more mature state will, however, need to take into account the possibility of qualitative differences in the nature of the positive alliance over time. During this phase of therapy, the investigator will be likely dealing with a truncated data set; clients who did not develop at least an adequate alliance with their therapist have probably dropped out already. The differences among the remaining clients are likely more subtle than those measured earlier. It is also possible that, over time, the alliance becomes more treatment specific; that is, some aspects of the alliance may be more critical for one form of therapy than another.[1] According to this hypothesis, we may need to explore specific aspects of the mature alliance critical for the type of treatment, rather than looking at the overall alliance picture to determine quality of long-term outcome.

To date, the research results have corroborated the importance of the alliance in the early stages of therapy. It appears that the concept of the alliance as a pantheoretical variable is a useful model of some important features of successful therapy and may, in the long term, assist us in better understanding the process of client change. Notwithstanding these encouraging results, a number of overarching concerns will need to be addressed. We will summarize these under three headings: (a) Measurement, (b) Prediction of Change, and (c) Alliance as a Target of Clinical Intervention.

---

[1] See Chapter 5 for a more extensive discussion of this issue.

MEASUREMENT

We have some concerns with the current heterogeneity of alliance measures. Although there is evidence of a broad consensus on "what the alliance is about," it is yet unclear how the different measures and the different perspectives of therapist, client, and observers relate to each other. We should take warning from the lessons taught to us by the research on empathy. Hindsight shows that the value of this corpus of work has been undermined by the failure of the measures used to converge on the same definition and the consequent lack of solid evidence of construct validity. The research results for the alliance indicate that the correlations between measures taken from the same perspective (i.e., clients, or therapist or observers) are only adequate (Bachelor, 1992; Safran & Wallner, 1991), and correlations between measurements taken from different perspectives, even with the same measure, are modest. Although the outcome variances predicted by measures taken from the same perspective are similar, we have no assurance that each measure assesses the *same* parts of the outcome. The therapists' and observers' measures are particularly in need of further refinement. The correlation of therapists' alliance scores with clients' measures (using the same instrument) range from $r = .0$ to $r = .40$; this value is too low. Also, compared with the client-based measures, therapists' estimate of the alliance is only distally related to outcome. This appears to be the case whether the outcome is evaluated from the client's, observer's, or therapist's perspective. There may be two sources of this problem. One is that the alliance measures currently in use are parallel forms derived from client scales. The epistomological assumption underlying such "scale translation" may be invalid. Indeed, it is quite conceivable that a therapist, viewing the relationship through the lens of a particular theoretical framework, may need to be asked substantially different questions than the client. Alternatively, therapists' initial expectation of the client's ability to trust, form positive personal attachments, and to collaborate may be unrealistic. In contrast, the clients, who can anchor their assessment on prior experience (i.e., "this is a *higher* level of collaboration, trust, liking etc. than I have been able to develop before"), can form more accurate comparative judgments.

The measurement of the alliance from the observers' perspective poses another set of challenges. The argument favoring this approach to assessment are twofold: Of all the measurement perspectives, the observer's data are the only one that permits replication: Using video- or audiotapes, the ratings can be repeated yielding data of greater reliability. The other putative advantage of obtaining raters' judgment is the assumption that this method yields information that is more objective, uncontaminated by the intersubjectivity of the therapist's and the client's report. In our view, only the first of these arguments can be supported; on closer examination, the presumed greater consensual reliability or objectivity of the rated as opposed to the self-reported data becomes, in fact, a strong potential disadvantage. The observer is forced to infer, on the basis of limited data (since the segments used for observation are subsets of the total material available to the participants), the participants' feelings, thoughts, and often motives. This is a complex inferential process, likely biased by the rater's theory. Before we can harness the potential advantage of the observer's perspective, we need more systematic investigation of the relation between observer's and participant's alliance data, and a careful delineation of specific aspects of the alliance that can be accurately captured by an observer.

The final measurement issue has to do with a need to define more precisely the time window through which we wish to observe the alliance. Most participant report measures are somewhat vague as to the time that the alliance experience is "summed over." Three practical time windows seem to be available, each likely revealing different kinds of information. The broadest perspective involves the time span the therapist and the client have spent together up to the time of measurement. Most of the self-report data reported in the literature is probably of this sort. The information obtained is quite useful, for example, in predicting outcome; however, alliance emerges as a static phenomenon using this approach. The next alternative is to use the individual session as the time window. This kind of data has also been collected and has yielded interesting sequential information not revealed by the open-ended approach. However, unless these measures are collected frequently and are treated as sequential data, there is a strong danger that the more recent ratings will be contaminated by previous experiences.

Last, there is a possibility of tracking the moment-to-moment therapy events that impact the development of the alliance. Although this approach is labor intensive, it permits the opening of the "black box" of the client's experiential world and the development of microtheories of alliance-building events. Such a bottom-up approach to understanding the alliance could lead to clinically important discoveries.

PREDICTION OF CHANGE

One of the strengths of the alliance research is the consistent finding that a good alliance is related to positive therapy outcome. This finding is uniform across a variety of treatment populations, kinds of therapies, and different perspectives on the alliance (Horvath & Symonds, 1991). Although many different types of outcome were successfully predicted, alliance may be more strongly associated with certain types of outcomes than others; we find this prospect neither a surprise nor a source of distress. It makes a great deal of conceptual sense that specific aspects of the therapy process are more directly linked to some unique outcomes than others. The identification of affinities between certain kinds of alliances and specific therapy results are potentially important areas of research.

The evidence is accumulating that alliance can be discriminated from early treatment gains and is predictive of outcome over and beyond these increments of progress (Horvath & Luborsky, 1993). These findings appear to be quite important since this question has been a source of controversy between those who saw the relationship as an important and real therapeutic factor (e.g., Frank, 1961) and those who believed it was merely an epiphenomenon. It is also noteworthy that the alliance/outcome relationship is not significantly related to length of treatment. This finding seems to offer further assurance that the variable is not just the first transient blush of success, but more likely a significant and important process factor.

ALLIANCE AS A TARGET OF INTERVENTION

The investigation of therapist activities that are directly responsible for the building or repair of the alliance has only emerged in the past 5 years. The most interesting research findings indicate that a here-and-now focus on the therapist/client relationship, affiliative and at the same time nondominant therapist behavior, and thematically focused activity, as well as interpretations dealing with the client's current wishes, will have a positive impact on the alliance. It seems, however, that all the research on the impact of therapist activities on the alliance have investigated the status of the alliance once it has been developed (midphase alliance); less is known about the transactions that enhance the initial buildup of the alliance (sessions 1 through 3).

Information on what does *not* influence the quality of the alliance is also being documented. It seems that more experienced therapists are not necessarily more successful in developing a good alliance, but they are more accurate in assessing the status of the relationship. Also, neither frequency nor accuracy of interpretations impacts the level of the alliance directly.

The overall picture supports the hypothesis that the relevance of the therapist activity (or the client's awareness of relevance) may be more obviously related to its impact on the alliance quality than specific behaviors per se. It also seems possible that research on the alliance-promoting factors within specific theoretical contexts might lead to the identification of specific therapist behaviors linked to good alliance.

For this book, we have asked a number of leading researchers to provide an up-to-date review of their theoretical positions, research results, and their views on the alliance in clinical practice. The first chapter by the late Edward Bordin outlines the basic aspects of the alliance model and offers guidelines for the course of future research. The next four chapters review the past and current work of the major alliance research groups involved in studying the alliance (Luborsky and his co-workers at the University of Pennsylvania; Hans Strupp and William Henry's team at Vanderbilt University; the group working on the California alliance scales—Louise

Gaston at McGill University and Charles Marmar based at the Langley Porter Institute; and Adam Horvath's group from Simon Fraser University in Vancouver). Each of these centers has developed a unique method of assessing the alliance and has generated considerable research data over the past 15 years. For these chapters, we asked the authors to address four major issues: (a) characteristics of the alliance, (b) measurement concerns, (c) the relationship of alliance to outcome, and (d) how to influence the quality of the alliance in clinical practice.

Chapters 6 through 8 are more theoretically based: the cognitive position is reviewed by Patrick Raue and Marvin Goldfried, the experiential perspective is explored by Jeanne Watson and Leslie Greenberg, and the family systemic view is presented by William Pinsof. In each chapter, research results illustrate the theoretical propositions.

Chapters 9 and 10 present the work of researchers who have been exploring the alliance process; they offer a more microscopic view of the relationship. The focus in these chapters is the intensive moment-to-moment exploration of therapist–client transactions impacting the alliance. Dr. Frieswyk et al. report on the work done at the Menninger Clinic in Topeka. They provide a detailed analysis of the alliance in psychoanalytic therapy. Members of Jeremy Safran's team, situated in New York, have been studying the progress of the alliance in the middle phase of therapy; this chapter focuses on the breaks (ruptures) and reestablishment of positive alliance.

The last chapter summarizes the state of knowledge with respect to the alliance: It offers a review of the research on alliance, discusses the strength of the evidence in relation to various theoretical propositions, possible future research agendas, and clinical issues.

REFERENCES

Bachelor, A. (1992, June). *Variability of Dimensions of the therapeutic alliance and alliance predictors of improvement.* Paper presented at the annual meeting of the Society for Psychotherapy Research, Berkeley, CA.

Bordin, E. S. (1975, August). *The working alliance: Basis for a general theory of psychotherapy.* Paper presented at the annual meeting of the Washington, DC.

Frank, J. D. (1961). *Persuasion and healing.* Baltimore, MD: Johns Hopkins Press.

Freud, S. (1913). On the beginning of treatment: Further recommendations on the technique of psychoanalysis. In J. Strachey (Eds.), *Standard edition of the complete psychological works of Sigmund Freud* (pp. 122–144). London, England: Hogarth Press.

Garfield, S. L., & Bergin, A. E. (Eds.). (1986). *Handbook of psychotherapy and behavior change* (3rd ed.). New York: Wiley.

Greenson, R. R. (1965). The working alliance and the transference neuroses. *Psychoanalysis Quarterly, 34,* 155–181.

Horvath, A. O., & Symonds, B. D. (1991). Relation between working alliance and outcome in psychotherapy: A meta-analysis. *Journal of Counseling Psychology, 38,* 139–149.

Luborsky, L. (1976). Helping alliances in psychotherapy. In J. L. Cleghhorn (Eds.), *Successful psychotherapy* (pp. 92–116). New York: Brunner/Mazel.

Luborsky, L., Singer, B., & Luborsky, L. (1975). Comparative studies of psychotherapies; "Is it true that everybody has won and all must have prizes?" *Archives of General Psychiatry, 32,* 995–1008.

Mitchell, K. M., Bozart, J. D., & Krauft, C. C. (1977). Reappraisal of the therapeutic effectiveness of accurate empathy, non-possessive warmth, and genuineness. In A. S. Gurman & A. M. Razin (Eds.), *Effective psychotherapy.* New York: Pergamon Press.

Safran, J. D., & Wallner, L. K. (1991). The relative predictive validity of two therapeutic alliance measures in cognitive therapy. *Psychological Assessment: A Journal of Consulting and Clinical Psychology, 3,* 188–195.

Smith, M. L., & Glass, G. V. (1977). Meta-analysis of psychotherapy outcome studies. *American Psychologist, 32,* 752–760.

Stiles, W. B., Shapiro, D., & Elliot, R. (1986). Are all psychotherapies equivalent? *American Psychologist, 41,* 165–180.

Zetzel, E. R. (1956). Current concepts of transference. *International Journal of Psychoanalysis, 37,* 369–376.

PART ONE

Conceptual and Research Perspectives

CHAPTER 1

Theory and Research on the Therapeutic Working Alliance: New Directions*

EDWARD S. BORDIN

At this time, a decade and a half after I first offered a formulation about the therapeutic working alliance that was partially responsible for stimulating a stream of research and found connection with many other visions regarding psychotherapy, it seems appropriate to take new sightings for the future. I will leave to others the detailed retrieval and assessment of what has been accomplished and its limits.

My efforts will be aimed in three directions:

1. Review the theory, clarify ambiguities, and offer additions.
2. Illuminate clinical applications of the theory.
3. Further explicate the function of therapeutic tasks and identify a "basic science" approach to research in psychotherapy.

In an earlier paper (Bordin, 1979), I proposed a formulation of the working alliance between the client seeking change and the therapist offering to act as a change agent that incorporated a mutual understanding and agreement about change goals and the necessary tasks to move toward these goals along with the establishment of bonds to maintain the partners' work. Further, I suggested that the power to achieve change was in good part a function of the strength of that alliance. Later (1980), I added that the interaction of therapeutic tasks with the problematic behaviors that brought the client to therapy would stimulate strains in the working partnership, I promised that the resolution of these strains would be an important key to change.

In pursuing the three directions of this chapter, I will discuss the following major topics: (a) an explication of both the process and therapeutic impact of selecting goals in collaboration with the client (I believe this process can result in increased client capacity to collaborate and even to

*I am greatly indebted to Adam Horvath for many suggestions for improved phrasing and for raising substantive questions that freed me to clear up ambiguities.

cope independently); (b) the differentiation between goals and tasks; (c) the relationship (and differences) between bond(ing) and transference (both are aspects of the capacity for object relations, but bonds sustain the alliance whereas transference ultimately strains it); (d) elaboration on how dealing with strains or ruptures contributes to the process of change; (e) a proposal for task-oriented research of the change process that, by combining experimental and clinical studies, will provide a knowledge base to better understand the factors underlying the outcome of psychotherapy.

THEORY REVISITED

There are many and varied formulations of therapeutic working alliance theory, partly because it is founded on earlier psychoanalytic terminology and partly because some aspects of the theory were concurrently developed as part of other psychotherapeutic approaches. Although my specific for-mulation of the theory built directly from Greenson's (1967) concepts of the real relationship and the alliance, it also reflects both Otto Rank (1945) and Carl Rogers (1951), who each in his own way, focused attention on the client (patient) as an active force in the change process. Indeed, both took the position that psychotherapy was not a process in which the therapist de-termines what is *really* wrong with the person seeking help and proceeds to treat the person so as to achieve the required changes. Instead they focused on the potential healing power of the therapeutic relationship. I was also aware other versions of alliance were developing concurrently. For example, Goldfried and Davison (1976) had moved from the emphasis on behavioral technique of establishing specific behavioral contracts to endorsing (after establishing the therapeutic goal), ". . . some sort of therapeutic contract, in which expected behaviors for both client and therapist are outlined, should be established" (p. 44). Similarly, Beck (1976), while emphasizing the cognitive side of emotional disorders and the cognitive process through which they are treated, also gives great attention to establishing therapeutic collaboration—he has called it "collaborative empiricism"—which allows the therapist to avoid turning the treatment into a debate.

The view that the person seeking change takes an active position in the change process is a key feature of my conceptualization. I assume that when the person consults a psychotherapist, the concerns and pains motivating this action reflect a lifelong search for safety as well as self-realization. I accept Rank's perspective that the reconciliation of the person's wish for fusion with others, to be part of a whole, with the wish to feel his or her own uniqueness is a lifelong developmental task to be reworked at each point of transition. This search is still ongoing for persons who present problems of pathological magnitude. Although Rogers recognized the indi-vidual's search for uniqueness, he assumed that the obstacle lies solely in the failure of caretakers to offer unconditional regard, thereby deflecting the search for a genuine self or organismic basis for self-regard. For Rogers, alliance building (I am not certain he ever used the term) required no formal processes but was simply the result of the undoing of the overdependence on the regard of others. Thus, questions of change goals and therapeutic tasks were of no concern to the client-centered therapist, since the client alone was responsible for the content of therapy. From this perspective, active participation by the therapist in the goal-setting process would interfere with his or her aim of freeing the person from too great a dependence on "other" based self-evaluation.

Even though the psychoanalytic view sees the patient in active terms, it underlines the self-defeating character of this activity. Perhaps because of its origins in medicine, an overweighting of the dynamics of self-defeat, or technical concerns about contamination of the transference, the psychoanalytic approach, with few exceptions, tended to advocate that the therapist take charge of the treatment: It is they who negotiate the goals and tasks. The radical reorganization of personality or its more limiting variants or compromises and the modifications in parameters of the associative task were not parts of the alliance-building process, though most of it might become pretty well understood by the patient as the treatment approached maturity.

I differ with both the client-centered and psychoanalytic methods in emphasizing the more explicit negotiation of detailed aspects of goals and tasks as important steps in alliance building and attaining the strength to overcome strains and ruptures.

Goal and Task

My view and my clinical use of the goal and task aspects of alliance building are somewhere between the silent or unilateral treatment by the client-centered and psychoanalytic approach and the very specific form it takes in cognitive and behavioral approaches. Later in this chapter, I will discuss clinical applications of the theory, but I want to emphasize my belief that a careful search with the patient for the change goal that most fully captures the person's struggle with pains and frustration relative to the story of his or her life is a key part of the building of a strong therapeutic alliance.[1] The element of negotiation is an integral part of alliance building. The arrival at a penetrating, meaningful change goal does not automatically lead to patient commitment, even though the client is often eager to pursue such objectives. The less frequent response has to be allowed for, that this goal is

---

[1] A strong alliance refers to a condition in which a person seeking change has found that the change agent can participate in the effort to shed light and open new doors without reducing the partnership to the pairing of a leader-therapist with an assistant-patient. Its strength revolves around the experience of new possibilities in the patient's struggle rather than faith in a charismatic therapist-magician.

more than the patient bargained for, the time is not right, and so forth. The possibility for such negotiation and the serious participation in it influence the therapist in identifying the correct change goal. The therapist is the major source in the selection of therapeutic tasks, but the patient must understand the relevance of these activities to change in order to maintain the role of an active partner.

I will try to dispel some of the confusions between goals and tasks and to extend theoretical distinctions. A common confusion between goals and tasks is illustrated when a therapist says, "My task is to help him forgive his parents so that he can live more fully in the present." This is really a statement of a change goal (whether or not negotiated with patient) that does not specify the means that will facilitate that change. When I speak of therapeutic tasks, I refer to the specific activities that the partnership will engage in to instigate or facilitate change. A major basis for differentiating various traditions of psychotherapy lies in the kinds of activities prescribed. These prescriptions represent proposals for patient action (e.g., practicing a different way of acting, with the therapist participating in the role of coach). This conceptualization of the therapeutic task is common in behavior therapy. Various forms of psychodynamic therapy make use of diverse versions of exploring a patient's observation of self-generated experience. An example of cognitive therapy tasks include the client keeping a diary.

We badly need more naturalistic observations designed to generate a taxonomy of therapeutic tasks with concrete descriptors. I anticipate certain subdivisions in tasks. An important distinction will be between tasks in the service of building a working alliance and tasks in the service of change. I will give further attention to these topics in the sections on clinical applications and on research on therapeutic tasks.

Bonding

Unlike the relative inattention paid to change goals and tasks in thinking about the working alliance, the bonding aspects have provoked both attention and controversy. Most of the debate focuses on the concepts of transference and real relationship and how these concepts differ from each other. I was and remain convinced that transference-powered relationships and real (meaning based in the actual experience with each other) relationships both exist, sometimes intertwined in a mutually augmented way, sometimes relatively independent, but in principle discriminable and subject to different dynamics of change. The bonding of the persons in a therapeutic alliance grows out of their experience of association in a shared activity. Partner compatibility (bonding) is likely to be expressed and felt in terms of liking, trusting, respect for each other, and a sense of common commitment and shared understanding in the activity. Thus, the specific nature of the bonds will vary as a function of the shared activity.

Gelso and Carter (1985) have selected out the liking part of the bonding aspect of what I called the real relationship as independent. I find it difficult to understand this distinction. Perhaps it is because this part of the real relationship and of bonding is also part of other real relationships outside of psychotherapy. It is a component of reactions to chance acquaintances, friends, lovers, and mates. But this very point strikes at the heart of another misconception, based in a more orthodox adherence to Freud's theory. Some (cf. *Hatcher, Hansell, & Leary,* 1990) start with an acceptance of Freud's distinction between inappropriate and appropriate transference, the latter being defined as realistically based feelings about another person. I believe that the addition of the latter term undermines the important contribution of the transference concept: the distorted perceptions of others.

Object relations theory, broadly conceived, provides a useful scaffolding for resolving the differences between various psychodynamic perspectives. From infancy, a person's experience in interacting with others provides the base for the individual's ability to form relationships, ranging from the primitive capacity to differentiate self from others to various levels and styles of connections. In a fully developed object relations theory, we will have a way of understanding how a person perceives, feels about, and reacts to other persons. It helps us to understand the relative importance of real characteristics and real events and the kinds of distortions that are appropriately labeled "inappropriate" (i.e., transference) and as such are vital concerns of psychodynamic therapy. Thus, I posit that the person who comes for psychotherapy brings the capacity to form both distorted and undistorted relationships.

When commitments to change goals and understandings of the tasks entailed are grounded in bonds of mutual sharing of liking, trust, and respect, they can provide the therapeutic leverage to deal with the strains and counterchange dynamic embedded in the pathological elements of transference. Thus, the building of a viable working alliance is a slow delicate process with individuals who have weak capacities for forming real relationships and strong transference propensities. Bonds heavily loaded with transference provide weak therapeutic leverage. I will return to this topic in the next part of the chapter dealing with the clinical aspects of building strong working alliances.

This proposition that there can be various proportions of transference and real relationship in the bonding aspects of the alliance identifies a psychometric issue that has been the target of much grumbling but little remedial action. Many express misgivings that what we measure as strength of the working alliance is heavily loaded with transference. This is a psychometric problem regarding measures of strength of the working alliance and calls for ingenuity in developing assessment procedures.

Recently, investigators have begun to examine some more distant aspects of object relations theory (e.g., attachment and separation), in relation to strength of alliance (cf. Mallinckrodt, 1992; Kivilighan & Schmitz, 1992).

These initial investigations have yielded some positive results. I would not want to discourage this line of study, but it is important to be aware that from a theoretical point of view defining the variable simply by the strength of alliance has limitations. Therapy facilitates the overcoming of obstacles toward building strong alliances. Except for the limiting case where the state of object relations precludes the formation of any meaningful partnership, the important functional relations to be investigated are between the capacity for object relations and the difficulties in achieving both viably strong working alliances and the kinds of goals and tasks embedded in them. Therapists fully committed to alliance theory and well schooled in the skills of alliance building will be able to sharply reduce variance in strength of alliance due to poor object relations. In these therapeutic situations the likelihood of forecasting strength of the alliance on the basis of a prior estimate of capacity for forming relationships is reduced.

Concept of Strain

Almost from the beginning of my research, I have given central importance to the events surrounding strain[2] in the therapeutic alliance and to the understanding of how and why change occurs. I may not have been clear and explicit enough about it. In my view, three key elements in therapeutic working alliance theory bear on change are: (a) strength of alliance, (b) the power of therapeutic tasks, and (c) the dynamics of strains in the alliance.

The psychoanalytic emphasis on interpretation of resistance is a major precursor of the strain part of the theory. As is well known, psychoanalytic theory presupposes that the patient's pathology will be expressed in transference or defense-based forms of opposition and interference with therapeutic work, and that the working through of such events is key to achieving the fundamental changes sought. If we strip this version of its reliance on psychodynamic terms, the kinds of problems (psychic pains) that stimulate a person to seek psychotherapy will be manifested either in the process of entering into a meaningful partnership and/or in participating in the work of therapy as represented by the therapeutic task. To the extent that this is true, the collaborative process represents an arena in which the patient once more encounters his self defeating propensities rather than a place where he reports on the problematic parts of his life outside of therapy. In therapy, the patient struggles with these problems with the therapist. To the extent that the patient achieves a different more self-fulfilling mode of response at a level that fosters generalization, this change will extend to other life situations and to relationships with other persons.

---

[2] *Strain* is only one of the terms that might be used to designate the appearance of a significant deviation in the patient's commitment to the working alliance, whether it is with regard to goals, tasks, or bonds. Temporary breaks or ruptures are among other possible terms.

Strains at Different Stages of Therapy

It is important to distinguish between strains as difficulties in the formation of the initial alliance and later appearing strains after the initial alliance has been established. In the preceding section, I spoke of object relations capacity as a factor in forming initial working alliances. I suggested that, except for the limiting case where relations incapacities preclude alliance formation, a skillful therapist will achieve a good level of strength of alliance, notwithstanding relatively poor objects relations capacities as shown by the usual measures applied at the third interview. The difference in initial object relations capacities will impact, however, the number of interviews required to reach a viable initial level of working alliance. My own experience suggests that with persons presenting mild to moderate neurotic problems, this level of alliance is almost invariably achievable in a single session. The more the pathology is embedded in close to primitive levels of object relation malformation, the more time will need to be spent on the alliance-building phase of therapy. As this alliance-building phase extends, changes of increasing import are at stake and achievable. As I have said elsewhere (Bordin, 1980), psychotherapy with extreme borderline and schizoid patients is best understood in these terms.

The strain aspect of alliance theory has been little addressed by research. Lansford (1983, 1986) carried out one of the first investigations. Using six cases conducted in Mann's (1973) pattern of time-limited therapy, she found that rated effectiveness in repairing strains arising after alliance formation correlated positively with independently judged outcome. Further, her data seemed to point more clearly to the patient factor in the alliance (e.g., patient-initiated attention to strains, patient ego strength), whereas the therapist factor in repair, as a whole, was unrelated to repair and outcome. But interventions in which the therapist articulated the similarities in the patient's therapy interactions and extratherapeutic behavior were most effective with good-outcome patients.

This factor of difficulties (strains) in forming alliances was addressed by Foreman and Marmar (1985). Out of a sample of 52 patients seeking psychotherapy after death of a parent or husband, they selected 6 patients who initially displayed poor working alliances. Of these patients, 3 achieved improvement and 3 were unimproved. Therapeutic actions that were strongly linked to the likelihood of improvement included addressing the patient's defenses, guilt, and expectations of punishment; the patient's problematic feelings in the relationship; and linking these feelings with the patient's defenses. Unfortunately, this report does not permit the separating out of the specific ways in which difficulties in forming alliances can be overcome from the ways of capitalizing on strains arising after alliance formation.

The lack of concern with the stage of therapy in which this strain occurs was illustrated by a panel at the 1989 annual meeting of the Society for Psychotherapy Research (SPR; Safran, 1989). Cases were presented illustrating the resolving of ruptures in the alliance, but in all instances, the strains seemed to reflect incompletely formed working alliances (e.g., the patient's conception of the change goal differed from that envisioned by the therapist, or the client was confused or unconvinced about the connection between assigned tasks and the goals of therapy).

A recent paper by Safran, Crocker, McMain, and Munay (1990) represents a major addition to the theory of the role of strains or ruptures in the change process. Safran and his collaborators have taken the important step of identifying process markers of ruptures. His approach can offer a guide to research on the phenomenon. Many of these markers are easily recognizable as examples of what psychoanalytic therapists would call resistance. It is important to realize that these markers are signaling glitches in the work of the partnership that are not attributable to some failure to establish a fully understood and agreed-to contract. Safran rightly emphasizes the opportunities for effecting change in the enduring dysfunctional interpersonal schemata of these ruptures and discusses how the therapist's participation can retard or facilitate such change. He asks (p. 163) whether it is important to distinguish ruptures appearing after an already established alliance from those in which an adequate alliance has never been established. My answer, as stated earlier, is that this is a vital distinction. I believe that a rupture's function as a vivid reflection of self-sabotage can be used to highlight the schema's dysfunctional properties. Thus, it must be brought to the person's attention at a point after he or she has fully committed to the change goal and understands the relevance of the ongoing work to its achievement. These conditions facilitate a recognition of the self-defeating character of the rupture event. This recognition is further facilitated if it happens to correspond with past behavior that is seen as self-defeating and has been accepted as connected with the change goal. This situation creates what I have called the "moment of truth" in the change process. At this point, the individual, fully in touch with the conflicting feelings and habits, experiences the pulls of the familiar—even though incompletely satisfying—behavior and pits these feelings and thoughts against the urge to try the new and the open ended. The clarity of this critical choice is clouded when the necessary conditions of alliance have not been fulfilled (i.e., there is an insufficient initial alliance). Safran and his co-workers have carefully examined the behaviors surrounding these events. It seems as though they tapped the inner experience of the participants.

Safran gives careful attention to how failures in empathy or attention to the alliance can give rise to or exacerbate ruptures and how the therapist's self-awareness and willingness to accept his or her contributions to the rupture will facilitate repair. Although Safran's classes of ruptures include those instigated by the simple collision of the person's patterns of self-sabotage with the situation, his discussions of the repair process tend to concentrate on the therapist's efforts to overcome his or her own contributions to the rupture. I am concerned that this emphasis will foster neglect of the sources of self-defeat originating in the client.

As the foregoing discussions suggest, research on the building of working alliances and the investigation of repair, ruptures, and strains need to proceed in tandem. The next section, on the clinical implications of alliance theory, will focus on the specifics of building strong alliances and the direction that further research might take. I will also add my ideas to Safran's to further specify the repair process.

CLINICAL IMPLICATIONS

This section will address the formation of an elementary (initial, viable) working alliance and especially the arrival at relevant change goals and related therapeutic tasks; it will also consider the vicissitudes of sensing and working with strains in the alliance in a way that fosters change.

Change Goals in the Building of Alliance

Reaching an understood and mutually agreed-on change goal is the key process in building an initial, viable alliance. On the therapist's side, it requires sensitive attention to the client's state of mind as well as the nature and direction of his or her struggle to maximize satisfaction and minimize pain and frustration. Thus, as do most clinicians, I pay careful attention to how the person formulates the reasons for seeking help (the events and experiences that led up to that decision). In my efforts to obtain contextual and longitudinal perspective, I introduce related questions in the natural flow of the client's own account so that the person experiences them as an amplification rather than an initiative of my own. For example, after a 31-year-old man had talked about the recurrence of guilt feelings that he had dealt with after breaking away from his attachment to a charismatic leader (who preached a social rather than a religious gospel) and had amplified the context of these guilt feelings in the role of both teacher and student (he was a doctoral candidate), I asked about his experience in opposing his father. His manner of giving the information about his Norwegian engineer-father had the flavor of joining with me in responding to its relevance.

Not only do such exchanges contribute to the search for a mutually understood change goal, they also help forge bonds of trust and respect. The client notes how carefully and sensitively I am listening and how seriously I am taking the voiced concerns. At the same time, while feeling that I raise pertinent questions, the client does not lose the sense of being an equal participant. When warranted, I will make clear my readiness to offer support and direction at points where the feeling of lack of resources represents a realistic block toward movement. But I am always careful to allow the person the full use of his or her own resources and to avoid having my support take the place of independent effort. Asking for help should not be experienced as either a state of helpless dependence or as a threat to the loss of independence.

My participations are directed toward identifying and agreeing on a change goal that is intimately related, if not identical with, the dominant themes in the individual's life story. Thus, in the case of the guilty man, our explorations led him to confront directly his enduring struggle between his wish for attachments and his equally strong need to be true to himself, for which he felt guilty. His conviction that these wishes were incompatible had, for example, kept him from being able to enter into any deep and enduring relationship with a woman. Thus, the meaningful change goal became to seek a reconciliation of these two seemingly irreconcilable wishes.

This way of thinking about change goals has much in common with some of the psychodynamic approaches proposed by Mann (1973) and the concept of Malan's (1979) case formulations. It is closer to Mann's approach in the sense that the focus is explicitly agreed to, whereas Malan's formulation of goals is in the head of the therapist and/or researcher. There is also a tangential connection with Sampson and Weiss's (1986) plan diagnosis and conception in that the possibilities of the therapist being useful depend on passing the patient's test, which is intimately related to the ultimate change goal.

A word might be said about mutual understanding. Similar to many other aspects of the intrinsically unequal therapeutic relationship, the understanding that the therapist shares with a partner may contain nuances that, while compatible with their shared understanding, go far beyond it. As the partner with greater knowledge and experience, these differences, when there, are to be expected. Instead of hidden agenda, which can be damaging to an alliance, they represent an asset of knowledge of the terrain over which a journey will pass.

Now, I want to return to the conceptualization of change goals as capturing the individual's struggle for an ideal mix of safety and self-realization and a sense of the inner and outer obstacles faced. This kind of mutual understanding is not a simple or brief process. I have already reported my own experience that a viable alliance can commonly be achieved in the first interview with persons presenting problems of mild to moderate magnitude. As I listen and seek to facilitate initial explorations, I find myself using family context as the basis for understanding the client's motives. This approach may be different from the usual, so I will elaborate. My own interest in personal development and vocational choice (Bordin, 1990) led me to pay attention to education and occupation in parents and other siblings as a clue to family atmospheres (e.g., who might have been the dominating parent, and the role of gender differences). When I see a pattern of mother as the high academic and occupational achiever and all three siblings, two sons and a daughter pursuing close or identical derivatives of her career line, it suggests a somewhat imbalanced family system. As I listen to my client, I am looking for evidence of the father's influence on the children and the part it has played in each one's identity development. More often, the system is not unipolar, but the client takes a direction different from the majority. I consider this information grist for the mill as I search for a statement of goals to offer the client.

This history provides a background for exploration of the kinds of changes, if any, the client seeks and for which I am willing to lend a hand. Of course, many persons do not seek change in themselves. They are dissatisfied with situations and see the sources of these dissatisfactions in situational factors of an impersonal or personal nature. In this case, they seek help with a decision (e.g., whether to move their family to another neighborhood, to change jobs or occupations, or to dissolve a marriage). These alternatives differ in the likelihood that not all the sources of dissatisfaction are external to what the individual brings to the situation. I happen to be willing to lend myself as a consultant on many external change decisions. But I am always interested in helping individuals assess how much of themselves as a source of difficulty they will bring to the new situation and test whether they are willing to include this possibility in our exploration. This in itself is not pressure toward accepting a change goal, but if we find personal issues, we would raise the question. At this point in our consultation, I seek a full understanding of how the client is grappling with aspirations and the satisfactions and frustrations being encountered. How enduring are the dissatisfactions and to what extent are they pointed toward a felt need for change?

The following example illustrates a way of building a working alliance around the finding of a mutually agreeable change goal.

Case Study

Nancy, a 30-year-old graduate student, sought an extension of a previous therapeutic effort at dealing with her problem with intimacy, especially with men. She was a tall, powerfully built woman who looked the athlete she had been in high school and college. She came of a large family with a long history in this country. From preliminary information, I knew that her father was a retired accountant, her mother a schoolteacher. Her brother, one year older, was a physician; two sisters, three and four years younger were, respectively, a teacher and a housewife/mother. Nancy was training for a human services profession.

This preliminary information suggested that there was a division along traditional sex role lines in the family with mother emphasizing nurturance and father emphasizing precision and control. All the daughters appeared to have followed mother fairly closely, whereas the oldest and only son struck out on his own, integrating aspects of both parents.

Nancy met me with a barrage of questions that reflected a cautiousness about getting involved as well as a seeking of a common ground; for example, what were my religious convictions? I do not avoid direct questions, but I am also curious and question how these bear on a client's problem. After only a few answers to specific questions, I could raise the issue of whether she had a very cautious approach to relationships, which in turn instigated a more directed exploration of how she acted in them and her dissatisfactions. She was always concerned with control, particularly with men. She saw men as seeking to retain power. This reminded me that her sibling position, one year behind her brother, made competition with a male very much a part of her early childhood experience. Previous therapeutic work in another part of the country, where Nancy had been working with troubled children, seemed to help her, for the first time, to get into a relationship with a man that had some sexual aspects, though it was far short of a full sexual relationship. In fact, she willingly acknowledged the likelihood that she had moved to escape that possibility and, moreover, had avoided further communication with him.

Exploration of her family showed a fearfulness of her father's temper and at the same time an identification with him. This identification carried with it a fearfulness of her own temper, which was reflected in her handling of unruly children under her care. As anticipated, her feelings about her brother were heavily ladened with competitiveness ("I think I was a better man than he"). Brother, in response to father's urging had gone into selling and then, with Nancy cheering, turned to medicine. Religion was an important concern in the family, especially to the two younger sisters. The older of these, contrary to my preliminary information, was an accountant; the younger one had the greater emotional expressiveness that Nancy seemed to want.

We agreed on a change goal that I stated as "achieving a fuller reconciliation between her wish for greater passion with her concern for planning and realism." This goal statement, while focusing attention on relationships, pointed to a therapeutic task emphasizing an established pattern of thought, feeling, and action as the center of our attention. This goal orientation allowed her to struggle in therapy with her revealed belief that intimate relationships must be forever and must be forgone. Since our work was conducted within a time-limited contract, a great deal of productive work centered around this facet of her problem. At the same time, this limit facilitated her grappling with her feelings about dependencies in intimate relationships. She hated the loss of freedom of action that she associated with attachment and hated even more the feeling that friendships or other intimate relationships represented a threat of becoming smothered by the other.

Although it is often easy to develop mutual goals, in some instances, several sessions, or even months of sessions, may be required to develop this aspect of the alliance. Earlier, I discussed the influence of poor object relations capacities and related difficulties in building working alliances. In the following case, the change goal was not reached until the third hour.

Case Study

Christine complained that her dependence on others made it difficult to concentrate on her studies. Further exploration revealed that the problem centered around men. Although she represented herself as shy, she was the initiator of relationships and seemed attracted by men already involved with others. But when the man became actively interested in her, she would break off the relationship. Yet, there was no evidence of an avoidance of sexuality per se. During the first hour, we agreed to explore the hows and whys of this running from attractive men after signs of their interest. Later in the first hour, she talked of two kinds of competition. If the man was outside her circle of friends, it became a competition between his and her friends. If he was in her circle, it became a problem of reassessing the competing attachments within the circle. From here, it was a natural move to talk about her experience of being a little more than two years younger than her sister, the only other sibling. When I pushed for the natural competitiveness of that situation, she grew silent and weepy. She acknowledged that this was the way she expressed anger, which we pursued further in the next hour. In between hours, she asked friends how they saw her handle anger. They replied: "You never get angry." Despite this active work on her problem, she seemed passive with me and unwilling to move further without my leading the way. When I called attention to what she was doing, she was once more weepy, but then associated to traveling in Europe and her sister's complaint that she was unwilling to propose activities for them. Jumping some intervening steps that elaborated and extended this picture, at the start of the third hour we were able to arrive at a goal to seek how she could enter into relationships marked by greater equality, allowing her to have wishes for herself without feeling that she was hurting the other or being selfish.

I am convinced that helping individuals to achieve the kind of understanding of change goals that I have described has great therapeutic power in itself. It can give them a momentum for change on their own. The experiences of some occasions, where circumstances have forced a week or more delay in starting therapy, after having reached this kind of understanding of the goal, have supported this impression of its power to foster change. Clients are likely to return reporting that they have been off and running during the intervening time. They have remembered other experiences that amplify and extend the understanding we had reached. They have been looking at their current experiences with new eyes. Invariably these changes are accompanied by considerably increased morale.

The empirical assessment of the validity of this hypothesis about the therapeutic power of arriving at change goals this way seems very feasible to me. For example, it would be possible to develop a manual for this style of achieving a change goal in the alliance. A minimally intrusive clinical investigation would introduce a pairing of two groups differing in conformity to the manual, all of whom have achieved the same initial level of working alliance.[3] Half of them would proceed directly into the therapy; the other half

---

[3] The current measures of working alliance, while including agreement on change goals, do not assess the quality of change goals of which I speak.

would be asked to delay two weeks. While the usual outcome measures would be of interest, measures of therapeutic work would also be valuable. Would the two groups differ in the quality and scope of their therapeutic work in the next hours?

Setting of Tasks in the Initial Alliance

As I suggested in discussing the case of Nancy, the very specification of the goal already defines the task(s). If exploration has resulted in uncovering a person's feeling of not trusting self, of being fearful of his or her impulses, of treating inner thoughts and experiences as mysterious and out of the person's control, to the extent that these are incorporated into the change goal, certain kinds of choices of therapeutic tasks become relevant. Free association is a way of giving inner experience a life of its own. Most of our experience of thoughts or feelings are responses to our own actions and the actions of others. Free association occurs under conditions of minimal physical movement; the client responds to his or her own preceding thought or feeling. The therapist in the classical parameters of psychoanalysis is a muted specific stimulus—though by nature of the circumstances, the therapist always has powerful influence, even in the absence of specific stimulation. There are, however, many other ways to direct the client's to attend to their inner experience. The client-centered therapist reinforces attention to the individual's own experience. This is another example of the same class of task. Gestalt-oriented techniques, such as double chairing and focusing on specific movements, and the self-experiencing exercises accompanying them, are also related tasks. What all these tasks have in common is that engaging in them is expected, according to the relevant theory, to have a particular effect on the person: In psychoanalysis, they reveal the dynamics of the person's defenses in the form of distortion of the free associative task; in client-centered thinking, they bring to the fore the person's struggle with self- versus other-based self-valuing; in the case of Gestalt, tasks confront self-alienation and help clients own their experiences, feelings, and actions.

More focused change goals (e.g., how to handle particular kinds of interpersonal situations or how to avoid certain patterns of thinking about self and others) are usually also associated with clearly indicated tasks, such as examining the particular thoughts or activities in detail. I will return to this topic when discussing "basic science" oriented research on therapeutic tasks.

Dealing with Alliance Strains and Ruptures

To me, the most important element in dealing with strains and ruptures in the working alliance is that they represent prime opportunities for change with persons whose psychological state creates the conditions most recalcitrant to alteration. With many garden varieties of clients, a basically adequate alliance will foster change with little accompanying strain or rupture. These are the mildly neurotic, sometimes situationally ascerbated help seekers. As we move past these groups in terms of severity, we enter the region where change will depend heavily on the utilization of strain and rupture episodes to foster the work of an individual overcoming firmly established inner obstacles toward change. Finally, there is a group so severely deprived in their object relations capacities—psychotic, schizophrenic, and borderline—for whom the development of the capacity to enter into an elementary working alliance is a critical, extended, and painful process.

To convert a strain or rupture into a significant part of the change experience, we must go beyond the simple restoration of the alliance. Safran et al. (1990) tend to concentrate attention on strains that therapists create through their expressed feelings, which indeed can be an important source of weakenings in the alliance. Although a client sometimes learns from such experiences, they do not seem to me to be the prime ones in helping a person regain control over deeply embedded self-defeating patterns. Rather, it seems likely that the experience induced by the individual's efforts to comply with a therapeutic task that the person recognizes as being relevant to the change goals carries with it greater opportunity to gain control over self-defeating behavior. During their work in the therapeutic partnership, clients may find themselves behaving in problematic ways that are strikingly similar (and with similar complexes of feelings) to those they had described in seeking out the change goals. Thus, the obstacles toward change become part of a shared event rather than one that clients will attribute to the therapist. Thus, although I would share Safran's concern with the feelings of therapists and their willingness to attend to that issue, I would also want therapists to be alert to the connection between problematic collaborative events and the kinds of behaviors that are central to the change goal. Therapists are vulnerable to feeling threats to their personal and professional self-esteem during such events. The perspective I offer, which sees these events as opportunities for change rather than threats to the self, can help reduce this vulnerability. With this perspective, these events can be experienced as necessary and understandable rather than as a glitch in the process. This can avoid the impression, often inadvertently given to patients, that this problem with the therapeutic task is being called to their attention as a criticism rather than as an opportunity for change.

RESEARCH ON THERAPEUTIC TASKS: TOWARD BASIC SCIENCE

In this section, I give free rein to my ambitious vision of the future of psychotherapy, still fertilized by our clinical experience, but firmly grounded in explicitly specified assumptions and derivations tested under controlled clinical or field observations and laboratory experiments. This is, for me, the hallmark of a basic science level of research in psychotherapy. The essence of the scientific method allows us to pick our way through the situational and personal factors that contribute to differing, even contradictory, beliefs held by individuals and sets of observers, each of whom remains convinced of the validity of these beliefs.

A sophisticated clinical trial, pitting non-treatment and alternative treatments against each other, while useful, does not in itself provide answers to questions about how, why, and under what conditions change does or does not occur. The main avenue for reaching that level of knowledge lies in research and theoretical development centered on therapeutic tasks. In this vision of the future, the psychotherapist will combine the personal qualities that make for a good partner with the accumulated knowledge about the relevance of various therapeutic tasks and the skill to implement these to induce change.

Formal Statement of Assumption

The technical aspects of psychotherapy as a change process reside in the validity of beliefs about what the engagement in therapeutic tasks does to the person seeking change. These beliefs often specify further conditions, situational and personal, that relate to the relevance of the task.

Implementing a Task-Oriented Program of Research

A therapeutic task-oriented program of research will be marked by the selection of particular tasks or sets of tasks as targets and the integration of all relevant parts of theory and research on behavior, feeling, and thought, drawn from clinical or developmental observation and laboratory data.

Such a program could comprise the following steps:

1. There must be a careful examination and explication of the tasks selected. These tasks should include only what the therapist explicitly or implicitly asks the patient to do in the service of change during the therapy[4] work, thus distinguishing those efforts from tasks in the service of building a working alliance. Briefly, these latter kinds of tasks, which were illustrated in the previous section, reduce to asking the person to explain why he or she sought help, to give the present context of difficulties, and to describe past precursors and contexts.

   Ideally, the selection of a target task or set of tasks will occur within a taxonomy of therapeutic tasks (as yet undeveloped). A curbstone first approximation of a collation of therapeutic tasks from various versions of psychotherapy follows:

---

[4] I will discuss a slightly different definition of task used by Rice and Greenberg later in this chapter.

    a. Practice of a particular response system in vivo or through imaging.

    b. Self-observation in the form of diaries and journals.

    c. Various forms of self-report ranging from that occurring in usual discourse to the more specified forms of experiencing and free association.

    d. Display of various aspects of cognitive processes.

    e. Various kinds of releasing actions such as double-chair experiences, exaggerating or simply repeating a just completed act, or extending an act.

2. The preceding period of field observation of the therapeutic task includes careful attention to state of the alliance in which it is embedded as well as the assumed relations, whether or not explicitly stated, between the task and the change goals. In all this, the researcher's convictions are based in various combinations of clinical experience and theoretical commitments. At this point, in addition to bringing assumptions into the open, it is crucial to look for possible basic psychological levels of task descriptions with the possibility of making contact with other streams of psychological knowledge. For example, in the task of free association, one aspect of the performance revolves around particular deployment of attention; the standard instruction is directed toward free-flowing as contrasted with purposefully directed attention. Because this is a significant distinction from the viewpoint of its therapeutic value, the vast literature of both theory and research on development of attention becomes important. This literature should be mined for fleshing out our understanding of deployment of attention as a facet of human functioning. (For a good example of drawing on theory and data from cognitive science, see Greenberg & Safran, 1980.) This is not a naive idealizing of "psychological science." There will be many formulations and laboratory or field observations that will be fatally flawed as possible contributors, but this judgment should not be made in a stereotypic reaction (e.g., "a laboratory situation could not capture what interests me"). We gain something from the concrete specification of perceived flaws. Laboratory studies are by their nature stripped-down versions of some events of interest, so it is important to identify left-out elements that we believe are vital to the events and to demonstrate their relevance in a way that makes the conclusion available to others than the believers.

3. This step goes along two parallel yet interacting paths. One path is the extended examination of persons engaging in the task and observation of them during a change sequence. It would be essential to observe the current state of the alliance and how it is affected by task instigated events. Thus, extended examination of the sequential patient–therapist interactions instigated by the task will provide

important systematic data about what engagement in the task will do to the person seeking change and what participations by the helper can influence that process.

The second path revolves around taking the therapeutic task situation out of its clinical context to look for the broad concepts and principles embedded in it. Avoidance of the error of oversimplification is a vital caveat (Bordin, 1965). Pretentious scientific aspirations to follow the path of the physical sciences can, and have in the past, seduced us into ungrounded use of research laboratory situations that were truer to scientism than to the scientific investigation of the objects of our curiosity. When we study therapeutic tasks outside a clinical setting, we must give critical attention to how our experimental situation differs from the clinical one. Where something is left out, we must be prepared to challenge, both theoretically and empirically, that the omitted factor is irrelevant to what we are seeking to learn. For example, it is difficult to imagine an experimental version of a therapeutic task that did not seek to include some reasonable facsimile of the motivational states that we contemplate as part of the state of alliance.

If we can achieve a reasonably credible experimental facsimile of a therapeutic task, it becomes feasible to investigate many factors without the encumbrances of the clinical study. We can look at how personality differences (e.g., diagnosis or personality measures) interact with performance in the task. We can examine how alternative therapeutic interventions influence the sequence and relate to short- or long-term outcomes. I believe this kind of backdrop of investigations will provide the stimulus for the most important formulations of basic psychological concepts. This type of research will make a fruitful contact with the rest of psychological science.

4. The question of whether a particular therapeutic task is one of a closely related family of tasks can arise anywhere during the preceding steps. It is important to consider this possibility. I have already indicated my belief that there is considerable overlap in a person's psychic process while experiencing (as in the client-centered task) and the various versions of the task of free association. In one relevant instance, scoring previously collected free associative protocols for experiencing produced highly correlated results, denoting overlap but not identity (Lansford & Bordin, 1983).

One of the products of the preceding approach will be a research series centering on a therapeutic task, or family of tasks. These investigations will bring together theoretical analysis and both clinical research and more generally related psychological theory and research. The previously cited paper by Greenberg and Safran (1980) is a good example of this type of investigation.

Roots of Task-Oriented Programs

Here, I intend to show that the basic science of psychotherapy has already been foreshadowed and to suggest ways for going further. Much of the following material has been adapted (to bring it up to date) from my Society for Research on Psychotherapy presidential address (1980):

1. The first example is the task or family of tasks utilized in the behavior-oriented approach to the treatment of phobias. The work of Peter Lang (1977) is a good example of the use of various combinations of clinical and laboratory or analogical investigations to unwrap the components of the task of asking a person to imagine a series of fear-related events under conditions of relaxation. A broadened perspective was brought in by Raimy (1975) when he devised experimental modifications from his client-centered view of the role of misconceptions of the self; Singer (1974) reinfused a whole line of theory and research on imagery; and Weitzman (1967) conducted clinical experiments aimed at expanding a too narrow view of what was occurring during the imaging process. Weitzman's observations led him to believe that many patients, during the silent period following the presentation of the image, used the image as the start of a free associative flight. Out of these diverse investigations has emerged a broad path of research and clinical practice under the cognitive-behavioral rubric with less clearly differentiated boundaries to other theoretical and clinical approaches.

I think a thorough up-to-date review of this line of research will reveal that relatively little has yet been done on the factor of individual differences. Some data relevant to the empathic qualities of the therapist and descriptive of diagnosis and severity in the patient as factors have been produced.

2. The client-centered task of experiencing-focusing illustrates a fairly full range of such therapeutic task research. This task has its roots in the client-centered conviction that the goal in psychotherapy is the enrichment of the individual's self-experience, which presumably is attained by modifying attitudes toward that experience. It is believed that a lack of such self-experience gave rise to barriers toward self-owning and authenticity.

In the normal course of client-centered therapy, this task is indirectly communicated by the therapist's increased responsiveness to expressions of feeling. Gendlin, following his program of study of experiencing behavior (Gendlin, Beebe, Cassena, Klein, & Oberlander, 1968) developed a modification of client-centered therapy by presenting explicit instructions of what he called focusing. He centered a clinical treatment around the performance of this task (Gendlin, 1978). It is interesting to note that his program of research took off from the measures of levels of experiencing developed by him, Klein, and others (Klein, Mathieu, Gendlin, & Kiesler, 1969). Also, he drew on the observations of Rice (1967) on voice quality (high levels of experiencing were marked by what was termed a focused voice quality). Gendlin's examination of the task of experiencing extended to analogue and laboratory investigations in which he examined individual differences in this kind of response. He later adapted the focusing instructions developed for these studies into a therapeutic approach that he found so teachable as to offer promise as a self-help method. His investigations of the individual differences factor gave evidence of personality correlates in a wide range of measures such as a Hidden Figures test, the TAT, and a personality inventory. This along with a previously accumulated set of clinical studies of experiencing give an important foundation for the usefulness of this task in psychotherapy. I believe the full potential of this line of investigation is not being realized because attention has been too narrowly focused on experiencing in the change process without enough attention to how such factors as differences in change goals, enduring personal characteristics, and/or diagnosis interact with the vicissitudes of the working alliance. Nevertheless, this series of task-oriented investigations represents a good example of how a therapeutic task can be empirically validated and can lead to changes in practice.

3. I have already suggested that free association and experiencing may be part of a closely related family of tasks. Even at this late date in the progress of research in psychotherapy, the major base of theory and observation regarding free association is embedded in what are basically clinical reports of particular events or groups of them. Bellak's (1961) excellent conceptual and clinical analysis of free association provides a fruitful platform for a program of research directed at this therapeutic task and its variants. He spells out carefully the differences and difficulties in performance to be expected on the basis of diagnostic and characterological differences in patients.

The 1960s saw attempts to research free association in the context of psychotherapy. Both Colby (1960) and I (Bordin, 1966a, 1966b), independently, chose to study in within the framework of an analogue in which the subject is given the standard rule of free association under conditions similar to the psychoanalytic situation. Because, as I have already suggested, taking therapeutic tasks into the laboratory or other highly controlled situations is such an important step in psychotherapy research and because it is so fraught with the many dangers of oversimplification, I will describe this investigation in detail. Considering that the therapeutic task of free association in the orthodox treatment occurs with the patient in a supine position on the coach with an unobtrusive therapist seated out of the center of vision, it seemed likely that laboratory conditions would provoke a succession of anxieties: First, the conventional concerns about the listener (is the person friendly? protective? punitive? moralistic?); then anxieties arising as the flow of associations inevitably, as the theory says, moves toward drive invested and conflictual areas; and finally the investment of the listener-analyst with characteristics associated with objects of infantile fixations. One of the decisions regarding the analogue was how long to make a session. Whereas a 50-minute session would have the virtue of veridicality, was that amount of time necessary? Preliminary trials convinced us that 30 minutes did not appreciably modify the subject's performance. Interestingly, Colby reached the same decision.

An important variation in the situation was how explicitly the subjects were forewarned of the task. Our initial studies were directed to the question of how personality influences the response to the task. The response in a single session looked like a natural starting place, but we wanted to keep out the influence of material prepared in anticipation. So we did not warn the participants of the task. Instead, during recruiting-selection interviews, we told our subjects that they would participate in a study of different methods of measuring personality including laboratory perceptual tasks, personality tests, and "an interview such as is sometimes conducted in psychotherapy." This is in contrast to Colby, whose research design required four sessions a week for 3 weeks and whose subjects were informed of the task during recruiting interviews.

A key test of the relevance of laboratory and analogue investigations is whether they come close enough to incorporating the working alliance factor. Even though we speak of individuals as subjects rather than as clients or patients in these investigations, it is important to incorporate some of the key elements of the therapeutic working alliance.

Our recruiting interview gave special attention to the volunteers' willingness and ability to enter into a therapeuticlike contract with us. They were given to understand that participation committed them to revealing themselves and were asked to consider whether they could participate in the study without constraint. The prospective subjects were given time to struggle with their doubts, and we helped them to voice such concerns. Almost without exception, these doubts consisted of concern with how the data would be used and by whom. In our assurances of confidentiality, we stated that our interest was in relationships of measures and that individuals would not be identified. Evidence of some success in stimulating this motive to fulfill the subjects' obligation to comply with the task was found in the interviews. One subject, finding himself unable to communicate and complaining of his mind being blank, commented that this was interfering with the purposes of the experiment. For the most part, such remarks appeared to be genuine expressions of regret rather than hostile taunts.

This analogue strategy for investigating the associative therapeutic task has, as far as I know, not received much research attention after the flurries in the 1960s. Colby found that the presence or absence in the room of an experimenter-therapist influenced the transferential quality of the associations. Further, in comparing questioning or interrogatives with interpretive interventions, he found that the latter were followed by greater freedom and expansion of association. This was a beginning at investigating the influence of various factors in the psychoanalytic situation. It would seem useful to look at the effects of having patient and therapist face each other, patient sitting up rather than lying on a couch, and so on. Similarly, it would be possible to look at the effects of minor or major variations in the basic task or the kinds of change goals associated with it. There are myriad complexities, especially those associated with successions of events in investigating the effects of alternative interventions.

My investigations were directed to the individual difference factor in response to the associative task. We found that flexibilities in perceptual response in the Rorschach and in a laboratory situation (reversible figures) were positively related to adequacy of response to the associative task. Yet in other exploratory studies, schizophrenic patients responded as adequately as our college sample in the analogue task. These results, if replicable, would seem to contradict assumptions and experiences that have led to the belief that the parameters of the psychoanalytic situation require modification for these and other clients with comparable or more severe kinds of psychopathology. Some further analyses of our data pool by Mann (1965) found support and surprise in relating diagnostic classification, arrived at by means of tests, to associative performance. Using the Rorschach and Minnesota Multiphasic tests, she classified subsets of the college subjects, all without known psychiatric history, into hysteric, obsessive, and borderline personality types.

Before leaving this particular line of research, I want to mention a direction that flows directly out of alliance theory. In accordance with this theory, the therapist selects this task because it taps into the kinds of pains and self-defeats that have been caught in the agreed-on change goals. It ought to be possible to design analogue studies in which free associative performance is perused for the degree to which it incorporates or reflects an independently derived set of self-defeating patterns. This kind of research design would seem to lend itself to a further extension of Colby's efforts to track the differential effects of various kinds of therapeutic interventions.

4. Another important, though potentially confusing, illustration of task-oriented research comes out of the collaboration of Rice and Greenberg (Greenberg, 1984). A source of confusion is their two uses of the term *task*. One version refers to task analysis of the resolution (by the client) of problematic reactions. Rice (Rice & Saperia, 1984) says, "The event (representing a change task) begins with a client's statement of a problematic reaction point (PRP), so named because it is a point at which the client recognizes that his or her reaction to a particular situation is problematic in some way" (p. 33). In this version of task, there is an intensive analysis of the client's operations in grappling with the problematic situation. I believe this emphasis on the client's mode of seeking change is intended as an antidote to overdependence on theory in psychotherapy. It can be said to rely on discovery by clients of the method of work that leads to change.

Earlier Greenberg (Greenberg & Clark, 1979) focused on splits as particular forms of problematic situations and proposed two-chair exercises as the kinds of client operations that facilitate resolution of the split (Greenberg & Kahn, 1979). This version of task corresponds to my definition of a therapeutic task in that it is suggested by the therapist as a means for the client to achieve change. In two investigations (Greenberg & Clarke, 1979;

Greenberg & Dompierre, 1981), he supported the hypothesis that, when the two-chair exercise was added to the underlying experiencing-empathic operation, deeper levels of experiencing would be reached and fuller resolution of the split would be obtained. During this period (1980), Greenberg more fully explicated the two-chair task than he had earlier (Greenberg & Kahn, 1978) when he spoke of it as constituting a "stimulation phase" of counseling. In the later paper, he gave fuller definition to the various forms of splits, offering three categories: (a) conflict, (b) self/object, and (c) attributions, with examples of each. In a manuallike exposition of the two-chair exercise, he described the stages a successful resolution must go through and the kinds (and) purposes of therapist interventions that facilitate this process.

For some reason, not much further work has been done in this direction. There might be some justification for concluding that most of the basic work has been completed. Yet, there is surely a need for examining more fully the factor of diagnostic and other personality differences.

SUMMARY

As I look back at this effort to identify new facets of theory and research on the working alliance, it seems to me that I have tried to make a case for two major directions. First, I hope to give new deeper meaning to the place of mutually understood change goals, particularly its capacity to empower the client or patient in seeking change. Second, I hope to revive my earlier effort to instigate a major basic science thrust to research in psychotherapy centered around the role of therapeutic tasks. My hopes for greater success this time arise partly from the availability of more compelling illustrations. Perhaps more importantly, clinical trials that have explored some aspects of the questions of social worth. It seems likely that the field is ready to renew these research efforts in light of fuller knowledge and understanding.

REFERENCES

Beck, A. T. (1976). *Cognitive therapy and the emotional disorders.* New York: International Universities Press.

Bellak, L. (1961). Free association: Conceptual and clinical aspects. *International Journal of Psychoanalysis, 42,* 9–20.

Bordin, E. S. (1965). Simplification as a strategy for research in psychotherapy. *Journal of Consulting Psychology, 12,* 339–345.

Bordin, E. S. (1966a). Personality and free association. *Journal of Consulting Psychology, 30,* 30–38.

Bordin, E. S. (1966b). Free association: An experimental analogue of the psychoanalytic situation. In L. A. Gottschalk & D. H. Averbach (Eds.), *Methods of*

Research in Psychotherapy (pp. 189–208). New York: Appleton-Century-Crofts.

Bordin, E. S. (1979). The generalizability of the psychoanalytic concept of the working alliance. *Psychotherapy, Theory Research and Practice, 16,* 252–260.

Bordin, E. S. (1980). Of human bonds that bind or free. Presidential Address to Tenth Annual Convention of Society for Research on Psychotherapy, Pacific Grove, California.

Bordin, E. S. (1990). Psychodynamic model of career choice and satisfaction. In D. Brown & L. Brooks (Eds.), *Career choice and development* (pp. 102–144). San Francisco, CA: Jossey-Bass.

Colby, K. M. (1960). Experiment on the effects of an observer's presence on the image system during psychoanalytic free association. *Behavioral Science, 5,* 197–210.

Foreman, S. A., & Marmar, C. R. (1985). Therapist actions that address initially poor therapeutic alliances in psychotherapy. *American Journal of Psychiatry, 142,* 922–926.

Gelso, C. J., & Carter, J. P. (1985). The relationship in counseling and psychotherapy: Components, consequences, and theoretical antecedents. *The Counseling Psychologist, 13*(2), 155–243.

Gendlin, E. T., Beebe, J., III, Cassena, J., Klein, M., & Oberlander, M. (1968). Focusing ability in psychotherapy, personality, and creativity. In J. M. Shlien (Ed.), *Research in Psychotherapy* (Vol. III). Washington, DC: American Psychological Association.

Gendlin, E. T. (1978). *Focusing.* New York: Everest House.

Goldfried, M. R., & Davison, G. C. (1976). *Clinical behavior therapy.* New York: Holt, Rinehart & Winston.

Greenberg, L. S. (1980). The intensive analysis of recurring events from the practice of Gestalt therapy. *Psychotherapy: Theory, Research, and Practice, 17,* 143–152.

Greenberg, L. S. (1984). A task analysis of intrapersonal conflict resolution. In L. N. Rice & L. S. Greenberg (Eds.), *Patterns of change* (pp. 66–123). New York: Guilford Press.

Greenberg, L. S., & Clarke, K. M. (1979). Differential effects of the two chair experiment and empathic reflection at a conflict marker. *Journal of Counseling Psychology, 26,* 1–6.

Greenberg, L. S., & Dompierre, L. M. (1981). Specific effects of Gestalt two chair dialogue on intrapsychic conflict in counseling. *Journal of Counseling Psychology, 28,* 288–294.

Greenberg, L. S., & Kahn, S. E. (1978). Experimentation: A Gestalt approach to counselling. *Canadian Counsellor, 13,* 23–27.

Greenberg, L. S., & Safran, J. D. (1980). Encoding information processing and cognitive behavioral therapies. *Canadian Psychology, 28,* 59–66.

Greenson, R. R. (1967). *The technique and practice of psychoanalysis* (Vol. 1). New York: International Universities Press.

Hatcher, R., Hansell, J., & Leary, K. (1990). *Transference and the therapeutic alliance.* Twenty-first Annual Conference of the Society for Psychotherapy Research, Wintergreen, VA.

Kivlighan, D. M., & Schmitz, P. J. (1992). Counselor technical activity in cases with improving working alliances and continuing-poor working alliances. *Journal of Counseling Psychology, 39*, 32–38.

Klein, M., Mathieu, P., Gendlin, E., & Kiesler, D. (1969). *The Experiencing Scale.* Madison, WI: Wisconsin Psychiatric Institute.

Lang, P. J. (1977). Imagery in therapy: An information processing of fear. *Behavior Therapy, 8*, 862–886.

Lansford, E., & Bordin, E. S. (1983). A research note on the relation between the free association and experiencing scales. *Journal of Consulting and Clinical Psychology, 51*, 367–369.

Lansford, E. (1986). Weakenings and repairs of the working alliance in short-term psychotherapy. *Professional Psychology: Research and Practice, 17*, 364–366.

Malan, D. C. (1979). *Toward the validation of dynamic psychotherapy.* New York: Plenum.

Malan, H. D. (1976). *Toward the validation of dynamic psychotherapy: A replication.* New York: Plenum Press.

Mallinckrodt, B. (1992). Client's representations of childhood emotional bonds with parents social support, and formation of the working alliance. *Journal of Counseling Psychology, 38*, 401–409.

Mann, J. (1973). *Time-limited psychotherapy.* Cambridge: Harvard Press.

Mann, N. D. (1965). *Free association and preferred defenses.* Unpublished doctoral dissertation. Ann Arbor, MI: University of Michigan.

Rank, O. (1945). *Will therapy and truth and reality.* New York: Knopf.

Raimy, V. (1975). *Misunderstandings of the self.* San Francisco, CA: Jossey-Bass.

Rice, L. (1967). Client voice quality and expressive style as indices of productive psychotherapy. *Journal of Consulting Psychology, 31*, 557–663.

Rice, L. N., & Greenberg, L. S. (1984). *Patterns of change* (pp. 29–66). New York: Guilford Press.

Rice, L. N., & Saperia, P. (1984). Task analysis of the resolution of problematic reactions. In L. N. Rice & L. S. Greenberg (Eds.), *Patterns of change* (pp. 29–66). New York: Guilford Press.

Rogers, C. R. (1951). *Client-centered therapy.* Boston, MA: Houghton-Mifflin.

Safran, J. D. (1989). Resolving ruptures in the therapeutic alliance. Panel at 20th Annual Meeting of SPR at Toronto, Canada.

Safran, J. D., Crocker, P., McMain, S., & Munay, P. (1990). Therapeutic alliance rupture as a therapy event for empirical investigation. *Psychotherapy, 27*, 154–164.

Sampson, H., & Weiss, J. (1986). Testing hypotheses: The approach of the Mount Zion psychotherapy research group. In L. S. Greenberg & L. O. Pinsof (Eds.), *The psychotherapeutic process.* New York: Guilford Press.

Singer, J. L. (1974). *Imagery and daydream methods in psychotherapy and behavior modification.* New York: Academic Press.

Weitzman, B. (1967). Behavior therapy and psychotherapy. *Psychological Review, 74*, 300–317.

CHAPTER 2

Therapeutic Alliances as Predictors of Psychotherapy Outcomes: Factors Explaining the Predictive Success

LESTER LUBORSKY

For the first 50 years after the beginning of the alliance concept (Freud 1912), clinical methods seemed to be the only ones that could explicate the alliance concept. Yet, bit by bit, for the next 30 years, especially for the last 15 of these, the clinical-quantitative genre has shown progressively more capacity to make significant discoveries on this topic.

By now, there are enough studies to satisfy the aims of this review: (a) to collate the predictive success of all alliance measures that have been correlated with outcomes of psychotherapy; (b) to review the influence of various factors on the predictive success of the alliance measures, for example, the type of alliance measure, and the type of treatment to which they are applied; and (c) to try to understand the basis for the trends in the alliance-outcome correlations (through leaps of interpretive gymnastics), within the mechanisms of action of dynamic psychotherapies.

This review concentrates on the period since 1976, for several good reasons: Up until then, the many studies had used one pioneer instrument, the Relationship Inventory by Barrett-Lennard (1962) for patient and therapist judgments of the relationship; 26 of these studies were summarized by Gurman (1977). Then beginning with Luborsky's (1976) research, a second type of method came into being: direct assessment of the sessions using operational measures of the alliance concept. It was after 1976 that a variety of methods appeared; both different types of questionnaires and different judgment-of-sessions methods, as part of a renewed generative period of research on the topic.

The preparation for a panel on the therapeutic alliance called together by Bordin (1975) led to the development of an operational measure of the alliance—the Helping Alliance Counting Signs (Luborsky, 1976; Morgan, Luborsky, Crits-Christoph, Curtis, & Solomon, 1982). The alliance measure was based on two types of signs found in sessions: Type 1 represents a helping relationship that depends on the patient's experiencing the therapist as helpful and supportive, and Type 2 represents a helping relationship based on a sense of working together in a joint struggle against whatever impedes the patient. Six signs were defined for Type 1:

1. The patient feels the therapist is warm and supportive.
2. The patient believes the therapist is helping.
3. The patient feels changed by the treatment.
4. The patient feels a rapport with the therapist.
5. The patient feels the therapist respects and values the patient.
6. The patient conveys a belief in the value of the treatment process.

Type 2 includes four signs:

1. The patient experiences the relationship as working together in a joint effort.
2. The patient shares similar conceptions about the source of the problems.
3. The patient expresses belief about being increasingly able to cooperate with the therapist.
4. The patient demonstrates abilities similar to those of the therapist in terms of being able to use the tools for understanding.

A related method was then developed based on the same signs but allowing the clinician to put together the signs into a global rating; this is the Helping Alliance Global Method (Luborsky, Crits-Christoph, Alexander, Margolis, & Cohen, 1983). A third method was developed also using the same signs but framing them in a self-report questionnaire format—the Helping Alliance Questionnaire method (Luborsky, McLellan, Woody, O'Brien, & Auerbach, 1985). The following concept of the alliance was generated by the studies using these three methods: The helping alliance is an expression of a patient's positive bond with the therapist who is perceived as a helpful and supportive person.

PREDICTIVE SUCCESS OF ALLIANCE MEASURES

All studies were surveyed for their predictive success, regardless of the alliance measuring methods used, and 24 samples were located within 18 studies. Each of these studies was briefly summarized by a categorization of the significance level of the study: "+" if significant and consistent in direction with the main trend; "0" if nonsignificant, and "−" if negatively significant. In this way, we were able to see how well the alliance measures

TABLE 2.1.   Alliance Measures as Predictors of Outcome (since 1976)

	Number of Samples	Number of Significant Findings
Alliance Questionnaires	18	14
Observer-rated on *session* (audio- or videotapes)	6	5
Total	24	19

related to the outcome measures. We found that in 19 of these 24 samples, an alliance measure of some sort achieved significantly positive prediction—an impressive record (see Table 2.1).*

FACTORS INFLUENCING PREDICTIVE SUCCESS OF THE ALLIANCE

After this multi-study predictive record, we can continue to learn more about the alliance by examining each of 11 factors that might influence the level of the prediction in each sample. These factors are described in the following sections.

Type of Measure

The main trend in the comparison of the relative prediction success of the two methods was not a surprise—there is no evidence that one type of alliance measure has a better record of success than the other. And even the two judgment-of-session methods (global ratings and counting signs) have predictive correlations with quite similar levels of success (Alexander & Luborsky, 1986; Luborsky, Crits-Christoph, Mintz, & Auerbach, 1988).

We were surprised, however, by the difference in the number of studies with the two methods. Before doing the review, we had thought there were many more of the observer judgment-of-sessions alliance studies, but of the 24 samples, only six are based on the use of judgment of sessions. The preference for the questionnaire may well have to do with its attractive ease of use—reliance on a questionnaire saves the work of transcribing the sessions and the time for assessment of the session. It must be pointed out though that the continued use of the questionnaire method was not based on the ample evidence that the two methods were correlated with each other.

---

* Only 14 of the 26 studies of the Barrett-Lennard Relationship Inventory assessed the relationship early in treatment, so that these could be examined predictively—twelve of the 14 appeared to have a positive relation with an outcome measure.

A few studies have begun to provide this necessary kind of information. Some of the more specific types of measures overlap in terms of what they measure. Using observer judgments of sessions, Titchner and Hill (1989) showed three measures to be overlapping, California Psychotherapy Alliance Scales (CALPAS; Marmar, Weiss, & Gaston, 1989), the Vanderbilt Therapeutic Alliance Scale (VTAS; Hartley & Strupp, 1983) and the Working Alliance Inventory-O (WAI-O; Horvath & Greenberg, 1986), whereas the Penn Helping Alliance Rating measure (Morgan et al., 1982) was related only to the Working Alliance Inventory-O. Further studies of the interrelation of measures are underway by MacKenzie (1989) Bachelor (1990), and Hatcher et al. (1990).

Type of Treatment

One of the most likely factors to investigate is the type of treatment. After all, the alliance concept came from dynamic theory and so it might be especially predictive for dynamic therapy. Also, the majority of the studies are still with dynamic therapies.

But, in fact, the evidence suggests instead that the alliance is significantly predictive in other therapies as well. Marmar, Gaston, Gallagher, and Thompson examined the alliance as a predictor in dynamic, cognitive, and behavioral therapies (1989). A sample of such results, using the Beck Depression Inventory (BDI) as the outcome measure, were as follows: For the therapist version of the alliance questionnaire, cognitive therapy had a mean correlation of .64, whereas behavior therapy had a mean correlation of .21 and dynamic therapy was .37. The results for the patient version of the alliance questionnaire follow: behavior therapy .40, cognitive therapy .36, and dynamic therapy .19. The study's conclusion for the therapist version was that cognitive therapy outcomes are well predicted, dynamic therapy moderately well and behavior therapy less well; for the patient version, the alliance was not as predictive for dynamic therapy. It is noteworthy that the CALPAS used in this study is a questionnaire method in the tradition of the Barrett-Lennard Relationship Inventory. Furthermore, for the results that are presented, its use as a predictor had a limitation—in treatments of 16 to 20 sessions, the CALPAS questionnaire was given at 3 points (Sessions 5, 10, and 15) but then was averaged. For a usual predictive study, these procedures should have been done separately so that the predictive correlations from the early sessions would be known.

The Penn Helping Alliance Questionnaire was first tried in a study with opiate-addicted patients (Luborsky et al., 1985) as rated by the patient and the therapist at the end of the third session for three groups: dynamic (supportive-expressive), cognitive, and drug counseling. The combination of the three groups showed significant prediction (.65), but the individual groups were insignificant.

The Penn Helping Alliance rating scale (Morgan et al. 1982) as applied to sessions of cognitive therapy (DeRubeis & Feely, 1991) was not significantly predictive of outcome (change in BDI). Their study reported the results of assessment of the alliance on only one early session, however.

Patients', Therapists', or Observers' Views

For the questionnaire method, the patient's view of the alliance appeared to predict better than the therapist's view; although not all studies showed this trend, Tichenor and Hill (1989) found a lack of relationship between client, therapist, and observer in judgment of sessions; the observer, however, is really judging the session whereas the client and therapist are responding on a questionnaire.

Positive versus Negative Alliance as a Predictor

The positive alliance was shown to be a better predictor than the negative alliance by Luborsky et al., (1983). The same was shown by Marziali (1984): P positive contribution .43; P negative contribution $-.29$. The findings were similar for the therapist: T positive contribution .28, T negative contribution $-.06$.

Overlap between the Alliance and Outcome Measures

The predictive power of the alliance probably benefits from its partial overlap with the outcome measures even with patients with the diagnosis of schizophrenia (Frank & Gunderson, in press). But the overlap is considered to be modest (by Luborsky et al., 1988) between the helping alliance rating items and the outcome measures, because the outcome measures are broadly based composites of patient, observer, and therapist measures. In contrast, the improvements represented by the helping alliance statements within the early sessions were only small improvements compared with the more substantial ones by the end of successful treatment.

Overlap between Alliance and Prior Improvement

If you were making a judgment about your alliance with your therapist, you would almost certainly be influenced by the improvement you had made so far. The only question would be, how much? You might have started to improve and might attribute some of the improvement to the positive alliance. Or, you might not have gained much, but you might feel you have a good alliance and have prospects of future benefits. We would expect therefore that the judgments of the alliance would correlate to some extent with the judgments of the prior improvement.

This factor was looked into by Gaston, Marmar, Thompson, and Gallagher (1988). For a sample of depressed patients, they identified the initial level of symptoms, the improvement up to the point when the alliance was measured by the CALPAS, and the patient's and therapist's CALPAS scores. At Session 5, for example, alliance scores accounted for 19% to 57% of outcome variance over and above the initial level of symptoms and the improvement. The alliance was found to contribute to the outcome variance for initial outcome levels and in-treatment symptom change.

DeRubeis and Feely (1991) also examined this factor. In one of the early sessions (either Session 2 or 3) of a 12-session cognitive therapy, *prior change* (improvement) on the Penn Helping Alliance rating scale correlated .28 (ns) with the BDI. The correlation was only .10 between the Penn helping alliance scale and *subsequent change* on the BDI. Their conclusion was that the relation of the alliance with the prior change was (insignificantly) greater than with the alliance and subsequent change.

Facilitation of the Alliance by the Therapist

The state of the alliance may often not need special help, but if it does, it can be fostered by specific alliance-stimulating behaviors of the therapist. Two moderately reliable measures of therapist facilitating behaviors (TFB) for the helping alliance, one a rated measure and the other a counting signs measure, have been constructed to test this possibility (Luborsky et al., 1988). The TFB measure was found to be associated with the helping alliance, which suggests that the therapist's facilitating behaviors do influence the formation of a positive helping alliance.

The TFB measures themselves, however, were not significantly correlated with the outcome measures. The only exception was the TFB-rated measure, which correlated .45 ($p < .05$) with the rated benefit outcome measures.

The ways the therapist can best influence the patient's alliance and deal with ruptures in the alliance have just begun to be systematically examined (Safran, Crocker, McMain, & Murray, 1990). In one study (Foreman & Marmar, 1985) of six patients in dynamic psychotherapy who had poor alliances at the beginning of therapy, three changed to better alliances and good outcomes and three continued with unimproved alliances and had poor outcomes. Among the therapist's techniques used most frequently with the improved patients were dealing with the patient's defenses, guilt, and feelings in relation to the therapist. In another study of five patients in cognitive therapy (Gaston, Marmar, & Ring, 1989) who started with poor alliances, the most frequent therapist interventions for those who improved in their alliance dealt with problematic relationships rather than with the solution of problematic situations.

All this evidence of the therapist's ability to help the alliance is reassuring, because therapists hope for a relation of the alliance to improvement during and after psychotherapy. But we have further evidence: There may even be differences among therapists in their capacity to establish the alliance. Such differences were suggested (Luborsky et al., 1985) by the correlation of each therapist's level of success of their case load with their patients' helping alliance questionnaire ratings.

Facilitation of the Alliance by Mental Health and by Quality of Object Relations

The patient's mental health is correlated with his or her ability in forming an alliance, which suggests that the capacity to form an alliance is partly a quality that the patient brings to the treatment. For example, the Health-Sickness Rating Scale (HSRS) (Luborsky, 1975) correlated with the positive helping alliance counting signs .44 ($p < .05$), although it was not significantly correlated with the helping alliance *rating* method.

The quality of interpersonal relationships tends to be highly associated with mental health (Luborsky, 1962) and is therefore included here. An interview measure of it was shown (Piper, Azim, Joyce, & McCallum, 1991) to be the best predictor of outcome but also to be significantly related to patient-rated and therapist-rated therapeutic alliance. All these factors were related to improvement in symptoms and in target complaints.

Facilitation by Basic Similarities between Patient and Therapist

Similarities of patient and therapist in certain basic demographic characteristics may be a factor conducive to forming an alliance. In the Penn study (Luborsky et al., 1983), similarities between patient and therapist (for the extreme groups of 10 more successful and 10 less successful patients) were significantly correlated with both the helping alliance rating method and helping alliance counting signs methods. The similarity score was based on 10 primarily demographic basic similarities: age, marital status, children, religion, religious activity, foreign-born parents, shared institutional affiliation (University of Pennsylvania), cognitive style, education, and occupation. One point was given for each similarity or "match." The sum score correlated .60 ($p < .01$) with positive helping alliance counting signs, .62 ($p < .01$) with a difference between positive and negative signs, and .53 ($p < .05$) with helping alliance rating. The age match and religious activity match contributed the most. These similarity scores and others like them should be further investigated because the presence of certain basic similarities between patient and therapist may facilitate the development of the alliance between them.

Time Course from Early to Late in Psychotherapy

Not enough evidence has been assembled yet on the variations in the time course of the alliance and the relation of such variation to outcome. Most studies have taken the early sessions as a predictor, and a few have averaged across the sessions as a predictor (e.g., Marmar, Gaston, Gallagher, & Thompson, 1989). Hartley and Strupp (1983) sampled the alliance across the sessions and found only one point that was significantly predictive—the 25% point. A similar result appeared in DeRubeis and Feely (1991)—the early session was predictive but the later one was not.

Size of the Sample of Sessions Needed

It is likely to be difficult to achieve significant prediction with a skimpy sample of the alliance. This limitation was noted even when the scores were inspected for the two sessions used by the Helping Alliance Counting signs method (Luborsky et al., 1983); it seemed likely that a third or fourth session might have produced more alliance scores and probably, in consequence, higher levels of prediction. This factor has not had sufficient research attention.

INTERPRETATION OF THE ALLIANCE-OUTCOME TRENDS

Psychotherapy research has made significant advances in the past 15 years in gaining knowledge about the therapeutic alliance through the mushrooming of operational measures of the concept. The main trend in the studies is that the measures generally predict the outcomes of psychotherapy: In 24 samples of patients (within 18 different studies done since 1976), the level of prediction has mostly been about .20 to .45. The therapeutic alliance is now the most popular in-treatment factor in terms of numbers of studies significantly predictive of the outcomes of psychotherapy. The only predictive factor that has more studies is a pretreatment factor, psychological health-sickness (Luborsky et al., 1988; Luborsky, Diguer, Luborsky, et al., 1993).

In summary, the 11 factors that may influence the level of the correlations of the alliance with outcomes are as follows (see Table 2.2):

1. The type of measure, whether it is a questionnaire or an observer judgment, appears not to make much difference in the level of predictability.
2. The type of treatment does not seem to be a special factor in its predictive capacity. Although most of the studies are with dynamic therapies, the alliance is also predictive in other therapies. More studies are needed, particularly with cognitive therapy and interpersonal therapy.
3. The main points of view are all predictive (patient's, therapist's, observer's) although the patient's point of view is especially predictive.
4. In part, the positive relationship capacity of the patient provides the foundation for the alliance; the positive alliance appears to be more

predictive than the negative alliance. This is not a surprising finding, because a basically positive alliance is therapeutically desirable and therefore, when it is achieved, is associated with a positive outcome; whereas the negative alliance may, after additional therapeutic work, give way to a more positive alliance and the greater likelihood of a positive outcome.

5. The alliance's overlap with outcome measures is only partial.

6. There is more evidence for overlap of the alliance and current improvement. This overlap is no surprise because the more the patient benefits, the more likely it is that an alliance will develop; and the more the alliance develops, the more benefits are likely to accrue.

7. The therapist can facilitate the therapeutic alliance. In addition to clinical armchair evidence, there is a correlation between therapist-facilitating behaviors and the alliance. Further facilitation may also come from the patient's side—those patients who are healthier may be more able to form an alliance. Additional facilitation may come from similarities in basic demographic characteristics between patient and therapist.

8. The association of mental health with the alliance suggests that mental health facilitates the formation of the alliance.

9. The findings of correlations between the alliance and similarities of patient and therapist (Luborsky et al., 1988) suggests that similarities facilitate the formation of the alliance.

10. Variations in the time course of the alliance result in inconsistently significant predictions.

11. Variations in the size of the database used for the alliance measure make prediction difficult. Some studies probably use too-brief samples of the alliance; a larger sample would likely produce higher correlations.

Enlarged Perspectives

It is time now to stand back a bit to try to gain more perspective on the meaning of the general trend of the correlations between the alliance and outcome measures. A primary benefit of the enlarged perspective is the ability to see that the trend of the correlations between the alliance and outcome measures is not strictly confined to measures of the alliance; it is also true for other positive relationship qualities, particularly from the patient's point of view. A grand-scale corroboration of this observation is provided by a review of other positive relationship qualities (Luborsky et al., 1988, pg. 350–351); in 10 such studies, all but one was significantly predictive of outcomes of psychotherapy. The significant positive relationship qualities included "a favorable patient-therapist relationship" (Parlof, 1961), "feeling understood by the therapist" (Feitel, 1968), and "feeling less resistant"

TABLE 2.2. Factors That May Influence the Association of Alliance with Outcome

Factors	Degree of Association
Type of alliance measure	Little or none
Type of treatment	Little or none
Views of patient, therapist, or observer	Moderate by all views, esp. patient's
Positive versus negative alliance	Positive is most predictive
Overlap of alliance and outcome measures	Some
Overlap of alliance and current improvement	Some
Facilitation by therapist's behavior	Much
Facilitation by mental health	Some
Facilitation by similarities of patient and therapist	Some
Time Course: Early vs. late	Not clear
Size of the sample needed	More than one session

(Crowder, 1972). The alliance, therefore, is only one type of instance of the broader category of positive relationship qualities, all of which are positively related to outcomes.

Since the earliest efforts to develop operational measures of the alliance (Luborsky, 1976), it has been viewed as only one component of a broader relationship pattern that eventually was recognized to be the transference. The therapeutic alliance is only that part of the pattern of relationships having to do with the therapist and only that part having to do with the positive bonds with the therapist. Later research on the alliance and the Core Conflictual Relationship Theme (CCRT) has revealed that patients who improve in psychotherapy tend to acquire more positive expectations from others and more positive responses from the self. The therapeutic alliance reflects the positive bonds with the therapist; these bonds tend to fluctuate in tandem with positive expectations from others.

A striking added increment to the enlarged perspective is gained by standing even further back to catch more light from the theory of the curative factors in dynamic psychotherapy. Three broad curative factors have been summarized (Luborsky, 1990):

1. The necessity to establish an at least partly positive relationship with the therapist.
2. The expression by the patient of the patient's conflicts and the working out by the patient and therapist of ways of coping with them.
3. The incorporation of the gains of treatment so that they are maintained after its termination.

Of these three curative factors, the first is consistent with the main trend in the alliance research. This first factor, the establishment of an at least partly positive alliance, has gained considerable support from this review of the predictive strength of the alliance measures. In fact, much more research supports this first factor than the other two factors (Luborsky et al., 1988).

The alliance serves the patient as a "transitional object"—a supportive helpful person who is experienced as having provided and is capable of providing necessary help in achieving the patient's goals. Backing this view are the findings of Orlinsky and Geller (Miller, Luborsky, Barber, & Docherty, 1993) on the development of increased representation of the therapist during psychotherapy. This review supports the conclusion that the therapist who can establish an at least partly positive alliance has fulfilled one main condition for the needed growth that typically occurs gradually during and after therapy. The other main therapeutic condition, related to the first, is the growth fostered by the working through of the relationship problems. The positive alliance ultimately is an essential curative factor that partly explains the hot-housed growth that occurs within the treatment environment.

REFERENCES

Alexander, L., & Luborsky, L. (1986). Research on the helping alliance. In L. Greenberg & W. Pinsof (Eds.), *The psychotherapeutic process: A research handbook* (pp. 325–366). New York: Guilford Press.

Bachelor, A. (1990). *Comparison and relationship to outcome of diverse dimensions of the Helping Alliance as seen by client and therapist.* Paper presented at the meeting of the Society for Psychotherapy Research, Wintergreen, VA.

Barrett-Lennard, G. (1962). Dimensions of the client's experience of his therapist associated with personality change. *Genetic Psychology Monographs, 76*(Monograph 43).

Bordin, E. (1975). The working alliance and bases for a general theory of psychotherapy. Paper given at the annual meeting of American Psychological Association, Washington, DC.

Crits-Christoph, P., Cooper, A., & Luborsky, L. (1988). The accuracy of therapists' interpretations and the outcome of dynamic psychotherapy. *Journal of Consulting and Clinical Psychology, 56,* 490–495.

Crowder, J. E. (1972). Relationships between therapist and client interpersonal behaviors and psychotherapy outcome. *Journal of Counseling Psychology, 19,* 68–75.

DeRubeis, R., & Feely, M. (1991). Determinants of change in cognitive therapy for depression. *Cognitive Therapy and Research, 14,* 469–482.

Feitel, B. (1968). Feeling understood as a function of a variety of therapist activity. Unpublished Ph.D. thesis. Teacher's College, Columbia University.

Foreman, S., & Marmar, C. R. (1985). Therapist actions that address initially poor therapeutic alliances in psychotherapy. *American Journal of Psychiatry, 142,* 922–926.

Frank, A., & Gunderson, J. (in press). The role of the therapeutic alliance in the treatment of schizophrenia: Effects on course and outcome.

Freud, S. (1912/1958). The dynamics of the transference. In J. Strachey (Ed. and Trans.), *The standard edition of the complete psychological works of Sigmund Freud* (Vol. 12, pp. 99–108). London, England: Hogarth Press.

Gaston, L., Marmar, C., & Ring, J. (1989, June). Engaging the difficult patient in cognitive therapy: Actions developing the therapeutic alliance. Paper given to the annual meeting of the Society for Psychotherapy Research, Toronto, Canada.

Gaston, L., Marmar, C. R., Thompson, L. W., & Gallagher, D. (1989). Relationship of patient pretreatment characteristics to the therapeutic alliance in diverse psychotherapies. *Journal of Consulting and Clinical Psychology, 56,* 483–489.

Gurman, A. (1977). The patient's perception of the therapeutic relationship. In A. Gurman and A. Razin (Eds.), *Effective Psychotherapy—A Handbook of Research* (pp. 503–543). Oxford: Pergamon Press.

Gurman, A., & Razin, A. (Eds.). (1977). *Effective psychotherapy.* Oxford: Pergamon.

Hatcher, R., Hansell, J., Barends, A., Leary, K., Stuart, J. & White, K. (1990, June). Comparison of psychotherapy alliance measures. Paper presented at the annual meeting of the Society for Psychotherapy Research, Wintergreen, VA.

Hartley, D., & Strupp, H. (1983). The therapeutic alliance: Its relationship to outcome in brief psychotherapy. In J. Masling (Ed.), *Empirical studies of psychoanalytic theories* (Vol. 1, pp. 1–27). Hillsdale, NJ: Erlbaum.

Horvath, A. O., & Greenberg, L. (1986). The development of the Working Alliance Inventory. In L. S. Greenberg & W. M. Pinsof (Eds.), *The psychotherapeutic process: A research handbook* (pp. 367–390). New York: Guilford Press.

Luborsky, L. (1962). Clinicians' judgments of mental health: A proposed scale. *Archives of General Psychiatry, 7,* 407–417.

Luborsky, L. (1975). Clinicians' judgments of mental health: Specimen case descriptions and forms for the Health-Sickness Rating Scale. *Bulletin of the Menninger Clinic, 35,* 448–480.

Luborsky, L. (1976). Helping alliances in psychotherapy: The groundwork for a study of their relationship to its outcome. In J. L. Claghorn (Ed.), *Successful psychotherapy* (pp. 92–116). New York: Brunner/Mazel.

Luborsky, L. (1990). Theory and technique in dynamic psychotherapy—Curative factors and training therapists to maximize them. *Psychotherapy & Psychosomatics, 53,* 50–57.

Luborsky, L., Crits-Christoph, P., Alexander, L., Margolis, M., & Cohen, M. (1983). Two helping alliance methods for predicting outcomes of psychotherapy: A counting signs versus a global rating method. *Journal of Nervous and Mental Disease, 171,* 480–492.

Luborsky, L., Crits-Christoph, P., Mintz, J., & Auerbach, A. (1988). *Who will benefit from psychotherapy? Predicting therapeutic outcomes.* New York: Basic Books.

Luborsky, L., Diguer, L., Luborsky, E., McLellan, A. T., Woody, G., & Alexander, L. (1993). Psychological health as a predictor of the outcomes in dynamic and other psychotherapies. *Journal of Consulting and Clinical Psychology, 61,* 542–548.

Luborsky, L., McLellan, A. T., Woody, G. E., O'Brien, C. P., & Auerbach, A. (1985). Therapist success and its determinants. *Archives of General Psychiatry, 42,* 602–611.

Mackenzie, R. (1989, May). *Comparing methods to assess patients for therapy.* Paper presented to the meeting of the American Psychiatric Association, San Francisco, CA.

Marmar, C. R., Gaston, L., Gallagher, D., & Thompson, L. W. (1989). Alliance and outcome in late-life depression. *Journal of Nervous and Mental Disease, 171,* 597–603.

Marmar, C. R., Weiss, D. S., & Gaston, L. (1989). Toward the validation of the California Therapeutic Alliance Rating System. *Psychological Assessment: A Journal of Consulting and Clinical Psychology, 1,* 46–52.

Marziali, E. (1984). Three viewpoints on the therapeutic alliance: Similarities, differences, and associations with psychotherapy outcome. *Journal of Nervous and Mental Disease, 172,* 417–423.

Miller, N., Luborsky, L., Barber, J., & Docherty, J. (1993). *Psychodynamic treatment research—A handbook for clinical practice.* New York: Basic Books.

Morgan, R., Luborsky, L., Crits-Christoph, P., Curtis, H., & Solomon, J. (1982). Predicting the outcomes of psychotherapy of the Penn Helping Alliance Rating Method. *Archives of General Psychiatry, 39,* 397–402.

Orlinsky, D., & Geller, J. (1993). Patients' representations of their therapists and therapy: A new focus of research. In N. Miller, L. Luborsky, J. Barber, & J. Docherty (Eds.), *Psychodynamic treatment research—A handbook for clinical practice.* New York: Basic Books.

Parlof, M. (1961). Patient-therapist relationships and outcome of psychotherapy. *Journal of Consulting Psychology, 25,* 29–38.

Piper, W. E., Azim, H. F., Joyce, A. S., & McCallum, M. (1991). Quality of object relations versus interpersonal functioning as predictors of therapeutic alliance and psychotherapy outcome. *Journal of Nervous and Mental Disease, 179,* 432–438.

Safran, J., Crocker, P., McMain, S. & Murray, P. (1990). The therapeutic alliance rupture as a therapy event for empirical investigation. *Psychotherapy, 27,* 154–165.

Tichenor, V., & Hill, C. E. (1989). *Working alliance: A comparison of the validity and reliability of several measures.* Manuscript submitted for publication.

CHAPTER 3

The Therapeutic Alliance as Interpersonal Process

WILLIAM P. HENRY and HANS H. STRUPP

Our interest in the therapeutic alliance has followed a natural progression from the second author's earliest writings (Strupp, 1958) to some of our most recent research (Henry, Schacht, & Strupp, 1990). Along the way, our conceptualization and empirical study of the alliance has evolved in a manner reflecting current trends in the broader field of psychotherapy research. That is, our research on the therapeutic alliance has moved from establishing *that* it is important to articulating more precisely *how* it may be important. Although we continue to operate from a psychodynamic perspective, our thinking has moved in the direction of common factors or processes operating in all therapies. Finally, we have focused increasingly on fine-grained measurements applied to a reduced number of selected dyads as opposed to global measures applied to group designs. In this regard, we have moved from scales designed to tap the general affective and attitudinal climate of the participants to a more highly structured examination of momentary interpersonal process. The result of this progression has been to narrow the conceptualization of the therapeutic alliance or relationship (we use the terms interchangeably) to permit a more operational definition with clear, empirically supported implications for clinical theory and training.

Certain questions are fundamental to any discussion of the therapeutic alliance:

1. What is it? Is it a type of relationship, a set of behaviors, an emotional bond, a consensus on goals and tasks?
2. Is the alliance a unidimensional or multidimensional construct?
3. How does the alliance develop over time?
4. What are the relative contributions of the therapist and patient?
5. Is the alliance directly or indirectly related to therapeutic change?
6. Does the alliance serve different functions in different types of therapy or during different phases of a given therapy?

7. How are "technique" and alliance related?
8. What are the implications of the alliance construct for clinical practice and training?

In this chapter, we will attempt to address all these questions, with special attention to a series of empirical studies spanning more than three decades of psychotherapy process and outcome research.

We have organized the chapter chronologically to provide a portrait of how research results, methodology, and conceptual thinking have evolved over time. We will begin by discussing the importance of the person of the therapist and the patient's perception of that person. This interpersonal framework emphasizes the parent-child aspects of the alliance, and the restructuring of the patient's self and object representations through the experiential learning processes afforded by the therapeutic relationship. How this relationship evolves over the early part of therapy, relative patient and therapist contributions, and the relationship of the alliance to outcome will be explored with reference to a number of empirical studies growing out of the Vanderbilt I and Vanderbilt II research projects. We conclude with a revised theoretical formulation based on interpersonal theory and discuss the relevance of our model and research results to clinical training.

EARLY DEVELOPMENT OF THE VANDERBILT PROJECTS

The Person of the Therapist

Our interest in the therapeutic alliance stems from an early conviction concerning the importance of the *person* of the therapist. Beginning in 1953, a series of studies was designed to explore the therapist's contribution to the treatment process. These analogue studies (Strupp, 1955a, 1955b, 1955c, 1960) demonstrated a wide range of therapist responses to a standardized patient interview. Results showed a systematic relationship between therapists' personal reactions to the patient and the quality of their communications, diagnostic impressions, and treatment plans. Negative attitudes toward the patient tended to be associated with unempathic communications and unfavorable clinical judgments. Because therapists were not neutral technicians, it seemed apparent that any meaningful definition of psychotherapy would have to accommodate personal qualities of the therapist that affect the therapeutic interaction with a given patient. To describe psychotherapy in terms of its theoretical orientations or techniques provided an artificially truncated view of what is essentially a complex human relationship in a specialized context. Thus, what came to be a focus on the therapeutic alliance grew originally out of a bias against seeing psychotherapy as the disembodied delivery of a "treatment." Extensive analyses of these early data made it clear that regardless of the therapist's level of technical expertise, psychotherapy was not effective when the therapist could not relate to the patient in a warm, empathic manner (Strupp, 1960).

The Patient's Perception of the Therapist

The emphasis on the therapist's contribution led to a study of the therapist's behavior as it influenced the development of the therapeutic relationship and therapeutic outcome. A composite picture of the "good" therapist emerged from studying patients' retrospective accounts of their therapy experience (Strupp, Fox, & Lessler, 1969). Positive attitudes toward the therapist were shown to be closely associated with success in therapy. Patients who had successful experiences in psychotherapy described their therapists as warm, attentive, interested, understanding, respectful, experienced, and active. Perhaps, in retrospect, this should come as little surprise. At the time, however, the focus of research was on the differential efficacy of theory-derived technical interventions, not the qualities of the therapist or the therapeutic relationship.

The studies of patients' perceptions of psychotherapy also led to another finding that was to guide subsequent research focus and conceptualization. In discussing therapeutic changes, patients placed relatively minor emphasis on the reduction of symptoms such as anxiety and depression. Rather they focused on improvements in their interpersonal relationships and self-esteem. In short, patients came to view their symptomatic difficulties in the context of their interpersonal relationships and developed ways to relate and interact more adaptively with others. These findings helped set the stage for what has become a strong interpersonal emphasis in defining the alliance and its function.

The Interpersonal Relationship as a Vehicle for Therapeutic Learning

Drawing on these early studies, Strupp began to sketch out his view of the nature and importance of the therapeutic relationship (Strupp, 1969, 1973a, 1973b, 1973c). He saw the therapeutic relationship as the basic framework for therapeutic change in all psychotherapies, from psychoanalysis to behavior therapy. The therapeutic alliance was seen as ameliorative in and of itself. Additionally, the emotional climate produced by and reflective of the therapeutic alliance was thought to serve as a vital catalyst mediating the effectiveness of specific technical interventions. In particular, Strupp emphasized:

> Learning in psychotherapy, almost by definition, occurs within the context of an interpersonal relationship, in the course of which the patient typically becomes dependent on the therapist as an authority, teacher and mentor. . . . Learning by identification and imitation is probably the

single most important aspect of the therapeutic influence. . . . the patient's learning is to a large part experiential but it is also cognitive. However, cognitive learning is seen as maximally effective when the feelings have become mobilized, most notably feelings about the therapist and the patient-therapist interaction. . . . I am convinced that the interpretations of resistances, that is, those roadblocks which the patient erects to prevent a more open and closer relationship to the therapist, are of the greatest significance and tremendously important in facilitating the identificatory process. . . . For therapeutic learning to occur, the most important precondition is the patient's *openness* to the therapist's influence. . . . in an important sense he [the patient] also complies to earn the therapist's approval which becomes an excruciatingly crucial leverage . . . [in] the agonizing process of subordinating himself to a powerful parent figure whom (following his past experiences) he never fully trusts. . . . (1969, pp. 209–210)

This view of the working alliance has four main features:

1. The therapist must possess certain facilitating human qualities, the qualities of a good parent (Strupp, 1973a).
2. These qualities permit the potential establishment of a power base for the therapist—modeled after the parent-child relationship—in which the therapist uses the patient's desire to please as leverage (the patient's yearning for a gratifying parent-child relationship).
3. Within the context of the therapeutic relationship, ameliorative experiential learning occurs through the normal developmental processes of imitation and identification.
4. The success of this relationship-based learning experience depends on preexisting patient qualities that permit at least a beginning level of trust and openness.

How does this framework relate to other views on the therapeutic alliance? Although not a formal definition of the alliance per se, this model closely resembles that of Zetzel (1956). She introduced the term "therapeutic alliance" and defined it as the patient's attachment to and identification with the therapist, emerging from the positive aspects of the mother-child relationship. In this view, the therapist's facilitating behaviors combine with patient capacities for attachment to permit the development of an alliance. The alliance itself is seen as a certain type of relationship—the bonded attachment to a primary caregiver.

This type of relationship necessarily involves therapist qualities and dyadic processes central to many other definitions of the alliance. For instance, therapist behaviors that facilitate the alliance are similar to Greenson's (1965) definition of the "real relationship," which is based on the therapist's decency, openness, and humane approach. The perception of these qualities by the patient would resemble Luborsky's (1976) Type 1 helping alliance (the experience of being helped). The resultant relationship, modeled after parent-child interactions, emphasizes the affective bond between patient and therapist, one of the three components of Bordin's (1979) alliance model.

The definition of the therapeutic alliance as a relationship implies an interactive model. This interaction might be said to be based on therapist contributions (facilitative behaviors) and patient capacities that enable the therapist's contributions to develop into a productive working alliance. The focus on therapist contributions runs counter in some sense, to Frieswyk et al.'s (1986) definition of the therapeutic alliance as the patient's collaboration on the tasks of therapy.[1] It is, however, quite similar to the multidimensional model of Gaston (1990), who breaks down this type of relationship into separate components: "Therapist empathic understanding and involvement," "Working Alliance" (patient's capacity to work purposely in therapy), and "Therapeutic Alliance" (the patient's affective bond to the therapist).

SPECIFIC VERSUS NONSPECIFIC FACTORS

Although the alliance was thought to provide both a direct and facilitating role in the change process, it was still viewed as a common or nonspecific factor. A logical question followed: what incremental therapeutic effectiveness was due to specific technical interventions over and above the benign effects of a healing relationship? Using the specific versus nonspecific factors paradigm dominant at the time, the Vanderbilt I study (Strupp & Hadley, 1979) was designed to explore the contribution to outcome made by professional training as a method for addressing the relative importance of technical skill versus relationship qualities. A comparable group of patients was treated in time-limited therapy by experienced psychotherapists and college professors chosen for their ability to form understanding relationships. The assumption was made that the therapists and alternate therapists would provide equivalent therapeutic relationships.

The results of this study are by now well known: Patients seen by the two groups of therapists did not differ significantly in their outcomes. The group data obscured the fact that professional therapists were often more effective than the college professors with patients who were highly motivated, able to quickly form a good working alliance, and who showed a relative absence of chronic maladaptive relationship patterns. Nonetheless, neither group was notably effective in treating patients with serious characterological problems such as pervasive distrust and hostility. A series of case studies (Strupp,

---

[1] Although Frieswyk et al. choose to define the alliance, in strict terms, as comprising the patient's contributions, they make clear that these patient contributions depend in part on therapist behaviors. In this sense, their model too is interactive.

1980a, 1980b, 1980c, 1980d) suggested that professional therapists gave little evidence of adapting their therapeutic approach or techniques in an attempt to work more productively with these difficult patients but did often respond with hostility of their own.

GLOBAL MEASUREMENT OF THERAPEUTIC PROCESS

The group results of the Vanderbilt I project served further to underscore the importance of therapeutic relationship factors. The project had also produced a rich database of therapies for further study. A variety of process rating instruments were developed in the following years, all designed to abstract and quantify characteristics of the patient, the therapist, and their interactions that might be related to outcome. These measures are described as "global rating methods" because they are based on summary judgments of session segments and involve the rating of general descriptors such as "authoritarian," "frustrated," "maintained focus," and "conveyed expertise." A brief summary of these studies as they relate to the therapeutic alliance follows.

The Vanderbilt Psychotherapy Process Scale (VPPS)

The majority of our studies relevant to the alliance have utilized the Vanderbilt Psychotherapy Process Scale (VPPS; Gomes-Schwartz, 1978; O'Malley, Suh, & Strupp, 1983). The VPPS took the Therapy Session Report (Orlinsky & Howard, 1967, 1975) as a point of departure and was designed to cover a range of theoretical orientations, built on general assumptions of psychotherapy as an interpersonal process. The 80 items, each rated on a 5-point Likert scale were designed to be unidimensional, primarily descriptive rather than evaluative, and require a relatively low level of inference. The quantitative indexes derived from these items were seen as a compromise between global clinical impressions of an entire session and atomistic assessments of single patient or therapist communications. The VPPS underwent a succession of refinements resulting in an instrument with eight stable factors derived from principal components analysis: Patient Participation, Patient Hostility (resistance), Patient Exploration, Patient Psychic Distress, Patient Dependency, Therapist Warmth and Friendliness, Therapist Negative Attitude, and Therapist Exploration. A complete description of the scale construction and psychometric properties can be found in Suh, Strupp, and O'Malley (1986).

Gomes-Schwartz (1978) combined the VPPS subscales into three main factors on a priori grounds: Therapist-Offered Relationship, Patient Involvement, and Exploratory Processes. These three factors closely mirrored Strupp's earlier formulation of the bases of the therapeutic alliance. The chief difference was that the patient's ego capacities reflective of early relationships thought necessary to the successful formation of the alliance were not measured directly, but were inferred from the patient's rated behavior. Gomes-Schwartz was interested in whether or not analytic, experiential and nonprofessional (alternate) therapists could be distinguished on these three dimensions. Her results indicated that analysts were significantly higher in Exploratory Processes, whereas the experiential and alternate therapists (college professors) were significantly more directive. Of prime importance, however, was her finding that the relationship between the three process dimensions and outcome was the same across all therapist groups. This suggests that the alliance dimensions tapped by the VPPS do not vary as a function of type of therapy, at least in terms of their relationship to outcome.

Patient Contributions

The dimension of Patient Involvement (reflected by items such as passive, spontaneous, inhibited, active, defensive, intellectualizing, hostile, initiating) was derived by subtracting the Patient Hostility subscale score from the Patient Participation subscale score. It measures a continuum of patient behavior from active, friendly collaboration to neutral passivity to overt hostility and resistance. Patient Involvement emerged consistently as the best predictor of outcome across all sources of outcome judgment (patient, therapist, and independent clinician). Furthermore, Patient Involvement was significantly correlated with outcome even after the effects of Therapist-Offered Relationship and Exploratory Processes were removed. In short, the patient's willingness and ability to become actively involved in the treatment process seemed to be the crucial factor in the alliance.

O'Malley, Suh, and Strupp (1983) replicated and expanded these findings by studying the same three process dimensions (utilizing a different set of raters) across the first three sessions of short-term therapy (approximately 25 sessions). Consistent with the results of Gomes-Schwartz (1978), Patient Involvement showed the strongest relationship to outcome. However, an interesting and very important additional discovery was made: the strength of the association between Patient Involvement and outcome increased linearly across sessions. No statistical relationship was observed at Session 1, a small relationship was obtained at Session 2, and a moderate (and significant) relationship occurred at Session 3. The lack of a relationship between outcome and Patient Involvement at Session 1, but the presence of a relationship by Session 3, suggested that the dimension of Patient Involvement was not solely an antecedent patient characteristic. Rather, it seemed to develop over the first few sessions, probably as a result of therapist functions.

Two related studies attempted to distinguish the variance in Patient Involvement attributable to antecedent patient variables versus emergent characteristics of the patient-therapist interaction. Moras and Strupp (1982) examined the relationship between patients' pretherapy interpersonal relationship history and the development of the therapeutic alliance (as measured by the Patient Involvement scale summed across four time points in therapy). Interpersonal history was assessed by an independent clinician prior to therapy, using a semistructured interview and rating format that yielded judgments in three areas: (a) current social functioning (the ability to form and sustain close interpersonal relationships), (b) family relationships (the amount of conflict and emotional isolation within the family system), and (c) generalized hostile attitudes toward others. Additionally, both pretherapy interpersonal relationships (IR) and the alliance (PI) were found to be related to outcome.

Results indicated a strong relationship between pretherapy IR and the patients' active involvement in therapy ($r = .50$, $p < .01$), accounting for 25% of the variance. Even after a pretherapy measure of overall psychological health was partialed out, the correlation, though diminished, remained significant ($r = .37$, $p < .05$). However, the association between pretherapy relationship history and outcome, while positive, was weak. Together, the studies by Moras and Strupp (1982) and O'Malley, Suh, and Strupp (1983) seemed to support an interactive view of the alliance—preexisting patient characteristics are an important base that permit a relationship to evolve with proper therapist input, and it is this interaction that is responsible for positive outcome.

Therapist Contributions

The findings of O'Malley, Suh, and Strupp (1983) suggested that something in addition to antecedent patient characteristics was responsible for a productive alliance by the third session of therapy. This "something" was presumed to be the therapist's contribution to the alliance. This assumption was supported by an additional finding by Moras and Strupp (1982). Patients judged to be in the top third of suitability for therapy based on relationship history, were invariably rated in the top third of active involvement in the therapeutic process. However, patients in the bottom two-thirds of suitability were quite variable in their Patient Involvement or alliance scores. Again, this at least suggested a differential emergent process based on interactions with the therapist.

From a theoretical standpoint, however, there remained a troublesome empirical fact; namely, the noticeable failure of these research studies to link the VPPS subscales measuring therapist-offered conditions to therapeutic outcome. Suh, Strupp, and O'Malley (1986) reasoned that this failure might be due to an exclusive reliance on statistical significance (e.g., correlation coefficients). Instead of attempting to demonstrate an overall relationship between a given variable (such as "therapist warmth and friendliness" or "negative therapist attitude") and outcome for an entire sample of cases, they chose to focus on "prediction failures." They believed that by isolating cases with significant discrepancies between expected and actual outcome, they might elucidate therapist characteristics associated with these unexpected results. Ratings on the VPPS subscale "Patient Participation" from the first session served to group patients into high and low prognostic categories. This scale was selected because it consistently predicted outcome from the third session but showed no relationship to outcome with the first session. Patients were also classified into high and low outcome, based on a composite outcome measure.

This 2 × 2 grouping resulted in four prognosis-outcome categories. When the therapist process scores were examined in each of these four categories, striking differences emerged. Different patterns of change in the therapists' behavior across the first three sessions, not the absolute level per se, seemed important. For patients with a high prognosis and high outcome, therapist behavior was characterized by an initially positive reaction, coupled with an increase in both warmth and exploration across early sessions. However, for the low-outcome patients, regardless of initial prognosis, therapist behavior was characterized by a high level of "negative attitude" and low warmth, which got worse across the first three sessions. Finally, of particular interest were the patients with low prognosis but high outcome. In these cases, positive outcome seemed to be a function of increasing participation by the patient that paralleled increases in therapist warmth and exploration. Thus, when therapist change scores were calculated, strong correlations between therapist-offered relationship conditions and outcome were obtained (ranging from .43 to .70 depending on the outcome variable and source).

VANDERBILT THERAPEUTIC ALLIANCE SCALE (VTAS)

Although the VPPS measures features of the patient-therapist interaction relevant to many different conceptualizations of the alliance, it was not constructed as an alliance scale per se. The Vanderbilt Therapeutic Alliance Scale (VTAS; Hartley & Strupp, 1983) was designed from the beginning as a measure of the therapeutic alliance from the perspective of expert clinical raters. Items were drawn from the theoretical and research writings of Bordin (1979), Greenson (1965), Langs (1976), and Luborsky (1976). The resultant 44 items were combined a priori into three subscales reflective of therapist contributions (18 items), patient contributions (14 items), and the interaction (12 items). The items on the VTAS were in many cases longer and more complex than items contained in the VPPS. For example, "Expects the therapist to change him/her without accepting his/her own responsibility for the session," as opposed to "patient is passive." In addition, the VTAS, unlike VPPS, contained specific items measuring patient-therapist agreement on goals and tasks, an alliance dimension stressed by Bordin (1979).

A principal components analysis of VTAS ratings from 124 sessions of short-term therapy was conducted to test the validity of the three-factor division. The results revealed a six-factor solution, however, and failed to confirm the a priori division of the alliance into three dimensions. While most factors contained items drawn primarily from just one of the original three scales, only two of the six factors contained "pure" therapist, patient, or interaction items. Consistent with earlier findings based on the VPPS, patient items seemed central. Of the six factors, four were deemed to represent primarily patient processes. In descending order of variance, these factors were:

1. Positive Climate (the therapist establishes a positive therapeutic climate by conveying expertise and treating the patient with understanding and respect).
2. Patient Resistance (the patient is actively hostile, defensive and/or engages in power struggles).
3. Therapist Intrusiveness (the therapist fosters dependency and imposes his/her own values and feelings).
4. Patient Motivation (the patient acknowledges problems, shows a desire to overcome them, works in an active and focused manner and agrees on therapeutic goals).
5. Patient Responsibility (the patient takes responsibility for the session and freely contributes).
6. Patient Anxiety (the patient exhibits passive defensiveness manifested as anxiety).

Interestingly, these six factors derived from the VTAS bear a strong resemblance to the seven VPPS subscales: Positive Climate is similar to a combination of the VPPS subscales Therapist Warmth and Friendliness and Therapist Exploration; Patient Resistance mirrors Patient Hostility; Therapist Intrusiveness reflects Negative Therapist Attitude; Patient Motivation is similar to Patient Exploration; Patient Responsibility taps Patient Participation; and Patient Anxiety resembles Patient Psychic Distress. The similarity in type and number of dimensions emerged despite a difference in raters, total number of items (44 vs. 80), item composition, and item complexity. The results suggest the presence of relatively stable dimensions of therapeutic process that would relate to or impact the alliance.

The initial study utilizing the VTAS (Hartley & Strupp, 1983) measured 15 minutes from each of five sessions across therapy for 28 dyads. It was designed to investigate (a) the relationship between the strength of the therapeutic alliance and outcome in brief individual psychotherapy, and (b) differences in the strength and patterning of the alliance across time in good outcome cases, poor outcome cases, and cases of premature termination. Analyses of variance were performed using outcome group as an independent variable and the a priori Patient, Therapist, and Interaction subscales as well as the derived factor scores as dependent variables.

The results indicated that the three outcome groups did not differ in their overall mean alliance scores. Some significant interactions between group and time, however, suggested a different pattern of alliance measures related to outcome. For those patients completing therapy, the total alliance score declined from the first to the last sessions, while it actually increased for the early termination group. The primary contributor to this increase in the alliance scores for the dropout group was the therapist subscale score. This may indicate that the therapists were somehow "trying harder" when they perceived that the therapies were not going well. There was also a significant drop in the Patient Motivation and Patient Resistance subscales from the first to last sessions across all groups, suggesting, perhaps, a natural rhythm to therapy. Interestingly, although dropouts were slightly (not significantly) more resistant, they were not more anxious or less motivated and responsible. Finally, the high-outcome group peaked on their total alliance scores at the 25% point (approximately Session 6), while the low-outcome group dropped slightly at this point.

The failure to find differences in the overall level of the alliance across groups was disappointing. However, there were still indications of a relationship between alliance dimensions and differential outcome. The divergence between low- and high-outcome groups at about Session 6 was of particular interest. On the whole, these data continue to underscore the importance of the early phase of therapy, and the fact that the alliance seems to develop (or fail to develop) relatively quickly, at least in short-term therapy. These data are consistent with those reported by Luborsky (1976) and are also consistent with the idea that formation of an alliance in the early phase of therapy is a crucial basis for the difficult work of the middle phase (Freud, 1912; Greenson, 1965; Langs, 1973, 1974).

THE ALLIANCE AS TECHNIQUE

To this point, the empirical research on the therapeutic relationship had led to a number of important conclusions. In broad strokes, it had been established that:

1. The alliance was formed relatively early and was predictive of eventual outcome.
2. The patient's contribution (or involvement) seemed crucial and was only partly based on antecedent or historical factors.
3. The therapist played an important role in the therapeutic realization of patient potential; in some cases, however, the therapist-offered facilitating conditions declined across early sessions, predicting poor outcome; and professional therapists were often surprisingly poor at establishing a good working alliance with difficult patients.

All these conclusions raised issues that were particularly germane to time-limited therapy. Thus it seemed to follow that the management and therapeutic use of the relationship should rightly be seen as a technique in and of itself. With the writing of a treatment manual for time-limited dynamic psychotherapy (TLDP; Strupp & Binder, 1984), the global paradigm of specific versus nonspecific factors was finally discarded and the role of the working alliance assumed center stage.

TLDP is a structured form of dynamic psychotherapy in which the patient and therapist agree initially on a set time limit (expected to be approximately 25 sessions). TLDP is designed to treat chronic interpersonal difficulties by defining them as the focus of therapeutic work. Thus, the therapist is expected to formulate at least one central cyclic maladaptive interpersonal pattern (CMP) to pursue therapeutically. The manner in which the CMP is manifested within the therapeutic relationship becomes a chief focus of exploration as the therapist actively solicits feedback about the patient's perception of the therapist. The presence of time limits facilitates working through emotions surrounding issues of loss and separation as they relate to the CMP.

TLDP principles embodied an important conceptual shift of emphasis regarding the alliance. The alliance had always been viewed as a crucial element in therapeutic change. However, the alliance was seen as a type of relationship that permitted the successful operation of direct (imitation and identification) and indirect (interpretation, confrontation, etc.) change processes. In short, the therapist (optimally) offered conditions enabling a patient to develop a productive working alliance, but the effectiveness of therapy then rested on the patient's ability to accept this offer of relatedness and assume a large share of the therapeutic task (Hartley & Strupp, 1983). This framework proves troublesome under two broad conditions: (a) if the patient is initially hostile and resistant, failing to form a productive early working alliance; and (b) if the therapist compounds the problem by succumbing to countertransferential pulls (see Strupp, 1980a, 1980b, 1980c, 1980d). To address both these problems, TLDP advocates that the transactions in the patient-therapist relationship should become a central content of therapy to be explored from the earliest sessions on. The emphasis on exploration of the working alliance as a modus operandi sets TLDP apart somewhat from more traditional dynamic therapy in which such exploration tends to occur later in therapy and in the form of confrontation of resistances and transference interpretations. By focusing on the transactions in the therapeutic relationship in an ongoing fashion, the therapist might be more likely to increase patients' involvement, strengthen weak alliances, and extend the range of patients who could benefit from psychotherapy (particularly short-term therapy). Furthermore, it was believed that the more effective management of the alliance was a technical skill that could be taught. Thus, the 5-year Vanderbilt II project (Strupp, 1993; Henry, Strupp, Butler, Schacht, & Binder, 1993; Henry, Schacht, Strupp, Butler, & Binder, 1993) was undertaken to study the effects of a year's training in TLDP on the process and outcome of short-term therapy. A brief summary of the results of the Vanderbilt II project will be presented in a later section.

First, however, we will discuss how the development of TLDP and related research have reshaped our definition of the alliance construct.

INTERPERSONAL PROCESS

In part, TLDP was designed to lower the level of theoretical abstraction associated with psychodynamic therapy. Although not totally eschewed, the emphasis on traditional concepts of defense mechanisms, psychosocial developmental stages, and wish-fear conflicts was minimized. In their place was a greater focus on observable interpersonal transactional behaviors and the effects of entrenched interpersonal patterns on the patient's introject (or thoughts about and actions toward the self). This emphasis on interpersonal transactions led us to select Benjamin's Structural Analysis of Social Behavior system (SASB; Benjamin, 1974) as the centerpiece for our latest process-outcome studies.

The SASB model comprises three interrelated circumplex surfaces that reflect transitive actions by one person toward another (focus on other), intransitive reactions to the other (focus on self), and intrapsychic actions by individuals directed toward themselves (introject). Each of the three circumplex surfaces contain behaviors arrayed in circular form, with each behavior representing a unique combination of the two underlying axes—affiliation and interdependence (or control). The system may be used in one of three ways:

1. A written form, the INTREX questionnaire (Benjamin, 1983), permits subjects to describe interpersonal relationships and intrapsychic states.
2. Independent raters may use the system to code moment-by-moment interpersonal process in fine-grained fashion.
3. The content of dialogue may also be scored for the interpersonal process contained in the narrative.

A major advantage of SASB is that it provides conceptual consistency by permitting the measurement of patient problems, therapeutic processes, and treatment outcomes in a common metric based on interpersonal transactions (cf. the principle of Problem-Treatment-Outcome [P-T-O] congruence; Strupp, Schacht, & Henry, 1988).

The global process rating instruments described earlier (VPPS and VTAS) may be thought of as reflecting the underlying alliance. Although such global scales have made (and continue to make) substantial contributions to our understanding, they tend to provide only a summary descriptive account of the interaction and overall therapeutic "climate." They do not pinpoint precise therapist behaviors that contribute to the quality of the relationship. Furthermore, although these scales are related to theoretical conceptualizations of the alliance, they were not designed for direct articulation with specific theories of change. Finally, global scales suffer from methodological problems having to do with summation of item ratings, which assumes equal importance of all rated items and an "additive" model of process (Hartley & Strupp, 1983).

The use of SASB as an alliance measure, on the other hand, offers the following advantages:

1. Interpersonal transactions between the patient and therapist are rated in very small units (usually a sentence or less). This isolates specific therapist statements or "process behaviors" that shape the alliance.
2. SASB process codes are context-sensitive and reflect momentary dyadic states, not simply unilateral behaviors by the patient or therapist (because the interpersonal process assigned to one participant cannot be judged without reference to the other).
3. There is no need to sum ratings across potentially different units of measurement.
4. SASB's grounding in interpersonal theory hypothesizes a direct theoretical mechanism to explain the relationship between interpersonal process in therapy and therapeutic change.

This direct change mechanism is based on the theory of interpersonal introjection, that the "self" comprises the reflective appraisals of others (Sullivan, 1953). People learn to treat themselves as they have been treated by important others early in life. The introject remains relatively stable because individuals tend to engage in cyclic interpersonal transactions that "pull for" introject confirming behaviors by others through the principle of interpersonal complementarity (Kiesler, 1982). Hence, the interpersonal process underlying therapeutic dialogue either ameliorates or entrenches negative introject structures. These introject states are in turn directly related to affective experience and behavior (Henry, Schacht, & Strupp, 1990).

For these reasons, we have come to conceptualize the therapeutic alliance as isomorphic with these interpersonal transactions. That is, the *interpersonal process in the patient-therapist dyad is the therapeutic relationship or alliance,* and the alliance so conceived is a sufficient agent of direct therapeutic change underlying all psychotherapies.[2] The function of interpersonal process in therapeutic change is both a specific *and* a common factor. Insofar as therapist interpersonal behavior is concerned, there can, be by definition, no such thing as an "inert ingredient" or "nonspecific factor." This position is similar to that taken by Kiesler, who stated that "Relationship is the momentary and cumulative result of the reciprocal messages, primarily

---

[2] This proposition does not rule out the important mediating role interpersonal process may play in simultaneously occurring change processes.

nonverbal, exchanged between the two interactants" (Kiesler, 1979, p. 301). Kiesler states that the primary therapeutic task is the therapist's metacommunication with the client about these messages, their impact, and their relationship to disordered interpersonal patterns. This position is highly consistent with TLDP's emphasis on the use of the therapeutic relationship itself as a technique to disrupt the transactional cycles maintaining a patient's distress. Our definition of the alliance as interpersonal process also posits a direct therapeutic effect on the patient's introject structure.

Empirical Evidence

Henry, Schacht, and Strupp (1986) used the SASB system to measure third session interpersonal process in a good-outcome and a poor-outcome case seen by each of four therapists (taken from Strupp, 1980a, 1980b, 1980c, 1980d). The results were striking and indicated that the same therapists engaged in markedly different interpersonal behaviors with different patients, despite a similarity in surface level techniques. Furthermore, the interpersonal processes associated with poor outcome were quite similar across therapists of divergent theoretical orientations (such as analytic and experiential). Therapists, when seeing their high-change cases, evidenced significantly more affiliative control (helping, teaching, and protecting) and affiliative autonomy granting (affirming and understanding), while exercising significantly less hostile control (blaming or belittling). Patients in the good-outcome group showed significantly more friendly autonomy (open disclosure and expression) and significantly less hostile separation (walling off and avoiding). Two additional findings were also of extreme importance. In the poor-outcome cases, the frequency of complementary exchanges between therapist and patient that were negative (interpersonally disaffiliative and/or separating) was significantly higher. The incidence of positive complementarity, however, was much higher in the good-outcome cases. Finally, the interpersonal process by both therapists and patients in the low-change conditions was significantly more complex. A complex communication is one that simultaneously conveys contradictory interpersonal processes (e.g., a message that conveys both acceptance and rejection). In the poor-outcome cases, the percentage of complex statements by the therapists and patients was 22% and 17% respectively, compared with 2% and 0% in the good-outcome cases.

Although these results cannot be used to conclude that interpersonal process caused poor outcome, it seemed clear that the alliance, defined as underlying interpersonal transactions, was related to differential outcome as predicted. Earlier research using global process measures had failed to relate therapist behavior in a single session to outcome. In this study, however, a very small sample of behavior (15 minutes of the third session) cleanly distinguished high- and low-change dyads. Encouraged by these results, we conducted a stricter test of the proposed role of the alliance as a change mechanism (Henry, Schacht, & Strupp, 1990). A larger sample of therapeutic dyads ($N = 14$) drawn from the Vanderbilt II project was separated into good- and poor-outcome groups based solely on introject change, as measured by the SASB INTREX questionnaire. All patients began therapy with similarly hostile introjects. We reasoned that the amount of change in the patients' introject would be directly related to the amount of confirming or disconfirming interpersonal process offered by the therapist. Our hypothesis was confirmed. Therapists whose patients' introject state remained unchanged engaged in significantly more disaffiliative interpersonal process, whereas the therapists of patients who did change showed an almost total absence of such process. The specific results were similar to those of our earlier study and have since been replicated at other universities (Coady, 1991a, 1991b).

In addition to the preceding results, other theoretically cogent evidence for an interpersonal definition of the alliance was observed. Introject theory would predict that therapists would tend to treat patients in accord with their own introjects. That is, through the same complementary dynamics that make introjects self-perpetuating for patients, therapists with hostile introjects would be expected to behave in a relatively more critical or neglectful manner toward others (including their patients). This is precisely what we observed: Therapists who acted with hostility toward themselves, engaged in three times as much disaffiliative interpersonal process with their patients (5.6% vs. 17.7%). Additionally, there was a strong correlation between the number of therapist statements that were hostile and controlling, and the number of self-blaming and critical statements made by patients ($r = .53$, $p < .05$). Finally, we have since linked therapists' ratings of interactions with their own parents in childhood to negative interpersonal process in therapy (Christensen, 1991). Taken together, these findings describe a theoretically coherent link between early actions by parents toward the therapist, the therapists' adult introject state, vulnerability to countertherapeutic interpersonal processes with their patients, and differential outcome.

Implications for Training

The results of our studies of interpersonal process have important and somewhat disturbing implications for clinical training. To begin with, we cannot help but be impressed by the relatively high level of potentially destructive interpersonal processes transpiring beneath the surface of many therapies. In one extreme case, over 60% of a therapist's communications were judged to be complex, and the patient in this case showed marked deterioration. It took fine-grained SASB analyses to reveal these negative processes. Simply listening to the session suggested a rather mild-mannered and well-meaning therapist struggling to be helpful with a difficult patient. It is our experience that although most therapists understand the importance of a good therapeutic alliance, many cannot adequately perceive the nuances of interpersonal process as it unfolds (Henry, Schacht, Strupp, Butler, & Binder, 1993).

The Vanderbilt II project (described earlier), in which therapists received extensive training in TLDP, was designed, in part, to address these perceptual and behavioral deficiencies related to interpersonal process. It was hypothesized that teaching therapists technical strategies for addressing the patient-therapist relationship as a regular modus operandi of therapeutic process would reduce therapists' expressions of negative countertransference feelings and help to strengthen the working alliance with difficult and resistant patients. The results indicated that therapists were able to learn this approach, as shown by adequate technical adherence to prescribed TLDP interventions (Henry, Strupp, Butler, Schacht, & Binder, 1993).

However, an unexpected and problematic set of additional findings emerged. Elements of the therapists' interpersonal behaviors did change, but in potentially countertherapeutic ways. VPPS data indicated that after training, therapists were significantly less optimistic, less supportive of patients' confidence, more defensive, and more authoritarian. SASB process analyses similar to the ones described earlier revealed a .52 effect size increase in therapist disaffiliative process and a .82 effect size increase in complex statements. The increase in negative interpersonal process as measured by SASB seems to have been primarily the result of a higher level of therapist activity after training. That is, the raw frequencies of negative process codes increased significantly, but the base rate (percentage of hostile and/or complex communications) remained about the same.

These findings are particularly striking and seemingly paradoxical in light of the TLDP focus on intensive scrutiny and management of the interpersonal patterns in the therapeutic relationship. Because the alliance is defined in terms of interpersonal process, we were forced to conclude that training had negative effects on at least the early alliance (third session). These results also have important implications for manual-guided treatments in general. In short, technical adherence to a treatment protocol may cause unexpected process changes along other dimensions, particularly those relevant to the alliance. If this is so, then the belief that the treatment variable is truly being specified and controlled with treatment manuals and technical adherence scales may be an illusion.

We have speculations as to some of the reasons for these unexpected findings, as well as an empirical study of therapist variables that seemed to mediate these changes. Unfortunately a complete treatment of these issues is beyond the scope of the current chapter. The interested reader is referred to Henry et al. (1993) and Henry, Schacht, Strupp, Butler, and Binder (1993). The implications for training and practice deserve some further comment. Traditional training methods (didactic lectures, supervision, etc.) may be sufficient to impart theoretical knowledge and guide the type of interventions made. However, such methods may not be sufficient to address the crucial underlying interpersonal processes that make up the alliance and constitute a common change mechanism. Therapists often proved unable to perceive the process as it unfolded, despite their abstract knowledge of its importance. This situation illustrates the difference between "inert knowledge" and "knowledge in action," a phenomenon explored in the cognitive literature. These results suggest that Horvath, Gaston, and Luborsky (1993) was correct when they speculated that therapists may frequently misjudge the alliance. We now believe that some type of fundamental training in the perception of moment-by-moment interpersonal process should be an initial foundation for later training in different theory-based therapies.

CURRENT THEORETICAL FORMULATION

Redefining the therapeutic alliance as interpersonal process answers two major questions confronting alliance theory and research: (a) What is the role of the alliance in affecting change? (b) What therapist actions can meaningfully be operationalized and measured? This definition is also consistent with Strupp's earlier formulation, with certain shifts of emphasis:

1. The facilitating qualities of a good parent are seen as an affiliative interpersonal process—communications that are straightforward, not complex and contradictory, and create a positive reflective appraisal.[3] These communications are mediated by the therapist's personal qualities reflected by his or her own introject state.
2. The therapist's power base—modeled after the parent-child relationship—increases the perceived importance of the underlying meanings contained in the therapist's interpersonal process transactions. This may increase the probability that the patient's introject structure will change as a result of the interpersonal process.
3. Therapeutic learning is still seen as primarily experiential. The normal developmental process emphasized in this view, however, is introjection of the interpersonal process.
4. The success of this relationship-based learning experience is dependent on the patient's antecedent relationship history.

It is hypothesized that the quality of early significant relationships determines the extent to which the patient's negative introject structure is entrenched and hence the degree to which it may be malleable by contemporary interpersonal process. This idea is consistent with Bowlby (1977a, p. 206), who stated, "There is a strong causal relationship between an individual's experiences with his parents and his later capacity to make

---

[3] This is not necessarily synonymous with "unconditional positive regard." It is possible to be challenging, even critical in a manner that is not interpersonally hostile and/or complex.

affectional bonds." Thus, even in the presence of benign and potentially ameliorative interpersonal process by the therapist, a resulting attachment or affective bond may not develop with some patients. Additionally, the relative rigidity of a patient's problematic interpersonal evoking style (Kiesler, 1979) may determine the likelihood that the therapist will respond with complementary and countertherapeutic interpersonal process. The negative interpersonal complementarity provided by the therapist may then prevent the formation of an attachment in those patients who might have had the capacity for bonding, despite their interpersonal dysfunction.

The alliance as interpersonal process does not distinguish "the real relationship" from the "transference relationship" or positive from negative transference. The nature of emergent interpersonal process may stem from a variety of patient and therapist sources, not the least of which is the process itself (interpersonal complementarity). The type of relationship that interpersonal process manifests at any given moment seems to be a secondary (though not unimportant) issue because we believe the *actual* process is responsible in part for therapeutic change, regardless of the etiology of that process. Horvath, Gaston, and Luborsky (1993) notes that a current chief controversy concerns whether or not the alliance is an intrapersonal or interpersonal phenomenon. This concern is theoretically central, because it relates to the degree to which past relationships influence the alliance. If the alliance is interpersonal (interactive), the therapist's skill may play an important role in shaping the quality of the alliance. If the alliance is intrapersonal, the quality of the therapeutic relationship may be predestined (at least initially) by the patient's history.

From our standpoint, resolving this question involves a distinction between the patient's absolute capacity to form an alliance, and the probability that a productive alliance will emerge if the capacity is present. Where a patient lacks the absolute capacity to form an attachment (which we believe is relatively rare), then the interpersonal process of therapy may be irrelevant. However, in the most common case, where some patient capacity is present, the alliance is seen to be the emergent result of interactive interpersonal process, and the interpersonal histories of both the patient and the therapist are highly relevant variables governing the probability of therapeutically beneficial or destructive interpersonal processes.

Direct Change Processes

The central theoretical mechanism that underlies an interpersonal definition of the alliance is the process of introjection whereby individuals intrapsychically represent past interpersonal relationships. Internal representations of others guide not only actions toward the self, but also tend to recreate the original interpersonal patterns in current relationships. These contemporary actions by others, in turn maintain the unhealthy introject. The importance of these processes in therapy has received growing empirical support. Rudy, McLemore, and Gorsuch (1985) found results similar to ours (Henry, Schacht, & Strupp, 1986, 1990): Disaffiliative complementary interactions between patient and therapist predicted little therapeutic change. Quintana and Meara (1990) administered the SASB INTREX questionnaire to patients and found a striking correspondence between patients' pattern of introject change and patients' reports of the therapists' interpersonal actions toward them. Over the course of therapy, there was increasing complementarity between therapists' actions toward the patient and the patients' actions toward themselves, suggesting an internalization of the therapeutic process. Alpher (1991) even presented the results from a patient's INTREX questionnaire rating of the therapeutic relationship to the patient during therapy, as a pivotal intervention or "change episode" in and of itself.

Although the descriptive language and context may vary, a wide range of theorists, from psychodynamic to cognitive-behavioral, have hypothesized that introjective actions are major correlates of emotional experience and interpersonal behavior (Henry, Schacht, & Strupp, 1990). Because of the introject's theoretically central role in maintaining problematic affective/interpersonal cycles, it would stand to reason that any successful therapy would likely alter a patient's introject state by some means. As noted earlier, we feel that the internalization or introjection of ameliorative interpersonal process is a common factor in all therapies. In fact, this process may account for the rather high success rate of all psychotherapies studied, as well as the failure to document (for the most part) the differential effectiveness of any particular approach. It might also be used to explain the success of lay counselors in the Vanderbilt I project.[4]

To view the therapeutic relationship as interpersonal process is somewhat different from, but certainly consistent with most major definitions of the alliance. Depending on the viewer's vantage point, underlying interpersonal processes may either reflect or directly shape goal and task agreement, the patient's active collaboration in accomplishing these goals and tasks, the patient's experience of being helped, and the affective bond between patient and therapist. Interpersonal processes that are complementary on the affiliation axis (either positive or negative) accumulate to establish the affective bond component of the alliance, and serve as a marker of its current state.[5]

---

[4] In purely interpersonal terms, professional therapists would still be expected (optimally) to produce superior outcomes due to their potentially greater power base, ability to perceive and metacommunicate about ongoing interpersonal process, and ability to avoid negative complementary cycles. The fact that our research indicates professional therapists often are unable to utilize these advantages speaks to the need for different approaches to training.
[5] The affective bond or attachment between patient and therapist and the dyadic interpersonal process are closely related. We place the affective bond as a secondary manifestation of primary interpersonal process for two reasons: (a) We postulate that the affective bond develops (or fails to develop) over time as the result of the interpersonal process history within the dyad; (b) as Ainsworth (1989) notes, affectional bonds are characteristics of individuals, not dyads. Our definition of the alliance as interpersonal process is based on a view of process defined in dyadic terms.

Affiliative complementarity on the interdependence axis (friendly influence followed by affiliative submission) may reflect goal and task agreement. Certainly, a predominance of such exchanges would not be expected in the absence of goal-related collaboration.

Indirect Influence

While we have chosen to emphasize a hypothetically direct effect of the alliance on change, we also believe that interpersonal process fulfills a crucial mediating role. Psychodynamic, interpersonal, and object relations theorists all posit a similar hypothesis to explain therapeutic change: Therapy is beneficial because the patient experiences a relationship that is qualitatively different from the early childhood relationships responsible for the maladaptive interpersonal patterns that ultimately led the patient to seek therapy. The underlying interpersonal process engaged in by the therapist may profoundly affect whether or not the therapeutic relationship is indeed perceived as qualitatively different. Bowlby states that the tasks of the psychotherapist are:

> (a) to provide the patient with a secure base from which he, the patient, can explore himself and his relationships; (b) and (c) to examine with the patient the ways in which he tends to construe current interpersonal relationships, including that with the therapist, and the resulting predictions he makes and actions he takes, and the extent to which some may be inappropriate. (1977b, p. 421)

A productive alliance may be seen, in Bowlby's terms, as a "secure base," and the successful discharge of these tasks requires that the therapist avoid certain interpersonal processes.

For example, a frequently observed occurrence is the forcing of an agenda by a therapist who subtly ignores a patient's statement or topic. Although the therapist may have well-meaning reasons, the underlying process (a complex combination of disaffiliative separation and control) may recapitulate the original unavailability of the primary attachment figure in time of need. Thus, the secure base may not be formed, which in turn curtails the process of exploration. As noted earlier, these interpersonal processes are often quite subtle, and are frequently engaged in by therapists who are attempting to help in a "warm" manner. We observed in the Vanderbilt II project, that even while the content of a therapist's intervention might address a problematic interpersonal pattern occurring in the session, the process of the intervention may inadvertently recreate that pattern. In short, the patient's "inappropriate" reaction to the therapist might actually be partly based on real, not distorted perceptions, creating an unrecognized and problematic situation for the therapist.

Even where a basically secure base and positive attachment have formed with the therapist, interpersonal process may mediate the effects of specific interventions. For example, the therapeutic effectiveness of an interpretation may depend in part on the interpersonal process that accompanies it. It is our experience that interpretations often come with an embedded blaming or pejorative element that might only entrench a patient's self-critical introject, regardless of the correctness of the interpretation. Likewise, interventions designed to enhance the immediacy and depth of emotional experiencing are likely to fail if the underlying process is one of hostile separation or interpersonal distance between patient and therapist. In these examples, the mediating role of therapist's interpersonal actions involves the momentary activation of a complementary, self-hostile patient introject state. Such a state is the theoretical antithesis of the introject state that reflects open self-exploration.

INTERPERSONAL PROCESS MODEL

Orlinsky and Howard (1986) set for themselves the lofty goal of developing an empirically based generic model of psychotherapy process, concerned with "active ingredients" rather than "brand names." Their proposed model contains five conceptual elements: the therapeutic contract, therapeutic interventions, the therapeutic bond, patient self-relatedness, and therapeutic realizations. We believe that the alliance as interpersonal process is a central mediating mechanism that influences the interactions of these five components. With some modification, the direct and indirect functions of interpersonal process fit rather cleanly into their model, potentially providing a further base of empirical support. Figure 3.1 presents an interpersonal adaptation of Orlinsky and Howard's generic process model.[6] This model is testable and capable of guiding both traditional group-based process-outcome research as well as providing a road map for individual case study. Space limitations prevent a complete detailing of this interpersonal model, but we will briefly highlight major features.

Patient Self-Relatedness

Patient self-relatedness is defined by Orlinsky and Howard (1986) as the "patient's psychological functioning during therapy . . . their affective and ideational responsiveness, their self-attunement and self-definition, their self-evaluation" (p. 313). In essence, self-relatedness can be seen as

---

[6] The therapeutic contract, defined as the purpose, format, terms, and limits of therapy, has been removed from our version of the model. It seems intuitively clear that interpersonal processes might shape the contract and certainly would be affected by it. For example, the imposition of time limits might lead to greater frustration (and problematic interpersonal process) in the face of limited progress. However, the present model was designed to address moment-by-moment process. Therefore, the therapeutic contract, envisioned as a relatively predetermined context, was omitted.

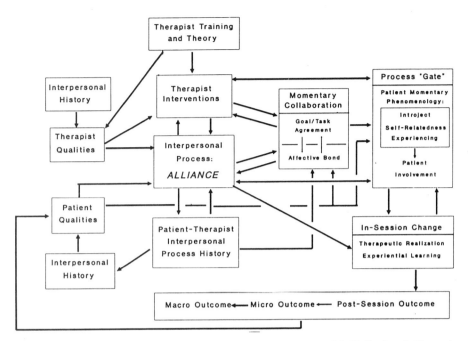

Figure 3.1. Interpersonal adaptation of Generic Process model (Orlinsky & Howard, 1986).

a crucial "gate," representing a momentary state of openness versus defensiveness that regulates the patient's ability to assimilate and accommodate therapeutic interventions and work collaboratively. Hypothesized patient states such as "self-definition," "self-attunement," and "self-evaluation" may be seen as momentary introject states influenced directly by the ongoing interpersonal process.

Patient self-relatedness is influenced by four factors:

1. The specific content of the therapist's intervention.
2. Preexisting patient qualities (e.g., defensive structure, developmental level).
3. The interpersonal process underlying the interventions in that session.
4. The state of momentary collaboration.

In this model, maximum facilitative conditions would include a well-timed, conceptually accurate, interpersonally affiliative therapist intervention offered in the context of a strong affective bond and task agreement, to a patient with the personal capacities to make use of it. Interpersonal process is so crucial because it is closely linked to each factor governing the patient's momentary state. Note too, that patient-therapist interpersonal process history is hypothesized to serve as an additional mediator of momentary interpersonal process. It seems reasonable to speculate that in a dyad with a long, positive interpersonal history, a momentarily poor process might be "filtered" through this history to produce less of a negative effect on subsequent interpersonal process and the affective bond. Conversely, a therapist statement with an embedded blaming element might produce greater disruption in patient self-relatedness in the case of a dyad with a history of such exchanges.

Momentary Collaboration

In the proposed interpersonal model, momentary collaboration[7] subsumes the factors (goal/task agreement and affective bond) typically used to define the alliance. The collaborative state is seen to be a function of therapist interventions, patient qualities, and interpersonal process. Although each of these three contributing factors directly affects momentary self-relatedness, it is necessary to posit the role of momentary collaboration as an additional mediational mechanism with independent effects to fully account for complex interactions of transient competing processes. For instance, a meaningful intervention accompanied by benign interpersonal process is likely to have less effect in the absence of goal and/or task agreement. Another possibility is the case in which a positive interpersonal process over time has led to the establishment of an affective bond. The emergence of the bond in turn contributes (with appropriate therapist interventions) to a shift toward greater goal agreement, when then increases the probability of a productive patient process in the session. In the early phases of therapy, interpersonal process might be benign and therapist interventions meaningful, but insufficient time has passed to permit the establishment of a true affective bond. Thus, the summation of forces pulling for openness or self-relatedness is reduced. Finally, a positive affective attachment and task consensus might maintain positive patient self-relatedness or exploration despite momentarily poor interpersonal process or tangential intervention.

Therapist Training and Qualities

We presented evidence earlier that the therapist's own introject state influences the quality of the interpersonal process, which in turn influences the patient's introject. We also cited evidence that the therapist's introject mediates response to training as evidenced in future interpersonal and technical

---

[7] We have labeled this factor "momentary" collaboration because it is possible for collaboration to vary from moment to moment, and also because it exerts its influence in moment-by-moment processes. However, after the early phases of therapy, it is likely to be a relatively stable influence.

behaviors. Thus, the therapist's introject can be seen as a vulnerability marker for poor process. The nature of the therapist's theoretical training may also be important. Many theories of psychopathology, particularly psychoanalytic theories, are subtly pejorative toward the patient (Wile, 1984). As Wile states, "Clients are seen as gratifying infantile impulses, being defensive, having developmental defects, and resisting the therapy . . . therapists who conceptualize people in these ways may have a hard time making interpretations that do not communicate at least some element of this pejorative view" (1984, p. 353). Thus, the therapist's clinical heuristics may also subtly shape the interpersonal transactions making up the alliance.

A CLINICAL EXAMPLE

A brief clinical vignette will help to illustrate some of our main theoretical formulations. The transcript passages presented are from the 16th of 25 sessions of time-limited dynamic psychotherapy with a male engineer in his late 30s. He had been involved in a long-term relationship with a woman and was highly ambivalent about marriage. The patient presented with a variety of complaints, including extreme lack of confidence, pervasive unhappiness with his job (accompanied by seeming inability to decide to switch careers), social withdrawal, and conflicts over commitment to a relationship. He described himself as "on hold," and admitted to frequent daydreaming. Diagnostically he was seen as Dysthymic and Avoidant (with Dependent and Passive-Aggressive features).

The central tendency of the patient's introject structure (as measured by the SASB INTREX questionnaire) was extremely self-critical (self-controlling and disaffiliative), but it also contained strong elements of self-neglect (self-separating or autonomy granting in a hostile manner). This introject structure likely represented a complex introjection of his relationship with his mother. The patient described her as nominally autonomy granting ("She always said it didn't matter what I wanted to be"), but in fact, she had rather clear-cut plans for him ("She was bitter about not having done more with her life . . . I think she was going to make sure we did . . . she drove us to feel like we had to do something special . . . and seem happy, and go to church and have kids and just be a well-adjusted citizen"). However, her plans ignored his needs, and she was also apparently quite critical toward the patient ("I can remember my mother screaming at me, how stupid I'd been . . ."). The patient's mother, then, acted toward him with control, using criticism when he did not meet her standards, and secondarily with neglect (her control overlooked his true developmental needs). The most important feature of the interpersonal process between mother and son seemed to have been the mother's complex messages on the control dimension, communications that simultaneously encouraged autonomy as well as submission.

The therapist, interestingly, had a similar introject structure with elements of hostile self-control and self-neglect. Based on this introject, we might predict that the therapist would be vulnerable to critical as well as neglectful behavior toward the patient (mirroring early acts by significant others toward the therapist). Furthermore, such acts with this particular patient would also replicate early interpersonal patterns between the patient and his mother, reinforcing the patient's problematic introject structure. If such interpersonal processes actually occurred between the patient and the therapist, we would expect to see a marginal affective bond, a struggle over goal agreement, and little introject change in the patient. Unfortunately, in this case, as the therapist explored the patient's relationship difficulties, the underlying interpersonal process did indeed mirror those same difficulties, and the outcome was poor (no introject or symptomatic change).[8]

The following brief exchanges help illustrate some of these problematic processes.[9] The patient had been explaining that, although he has spent over 8 years with his girlfriend, he doesn't truly love her and doesn't want to get married, but cannot end the relationship because of guilt and fears that he will hurt her. The therapist, like the patient's mother, is nominally autonomy granting ("Tell me about your relationship"). However, the therapist seems to have his own agenda which is at odds with the patient's explanation. The therapist believes that the patient truly cares for his girlfriend, is afraid to admit it, and is actually quite dependent on her.

P: I haven't been able to yet [leave his girlfriend].
T: So in a way, you care very much about how she feels.
P: No, I care what I feel because it hasn't been a real fun-filled eight and a half years.

In this brief exchange, with one sentence, the therapist begins to engage in a complex interpersonal process similar to the patient's early history. The surface structure of the therapist's comment is a reflective restatement (affiliative autonomy granting). However, it misses the true intent of the patient's earlier statements and instead reflects the therapist's vision of events (a process of disaffiliative autonomy granting or neglect). This represents a recapitulation of the patient's relationship with his mother. In response, the patient attempts to separate ("No, I care because . . ."). Although this interchange sounds benign on first reading, it is charged with meaning and accompanied by a rather hard edge from both participants. Several lines

---

[8] The therapist in this case had been observed with other patients to be a warm and understanding man who did not engage in hostile control and neglect. This case illustrates the importance of the interaction between patient and therapist introject structure, interpersonal history, and therapeutic process.
[9] Tone of voice and inflection are crucial to the accurate rating of interpersonal process and cannot be captured by a written transcript alone.

later, this process repeats itself, as the therapist begins to have a critical tone in his voice.

T: Well, one could, from the outside looking in, say something like, "It appears John needs Carol a lot," how would that statement strike you?

P: Maybe I need what she gives me a lot, but I don't know if I need her.

T: All right, let me add another phrase on that statement. "It appears John needs Carol a lot, but it's very difficult for him to admit it to himself."

P: Well, I'm not sure, I really felt like I could get more done without her . . .

At this point, the therapist seems to become more noticeably irritated and critical and his interpersonal process becomes more overtly controlling and critical. As the patient continues to respond with hostile separation, something of a "battle" for control over the patient's beliefs is recreated.

T: I guess the part that's mysterious to me is that uh, need for her is not there, it's hard to understand what has kept you hanging in, because you are extraordinarily concerned about her feelings and her experience and how she's doing and how she is. You care about that very much. You extend yourself greatly . . .

P: No, stopped being for a long time ago (sic).

T: But something keeps you hanging in there, it appears that you need her, but at the same time, it is difficult to admit that.

P: Well, maybe I need what she gives me, but I consider her not being good enough for me for the rest of my life . . .

T: But see, I think all those considerations are ways of, of protecting yourself a little bit. I mean like if you thought she were absolutely beautiful and smart and capable and independent and everything was perfect.

P: Then I'd probably want to marry her. . . . That would be motivation enough to make me try to be the best I could be . . .

T: (cuts patient off) See, the scary part about that would be what if she were all those things, she might not need you, she might not want you . . .

P: (cuts therapist off) Uh huh, well that's the gamble I'd be taking.

T: But that's a gamble you've not taken.

In these exchanges, the therapist has more and more overtly ignored what the patient has been saying, and has done so in a critical manner. The communications that are complex on the control dimension are similar to the patient's description of his mother's style, as well as structurally isomorphic to the patient's introject (i.e., confirming of it). This interpersonal process is resulting in little depth of experiencing or exploration on the part of the patient. The therapist and patient seem to have very different goals, and their collaboration is poor—both reflecting and creating poor interpersonal process. Ultimately, this process results in the patient making a series of self-critical remarks ("What makes me so foolish is that . . ."), suggesting the activation of his hostile, critical introject. In fact, a measure of short-term outcome taken following this session showed deterioration from intake status (up until this point the short-term measures had indicated no change). This example helps to illustrate some of the hypothesized features of the generic interpersonal process model.

SUMMARY AND CONCLUSIONS

The highlights of our empirical research on the alliance might be summarized as following:

1. Therapists' personal reactions to patients color their communications, diagnostic impressions and treatment plans (Strupp, 1955a, 1955b, 1955c, 1960).
2. Patients' retrospective accounts of their therapeutic experiences were similar in that they focused on positive therapist qualities (empathy, warmth, respect, interest, etc.) and linked these to successful outcomes (Strupp, Fox, & Lessler, 1969).
3. The relationship between alliance dimensions and outcome does not seem to vary as a function of type of therapy (Gomes-Schwartz, 1978).
4. The dimension of patient involvement—the patient's willingness and ability to become actively involved in treatment—seems to be the best predictor of outcome (Gomes-Schwartz, 1978; O'Malley, Suh, & Strupp, 1983). The relationship between patient involvement and outcome remains significant even after the therapist-offered conditions are partialed out.
5. The relationship between patient involvement and outcome increases linearly across the first three sessions, suggesting that the dimension of patient involvement is not solely an antecedent characteristic, but also an emergent one in collaboration with certain therapist contributions. (O'Malley, Suh, & Strupp, 1983; Moras & Strupp, 1982).
6. The pattern of therapist-offered relationship conditions over the first three sessions showed high correlations with outcome, whereas ratings from a single time point did not (Suh, Strupp, & O'Malley 1986).
7. Taken together, these findings suggest that the alliance is either well-formed or fails to form early in therapy (the first three sessions).
8. The similarity in factor structure of two different instruments (VPPS and VTAS) suggests relatively stable process dimensions

related to the alliance. The number of dimensions that reflect patient behaviors seems to be greater than the number that reflect therapist contributions (Hartley & Strupp, 1983).

9. Patient motivation and resistance seem to drop over the course of therapy, regardless of outcome. Overall alliance scores peak at about the 25% point of therapy, with high- and low-outcome cases being maximally differentiated at this point (Hartley & Strupp, 1983).

10. Even well-trained therapists may have considerable difficulty forming productive alliances, and they show surprising vulnerability to countertransference reactions with hostile, resistant patients (Strupp, 1980a, 1980b, 1980c, 1980d).

11. The same therapists, employing similar technical strategies, nonetheless engaged in marked different interpersonal processes with their high- and low-change cases (Henry, Schacht, & Strupp, 1986).

12. Countertherapeutic interpersonal process, thought to be a measure of a poor working alliance, is marked by relatively high levels of subtle therapist hostility, complex communications, and negative complementarity (Henry, 1986; Henry, Schacht, & Strupp, 1986, 1990).

13. Although the absence of negative interpersonal process may not be sufficient in some cases to produce positive therapeutic change, the presence of even relatively low frequencies of countertherapeutic interpersonal process does seem sufficient to prevent change. A little bit of bad process goes a long way (Henry, Schacht, & Strupp, 1986).

14. Predictions drawn from interpersonal theory were supported. Links between the therapists' own interpersonal history, therapists' introject state, therapeutic process, and patient introject change (Henry, Schacht, & Strupp, 1990) provided an empirical base for an interpersonal definition of the alliance.

15. Additional technical training designed to promote a collaborative alliance with difficult patients did not successfully alter the problematic underlying interpersonal process, and may actually have increased it (Henry, Strupp, Butler, Schacht, & Binder, 1993).

With this empirical base, we now return to the basic questions about the alliance detailed at the beginning of this chapter. At this point, we have chosen to offer a unidimensional definition of the alliance as interpersonal process reflecting a cumulative succession of momentary dyadic states. This process both affects and reflects an emergent set of secondary alliance dimensions such as affective bond and task agreement and is a crucial variable determining the nature of the "working model" or internal representation of the therapist formed by the patient. The patient and therapist both contribute to the ongoing interpersonal process, which is in part mediated by each participant's interpersonal history, as well as by the basic transactional "pull" for complementarity. The alliance as interpersonal process is theoretically sufficient to produce direct change through the process of introjection.[10] The momentary dyadic state, as reflected in interpersonal process, also serves a gating function that either potentiates or blocks the effectiveness of specific interventions. In turn, certain techniques (particularly interpretations and confrontations) may inadvertently create a negative interpersonal process that weakens the alliance. The nature of the alliance seems to be formed within the first few sessions, and whereas the absence of negative interpersonal processes may not suffice for change in all cases, the presence of even relatively low levels of negative therapist behavior may prevent change. Although the theoretical mechanisms by which the alliance effects change should not vary as a function of the phase of therapy, these early sessions are likely a critical period. This is so because the introject may be construed as rigid, overleaned beliefs or stereotypes about the self (Henry, Schacht, & Strupp, 1990) that require little affirmative interpersonal evidence for reinforcement. These processes are thought to be a common change mechanism, equally important to all therapies.

Our definition of the alliance is in some ways arbitrary, as the therapeutic alliance is a conceptual construct with many possible definitions. Frieswyk et al. (1986) make a cogent argument for limiting the definition of the alliance to patient contributions on the grounds that this offers greater research utility. We argue for our viewpoint on similar grounds. The definition of the alliance as interpersonal process permits a unified research metric and underlying theory to link patient and therapist characteristics, therapeutic process, and outcome. Nonetheless, we feel our approach should complement, not compete with other methods of studying and defining the alliance. We are entering a potentially fruitful era in the history of psychotherapy research—one more focused on common factors as important change mechanisms worthy of study themselves. Accompanying this shift has been a reduction in "theoretical warfare" among proponents of different therapeutic approaches.

In some ways, our research has come full circle. We began our research intuitively convinced of the importance of the person of the therapist, and the quality of the therapeutic relationship. Such thinking was dismissed by some as anti-theoretical or nonscientific because it did not focus on the technical interventions linked to specific theories of therapy. After more than 30 years, our most recent research on the role of the therapist's introject structure in therapeutic process and outcome continues to underscore the importance of therapists' personal qualities and the central role of the alliance in therapeutic change processes. Our hope is that these studies of the alliance have ultimately demonstrated that concepts such as *personal qualities* and *relationship variables* are indeed quite at home with scientific theory.

---

[10] We recognize, however, that there are likely patients with deeply entrenched introject structures who will not change even under optimal therapist-offered process conditions.

REFERENCES

Ainsworth, M. D. S. (1989). Attachments beyond infancy. *American Psychologist, 44*, 709–716.

Alpher, V. S. (1991). Interpersonal process in psychotherapy: Application to a case study of conflict in the therapeutic relationship. *Psychotherapy, 28*(4), 550–562.

Benjamin, L. S. (1974). Structural analysis of social behavior. *Psychological Review, 81*, 392–425.

Benjamin, L. S. (1983). *The INTREX user's manual, Parts I and II.* (Available from Intrex Interpersonal Institute, Inc., P.O. Box 55218, Madison, WI 53705).

Bordin, E. S. (1979). The generalizability of the psychoanalytic concept of the working alliance. *Psychotherapy: Theory, Research and Practice, 16*, 252–260.

Bowlby, J. (1977a). The making and breaking of affectional bonds: I. Aetiology and psychopathology in the light of attachment theory. *British Journal of Psychiatry, 130*, 201–210.

Bowlby, J. (1977b). The making and breaking of affectional bonds: II. Attachment, communication, and the therapeutic process. *British Journal of Psychiatry, 130*, 421–431.

Christianson, J. (1991). *Understanding the patient–therapist interaction and therapeutic change in light of pre-therapy interpersonal relations.* Unpublished doctoral dissertation, Vanderbilt University, Nashville, TN.

Coady, N. J. (1991a). The association between client and therapist interpersonal processes and outcomes in psychodynamic psychotherapy. *Research on Social Work Practice, 1*(2), 122–138.

Coady, N. J. (1991b). The association between complex types of therapist interventions and outcomes in psychodynamic psychotherapy. *Research on Social Work Practice, 1*(3), 257–277.

Freud, S. (1912/1966). On beginning the treatment. In J. Strachey (Ed.), *The standard edition of the complete psychological works of Sigmund Freud* (Vol. 12). London, England: Hogarth Press.

Frieswyk, S. H., Allen, J. G., Colson, D. B., Coyne, L., Gabbard, G. O., Horowitz, L., & Newsom, G. (1986). Therapeutic alliance: Its place as a process and outcome variable in dynamic psychotherapy research. *Journal of Consulting and Clinical Psychology, 54*(1), 32–38.

Gaston, L. (1990). The concept of the alliance and its role in psychotherapy: Theoretical and empirical considerations. *Psychotherapy, 27*(2), 143–153.

Gomes-Schwartz, B. (1978). Effective ingredients in psychotherapy: Prediction of outcome from process variables. *Journal of Consulting and Clinical Psychology, 46*(5), 1023–1035.

Greenson, R. R. (1965). The working alliance and the transference neuroses. *The Psychoanalytic Quarterly, 34*, 155–181.

Hartley, D. E., & Strupp, H. H. (1983). The therapeutic alliance: Its relationship to outcome in brief psychotherapy. In J. Masling (Ed.), *Empirical studies of psychoanalytical theories,* Vol. 1; pp. 1–38. Hillsdale, NJ: Analytical Press.

Henry, W. P. (1986). *Interpersonal process in psychotherapy*. Unpublished doctoral dissertation, Vanderbilt University, Nashville, TN.

Henry, W. P., Schacht, T. E., & Strupp, H. H. (1986). Structural analysis of social behavior: Application to a study of interpersonal process in differential psychotherapeutic outcome. *Journal of Consulting and Clinical Psychology, 54*(1), 27–31.

Henry, W. P., Schacht, T. E., & Strupp, H. H. (1990). Patient and therapist introject, interpersonal process, and differential psychotherapy outcome. *Journal of Consulting and Clinical Psychology, 58*(6), 768–774.

Henry, W. P., Strupp, H. H., Butler, S. F., Schacht, T. E., & Binder, J. L. (1993). Effects of training in time-limited dynamic psychotherapy: Changes in therapist behavior. *Journal of Consulting and Clinical Psychology, 61*, 434–440.

Henry, W. P., Schacht, T. E., Strupp, H. H., Butler, S. F., & Binder, J. L. (1993). Effects of training in time-limited dynamic psychotherapy: Mediators of therapists' responses to training. *Journal of Consulting and Clinical Psychology, 61*, 441–447.

Horvath, A. O., Gaston, L., & Luborsky, L. (1993). The therapeutic alliance and its measures. In N. E. Miller, L. Luborsky, J. P. Barber, & J. P. Docherty (Eds.), *Psychoanalytic treatment research: A handbook for clinical practice* (pp. 247–273). New York: Basic Books.

Kiesler, D. J. (1979). An interpersonal communication analysis of relationship in psychotherapy. *Psychiatry, 42*, 299–311.

Kiesler, D. J. (1982). Interpersonal theory for personality and psychotherapy. In J. C. Anchin & D. J. Kiesler (Eds.), *Handbook of interpersonal psychotherapy* (pp. 3–24). New York: Pergamon Press.

Langs, R. (1973). *The technique of psychoanalytic psychotherapy* (Vol. 1). New York: Aronson.

Langs, R. (1974). *The technique of psychoanalytic psychotherapy* (Vol. 2). New York: Aronson.

Langs, R. (1976). *The therapeutic interaction* (Vol. 2). New York: Aronson.

Luborsky, L. (1976). Helping alliance in psychotherapy. In J. L. Claghorn (Ed.), *Successful psychotherapy*. New York: Bruner/Mazel.

Moras, K., & Strupp, H. H. (1982). Pretherapy interpersonal relations, patients' alliance, and outcome in brief therapy. *Archives of General Psychiatry, 39*, 405–409.

O'Malley, S. S., Suh, C. S., & Strupp, H. H. (1983). The Vanderbilt Psychotherapy Process Scale: A report on the scale development and a process-outcome study. *Journal of Consulting and Clinical Psychology, 51*(4), 581–586.

Orlinsky, D. E., & Howard, K. I. (1967). The good therapy hour. *Archives of General Psychiatry, 16*, 621–632.

Orlinsky, D. E., & Howard, K. I. (1975). *Varieties of psychotherapeutic experience*. New York: Teacher's College Press.

Orlinsky, D. E., & Howard, K. I. (1986). Process and outcome in psychotherapy. In S. L. Garfield & A. E. Bergin (Eds.), *Handbook of psychotherapy and behavior change* (3rd ed., pp. 311–381). New York: Wiley.

Quintana, S. M., & Meara, N. M. (1990). Internalization of therapeutic relationships in short-term psychotherapy. *Journal of Counseling Psychology, 37*(2), 123–130.

Rudy, J. P., McLemore, C. W., & Gorsuch, R. L. (1985). Interpersonal behavior and therapeutic progress: Therapists and clients rate themselves and each other. *Psychiatry: Interpersonal and Biological Processes, 48,* 264–281.

Strupp, H. H. (1955a). An objective comparison of Rogerian and psychoanalytic techniques. *Journal of Consulting Psychology, 19,* 1–7.

Strupp, H. H. (1955b). Psychotherapeutic technique, professional affiliation, and experience level. *Journal of Consulting Psychology, 19,* 97–102.

Strupp, H. H. (1955c). The effects of the psychotherapist's personal analysis upon his techniques. *Journal of Consulting Psychology, 19,* 197–204.

Strupp, H. H. (1958). The psychotherapist's contribution to the treatment process. *Behavioral Science, 3*(1), 34–67.

Strupp, H. H. (1960). Nature of psychotherapist's contribution to treatment process. *Archives of General Psychiatry, 3,* 219–231.

Strupp, H. H. (1969). Toward a specification of teaching and learning in psychotherapy. *Archives of General Psychiatry, 21,* 203–212.

Strupp, H. H. (1973a). The interpersonal relationship as a vehicle for therapeutic learning. *Journal of Consulting and Clinical Psychology, 41*(1), 13–15.

Strupp, H. H. (1973b). On the basic ingredients of psychotherapy. *Psychotherapy and Psychosomatics, 24,* 249–260.

Strupp, H. H. (1973c). Toward a reformulation of the psychotherapeutic influence. *International Journal of Psychiatry, 11,* 263–365.

Strupp, H. H. (1980a). Success and failure in time-limited psychotherapy: A systematic comparison of two cases (Comparison 1). *Archives of General Psychiatry, 37,* 595–603.

Strupp, H. H. (1980b). Success and failure in time-limited psychotherapy: A systematic comparison of two cases (Comparison 2). *Archives of General Psychiatry, 37,* 708–716.

Strupp, H. H. (1980c). Success and failure in time-limited psychotherapy: With special reference to the performance of a lay counselor (Comparison 3). *Archives of General Psychiatry, 37,* 831–841.

Strupp, H. H. (1980d). Success and failure in time-limited psychotherapy: Further evidence (Comparison 4). *Archives in General Psychiatry, 37,* 947–954.

Strupp, H. H. (1993). The Vanderbilt psychotherapy studies: Synopsis. *Journal of Consulting and Clinical Psychology, 61,* 431–433.

Strupp, H. H., & Binder, J. L. (1984). *Psychotherapy in a new key: A guide to time-limited dynamic psychotherapy.* New York: Basic Books.

Strupp, H. H., Fox, R. E., & Lessler, K. (1969). *Patient's view their psychotherapy.* Baltimore, MD: Johns Hopkins Press.

Strupp, H. H., & Hadley, S. W. (1979). Specific vs. nonspecific factors in psychotherapy. *Archives in General Psychiatry, 36,* 1125–1136.

Strupp, H. H., Schacht, T. E., & Henry, W. P. (1988). Problem-treatment-outcome congruence: A principle whose time has come. In H. Dahl, H. Kachele, &

H. Thoma (Eds.), *Psychoanalytic process research strategies* (pp. 1–14). Berlin, Germany: Springer-Verlag.

Suh, C. S., Strupp, H. H., & O'Malley, S. S. (1986). The Vanderbilt Process Measures: The Psychotherapy Process Scale (VPPS) and the Negative Indicators Scale (VNIS). In L. S. Greenberg & W. M. Pinsof (Eds.), *The psychotherapeutic process: A research handbook* (pp. 285–324). New York: Guilford.

Sullivan, H. S. (1953). *The interpersonal theory of psychiatry.* New York: Norton.

Wile, D. B. (1984). Kohut, Kernberg, and accusatory interpretations. *Psychotherapy, 21,* 353–364.

Zetzel, E. (1956). Current concepts of transference. *International Journal of Psychoanalysis, 37,* 369–375.

CHAPTER 4

The California Psychotherapy Alliance Scales*

LOUISE GASTON and CHARLES R. MARMAR

The California Psychotherapy Alliance Scales, or CALPAS, comprise an alliance measure derived from theory and for which construct validity is somewhat supported by empirical results. Most other alliance measures were constructed by developing clinically sound items, and their underlying dimensions were identified through exploratory factor analysis (Hartley & Strupp, 1983; Horvath & Greenberg, 1989; Luborsky, Crits-Christoph, Alexander, Margolis, & Cohen, 1983; Marmar, Horowitz, Weiss, & Marziali, 1986), with the exception of the Working Alliance Inventory (Horvath & Greenberg, 1989), which was explicitly based on Bordin's (1979) conceptualization. The development of these alliance measures was pivotal because they led to the recognition of the predictive value of the alliance concept and to its multidimensional nature. Nevertheless, theoretically derived alliance measures are needed for the identification of a potentially generic change factor in psychotherapy, which may later assist psychotherapists in better applying techniques and improving the efficacy of psychotherapy.

HISTORICAL OVERVIEW

The CALPAS is based on alliance measures previously developed at the Langley Porter Psychiatric Institute, San Francisco. A 41-item measure to be rated by independent judges, CALTARS, was first developed to tap patient's and therapist's positive and negative contributions to the alliance (Horowitz, Marmar, Weiss, DeWitt, & Rosenbaum, 1984; Marmar, Weiss, & Gaston, 1989).

Marmar revised this measure to propose the original version of the CALPAS, which contained 31 items for the patient version and 5 items for the therapist and rater versions (Marmar, Gaston, Thompson, & Gallagher,

---

* Requests for reprints should be sent to Louise Gaston, Ph.D., Department of Psychiatry, McGill University, 1033 Pine Ave. West, Montreal (Quebec), Canada, H3A 1A1.

1989). In parallel, at Clark Institute in Toronto, Marziali (1984) further developed the CALTARS into the TARS, and she introduced additional versions for patients and therapists. Principal component factor analyses of the patient versions of both the CALTARS and the 31-item CALPAS revealed four alliance factors along with factors of either patient or therapist negative contributions.

Taking into account both the empirical findings and theoretical formulations, Marmar and Gaston (1988) developed a 24-item CALPAS, with patient, therapist, and independent rater versions of the instrument. This chapter mostly focuses on this latest effort.

DEFINITION OF ALLIANCE

Given the numerous alliance definitions proposed in the literature, the validity of the alliance concept remains controversial. Much of the actual controversy is probably because the alliance as a construct is not embedded within a larger theory of the change process in psychotherapy. One proposed solution to the conceptual confusion created by the recent proliferation of alliance measures is to view the various alliance definitions as each reflecting a relatively independent dimension of the alliance (Gaston, 1990; Marmar, 1990). Consequently, the CALPAS was developed to measure four relatively independent alliance dimensions: (a) the therapeutic alliance; (b) the working alliance; (c) the therapist's understanding and involvement; and (d) the patient-therapist agreement on goals and strategies. The following paragraphs present the rationale for each of these alliance dimensions.

The CALPAS scale reflecting the *therapeutic alliance* is based on Freud's early papers on transference where he wrote, "The first aim of treatment is to attach the person of the patient to the person of the therapist" (1913/ 1966a, p. 139), as well as on Zetzel's (1956) introduction of the term "therapeutic alliance," which she viewed as stemming from the patient's attachment to and identification with the analyst. The Penn Helping Alliance Rating Scale already reflects this dimension of the alliance concept (Luborsky et al., 1983), although it contains items reflecting satisfaction in therapy, as does the 31-item CALPAS (Marmar, Gaston, et al., 1989), which are contaminated with outcome.

The CALPAS scale reflecting the *working alliance* emerged from Sterba's (1934) writings. He labeled this phenomenon as an "ego alliance," referring to the need for an alliance between the patient's mature ego functioning and the working style of the therapist. He stressed the importance of the patient's capacity to work in analysis through an oscillation between experiencing and observing.

Although Greenson (1965) introduced the term "working alliance," he employed it interchangeably with the term "therapeutic alliance," which led to some confusion. To reduce the conceptual ambiguities, we view the therapeutic alliance and the working alliance as distinct but yet somewhat related dimensions of the patient's contribution to the alliance (Gaston, 1990; Kanzer, 1975). Therefore, the CALPAS incorporates this distinction by providing scales purporting to measure these two alliance dimensions separately; the therapeutic alliance is defined as affective aspects of the patient's collaboration that are oriented toward the person of the therapist, and the working alliance is defined as the skillful aspects of the patient's collaboration that are directed toward the tasks of therapy.

By focusing only on the patient's contribution to the alliance in developing alliance measures (e.g., Frieswyk et al., 1986), some authors have adopted the implicit hypothesis that therapists behave in a uniformly benevolent and involved fashion. As pointed out by Bowlby (1988), when only the patient's reasonable rapport with the therapist is considered, the qualities and attitudes of the person of the therapist toward the patient tend to be lost. The CALPAS scale of *therapist's understanding and involvement* reflects the work of authors who argued that the therapist plays an important role in forging the alliance in psychotherapy (e.g., Bowlby, 1988; Freud, 1912/1966b; Rogers, 1957).

The CALPAS dimension of *patient-therapist agreement on goals and strategies* is based on Bordin's (1979) eclectic definition of the alliance. He proposed that there are three main alliance components: the bond between patient and therapist; the agreement on goals; and the agreement on tasks. Although the bonding dimension reiterates the importance of the affective aspects of the alliance (Bowlby, 1988; Freud, 1913/1966a; Zetzel, 1956), the agreement on goals and tasks is likely to refer to the more cognitive aspects by focusing on the congruence of the patient's and therapist's beliefs about how people change in psychotherapy. We therefore retain the latter aspects to form a separate alliance scale.

Empirically, these four alliance dimensions (working alliance, therapeutic alliance, therapist understanding and involvement, and agreement on goals and tasks) were found to be tapped by alliance measures when they contained items reflecting these respective dimensions. Relatively separate dimensions of therapeutic and working alliances were found when alliance scales encompassed items reflecting both affective and working aspects of the patient's collaboration in psychotherapy (Gomes-Schwartz, 1978; Hartley & Strupp, 1983; Marmar, Gaston, et al., 1989; Marmar, Weiss, et al., 1989). When items reflecting aspects of the therapist's empathic understanding were included, a dimension of the therapist's positive contribution to the alliance was also repeatedly identified as a component distinct from those of the patient's contribution (Gomes-Schwartz, 1978; Hartley & Strupp, 1983; Marmar, Gaston, et al., 1989; Marmar, Weiss, et al., 1989). Finally, alliance scales assessing agreement on goals and tasks have not been empirically found to be distinct (Horvath & Greenberg, 1989; Marmar, Gaston, et al., 1989; Tracey & Kokotovic, 1989), supporting a single agreement dimension.

VERSIONS OF THE CALPAS

Findings with Previous Versions

In previous versions of the CALPAS, consistent with the preceding theorization, exploratory factor analyses with varimax rotation have repeatedly identified the aforementioned dimensions. The first measure (a 41-item rater version) was named the California Therapeutic Alliance Rating Scale (CALTARS). Although the CALTARS was designed to assess the patient's and therapist's positive and negative contributions to the alliance, a principal component factor analysis yielded a solution with five factors: (a) Patient Commitment; (b) Patient Working Capacity; (c) Therapist Understanding and Involvement; (d) Patient Hostile Resistance; and (e) Therapist Negative Contribution (Marmar, Weiss, et al., 1989).

Another previous measure, a 31-item patient version designated as the CALPAS was factor analyzed, yielding five components: (a) Patient Commitment; (b) Patient Working Capacity; (c) Therapist Understanding and Involvement; (d) Goal Disagreement; and (e) Therapist Negative Contribution (Marmar, Gaston, et al., 1989). Because the latter component tended to reflect more countertransference reactions than alliance expressions, it was not included in the 24-item CALPAS.

The previous CALPAS therapist version was composed of five items, each reflecting an alliance dimension and each rated on a 7-point scale. The scale points were defined by detailed anchored clinical descriptors. Although this approach was clinically attractive, this methodological strategy was revised in the latest version to include more than one item per scale because intercorrelations between the five dimensions or items were found to be too high (.73 to .87) (Marmar, Gaston, et al., 1989).

Current Versions

The 24-item CALPAS was designed to assess four theoretically derived alliance dimensions. It contains four scales: (a) a Patient Commitment (PC) scale reflecting the "therapeutic alliance"; (b) a Patient Working Capacity (PWC) scale reflecting the "working alliance"; (c) a Therapist Understanding and Involvement (TUI) scale reflecting the therapist's contribution to the alliance; and (d) a Working Strategy Consensus (WSC) scale reflecting the agreement on goals and tasks of therapy. While certain of these scales stress either the contribution of the therapist or the patient, all ratings are viewed as being influenced by the interactive context.

The current CALPAS version was elaborated in three steps. First, alliance dimensions were identified by reviewing theoretical and empirical studies (Gaston, 1990). Efforts were directed at developing a comprehensive alliance measure that would not favor any particular therapeutic approach. Instead of using an eclectic definition of the alliance, complementary alliance definitions were borrowed from various theoretical perspectives; that is, analytic (e.g., Sterba, 1934), neoanalytic (e.g., Bowlby, 1988), humanistic (i.e., Rogers, 1957), and eclectic (i.e., Bordin, 1979).

Second, each alliance dimension was operationalized into six components. For the PC scale, they are the patient's confidence that efforts will lead to change, willingness to make sacrifices such as time and money, view of therapy as an important experience, trust in therapy and therapist, participation in therapy despite painful moments, and commitment to complete the therapy process. The PWC scale comprises the patient's capacity to self-disclose intimate and salient information, to self-observe one's reactions, to explore contributions to problems, to experience emotions in a modulated fashion, to work actively with the therapist's comments, to deepen the exploration of salient themes, and to purposefully work toward resolution of problems. The TUI scale reflects the therapist's capacity to understand the patient's subjective point of view and sufferings, to demonstrate a nonjudgmental acceptance of the patient, to address the patient's core difficulties, to intervene with tact and timing, to not misuse therapy for own needs, and to show commitment to help the patient overcome problems. The WSC scale encompasses the similarity of patient and therapist goals, joint effort, and agreement on how people are helped, how people change in therapy, and how therapy should proceed.

Third, parallel forms of the CALPAS were created to be completed by patients (CALPAS-P), therapists (CALPAS-T), or trained clinical raters (CALPAS-R). According to the previously listed alliance components, 24 respective items were constructed for each of these three parallel forms, with six items for each of the four scales. In the patient version, half the items were positively phrased and half were negatively phrased in an attempt to counter the tendency of providing positive responses. Although some CALPAS items were derived from the original scales (Marmar, Gaston, et al., 1989; Marmar, Weiss, et al., 1989), others were developed to take into account expressions of alliance emphasized in theoretical papers (Greenson, 1965; Sterba, 1934) but omitted in previous alliance measures.

CALPAS-R Rating Procedure

The procedure to rate the CALPAS-R is described in a manual to allow standardization of the training and rating procedure (Marmar & Gaston, 1988). In a study requiring complex clinical ratings, it is important to ensure that the raters produce reliable and potentially valid ratings of the phenomena of interest. With the CALPAS, raters need to make inferences about complex observable behaviors. To increase the likelihood that ratings are valid, relatively experienced psychotherapists need to serve as raters.

To promote rater reliability and potential validity, the training of the raters should encompass three steps: (a) learning the concept to be assessed through presentations and readings; (b) group practice ratings of 10 precalibrated therapy sessions; and (c) independent ratings of 10 therapy sessions followed by a reliability check. An acceptable reliability estimate is considered to be greater or equal to .70 (Kraemer, 1981).

To further ensure reliable ratings, the use of three trained eclectic clinical raters is recommended. The use of several raters increases reliability (Shrout & Fleiss, 1979) and protects against rater drift (Kazdin, 1977) or dropout. In the training phase of a study, if one rater consistently shows discrepant ratings with those of the other raters, supplementary training is desirable. If the problem remains, however (that is, leading to reliability coefficients lower than .70), we recommend that this rater is dropped. During a study, recalibration training sessions should be conducted after the completion of every 10 consecutive ratings to ensure against possible rater drift, and reliability checks should also be performed throughout the study.

Following such a training and rating procedure, rater reliability was tested for the CALPAS-R (Gaston, Piper, Debbane, Bienvenu, & Garant, 1991). Intraclass coefficients ICC [2,2] were found to yield excellent estimates of interrater reliability for the four scales: PWC (.94); PC (.94); WSC (.89); and TUI (.97).

CALPAS Validity

An important way of evaluating the construct validity of the CALPAS is to assess its association with other scales purporting to measure the same construct. Sabourin, Coallier, Cournoyer, and Gaston (1990) found moderate-to-high correlations between CALPAS-P scales and the Penn Helping Alliance Rating Scale, Penn HA-P (range from .37 to .60). Hatcher et al. (1990) reported high correlations between the total CALPAS-P score and both the Working Alliance Inventory, WAI-P, (.83) and the Penn HA-P (.79). Similarly, the CALPAS-T total score correlated highly with the WAI-T (.79) and the Penn HA-T (.71) (Hatcher et al., 1990). Finally, Tichenor and Hill (1989) reported that the 5-item CALPAS-R correlated strongly with the rater versions of the WAI (.82) and of the Vanderbilt Therapeutic Alliance Scale (.80), but only moderately with Penn HA-R (.34). These studies were conducted at university counseling centers.

Although these findings are important in supporting the construct validity of the CALPAS, it is also crucial to show that the alliance, as measured by the CALPAS, differs from other related constructs. Sabourin et al. (1990) conducted an exploratory factor analysis with oblique rotation. The included variables were the four CALPAS-P scales and three subscales of Attractiveness, Expertness, and Trustworthiness. It yielded two factors: an alliance factor composed of the four CALPAS scales; and a perceived therapist influence factor where the other three variables mostly loaded. These factors were correlated at .41. These findings, therefore, support the construct validity of the CALPAS-P (the CALPAS-P scales grouped together), and they were found to be relatively distinct from those of a related construct of the psychotherapeutic process.

STRUCTURE OF THE CALPAS

But does the CALPAS truly assess four relatively independent alliance dimensions? To answer this question, it is important to determine that each CALPAS scale assesses a relatively homogeneous alliance dimension, and that the four CALPAS scales are not highly correlated.

Reliability

In a study of 147 psychotherapy patients who completed the CALPAS-P (Gaston, 1991), Cronbach's coefficients for the four alliance scales were found to vary from .43 to .73, with lowest coefficients associated with the PWC and TUI scales (Gaston, 1991). For each of these two scales, one item was responsible for reducing the internal consistency; without this item, the Cronbach alpha would have equaled .58. These results could not be explained by restricted variance associated with these two items. Whether these estimates are adequate is debatable.

For the CALPAS-R, Cronbach's alpha coefficient were found to be as follows: PWC (.95); PC (.96); WSC (.95); and TUI (.97) (Gaston, Piper, et al., 1991). Although these estimates are definitively adequate in a traditional psychometric sense, they also indicate that only one item per scale might have been sufficient to reliably assess each alliance dimension.

Interscale Correlations

Correlations among CALPAS-P scales were found to range from .37 to .62. The greatest differentiation was found between the PWC scale and other scales. The highest common variance was shared by the WSC and TUI scales. This latter result is consistent with previous findings indicating that scales reflecting patient-therapist agreement on goals and tasks were highly related to other alliance dimensions (Horvath & Greenberg, 1989). Similar correlations among CALPAS-P scales were observed in another study (Sabourin et al., 1990), whereas mostly large correlations were obtained in another one, that is, .59 to .81 for the alliance within the session just completed and .22 to .81 for the psychotherapy received so far (Hansell, 1990).

In a study of 32 patients (Gaston, Piper, et al., 1991), correlations among CALPAS-R scales were found to range from .33 to .83. The lowest correlations were observed between the TUI scale and the other CALPAS-R scales.

Taken together, these findings might indicate that patients are better at differentiating their working capacity from the other aspects of the alliance on the CALPAS-P, which might be filtered by their affective contribution to the alliance. Trained clinical judges appear to be better at differentiating the therapist's contribution to the alliance from the patient's contributions on the CALPAS-R. These results are of interest because each participant (patient, therapist, or external observer) has a different vantage point, and each vantage point might yield greater differentiation of certain aspects of the alliance. Examination of the internal structure of the CALPAS-T has not yet been conducted, but it should be done.

In most studies, the moderate-to-high correlations among CALPAS scales challenge the proposed multidimensionality of the alliance. Defining the alliance as a monolithic construct would, however, be premature at this stage. For example, the study reporting mostly high correlations was conducted on a sample of relatively homogeneous individuals (Hatcher et al., 1990), which is likely to increase correlations. When studies recruited a more heterogeneous sample (Gaston, 1991), greater distinctiveness was found among CALPAS scales.

Confirmatory Factor Analysis

More recently, confirmatory factor analysis, CFA, was employed to examine the structure of the CALPAS-P on 308 patients who were being treated using different kinds of psychotherapy and for different lengths of time (Gaston, Sabourin, Hatcher, & Hansell, 1992). A monolithic alliance model composed of a single factor was tested against a bilevel model where four alliance factors were embedded within a general alliance factor. Results indicated that the bilevel model was the best fit to the data, although it was not a good fit. When the CALPAS-P was reduced to the 12 most discriminative items of the four alliance dimensions, the bilevel model appeared indeed to be a good fit to the data, supporting the theoretical model on which the CALPAS was elaborated. The construct validity of this 12-item CALPAS-P version was also supported.

Besides these internal structure considerations, the dimensionality of the CALPAS needs to be examined by investigating the differential associations of its scales across an array of process and outcome dimensions, as well as across a diversity of therapy modalities.

ROLES OF ALLIANCE

Theoretical Considerations

We view the roles played by the alliance in psychotherapy as being threefold: (a) The alliance can be therapeutic in and of itself; (b) the alliance can be a prerequisite for the effectiveness of the therapist's interpretations; and (c) the alliance can interact with different types of therapist interventions (exploratory vs. supportive) in determining success in psychotherapy (Gaston, 1990). As shown in the following paragraphs, these hypotheses can be viewed as complementary.

The view of the alliance as therapeutic in and of itself is based on Rogers' (1957) model of client-centered psychotherapy. A central postulate is that the therapist-offered relationship represents a necessary *and* sufficient ingredient for therapeutic changes to occur. Some analytically oriented authors also came to consider the development of an alliance as therapeutic in its own right. For example, Balint (1968) has extensively written on the developmental function of the therapeutic relationship. Bowlby (1988) also regards the patient-therapist alliance as producing change in and of itself by providing the patient with a corrective emotional experience.

Most analytic authors, however, conceptualize the alliance as a necessary but not sufficient ingredient of successful psychotherapy. The establishment of an alliance is regarded as a prerequisite for the efficiency of interpretations; the alliance would allow the patient to work actively with the interpretations provided by the therapist, and would assist the therapist in elaborating accurate interpretations (Freud, 1913/1966a; Greenson, 1965). From this point of view, the alliance does not uniquely contribute to the acquisition of therapeutic benefits, but rather mediates the efficacy of interpretations by providing the context in which they can promote change. Some authors consider this hypothesis to be complementary to the former. For example, Bowlby (1988) agrees that a therapeutic alliance, although therapeutic in and of itself, would permit the patient to tolerate the anxiety of the exploration elicited by interpretations.

A further complementary hypothesis emerges from the work of Zetzel (1956), who proposed that, for patients presenting difficulties in becoming engaged in therapy, analysts needed to adapt their technical style by using more supportive strategies instead of focusing exclusively on interpretations. Balint (1968) also pointed out that for some patients, whose problems lie at an earlier level of developmental stage, the overuse of interpretation carries particular risks of leaving them feeling rejected by the therapist, and that more supportive interventions would be useful. The clinical implications of attachment theory also include this hypothesis; that is, poor alliances might require supportive interventions to achieve therapeutic success (Bowlby, 1988).

Taken together, the last two hypotheses suggest that exploratory interventions might be more effective in the context of better alliances, and supportive interventions might be more effective when in the context of poorer alliances. In our empirical work, we attempt to test the previously mentioned hypotheses.

Association with Outcome

Findings on the CALPAS and its related alliance scales repeatedly provided empirical support for the predictive validity of the alliance. Of importance, correlations of CALPAS scores with outcome were computed in each study only after controlling for initial levels of outcome.

Using the latest CALPAS-P, Gaston (1991) reported the following correlations between alliance scores and estimates of patient satisfaction with psychotherapy in diverse modalities: PC (.43); PWC (.39); TUI (.65); and WSC (.65), $p < .05$ with 145 degrees of freedom. With the 31-item CALPAS-P, Marmar, Gaston, et al. (1989) found that scores reflecting the therapeutic alliance were associated with symptomatology in cognitive therapy ($r(20) = -.73$, $p < .01$), but they were not associated with outcome in brief dynamic and behavioral therapy. PWC scores tended to be related to symptomatology in both cognitive and brief dynamic psychotherapy ($r(20) = -.34$, $p > .05$; and $r(18) = -.29$, $p > .05$), but not in behavior therapy.

So far, only one study has examined the predictive validity of the CALPAS-T. Marmar, Gaston, et al. (1989) observed only trends toward an association between alliance and symptomatology scores in brief dynamic therapy ($r(18) = -.38$, $p > .05$).

With CALPAS-R ratings, Gaston, Piper, et al. (1991) found that the scale reflecting the therapeutic alliance tended to be correlated with the severity of target objectives as assessed by patients at the termination of short-term psychotherapy ($r(15) = -.44$, $p = .09$), but not with an independent assessor evaluation of the severity of target objectives ($r(15) = -.10$, $p > .05$). In a previous study with the CALTARS, Marmar, Weiss, et al. (1989) reported significant correlations with the scale reflecting the working alliance; outcome consisted of symptomatic improvement ($r(48) = -.29$, $p < .05$) and interpersonal functioning ($r(45) = .39$, $p < .05$).

These findings are consistent with the hypothesis that the alliance could be therapeutic in and of itself. A plausible alternative hypothesis could, however, account for these alliance-outcome associations. It could be argued that the alliance is not an active ingredient of psychotherapy contributing independently to outcome, but rather is a function of in-treatment improvement; patients who experience improvement during therapy would be more likely to have positive feelings toward their therapist, be more committed to treatment, and work more collaboratively.

To test this hypothesis, Gaston, Marmar, Thompson, and Gallagher (1991) examined the association of alliance to outcome after controlling for initial symptomatology and in-treatment symptomatic change. In a sample of elderly depressed patients treated in behavioral, cognitive, or brief dynamic therapy, CALPAS scores provided by both patients and therapists were found to contribute to large amounts of outcome variance, over and above initial symptomatology and in-treatment symptomatic change. For the whole sample, alliance scores were found to contribute to the variance of Beck Depression Inventory scores at termination as follows: 18% by the alliance at the 5th session, 5% by the alliance at the 10th session, and 13% by the alliance at the 15th session. Those results were not statistically significant. Because such findings could be due to differential associations of alliance dimensions with outcome across these psychotherapy modalities, analyses were conducted separately in behavioral, cognitive, and brief dynamic therapy. Within treatment conditions, CALPAS scores were found to account for substantial amounts of outcome variance for CALPAS scores gathered at early, middle, and late sessions respectively: 32%, 57%, and 55% in behavioral therapy; 23%, 49%, and 57% in cognitive therapy; and 18%, 20%, and 36% in brief dynamic therapy. Most results were not statistically significant, however, due to limited power within each treatment condition.

Drawing the conclusion that the alliance is therapeutic in and of itself would be premature at this point. For example, an association between alliance and outcome was not consistently observed in long-term psychotherapy (Gaston, Piper, et al., 1991), and only some alliance scales were predictive of outcome across studies (Gaston, Marmar, et al., 1991; Marmar, Gaston, et al., 1989; Marmar, Weiss, et al., 1989). Therefore, the alliance role in psychotherapy might also allow therapist interventions to be effective.

In a study of bereaved patients, Horowitz, Marmar, Weiss, et al. (1984) reported that the patient's capacity for establishing an alliance in a pretreatment evaluation session interacted inversely with exploratory and supportive interventions in predicting outcome of brief dynamic therapy. Employing a different method of assessing the alliance and interventions but using the same sample, Jones, Cummings, and Horowitz (1988) found similar results. In a preliminary study, Gaston and Ring (in press) further examined this question within a sample of elderly depressed patients, and also found that exploratory interventions interacted with the alliance in determining outcome of cognitive therapy. Although these studies provided some preliminary support for the hypothesis that the alliance interacts with different types of therapist interventions in determining the outcome of brief psychotherapy, further studies are needed in both short-term and long-term psychotherapy.

In a recent study, Gaston, Piper, et al. (1991) examined the impact of both the alliance and therapist interventions, as well as their interaction, on the outcome of both short-term and long-term psychotherapy. CALPAS-R ratings were expected to account for substantial amounts of outcome variance, over and above initial outcome levels, and to interact with exploratory and supportive ratings to explain substantial amounts of outcome variance. Although alliance ratings did not vary across conditions and over time, better alliances tended to be predictive of better outcomes in short-term psychotherapy (accounting for an average 11% of outcome variance). In long-term psychotherapy, interactions terms accounted for substantial outcome variance; more exploratory interventions in the context of better alliances *tended* to lead to better outcomes (accounting for an average 19% of outcome variance), whereas more supportive interventions provided in the context of poorer alliances led to better outcomes (accounting for an average 15% of outcome variance). Although some of the outcome variance accounted for was comparatively large, most findings were not statistically significant due to the small sample sizes.

These findings are consistent with the clinical recommendations by Bowlby (1988), Wallerstein (1989), and Zetzel (1956). Due to very limited power and the low observations-to-variables ratio, these findings can only be considered as preliminary, however. What strengthens these findings is that these relationships were predicted a priori.

ROLES OF ALLIANCE OVER TIME

The examination of alliance variations over time is relevant for understanding the roles played by the alliance in psychotherapy. If alliance improvements were found to be associated with decreases in symptomatology, the hypothesis that the alliance is effective in and of itself could be further supported. A similar conclusion could be drawn if the alliance assessed late in therapy were shown to be more predictive of outcome than when assessed early in therapy.

Before examining empirical results addressing this question, it should be noted that no changes in CALPAS levels over time were observed (Gaston, Marmar, et al., 1991; Marmar, Gaston, et al., 1989; Marmar, Weiss, et al., 1989). Although these findings indicate that the alliance does not vary in average across patients as psychotherapy progresses, another approach is required to investigate whether there are individual alliance shifts and whether they are related to outcome.

Substantial associations were observed between increases of TARS alliance ratings and symptomatology in previous studies (Eaton, Abeles, & Gutfreund, 1988; Klee, Abeles, & Muller, 1990). When CALPAS-R shifts were considered over time, 41% of patients of short-term psychotherapy and 33% of patients in long-term psychotherapy were judged as either having increased or decreased their alliance by at least 1 point on the 7-point scale of the CALPAS-R, but no association was found with outcome (Gaston, 1992a).

When alliance-outcome associations were examined at different time-points in therapy, variable findings were obtained. In a sample of elderly depressed patients, substantial increases of outcome variance were found to be uniquely accounted for by CALPAS-P and CALPAS-T scores from early and late sessions: 23% in behavioral therapy; 34% in cognitive therapy; and 18% in brief dynamic therapy (Gaston, Marmar, et al., 1991). These increases were not found, however, to be statistically significant due to limited power, which equaled about .15, emphasizing the preliminary nature of these findings. In another study, no increment of outcome variance accounted for by CALPAS-R ratings was observed over time (Gaston, Piper, et al., 1991).

Of interest, ratings of positive transference were found to be associated with outcome, but only at the end of therapy. In short-term psychotherapy, partial rs were found to equal .10 and $-.63$ from early to late sessions, and in long-term psychotherapy, partial rs were .13 and .69 from early to late sessions (Gaston, unpublished data). This pattern is similar to the one observed using CALPAS-P ratings, that is, patients' ratings of alliance (Gaston, Marmar, et al., 1991). Taken together, these findings may suggest that CALPAS-P ratings are influenced by elements of positive transference, and that such filter is not likely to occur with CALPAS-R ratings because they are made by external observers. These findings might suggest the importance of individual differences in alliance variations over the course of psychotherapy. As therapy progresses, for some patients the alliance may improve over time, for some it may remain stable, and for others it may deteriorate. It therefore becomes crucial to identify therapist interventions that are associated with alliance improvements, as well as those that could be detrimental for the patient-therapist collaboration.

PATIENT CONTRIBUTIONS TO THE ALLIANCE

In the conceptual framework of the CALPAS, alliance dimensions are viewed as being impacted by each patient's characteristics, as well as by therapist interventions.

Pretreatment Characteristics

The therapeutic alliance is viewed as partially emerging from the patient's early positive experiences with parental figures and quality of object relations (Bowlby, 1988; Freud, 1912/1966b; Zetzel, 1956). The working alliance is conceptualized as also emerging from the patient's mature ego functioning and therapist's interventions (Sterba, 1934). Empirical evidence is accumulating in support of these hypotheses using the latest CALPAS or its predecessors.

Scales reflecting the therapeutic and working alliance were found to be moderately associated with patients' pretreatment interpersonal functioning (Gaston, 1991; Marmar, Weiss, et al., 1989). Although a nonsignificant association between these variables was found in another study, a moderate correlation was revealed between the therapeutic alliance and the quality of social support received by patients (Gaston, Marmar, Gallagher, & Thompson, 1988). Moreover, judges' ratings of the therapeutic alliance were found to be moderately related to patients' level of object relations ($r(32) = .33$, $p = .06$) (Gaston, 1992b).

It is important to note that only moderate correlations were found when significant findings were observed. These moderate correlations between patients' pretreatment characteristics and alliance are clinically encouraging because they suggest that the therapeutic and working alliances are malleable phenomena and are not solely driven by the personality of the patient. As Bowlby (1988) suggested, the association between the patient's quality of attachments and the therapeutic alliance may be mediated by the therapist's understanding and involvement.

Therapists' characteristics and attitudes in treatment were also repeatedly reported to be correlated with therapeutic and working alliances. The TUI scale was repeatedly found to be moderately to highly associated with the PC and PWC scales (Gaston, 1991; Hatcher et al., 1990; Marmar, Gaston, et al., 1989; Marmar, Weiss, et al., 1989; Sabourin et al., 1990).

The association between the patient's alliance and the patient's ego functioning was only indirectly supported by empirical findings. Ratings of therapeutic and working alliances were found to be positively related to patients' experiencing in therapy (Marmar, Weiss, et al., 1989) and negatively related to patients' tendency to avoid dealing with problems (Gaston et al., 1988). Finally, patients' capacity to express appropriate affects and to respond to interpretations were found to be related to the working alliance scale ($r(32) = .34$ and $.38$, $p < .05$), and patients' verbal skills were found to be associated with scales reflecting both the therapeutic and working alliances ($r(32) = .44$ and $.45$, $p < .01$) (Gaston, 1992b).

Whereas these findings provide support to the construct validity of the alliance concept, empirical evidence is also accumulating regarding its discriminant validity. In future studies, direct measures of ego strength should be employed to directly test this hypothesis.

With respect to sociodemographic characteristics, no association was found with scores of therapeutic and working alliances (Gaston et al., 1988; Marmar, Weiss, et al., 1989; Sabourin et al., 1990), but with the exception of one association between therapeutic alliance and level of education (Marmar, Weiss, et al., 1989).

Moderate correlations were, however, sometimes observed between the alliance and level of psychological distress or symptomatology (Gaston, 1991; Gaston, 1992b; Gaston et al., 1988; Marmar, Weiss, et al., 1989; Sabourin et al., 1990); that is, greater pretreatment symptomatology was related to a diminished capacity of the patient to become engaged in therapy, to work in therapy, and to have a sense of working with the therapist toward agreed-on goals.

Most importantly, neither significant nor substantial association was found between CALPAS-P scales and estimates of social desirability (Gaston, 1991), indicating that patients' responses are not merely a reflection of their need to present themselves favorably.

Transference

A major conceptual ambiguity exists regarding the distinctiveness of alliance and transference, in particular the differentiation of the alliance from positive transference. Some psychoanalytic authors have asserted that the alliance concept is neither valid nor useful (Brenner, 1979), or that it may be misleading (Curtis, 1979). These arguments were criticized for being based on a conviction that paying attention to any aspects of the therapeutic relationship other than transference would lead to a shift away from interpretation as the main technique, rather than being based on strong theoretical assertions (Bienvenu & DeCarufel, 1989). The alliance versus transference controversy is not without theoretical basis, especially with respect to the therapeutic alliance, which relies more on affectionate aspects.

Ratings of positive transference were, however, found to not be related to ratings of therapeutic or working alliance in short-term and long-term analytically oriented psychotherapy (Gaston, 1990). In this study, items reflecting positive transference were as follows: The patient tends to overestimate the therapist; the patient tends to look for the therapist's approval; the patient tends to be frustrated by the limits of therapy; the patient tends to be seductive toward the therapist; the patient tends to show interest in the person of the therapist; and the patient tends to wish to be closer to the therapist. This lack of association was obtained even if alliance and transference ratings were performed by the same clinical judges, a strategy that usually produces an halo effect inflating correlations. Although these findings differentiate judges' ratings of alliance and transference, it remains to be determined whether patients' alliance ratings are influenced by positive transference.

Furthermore, CALPAS scales could be tapping aspects of negative transference. When hostility items were included in CALPAS measures as representing negative contributions to the alliance, independent clustering was repeatedly found. Items of patient's hostility toward the therapist were repeatedly distinguished from those representing the therapeutic and working alliance (Marmar, Gaston, et al., 1989; Marmar, Weiss, et al., 1989). Furthermore, items reflecting the therapist's hostility toward the patient were also distinctly clustered from items of therapist's understanding and involvement (Marmar, Gaston, et al., 1989; Marmar, Weiss, et al., 1989), and therapist's hostility is usually conceptualized as an expression of countertransference (Greenson, 1965). This empirical distinction between collaboration and hostility may indicate that the alliance as assessed by the CALPAS represents a phenomenon distinct from the negative aspects of the therapeutic relationship. Given these findings, the latest CALPAS did not include items reflecting patient's negative reactions in therapy; instead, these reactions were tapped in a distinct scale named Patient Overt Negative Transference-like Reactions (Gaston & Marmar, 1991).

THERAPIST'S CONTRIBUTIONS TO THE ALLIANCE

One way of verifying whether an alliance measure is likely to be useful in assessing the collaborative components of various psychotherapy modalities, is to test whether alliance scores vary in average across modalities. In two studies, CALPAS-P levels were not found to be different in behavioral, cognitive, humanistic, and/or dynamic psychotherapy (Gaston, 1991; Gaston, Marmar, et al., 1991). CALPAS-T ratings were also found to not vary across behavioral, cognitive, and brief dynamic psychotherapy (Marmar, Gaston, et al., 1989). CALPAS-R ratings were found to be similar in short-term and long-term psychotherapy (Gaston, Piper et al., 1991). In addition, given that CALPAS ratings were not found to differ at different time points in psychotherapy (Gaston, 1991; Gaston, Marmar, et al., 1991; Marmar, Gaston, et al., 1989; Marmar, Weiss, et al., 1989), these findings might suggest that the CALPAS could be useful in assessing the alliance across diverse psychotherapy modalities.

But does the CALPAS tap alliance dimensions that are differentially related to outcome across diverse psychotherapy approaches? When CALPAS-P associations were computed with satisfaction with treatment across three types of psychotherapy modalities, findings tended to suggest a potentially greater role played by the working alliance (Patient Working Capacity) in dynamic psychotherapy in comparison with behavioral/cognitive therapy (Gaston, 1991). Furthermore, Gaston, Marmar, et al. (1991) reported that CALPAS dimensions tended to be differentially associated with outcome in behavioral, cognitive, and brief dynamic psychotherapy.

With respect to therapists' sociodemographic characteristics, no association was observed with alliance ratings (Gaston et al., 1988). Furthermore, alliance levels were not found to significantly differ across the three psychotherapists who participated in the Gaston, Piper, et al. (1991) study, although trends were observed.

IMPACT OF TECHNIQUE ON THE ALLIANCE

We conceptualize the alliance as a dynamic process that is influenced by the characteristics and efforts of both parties and that can evolve into an active purposeful collaboration or deteriorate into a difficult struggle between patient and therapist. As therapy progresses, for some patients the alliance improves over time, for some it remains stable, and for others it deteriorates. It therefore becomes crucial to identify therapist interventions that are associated with alliance improvements, as well as those that could be detrimental for the patient-therapist collaboration.

Theoretical viewpoints differ greatly with respect to the technical handling of the alliance. Some authors argue that interpretations remain the solely useful technique either to develop good-enough alliances or to repair difficult alliances (Bienvenu & DeCarufel, 1989; Freud, 1912/1966b). Others recommend the use of more supportive and/or educational interventions in combination with exploratory strategies (Balint, 1968; Bowlby, 1988; Dickes, 1975; Greenson, 1965; Kanzer, 1975; Safran, Crocker, McMain, & Murray, 1990; Zetzel, 1956).

In preliminary studies, Foreman and Marmar (1985) reported that, in brief dynamic therapy, interpretations of transference and defenses were associated with alliance improvements on the CALTARS. Gaston and Ring (in press) observed that, in cognitive therapy, interpretations of interpersonal problems were useful in differentiating patients who improved their alliance from those who did not. These studies, however, have methodological flaws and are based on very small sample sizes.

In a larger study, Marmar, Weiss, et al. (1989) reported that the scales reflecting therapeutic and working alliances were negatively associated with the frequency of transference interpretations in brief dynamic therapy of bereaved patients. In contrast, similar scales were not found to be correlated with the frequency of transference interpretations, or of supportive interventions, in short-term and long-term dynamic psychotherapy (Gaston, 1992c). These correlational results do not indicate, however, that these interventions were instrumental in deteriorating the patients' alliance. They might simply mean that therapists employed more or less of certain types of interventions to address problematic alliances.

The impact of therapist interventions on the patient's alliance might be best understood by using estimates of alliance shifts over time. Gaston (1992c) computed shifts of alliance over the course of short- and long-term psychotherapy; that is, whether ratings of therapeutic and working alliances increased or decreased between the early and late sessions. These alliance shifts were correlated with the frequency of exploratory and supportive interventions, as employed throughout therapy, and no association was revealed. Sequential analysis may need to be employed to determine therapist interventions that can alter alliance levels.

The technical handling of the alliance is likely to be more complex than previously thought. Interpretations may be instrumental in improving poor alliances when they are provided in the context of supportive comments. The relation between alliance and transference interpretations might also be curvilinear (e.g., Piper, Azim, Joyce, & McCallum, 1990). The impact of interventions might depend on the initial alliance level; low levels might require more support due to functional deficits in patients, and somewhat good alliances might necessitate more interpretations due to patients' inner conflicts. In addition, it is plausible that a phenomenon of circularity exists between alliance and technique. Therefore, the empirical exploration of this highly relevant clinical question requires imaginative strategies to successfully address the complex relations among its numerous variables. Time-series designs are likely to be necessary to identify the timing impact of therapist interventions on alliance; that is, whether there is an immediate impact, a within-session impact, or a session-to-session impact.

CLINICAL IMPLICATIONS

Research findings on the alliance can lead to practical considerations. As therapists were not found to make alliance ratings that were predictive of outcome (Horvath & Symonds, 1991), therapists do not appear to be good judges of the collaborative aspects of psychotherapy. These findings suggest that therapists need to be adequately trained to assess the alliance, which could then improve their efficiency.

It was found that thoroughly trained therapists could become good judges of the alliance (e.g., Marmar, Gaston, et al., 1989). Marmar, Gaston, et al. (1989) observed trends toward an association between CALPAS-T and symptomatology scores in brief dynamic therapy ($r(18) = -.38, p > .05$). This latter finding is of interest because only dynamic therapists tended to make alliance ratings that were predictive of outcome in this clinical trial (in comparison with behavioral and cognitive therapists), and they were the only therapists who were thoroughly trained in assessing the alliance. In fact, the dynamic therapists were trained to conduct brief dynamic therapy according to the model outlined by Horowitz, Marmar, Krupnick, et al. (1984), which emphasizes the importance of establishing an alliance at the beginning of therapy.

Could it be that therapists who have been trained at recognizing the alliance during their psychotherapy training are better at assessing it later? If so, it would be of importance to train therapists in assessing the alliance. Therapists need to be educated about (a) evaluating the degree of their patients' commitment as well as their capacity to work in treatment, (b) recognizing their own level of understanding and involvement (as well as their countertransference), (c) questioning whether their strategies are suitable for best assisting their patients, and (d) examining whether they strive toward similar goals as those of their patients.

Therapists could, therefore, attempt to improve problematic alliances and/or to adapt their technique to the alliance status presented by patients. Ultimately, it is a question of increasing the efficacy of psychotherapy. The most malleable factor in psychotherapy remains therapist interventions. Although research findings are meager regarding how to handle patients' difficulties in developing a good-enough alliance and empirical efforts need to be pursued, there is sufficient evidence, nevertheless, to support the predictive validity of the alliance to start training therapists immediately in assessing the diverse alliance dimensions. It will be of interest to see how therapists integrate the information provided by these assessments, and to determine which training interventions are the most productive.

RESEARCH DIRECTIONS

Empirical evidence is accumulating to support the validity of the CALPAS across a variety of symptomatic disorders and from different sources of information. The predictive validity of the CALPAS remains to be examined on specific populations such as children, inpatients, and patients presenting with severe personality disorders. Testing hypotheses about the roles of alliance in psychotherapy are important steps, and this line of re-search needs to be continued because it is likely to be the most fruitful avenue in terms of increasing efficacy and of understanding the change process in psychotherapy.

Gaston, Marmar, et al. (1991) provided preliminary evidence supporting the hypothesis that the alliance makes a unique contribution to outcome across a diversity of psychotherapies, and that this contribution is not merely a reflection of in-treatment improvement. Because substantial asso-ciations were observed only within behavioral, cognitive, or brief dynamic psychotherapy, these findings may also suggest that different alliance di-mensions may play various roles across these diverse psychotherapy ap-proaches. Although interesting and clinically meaningful, these results are based on small sample sizes that await replication in larger samples. Re-search is thus needed to clarify whether the diverse CALPAS dimensions influence outcome differentially across various psychotherapy approaches (Wolfe & Goldfried, 1988).

The examination of the role played by the interaction of alliance and ther-apist interventions appears to be a promising avenue and should be pursued. Nonetheless, the clinical reality is probably far more complex than interac-tion effects; for example, when the accuracy of interpretations is consid-ered, the alliance does not seem to interact with interpretations in promoting change (Crits-Christoph, Cooper, & Luborsky, 1988). Furthermore, as much as the alliance interacts with different types of interventions in promoting change, the alliance is also likely to be influenced by interventions. Creative research strategies are needed to disentangle these effects. In an attempt to do so, the rater version of the CALPAS is now being used by the senior au-thor to study the alliance as reflected in each patient statement, and this data is entered in a sequential analysis to identify the therapist interventions most likely to increase or decrease a patient's alliance level.

The concept of alliance also needs to be adapted to other contexts where it is likely to play a role, such as group psychotherapy and pharmacotherapy. A version of the CALPAS has been elaborated to be adapted to the realities of group psychotherapy and is now being used. In a study conducted by John Schneider at Stanford University, patients fill out a CALPAS-P describing the alliance with the group and two CALPAS-P describing the alliance with each of the two co-therapists. The two co-therapists fill out a CALPAS-T for each patient. In several studies being conducted in Canada and United States, CALPAS versions adapted to pharmacotherapy are used to tap the alliance in pharmacotherapy per se, as well as during the usual placebo washout phase conducted at the beginning of clinical trials.

Of greatest importance, the new research directions should be theoreti-cally driven. By testing theoretically guided hypotheses about the roles of the alliance in psychotherapy, researchers contribute to testing theories about the change process in psychotherapy and ultimately to increasing effi-cacy of psychotherapy.

CONCLUSION

The concept of the alliance is a promising construct for the study of the change process in psychotherapy. Empirical findings provide partial support for the validity of the three CALPAS versions in assessing this construct. Although the alliance concept has emerged from clinical observations, research findings are starting to pay back by indicating that the relational and collaborative components of psychotherapy can substantially contribute to helping patients overcome their difficulties. Research efforts have yet to be pursued before the alliance concept can further our understanding of the change process in psychotherapy, but actual findings could immediately benefit the practice of psychotherapy.

Although preliminary findings were provided using the CALPAS, it has yet to be determined whether the roles of the alliance differ in short-term versus long-term psychotherapy, as well as across psychotherapy modalities. Moreover, to fully integrate the alliance concept within the analytical framework, further studies are required on the distinctiveness of the alliance versus positive transference. This distinction needs to be made before the analytical guideline of focusing on transference interpretations can be modified. The roles of the alliance in psychotherapy also need to be investigated more specifically.

To fully examine the value of the alliance concept and its roles in psychotherapy, the alliance construct will ultimately need to be embedded within a theory of the change process in psychotherapy. As the alliance construct emphasizes the relational aspects of psychotherapy, a theory of development such as the attachment theory proposed by Bowlby (1988) might represent an adequate stepping-stone in that direction.

Bowlby (1988) asserts that a child must engage in the following two central developmental tasks to become a healthy individual: (a) develop a secure attachment to a parental figure, and (b) explore the world using this attachment as a secure base. The success of the child's development is viewed as being dependent on the reciprocal attachment of the parental figure to the child, which encompasses immediate empathic emotional responses to the child's needs and a tolerance of the child's exploration. These processes are paralleled in the psychotherapeutic situation by the therapeutic alliance, which consists of the patient's formation of a secure attachment with the therapist; by the working alliance, which involves the patient's exploration of his or her inner and outer world; and by the therapist's empathic understanding and involvement. Some innovative theoretical speculations in that area would help foster the usefulness of the alliance concept in improving the efficacy of psychotherapy. Such theorization could also gain by attempting to integrate the more classical libidinal theory with alliance-related phenomena in psychotherapy. For example, it remains to be seen whether positive transference plays a role in establishing an alliance in psychotherapy for those patients who have already developed a secure-enough attachment, and whether this role differs in short- and long-term psychotherapy.

Definitively, psychotherapy researchers and psychotherapists are at the beginning of an exciting and unfolding adventure in the understanding of the change process in psychotherapy. Those who stand to benefit most from this adventure will be the patients themselves as well as their therapists, who will have more solid grounds on which to base their interventions.

REFERENCES

Balint, M. (1968). *The basic fault.* London, England: Tavistock.

Bienvenu, J. P., & DeCarufel, F. (1989, October). *Transference, therapeutic alliance and working alliance revisited.* Paper presented at the Canadian Psychoanalytic Society, Montreal, Canada.

Bordin, E. S. (1979). The generalizability of the psychoanalytic concept of the working alliance. *Psychotherapy: Theory, Research, and Practice, 16,* 252–260.

Bowlby, J. (1988). *A secure base: Clinical applications of attachment theory.* London, England: Routledge.

Brenner, C. (1979). Working alliance, therapeutic alliance, and transference. *Journal of the American Psychoanalytic Association, 27,* 136–158.

Crits-Christoph, P., Cooper, A., & Luborsky, L. (1988). The accuracy of therapists' interpretations and the outcome of dynamic psychotherapy. *Archives of General Psychiatry, 56,* 490–495.

Curtis, H. C. (1979). The concept of the therapeutic alliance: Implications for the "widening scope". *Journal of the American Psychoanalytic Association, 27,* 159–192.

Dickes, R. (1975). Technical consideration of the therapeutic and working alliances. *International Journal of Psychoanalytic Psychotherapy, 4,* 1–47.

Eaton, T. T., Abeles, N., & Gutfreund, M. J. (1988). Therapeutic alliance and outcome: Impact of treatment length and pretreatment symptomatology. *Psychotherapy, 25,* 536–542.

Foreman, S., & Marmar, C. R. (1985). Therapist actions that address initially poor therapeutic alliances in psychotherapy. *American Journal of Psychiatry, 142,* 922–926.

Frieswyk, S. H., Allen, J. G., Colson, D. B., Coyne, L., Gabbard, G. O., Horwitz, L., & Newsom, G. (1986). Therapeutic alliance: Its place as a process and outcome variable in dynamic psychotherapy research. *Journal of Consulting and Clinical Psychology, 54,* 32–38.

Freud, S. (1966a). On beginning the treatment. In J. Strachey (Ed. and Trans.), *The standard edition of the complete psychological works of Sigmund Freud* (Vol. 12, pp. 112–144). London, England: Hogarth Press. (Original work published 1913)

Freud, S. (1966b). The dynamics of transference. In J. Strachey (Ed. and Trans.), *The standard edition of the complete psychological works of Sigmund Freud*

(Vol. 12, pp. 99–108). London, England: Hogarth Press. (Original work published 1912)

Gaston, L. (1990). The role of the alliance in psychotherapy: Theoretical and empirical considerations. *Psychotherapy, 27,* 143–153.

Gaston, L. (1991). Reliability and criterion-related validity of the California Psychotherapy Alliance Scales. *Psychological Assessment: A Journal of Consulting and Clinical Psychology, 3,* 68–74.

Gaston, L. (1992a). [Alliance shifts and outcome in short- and long-term psychotherapy]. Unpublished data.

Gaston, L. (1992b). [Association of patient's pretreatment characteristics with alliance in short- and long-term psychotherapy]. Unpublished data.

Gaston, L. (1992c). [Alliance and therapist interventions in short- and long-term psychotherapy]. Unpublished data.

Gaston, L., & Marmar, C. R. (1991). *Manual for the California Psychotherapy Alliance Scales-CALPAS.* Unpublished manuscript. Department of Psychiatry, McGill University, Montreal, Canada.

Gaston, L., Marmar, C., Thompson, L., & Gallagher, D. (1988). Relation of patient pretreatment characteristics to the therapeutic alliance in diverse psychotherapies. *Journal of Consulting and Clinical Psychology, 56,* 483–489.

Gaston, L., Marmar, C. R., Thompson, L. W., & Gallagher, D. (1991). Alliance prediction of outcome beyond in-treatment symptomatic change as psychotherapy progresses. *Psychotherapy Research, 1,* 104–113.

Gaston, L., Piper, W. E., Debbane, E. G., Bienvenu, J. P., & Garant, J. (1991, July). *Alliance and technique in predicting outcome of short- and long-term psychotherapy.* Paper presented at the annual meeting of the Society for Psychotherapy Research, Lyon, France.

Gaston, L., & Ring, J. M. (in press). Preliminary results on the Inventory of Therapeutic Strategies. *Journal of Psychotherapy Practice and Research.*

Gaston, L., Sabourin, S., Hatcher, R., & Hansell, J. (1992, June). *Confirmatory factor analysis of the CALPAS-P and its short version.* Paper presented at the meeting of the International Society for Psychotherapy Research, Berkeley, CA.

Gomes-Schwartz, B. (1978). Effective ingredients in psychotherapy: Prediction of outcome from process variables. *Journal of Consulting and Clinical Psychology, 46,* 1023–1035.

Greenson, R. R. (1965). The working alliance and the transference neuroses. *Psychoanalysis Quarterly, 34,* 155–181.

Hansell, J. (1990). *The relationship of the CALPAS to other measures of the alliance.* Paper presented at the meeting of the Society for Psychotherapy Research, Wintergreen, VA.

Hartley, D., & Strupp, H. (1983). The therapeutic alliance: Its relationship to outcome in brief psychotherapy. In J. Masling (Ed.), *Empirical studies of psychoanalytic theories* (Vol. 1, pp. 1–27). Hillsdale, NJ: Erlbaum.

Hatcher, R., Hansell, J., Barends, A., Leary, K., Stuart, J., & White, K. (1990, June). *Comparison of several psychotherapy alliance measures.* Paper presented at the meeting of the Society for Psychotherapy Research, Wintergreen, VA.

Horowitz, M., Marmar, C. R., Krupnick, J., Wilner, N., Kaltreider, N., & Waller-stein, R. (1984). *Personality styles and brief psychotherapy.* New York: Basic Books.

Horowitz, M. J., Marmar, C. R., Weiss, D. S., DeWitt, K. N., & Rosenbaum, R. (1984). Brief psychotherapy of bereavement reactions: The relationships of process to outcome. *Archives of General Psychiatry, 41,* 438–448.

Horvath, A. O., & Greenberg, L. (1989). Development and validation of the Working Alliance Inventory. *Journal of Counseling Psychology, 36,* 223–233.

Horvath, A. O., & Symonds, B. D. (1991). Relationship between working alliance and outcome in psychotherapy: A meta-analysis. *Journal of Counseling Psychology, 38,* 139–149.

Jones, E. E., Cummings, J. D., & Horowitz, M. J. (1988). Another look at the non-specific hypothesis of therapeutic effectiveness. *Journal of Consulting and Clinical Psychology, 56,* 48–55.

Kanzer, M. (1975). The therapeutic and working alliances. *International Journal of Psychoanalytic Psychotherapy, 5,* 48–76.

Kazdin, A. E. (1977). Artifact, bias, and complexity of assessment: The ABCs of reliability. *Journal of Applied Behavior Analysis, 10,* 141–150.

Klee, M. R., Abeles, N., & Muller, R. T. (1990). Therapeutic alliance: Early indicators, course, and outcome. *Psychotherapy, 27,* 166–174.

Kraemer, H. C. (1981). Coping Strategies in Psychiatric Clinical Research. *Journal of Consulting and Clinical Psychology, 49,* 309–319.

Luborsky, L., Crits-Christoph, P., Alexander, L., Margolis, M., & Cohen, M. (1983). Two helping alliance methods of predicting outcomes of psychotherapy. *Journal of Nervous and Mental Disease, 171,* 480–491.

Marmar, C. R. (1990). Psychotherapy process research: Progress, dilemmas, and future directions. *Journal of Consulting and Clinical Psychology, 58,* 265–272.

Marmar, C. R., & Gaston, L. (1988). *Manual for the California Psychotherapy Scales-CALPAS.* Unpublished manuscript. Department of Psychiatry, University of California, San Francisco, CA.

Marmar, C. R., Gaston, L., Thompson, L. W., & Gallagher, D. (1989). Alliance and outcome in late-life depression. *Journal of Nervous and Mental Disease, 177,* 464–472.

Marmar, C. R., Horowitz, M. J., Weiss, D. S., & Marziali, E. (1986). Development of the Therapeutic Rating System. In L. S. Greenberg and W. M. Pinsof (Eds.), *The psychotherapeutic process: A research handbook* (pp. 367–390). New York: Guilford Press.

Marmar, C. R., Weiss, D. S., & Gaston, L. (1989). Towards the validation of the California Therapeutic Alliance Rating System. *Journal of Consulting and Clinical Psychology, 1,* 46–52.

Marziali, E. (1984). Three view points on the therapeutic alliance: Similarities, differences and associations with psychotherapy outcome. *Journal of Nervous and Mental Disease, 172,* 417–423.

Piper, W. E., Azim, F. A., Joyce, S. A., & McCallum, M. (1990, June). *Transference interpretations, therapeutic alliance and outcome in short-term individual psychotherapy.* Paper presented at the meeting of the Society for Psychotherapy Research, Wintergreen, VA.

Rogers, C. R. (1957). The necessary and sufficient conditions of therapeutic personality change. *Journal of Consulting Psychology, 21,* 95–103.

Sabourin, S., Coallier, J. C., Cournoyer, L. G., & Gaston, L. (1990, June). *Further aspects of the validity of the California Psychotherapy Alliance Scales.* Paper presented at the meeting of the Society for Psychotherapy Research, Wintergreen, VA.

Safran, J., Crocker, P., McMain, S., & Murray, P. (1990). Therapeutic alliance rupture as therapy event for empirical investigation. *Psychotherapy, 27,* 154–165.

Shrout, P. E., & Fleiss, J. L. (1979). Intraclass correlations: Uses in assessing rater reliability. *Psychological Bulletin, 86,* 420–428.

Sterba, R. (1934). The fate of the ego in analytic therapy. *International Journal of Psychoanalysis, 15,* 117–126.

Tichenor, V., & Hill, C. E. (1989). A comparison of six measures of working alliance. *Psychotherapy, 26,* 195–199.

Tracey, T. J., & Kokotovic, A. M. (1989). Factor structure of the Working Alliance Inventory. *Psychological Assessment: A Journal of Consulting and Clinical Psychology, 1,* 207–210.

Wallerstein, R. S. (1989). The psychotherapy project of the Menninger Foundation: An overview. *Journal of Consulting and Clinical Psychology, 57,* 195–205.

Wolfe, B. E., & Goldfried, M. R. (1988). Research on psychotherapy integration: Recommendations and conclusions from an NIMH workshop. *Journal of Consulting and Clinical Psychology, 56,* 448–451.

Zetzel, E. (1956). Current concepts of transference. *International Journal of Psychoanalysis, 37,* 369–375.

CHAPTER 5

Empirical Validation of Bordin's Pantheoretical Model of the Alliance: The Working Alliance Inventory Perspective

ADAM O. HORVATH

Although the results of the past 15 years of research on the alliance converge on some important issues (e.g., the relation between good alliance and positive therapy outcome), the diverse ways the alliance construct has been measured give rise to the possibility that different measures tap into distinct aspects of the therapeutic relationship (Horvath & Symonds, 1991). The various measuring scales offer a number of de facto definitions of the alliance; some are directly related to a specific theoretical formulation, whereas others are more or less empirically derived. Although all these measures provide a related view of the alliance, the interpretation of the corpus of research is made more difficult by this underlying heterogeneity.

In this chapter, the alliance will be examined through a more focused perspective provided by a unitary vision of the construct—the Working Alliance Inventory (WAI; Horvath, 1981, 1982). This WAI-based synthesis of the studies provides not only a clear, focused, conceptual point of reference but also an opportunity to evaluate Bordin's (1975, 1976, 1980) model of the alliance, because the instrument was developed and validated using his definitions of the construct (Horvath, 1981; Horvath & Greenberg, 1989; Horvath & Marx, 1991). The WAI can be used to assess the working alliance from the therapist's, client's, and independent observer's perspective. This chapter however, will concentrate on data based on clients' and observers' reports because the therapist's view of the working alliance may reference a different phenomenon from that of the other perspectives and therefore is best discussed independently (Horvath & Luborsky, 1993).

The chapter is organized in two major sections: The first part discusses the instrument itself including the theoretical rationale and psychometric procedures used to develop the scale, as well as some validity and reliability data; the second part of the chapter is a topically organized synthesis of more than 30 empirical studies that used the WAI to measure the alliance.

THE RATIONALE BEHIND THE MEASURE

Development of the WAI began in 1979. At that time, instruments were already available to assess the alliance. The reason to develop a new scale was threefold: First, the overarching goal of the project was to investigate therapeutically active factor(s) shared by all forms of therapies. Thus, a measure that evaluated the alliance from a pantheoretical perspective was needed. Second, because the focus of the investigation was the process of therapeutic change, the relationship between the alliance measure and the theoretical construct on which it was based had to be well documented. It was apparent that without clear and convincing evidence of such a link between the definition of the alliance and the measure, the interpretation of the results of the research would be difficult. For example, if the data did not support the hypothesized link between quality of alliance and outcome in a particular therapeutic context, the finding might be alternatively attributed to the inadequacy of the theory or to the possibility that the measure failed to capture completely the alliance as defined by the theory. Last, it was important to base the measure on a definition of the alliance that was linked to a general theory of therapy and change. It seemed evident that without integrating the alliance in such nomothetic network, the understandings gleaned through the working alliance studies would be isolated from the larger body of therapy research. It was our intent to investigate of the working alliance within the broader context of psychotherapy process research. Moreover, lack of integration with the broader notions of therapy and change would also limit the utility for practitioners of any conclusion based on such investigation.

After careful review of the literature, it was concluded that none of the available measures met all the preceding criteria, so we decided to develop a new instrument to better serve these objectives.

THE THEORETICAL MODEL

The Working Alliance Inventory (WAI) is based on a theoretical model of the alliance developed by Bordin (1975, 1976, 1980, 1989). The salient features of this model are presented in detail elsewhere in this volume; what follows is a brief summary of Bordin's alliance schema.

Bordin (1975) defined the working alliance as the active relational element in *all* change-inducing relationships. In a sequence of papers, Bordin put forward a conceptualization of the therapeutic relationship that distinguished between the unconscious projections of the client (transference) and the alliance. His formulation emphasizes the role of the client's positive *collaboration* with the therapist against the common foe of the client's pain and self-defeating behavior. According to this model, the alliance has three constituent elements: Task, Bond and Goal. *Task* refers to

the in-therapy activities that form the substance of the therapeutic process. In a well-functioning relationship, both parties must perceive these
tasks as relevant and effective; furthermore, each must accept the responsibility to perform these acts. *Goal* refers to the therapist and the client
mutually endorsing and valuing the aims (outcomes) that are the target of
the intervention. *Bond* embraces the complex network of positive personal
attachments between client and therapist including issues such as mutual
trust, acceptance, and confidence.

The model also speaks to the role of the alliance in therapy. According to
Bordin, the alliance does not replace the therapist's techniques as the active
ingredient in healing: "[It is what] makes it possible for the patient to accept
and follow treatment faithfully" (1980, p. 2). Moreover, Bordin's model
clarifies the link between alliance and the change process in therapy:

> . . . the means by which change is achieved resides in the building and repair
> of strong working alliance . . . . To the degree to which the therapeutic task
> or tasks succeeds in tapping into [these] self-defeating habits of feeling,
> thought and action, breaks in the working alliance that are representative of
> other ways in which the person's habits function in a self defeat[ing way] will
> inevitably occur during the therapeutic collaboration. The overcoming of
> these obstacles will then provide the person with those new ways of thinking,
> feeling or acting which, under the right circumstances will generalize to
> other areas of his or her life. (1980, p. 3)

Thus, this conceptualization provides an important bridge between the
"relationship" and "technique" aspects of therapy. The Goals negotiated
and agreed on frame the client's wishes within the therapist's theoretical
and practical wisdom, the Tasks represent both the means to achieve these
ends and the client's willingness to engage in solving the problem in a new
way. This relationship is not seen as a separate or independent process, but
as a form of active collaboration, the development of which is directly
linked to the therapeutic agenda. The very act of negotiating and defining
this agenda is central to the development of the positive alliance *and* to the
therapeutic change process. Thus, although the working alliance takes account of generic factors that are common to the universe of positive relationships, such as liking, trust, and compatibility (i.e., Bond), it emphasizes
those components of the interpersonal dynamic that are specific to the therapeutic enterprise such as the commitment to therapeutically sound and realistic goals and active endorsement of a set of procedures or tasks that will
enable the client to reach those objectives.

MEASUREMENT ISSUES IN ASSESSING THE ALLIANCE

The fundamental challenge confronting the developer of a measure of a psychological construct is to generate an instrument that is (a) *reliable* (i.e.,

yields stable results) and (b) *valid* (i.e., fully samples the construct under investigation and, at the same time, is free of the influence of other, theoretically distinct variables) (Cronbach, 1975). Although the former criterion has been met by most alliance scales, the issue of documenting validity remains a challenge for many measures (Bachelor, 1991, 1992).

There are diverse roads to demonstrate an instrument's validity. Most alliance measures use one of two criteria: (a) Because alliance is thought to facilitate successful outcome in therapy, instrument developers have used *positive relationship with outcome* both as evidence of criterion validity and to refine the instrument by culling items that failed to relate to outcome (e.g., California Psychotherapy Alliance Scales—CALPAS—Gaston, 1991; Therapeutic Alliance Scales—TAS—Marziali, Marmar, & Krupnick, 1981); (b) A number of the instruments were developed or refined using factor analytic procedures.

The latent-trait theory underlying the factor analytic procedure is based on the assumption that a theoretical variable (such as the alliance) may be, in reality, a product of a number of more elemental but invisible factors. The statistical procedure used identifies these latent traits by inspecting the relation among the items: Each trait (in this case subscale) is indicated by clusters of items that strongly correlated in this set of data. The number of factors (subscales) discovered through such procedures is dependent, in part, on the researcher's notion of the type of relations (orthogonal, oblique, etc.) that exists among the subscales. Moreover, the researcher also has to specify what is a "strong enough" correlation among the items. (Unfortunately, these parameters are precisely what the investigator wishes to discover!)

The development of the WAI was guided by a different philosophy than the latent-trait approach. We wanted to construct a scale that first and foremost implemented Bordin's theoretical formulations. To document this relationship, the primary objective in instrument development was to confirm the inventory's *content validity*. The relation between the proposed inventory items and Bordin's definitions was quantified by repeated rating procedures until consensual agreement was reached that these items were representing the theoretical parameters (for a detailed discussion of these procedures, see Horvath, 1981; Horvath, & Greenberg, 1989). It was felt that by following this procedure (deciding on the content of the scale before testing the item's relation to outcome or looking at the factor structure), the theoretical model could be more accurately tested. Only after content validity was investigated and the scale was developed did we explore the relation between the WAI and outcome. Doing otherwise—letting outcome-alliance relations influence the scale content and then validating the relationships using the scale—would have confounded the process.

In pursuing this path, we were mindful that this approach, too, has drawbacks. Selecting the content of the scale based on theory rather than on empirical observations leaves the onus on the instrument developer to seek evidence of the measures' proximity to the construct of the alliance as it is currently measured and understood. Moreover, if some aspects of the theory on which the instrument is based are not supported empirically, the question still remains: Would a measure with an even better content have confirmed the hypothesis?

THE DEVELOPMENT OF THE WAI

The focal task in the development of the instrument was to validate its content with respect to Bordin's definition of the alliance. Moreover, it was decided to generate items from each of three reference points: (a) The self—the client's own thoughts and feelings; (b) the other—the client's belief about the quality of the interaction and about the therapist's experiences, thoughts, and feelings; and (c) the respondent's thoughts and beliefs about the quality of the relationship between him- or herself and the therapist. To this end, a large pool of alliance items was generated from each perspective on the basis of a careful content analysis of Bordin's model. This item pool was sequentially evaluated twice. The first set of raters consisted of experts; the second group was randomly selected from the membership list of the local licensing body for psychologists. Each set of raters evaluated each item twice; once for the degree of fit between the item and Bordin's definition of the working alliance, and a second time to identify whether the item referred to the Task, Bond, or Goal component of the alliance. A rewording of the clients' scale was used as the therapists' scale (WAI_t).

The WAI has been revised once; this revision involved minor editorial changes in three items and the original 5-point Likert rating scale was lengthened to 7 points in the interest of increased variability. Besides the original client and therapist version, the Working Alliance Inventory is now available as an observer's (rater's) instrument (WAI_o), based on the work of Tichenor and Hill (1989), and a short version (12 items) was developed (WAI_s), based on data reported by Tracey and Kokotovic (1989). Other researchers have adapted the instrument for special populations (e.g., supervisory relationship, inpatient population). In addition, French, Spanish, Finnish, and Dutch translations have been made of the instrument. We are also currently validating a couples/family form of the WAI.

THE PSYCHOMETRIC PROPERTIES OF THE WAI

Content Validity

As noted earlier, the validity of this instrument rests primarily on the content rating procedures described earlier. On these bases, there appears to be reasonable evidence that the WAI fairly represents the alliance construct and its constituent elements, as specified by Bordin.

Convergent and Discriminant Validity

Although the WAI is specifically designed to measure the alliance as defined by Bordin, if the scale is indeed measuring the concept accurately, it is expected that the WAI scores would correlate positively with other alliance measures. A number of investigators have explored this relationship (Adler, 1988; Bachelor, 1992; Greenberg & Adler, 1989; Hansell, 1990; Horvath, 1981; Horvath & Greenberg, 1989; Leary et al., 1991; Moseley, 1983; Plotnicov, 1990; Safran & Wallner, 1991; Tichenor & Hill, 1989). Safran's findings are typical of the results. They report correlations between the global CALPAS scores and the WAI of .84, .79, and .72, for the Goal, Task, and Bond scales respectively. The correlations between the WAI (client's version) and the Helping Alliance and the Vanderbilt scales are also significant though slightly lower (Greenberg & Adler, 1989; Tichenor & Hill, 1989).

Somewhat lower overlap was anticipated between the WAI and more global measures of the therapeutic relationship. The relation between the Rogerian dimensions of the therapeutic relationship (Relationship Inventory—RI—Barrett-Lennard, 1978) has been tested in several studies (e.g., Adler, 1988; Babin, 1991; Horvath, 1981; Jones, 1988; Moseley, 1983; Webster, 1981). Jones's (1988) results are the most detailed of these investigations and are representative of the findings: Task is the most independent of empathy, positive regard, unconditionality, and congruence (correlations ranging from .3 to .49), the Goal dimension is more overlapping (correlations ranging from .43 to .59), and Bond is the most correlated (r's between .6 to 74) to the RI scales.

Based on the same logic, the validity of the instrument would be supported if the WAI were less related to instruments that measure theoretically distinct aspects of the therapist-client relationship. This question of discriminant validity was also investigated by a number of researchers (e.g., Adler, 1988; Greenberg & Webster, 1982; Horvath, 1981; Moseley, 1983; Safran & Wallner, 1991). Most of these studies contrast the relation of the WAI to instruments measuring the alliance with its relation to the Counselor Rating Form (CRF; LaCrosse, 1980)—an instrument assessing relationship dimensions of expertness, attractiveness, and trustworthiness—based on Strong's (1968) interpersonal influence model. The results indicate that the relation between the WAI and the CRF is indeed significantly lower than the relation between the WAI and other alliance measures (Adler, 1988; Horvath & Greenberg, 1989; Moseley, 1983). Moreover, the results suggest that the two instruments (CRF and WAI) correlate with *different* measures of outcome (Greenberg & Adler, 1989; Safran & Wallner, 1991).

Thus it appears that a number of separate investigations provide support of the WAI's validity (data relating to criterion validity will be presented later in this chapter).

Reliability

Reliability estimates for the whole instrument, based on item homogeneity (Cronbach's Alpha), range from .93 to .84, with most reported coefficients in the upper range (Adler, 1988; Horvath, 1981; Moseley, 1983; Plotnicov, 1990; Watkins, 1987). Reliability estimates for the subscales are lower, but in the similar range (.92 to .68). Test-retest reliability for the whole scale across a 3-week interval is .80; and for the component scales, the range is between .74 and .66 (Plotnicov, 1990). We obtained reliability data based on two administrations of the short (12-item) form of the WAI across an average span of 2 weeks and obtained a test-retest index of .83 for the whole instrument (Horvath, in press). Taken together, these results support the scale's reliability.

Structure of the WAI

The three WAI dimensions—Bond, Goal, and Task—are strongly correlated; scale intercorrelations ranging from the low .60s to the high .80s were reported (Horvath & Greenberg, 1989; Plotnicov, 1990; Safran & Wallner, 1991; Tichenor & Hill, 1989; Tracey & Kokotovic, 1989). Notwithstanding the magnitude of these relations, there is also empirical evidence that the three working alliance components hypothesized by Bordin may be distinct: Tracey and colleagues (1989) gathered alliance information from 140 students after their first counseling session. The researchers analyzed the data using a bilevel confirmatory factor analysis and found a general alliance factor plus three second-level factors corresponding to the Bond, Goal, and Task subscales respectively. The authors also reported that the adequacy of this bilevel model has met the standards of three conservative statistical criteria. This finding fits well with Bordin's (1980) prediction that alliance in the early phases of therapy would be largely undifferentiated and global, based on initial impressions, trust, and liking. He hypothesized that, as therapy progressed, the three subdimensions would be more distinct and the relative significance of each would depend on the type of therapy used. Unfortunately, this aspect of the model has not been tested.

THE RELATION BETWEEN THE WAI AND OUTCOME

Recent reviews of the road spectrum of the alliance literature support the hypothesis that there is a positive relation between the alliance and outcome (Gaston, Marmar, Gallagher, & Thompson, 1990; Horvath & Symonds, 1991; Luborsky, 1990). Eight studies that investigated Bordin's model alliance using the WAI are presented in Table 5.1. A meta-analytic synthesis of these research results indicates that the average effect size

TABLE 5.1. Relation between Working Alliance
Inventory Scores and Outcome

Author	Year	No. of Participants	Correlation
Adler	1988	44	.23
Horvath	1981	29	.42
Kokotovic & Tracey	1990	144	.11
Moseley	1983	25	.24
Tichenor & Hill	1989	8	.11
Webster	1982	31	.62
Safran & Wallner	1991	22	.35
Plotnicov	1990	31	.87

Note: Average weighted effect size: .33; 95% confidence interval about the ES: .23 to .43.

(ES) expressed as a correlation coefficient is .33 for the client-based measures (the mathematical model used to compute the effect size is more fully discussed in Horvath & Symonds, 1991). The procedure used to estimate the ES is conservative: The 95% confidence interval drawn around the estimated ES spans .23 to .43, where the upper limit is more likely representative of the true value. This suggests a robust link between the client's estimate of the working alliance and the outcome of therapy. Although the general alliance outcome relation has been documented before, the more focused nature of this data set invites the closer examination of the way the working alliance impacts outcome.

Early versus Late Alliance

The research indicate that alliance measures taken early in therapy tend to be the best prognosticators of final outcome (Adler, 1988; Horvath, 1981; Moseley, 1983; Plotnicov, 1990). It is also evident that, in limited-term interventions, the client's evaluation of the working alliance measured as early as the first session can be a good predictor of premature termination (Kokotovic & Tracey, 1990; Plotnicov, 1990) and can distinguish between clients who will benefit from treatment and those who will not (Plotnicov, 1990). These findings are corroborated by the general trend noted in the alliance literature as a whole (Horvath & Symonds, 1991).

There may be several reasons for the relative predictive superiority of the early measures compared with assessments obtained at the middle or near the end of therapy. The most obvious one is the possibility that the range of working alliance scores obtained later in therapy may be truncated. As noted earlier, clients with poor working alliances tend to drop out of therapy early; consequently, subsequent measures deal with only the upper half of the alliance range. Such restrictions in range are known to diminish the magnitude of correlation coefficients (Glass & Stanley, 1970).

Another reason may have to do with the course of the alliance across time. A number of studies report a slight but definite increase of the working alliance scores from Session 1 through Session 5, but the amount of alliance growth in these early sessions is not strongly related to outcome (Adler, 1988; Bachelor, 1992; Plotnicov, 1990). Thus, the quality of the working alliance (at least in relatively short-term treatments) seems likely to build through the early sessions. It has been found that in the beginning phase of therapy, the Task scale is most strongly correlated with outcome. Research results also indicate that the Goal scale's relation to outcome increases between Sessions 1 and 5 (Bachelor, 1992; Plotnicov, 1990).

As therapy progress, the situation becomes more complex: Bordin predicted that the alliance would, in the later stages, itself be the host of the client's past habitual self-damaging interpersonal habits. The "work of the alliance" becomes the rebuilding of the damaged alliance and thus the acquisition of new ideas about self and relationships (Bordin, 1976, 1989). This labile state of the working alliance in the midphase of therapy was confirmed in a longitudinal study by Horvath and Marx (1991), and the rupture and repair sequences have been documented by a series of studies published by Safran and his colleagues (Muran, Segal, Wallner Samstag, & Schuman, 1992; Safran, 1990; Safran et al., Chapter 10, this volume). Measurements taken amidst such fluctuations are likely to either under- or overestimate the true state of the working alliance; thus the relation of these assessments to outcome is less strong.

The third possible reason may be that the alliance measures (including the WAI) are most efficacious in measuring the construct in its early, relatively undifferentiated state. Both Luborsky (1976) and Bordin (1980) predicted that the qualities of the good alliance become more therapy-specific as the treatment progresses. The tasks of a particular therapy impose unique demands and differential values on certain aspects of the relationship. For example, in psychodynamic treatment, the client's willingness to free associate (endorse the task of expressing uncensored thoughts) is critical to success. But a client in treatment with a therapist using paradoxical interventions may benefit in spite of resisting the prescribed tasks. Instruments (or observations) based on simplified, generic descriptors of the alliance may fail to assess accurately the strength of the therapeutic relationship at more differentiated levels.

Working Alliance and Early Improvements

Another important issue that needs careful examination is the relation between the alliance and increments of ongoing therapeutic gain: If the working alliance captures no more than the initial therapeutic achievements of the client, then it is merely an epiphenomenon (a rose by a different name) and, as a concept, is unlikely to add to our efforts to understand the dynamics of change and improve therapy. The evidence, however, seems to indicate that we are dealing with a phenomenon that is quite distinct from therapeutic progress. In fact, research results indicate the relation between session level outcome and working alliance measured at the same time is rather weak. On the other hand, working alliance seems to be able to predict subsequent session level outcome. Moreover, although there is a positive association between clients' session level outcome evaluation and their own final outcome rating, only their working alliance scores predicted the counselors' outcome scores (Horvath, 1991; Horvath, Gaston, & Luborsky, in press; Mallinckrodt, in press). Thus it appears that the working alliance is not a reflection of the current level of therapeutic progress, but rather a true window into the dynamics between the participants. The quality of the client's sense of Bond, Task, and Goal early in therapy is related to the potential viability of the therapeutic effort. However, because of the way this definition of the working alliance is framed, the quality of the therapeutic relationship cannot be completely disentangled from the kind of therapy offered. Both the Goal and Task aspects of the alliance (i.e., the type of outcomes seen as worthwhile and the particular techniques used in therapy) are influenced by the theoretical orientation of the therapist. Therefore, the question whether this client with the same therapist would develop the same quality of alliance if a different kind of therapy were offered is yet unanswered.

THE INGREDIENTS OF A GOOD WORKING ALLIANCE

Client Factors

Although evidence of the relation between alliance and outcome is of major scientific importance, this fact alone does not help us provide better therapy. To improve therapy efficacy and to better understand how the good alliance helps the client change, we must discover the pretreatment factors that help or hinder the development of the relationship, learn their etiology, and examine the kinds of variables that positively influence the alliance.

Wallner Samstag and her colleagues contrasted the characteristics of clients with poor and good alliances (Wallner Samstag et al., 1992) using data based on 31 outpatient clients receiving cognitive therapy. With symptom severity statistically controlled, the clients who were more submissive, isolated, and friendly were more likely to develop strong alliances compared with the more hostile, aggressive, and dominant individuals. In a somewhat similar vain, Reandeu and colleagues examined sequences of interactions of clients with improving and nonimproving working alliances (Reandeu & Wampold, 1991). They found that clients who were able to respond to the therapist's confronting messages with positive energy were more likely to improve the relationship than individuals who withdrew from these transactions. Likewise, Safran found that the client's ability to engage with the therapist in the examination of the here-and-now relationship in therapy is a necessary component of resolving alliance ruptures (Safran, Crocker, McMain, & Murray, 1990; Safran, Muran, & Wallner Samstag, 1994).

Clients' relational capacities are another potentially important group of variables impacting the development of the working alliance. There are at least two conceptually distinct possible links: First, clients' early experiences may developmentally predispose them to have good or poor object relations, and these general dispositions in turn may affect the therapeutic alliance; second, the level of current social support and satisfaction with present relationships may impact the clients' capacity to form a collaborative alliance with the therapist. Research on the influence of early object relations has yielded complex results: Mallinckrodt (1992) found that the client's current level of social support was more influential in determining the quality of the working alliance (5% of the unique variance) than parental bonds (1% of variance explained). However, therapists' ratings were more related to the quality of early parental bond (13%). The interaction between these variables (parental bond and current social support) explained an additional 10% of variance in the working alliance ratings. The nature of this interaction is as yet somewhat unclear, but it seems likely that the pattern may be different for male and female clients. This may indicate that the eventual impact of parental relations is different from men and women and that they develop and use social relationship in different ways (Mallinckrodt & Leong, in press).

These findings broadly parallel the results of investigations using other instruments: A meta-analysis of the research on the antecedents of good alliance (Horvath & Symonds, 1990) indicated that across a variety of therapeutic contexts pretherapy client factors had an effect size of approximately .32 as a determinant of subsequent measure of the quality of the alliance. Researchers have found fairly consistent indications that the client's early object relations exert a significant influence on the development of the alliance (Piper, in press). Moreover, the idea that aspects of these early unsuccessful experiences tend to reemerge in therapy is consistent with the findings of several investigations (e.g., Luborsky, 1985; Quintana & Meara, 1990; Safran et al., 1990). Bordin (see Chapter 1, this volume), however, suggests that the influence of these variables will be more important in the early than in later phases of therapy, and sees these initial relational difficulties of the client as valid goals for therapy rather than as determinants of the alliance.

The potential impact of several other client variables on the working alliance has been investigated but these variables were found to exert little influence: Pretreatment symptom severity by itself is not a good predictor of working alliance development (Adler, 1988; Plotnicov, 1990). Moreover, early levels of working alliance predict outcome even if symptom severity is partialed out to control for this factor (Safran & Wallner, 1991; Wallner Samstag, 1992). Similarly, the client's preferences or expectations have negligible impact on the subsequent working alliance levels (Jones, 1988).

Gender Differences

A superficial compilation of the alliance-positive client characteristics (submissive, nonhostile, affiliative), suggests a gender factor may be embedded in the definition of the positive working alliance. Goren (1991) explored this issue directly and found that the overall working alliance scores of men and women did not differ significantly. Moreover, there were no differences due to the cross-gender combinations of client and therapist (male therapist-female client, female therapist-male client, etc.). The level of androgyny of either participant was likewise not related to the strength of the working alliance. She also investigated the possibility that gender might be a factor in the *kind* of working alliance developed (i.e., the relative strengths of the alliance components). No difference was noted along the Bond dimension; however, female clients with female therapists tended to rate the Task and Goal scales higher than other gender combinations.[1]

THERAPIST'S IMPACT ON THE WORKING ALLIANCE

Rogers hypothesized that the therapist's ability to offer an empathic, prizing, and congruent relationship was a necessary and sufficient cause of client improvement (Rogers, 1957). The alliance perspective of the therapeutic relationship is much more interactional: It is the product of each of the participants' contributions to the process. Nonetheless, understanding of the therapist's role and the delineation of therapist's actions that contribute to positive alliance are of vital interest. Empirical information on the impact of therapist variables is beginning to emerge.

Safran and his colleagues presented the most detailed model of transactions that impact the positive alliance. A full description of this schema is beyond the scope of this chapter (see Safran et al., 1990; also Chapter 20, this volume), but in essence, the model emphasizes three features:

1. The recognition by the therapist of the significance of here-and-now relationship problems as they occur during therapy.
2. Use of this alliance rupture to emphatically explore the client's negative experiences and feelings in the relationship.

---

[1] However, Mallinckrodt's (1993) research raises the possibility of a three way interaction between social support, early object relations and therapist/client gender combinations.

3. The therapist's need to take ownership of his or her own struggles in the therapeutic relationship, thus validating the client's painful experience and promoting an insight into recurring relationship patterns.

The model offers a rich, highly detailed flowchart of the sequences that will result in improved working alliance. His research group is currently implementing a programmatic investigation of the resolution of alliance ruptures and has presented preliminary evidence validating some of the key sequences (Safran, Muran, & Wallner Samstag, 1992).

The salutary value of the therapist focusing on the here-and-now relationship is further supported by the results of a recent analogue study (Kivlighan & Schmitz, 1992). Their findings also suggest that thematically focused, challenging, distant rather than intimate therapists are most likely to improve the working alliance. Additional support for the alliance building and therapeutic benefit resulting from focusing on the relationship issues between the therapeutic dyad comes from an investigation that contrasted the relation of early working alliance scores to outcome in cognitive and psychodynamic therapies (Raue, 1991). The stronger link between working alliance and outcome in the more here-and-now focused approach (cognitive therapy) may be construed to support the preceding findings.

Bordin's (1980) model hypothesized that the therapist's empathy and trustworthiness are prerequisites for alliance development, particularly in the early stages of therapy. Evidence appears to support this position. The WAI scores measured early in therapy correlate positively with empathy ($r = .60$ to $.80$); however, the working alliance has a stronger relation to outcome than empathy and accounts for an additional portion of outcome variance after the level of empathy has been statistically controlled (Adler, 1988; Horvath, 1981; Plotnicov, 1990). These client-centered dimensions tap into factors that prognosticate the therapist's capacity to develop a good working alliance, whereas the WAI measures whether the alliance has been actually developed.

It seems likely that specific therapist behaviors contribute positively to the development of the working alliance; moreover, the evidence appears to converge on at least some of the desirable alliance-enhancing moves. The logical next step is to put this knowledge to use by training therapists to develop better alliances. However, evaluation of therapists' training to develop better alliances with their clients yielded somewhat puzzling findings. Overall, attempts to link training focused on therapists' alliance-promoting behavior to outcome have been less than successful (see Chapter 3, this volume). The effect of generic therapist skill training on the quality of therapists' working alliance has also produced nonsignificant results (Babin, 1991). And therapists with more advanced training and experience do not necessarily have better working alliances, although there appears to be a positive curvilinear relation between level of training and ability to accurately assess the level of working alliance (Mallinckrodt & Nelson, 1991).

Safran and others have demonstrated that therapists' actions do influence the quality of the alliance; how then can we explain the apparent lack of training effect? It is possible that the therapists' own relational dispositions filter out any training effect (Henry, Chapter 3 this volume). Additionally, the notion of generic relationship training might have been too simplistic. Therapists' training may need to be more contextualized by specifically identifying therapist activities that are alliance building *within the context of that therapy.* There is an urgent need to explore the reasons for these generally disappointing initial findings: Research on the alliance will greatly diminish in practical importance if clinically viable methods of training therapists how to influence the development of the working alliance are not discovered.

INTERACTIONAL EFFECTS

One of the features that sets the alliance concept apart from previous formulations of the effective ingredient in the therapeutic relationship is its emphasis on collaboration (Bordin, 1980; Bordin, 1989; Frieswyk et al., 1986). The working alliance is understood to be interactive, a measure of the strength of the partnership that has joined the participants to achieve a common goal. What do we know of the "fit" or kinds of complementarity that would be conducive to forming a good partnership? Kiesler and Watkins (1989) examined 36 therapist-client relationships and report that complementarity, particularly in the "hostile" half of Keisler's circumplex Interpersonal Circle model, predicted positive working alliances. They also found evidence that the more extreme the therapist perceived the client's behavior to be, the less likely that a strong working alliance would develop. Interestingly, from the client's point of view, only negative complementarity predicted the quality of the relationship. The therapists' rating of complementarity, however, was predictive on both the hostile and friendly half of the circle.

Several investigators supported Bordin's hypothesis that the alliance will be host to the client's past relational difficulties (Kivlighan, 1992; Mallinckrodt, 1992; Safran, Crocker, McMain, & Murray, 1990; Safran, Muran, & Wallner Samstag, 1992). The idea that the clients' pathology will resurface in the context of the therapeutic relationship is also in accord with other hypotheses of the generic change process currently under development (i.e., Luborsky's Core Themes and Orlinsky & Howard's generic model of therapy). Preliminary evidence indicates that if the therapeutic dyad can avoid repeating the client's past patterns of dealing with such relational issues, therapy will move forward. In this context, the ability of each participant to affirm the other's experience is probably an essential ingredient to the development of the kinds of mutual understandings and collaborative undertakings that the alliance involves. In this light, the capacity to achieve

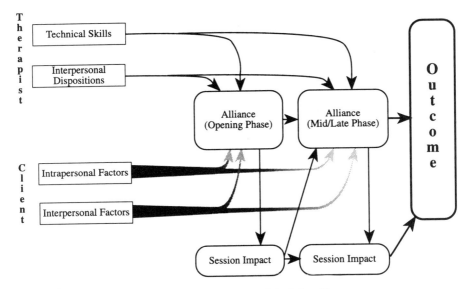

Figure 5.1.   A working model of the alliance.

this level of understanding with respect to the more negative or hostile client characteristics fits well with Safran's notion that the therapist needs to empathize and validate the client's negative experiences. Figure 5.1 illustrates the model of the working alliance.

CONCLUSIONS

The past decade and a half of research has lent considerable support for a number of Bordin's (1980) original hypotheses. It has also raised some complex new questions.

It now seems evident that if the client experiences a positive working alliance with the therapist early in therapy, success is more likely. Very early (3rd session), measures of the degree of support and consensus on the therapeutic tasks appear to be the most proportional to final outcome. Moreover, working alliance readings taken after the first session are reliable indicators of the likelihood of premature termination. Most evidence also suggests that the working alliance is associated more with final outcome than with concurrent session satisfaction.

The concept of the rupture-repair cycle also seems to be supported as originally predicted, at least in the middle phase of therapy. The idea that the work of building the alliance will capture the client's core dilemmas and that the focus of building or repairing the alliance and helping the client to deal with problems more effectively will overlap has also received research support. However, the notion that different therapies will engender qualitatively different alliances has only indirect endorsement so far.

The role of clients' object relations and current social experiences or support is emerging as a significant factor influencing the working alliance, at least in its early stages. Although a number of independent investigations support the impact of this factor (e.g., Mallinckrodt, 1992; Piper et al., 1991), the *way* these client factors interact with other variables appears to be complex and poses a challenge for the next generation of research. The possibility that the therapist's self-issues and relational patterns play a significant role is also emerging as an important research question. It is likely that these client and therapist pretherapy factors interact and will need to be carefully monitored in future studies.

The research results point to qualitative differences in the working alliance over time. Distinctions between early and later alliance were predicted by Luborsky as early as 1976. However, whereas the positive working alliance in the early phases of therapy can be accurately modeled by Bordin's Task, Bond, and Goal structure, it may become more difficult to capture all its salient features in a generic model as therapy progresses. Current evidence is consistent with the possibility that although all helping relations need a good working alliance to succeed and all therapeutic relations have the similar essential features in the beginning of therapy, the therapeutic environment becomes more treatment specific and complex as therapy moves toward its later phases. This possibility may be construed in terms of more differentiated therapeutic tasks: These tasks become less generic and more sophisticated as treatment moves along, refining the parameters of the successful therapeutic relationship more and more narrowly in terms of the model that guides the therapist's behavior.

REFERENCES

Adler, J. V. (1988). *A study of the working alliance in psychotherapy.* Unpublished doctoral dissertation thesis, University of British Columbia, Canada.

Babin, R. J. (1991). *Basic counselor skills scoring method as a predictor of the counselor trainee's effectiveness in establishing a working alliance.* Unpublished master's thesis, Nicholls State University, Thibodaux, LA.

Bachelor, A. (1991). Comparison and relationship to outcome of diverse dimensions of the helping alliance as seen by client and therapist. *Psychotherapy: Theory Research and Practice, 28,* 534–539.

Bachelor, A. (1992, June). *Variability of dimensions of the therapeutic alliance and alliance predictors of improvement.* Paper presented at the annual meeting of the Society for Psychotherapy Research, Berkeley, CA.

Barrett-Lennard, G. T. (1978). *The Relationship Inventory: Later development and adaptations* (Nos. 8, 68). JSAS Catalog of Selected Documents in Psychology.

Bordin, E. S. (1975, September). *The working alliance: Basis for a general theory of psychotherapy.* Paper presented at the annual meeting of the American Psychological Association, Washington, DC.

Bordin, E. S. (1976). The generalizability of the psychoanalytic concept of the working alliance. *Psychotherapy: Theory Research and Practice, 16,* 252–260.

Bordin, E. S. (1980, June). *Of human bonds that bind or free.* Paper presented at the annual meeting of the Society for Psychotherapy Research, Pacific Grove, CA.

Bordin, E. S. (1989). *Building therapeutic alliances: The base for integration.* Paper presented at the annual meeting of the Society for Psychotherapy Research, Berkeley, CA.

Cronbach, L. J. (1975). Five decades of public controversy over mental testing. *American Psychologist, 30,* 1–4.

Frieswyk, S. H., Allen, J. G., Colson, D. B., Coyne, L., Gabbard, G. O., Horwitz, L., & Newsom, G. (1986). Therapeutic alliance: Its place as process and outcome variable in dynamic psychotherapy research. *Journal of Consulting and Clinical Psychology, 1,* 32–39.

Gaston, L. (1991). Reliability and criterion-related validity of the California Psychotherapy Alliance Scales—patient version. *Psychological Assessment: A Journal of Consulting and Clinical Psychology, 3,* 68–74.

Gaston, L., Marmar, C., Gallagher, D., & Thompson, L. W. (1990). *Alliance prediction of outcome: Beyond initial symptomology and symptomatic change.* Paper presented at the annual meeting of the Society for Psychotherapy Research, Philadelphia, PA.

Glass, G. V., & Stanley, J. C. (1970). *Statistical methods in education and psychology.* Englewood Cliffs, NJ: Prentice-Hall.

Goren, L. (1991). *The relationship of counselor androgyny to the working alliance.* Unpublished doctoral dissertation thesis, University of Southern California, Los Angeles, CA.

Greenberg, L. S., & Adler, J. (1989, June). *The working alliance and outcome: A client report study.* Paper presented at the annual meeting of the Society for Psychotherapy Research, Toronto, Ont., Canada.

Greenberg, L. S., & Webster, M. C. (1982). Resolving decisional conflict by Gestalt two-chair dialogue: Relating process to outcome. *Journal of Counseling Psychology, 29,* 468–477.

Hansell, J. (1990). *The relationship of the California Psychotherapy Alliance Scales to other measures of the alliance.* Paper presented at the annual meeting of the Society for Psychotherapy Research, Wintergreen, VA.

Horvath, A. O. (1981). *An exploratory study of the working alliance: Its measurement and relationship to outcome.* Unpublished doctoral dissertation thesis, Vancouver, Canada.

Horvath, A. O. (1982). *Users' manual of the Working Alliance Inventory.* Unpublished manuscript No. 82:2, Simon Fraser University, Canada.

Horvath, A. O. (1991, June). *What do we know about the alliance and what do we still have to find out?* Paper presented at the annual meeting of the Society for Psychotherapy Research, Lyon, France.

Horvath, A. O. (in press). *Manual for the use of the Working Alliance Inventory (2nd Ed.)* No. 93:1, Simon Fraser University, Canada.

Horvath, A. O., Gaston, L., & Luborsky, L. (in press). The role of alliance in psychotherapy. In L. Luborsky, N. Miller, & J. Barber (Eds.), *Psychotherapy: Research and Practice*. Basic Books: NY.

Horvath, A. O., & Greenberg, L. S. (1989). The development and validation of the Working Alliance Inventory. *Journal of Counseling Psychology, 36,* 223–233.

Horvath, A. O., & Luborsky, L. (1993). The role of the therapeutic alliance in psychotherapy. *Journal of Consulting and Clinical Psychology, 61,* 561–573.

Horvath, A. O., & Marx, R. W. (1991). The development and decay of the working alliance during time-limited counselling. *Canadian Journal of Counselling, 24,* 240–259.

Horvath, A. O., & Symonds, B. D. (1990, June). *Relation among counsellor and client variables, working alliance, and outcome in counselling and psychotherapy: An empirical review.* Paper presented at the annual meeting of the Society for Psychotherapy Research, Wintergreen, VA.

Horvath, A. O., & Symonds, B. D. (1991). Relation between working alliance and outcome in psychotherapy: A meta-analysis. *Journal of Counseling Psychology, 38,* 139–149.

Jones, S. S. (1988). *An exploration of the relationship between client expectations and the working alliance.* Unpublished doctoral dissertation thesis, University of Mississippi, Mississippi, MS.

Kiesler, D. J., & Watkins, L. M. (1989). Interpersonal complementarity and the therapeutic alliance: A study in relationship in psychotherapy. *Psychotherapy: Theory Research and Practice, 26,* 183–194.

Kivlighan, D. M., & Schmitz, P. J. (1992). Counselor technical activity in cases with improving working alliances and continuing-poor working alliances. *Journal of Counseling Psychology, 39,* 32–38.

Kokotovic, A. M., & Tracey, T. J. (1990). Working alliance in the early phase of counseling. *Journal of Counseling Psychology, 37,* 16–21.

LaCrosse, M. B. (1980). Perceived counselor social influence and counseling outcomes: Validity of the Counselor Rating Form. *Journal of Counseling Psychology, 27,* 320–327.

Leary, K., Gutfreund, J. M., Hatcher, R., Barends, A., Davies, J., Gittleman, M., Hansell, J., & Stuart, J. (1991, July). *The relationship between transference and working alliance.* Paper presented at the annual meeting of the Society for Psychotherapy Research, Lyon, France.

Luborsky, L. (1976). Helping alliances in psychotherapy. In J. L. Cleghhorn (Eds.), *Successful psychotherapy* (pp. 92–116). New York: Brunner/Mazel.

Luborsky, L. (1990, June). *Therapeutic alliance measures as predictors of future benefits of psychotherapy.* Paper presented at the annual meeting of the Society for Psychotherapy Research, Wintergreen, VA.

Mallinckrodt, B. (1992). Client's representations of childhood emotional bonds with parents social support, and formation of the working alliance. *Journal of Counseling Psychology, 38,* 401–409.

Mallinckrodt, B. (1993). Session impact, working alliance, and treatment outcome in brief counseling. *Journal of Counseling Psychology, 40,* 25–32.

Mallinckrodt, B., & Leong, F. T. L. (in press). Social support in academic programs and family environments. *Journal of Counseling and Development.*

Mallinckrodt, B., & Nelson, M. L. (1991). Counselor training level and the formation of the therapeutic working alliance. *Journal of Counseling Psychology, 38,* 14–19.

Marziali, E., Marmar, C., & Krupnick, J. (1981). Therapeutic Alliance Scales: Development and relationship to psychotherapy outcome. *American Journal of Psychiatry, 138,* 361–364.

Moseley, D. (1983). *The therapeutic relationship and its association with outcome.* Unpublished master's thesis, Vancouver, Canada.

Muran, J. C., Segal, Z. V., Wallner Samstag, L., & Schuman, C. E. (1992, June). *Patient pretreatment interpersonal problems and therapeutic alliance in short-term cognitive therapy.* Paper presented at the annual meeting of the Society for Psychotherapy Research, Berkeley, CA.

Piper, W. E., Azim, H. F. A., Joyce, A. S., MacCallum, M., Nixon, G. W. H., & Segal, P. S. (1991). Quality of object relations vs. interpersonal functioning as predictor of therapeutic alliance and psychotherapy outcome. *Journal of Nervous and Mental Disease, 179,* 432–438.

Plotnicov, K. H. (1990). *Early termination from counseling: The client's perspective.* Unpublished doctoral dissertation thesis, University of Pittsburgh, PA.

Quintana, S. M., & Meara, N. M. (1990). Internalization of therapeutic relationships in short-term psychotherapy. *Journal of Counseling Psychology, 37,* 123–130.

Raue, P. J., Castunguay, L. G., & Goldfried, M. R. (1991). *The working alliance: a comparison of two therapies.* Paper presented at the annual meeting of the Society for Psychotherapy Integration, London.

Reandeu, S. G., & Wampold, B. E. (1991). Relationship of power and involvement to working alliance: A multiple-case sequential analysis of brief therapy. *Journal of Counseling Psychology, 38,* 107–114.

Rogers, C. R. (1957). The necessary and sufficient conditions of therapeutic personality change. *Journal of Consulting and Clinical Psychology, 22,* 95–103.

Safran, J. D., Crocker, P., McMain, S., & Murray, P. (1990). The therapeutic alliance rupture as a therapy event for empirical investigation. *Psychotherapy: Theory Research and Practice, 27,* 154–165.

Safran, J. D., Muran, J. C., & Wallner Samstag, L. (1992, June). *A comparison of therapeutic alliance rupture resolution and nonresolution events.* Paper presented at the annual meeting of the Society for Psychotherapy Research, Berkeley, CA.

Safran, J. D., Muran, J. C., & Wallner Samstag, L. (1994). Resolving therapeutic ruptures: A task analytic investigation. In A. O. Horvath & L. S. Greenberg (Eds.), *The working alliance: Theory, research, and practice.* New York: Wiley.

Safran, J. D., & Wallner, L. K. (1991). The relative predictive validity of two therapeutic alliance measures in cognitive therapy. *Psychological Assessment: A Journal of Consulting and Clinical Psychology, 3,* 188–195.

Strong, S. R. (1968). Counseling: An interpersonal influence process. *Journal of Counseling Psychology, 15,* 215–224.

Tichenor, V., & Hill, C. E. (1989). A comparison of six measures of working alliance. *Psychotherapy: Theory Research and Practice, 26,* 195–199.

Tracey, T. J., & Kokotovic, A. M. (1989). Factor structure of the Working Alliance Inventory. *Psychological Assessment: A Journal of Consulting and Clinical Psychology, 37,* 369–375.

Wallner Samstag, L., Muran, C., Zindel, V., Segal, Z., & Schuman, C. (1992). *Patient pretreatment interpersonal problems and therapeutic alliance in short-term cognitive therapy.* Paper presented at the annual meeting of the Society for Psychotherapy Research, Berkeley, CA.

Watkins, L. M. (1987). *Interpersonal complementarity and the therapeutic alliance: A study of relationship in psychotherapy.* Unpublished doctoral dissertation thesis, Virginia Commonwealth University, Richmond, VA.

Webster, M. C. (1981). *Resolving decisional conflict by Gestalt two-chair dialogue.* Unpublished Doctoral dissertation thesis, University of British Columbia, Canada.

PART TWO

The Alliance in Diverse Therapies

CHAPTER 6

The Therapeutic Alliance in Cognitive-Behavior Therapy*

PATRICK J. RAUE and MARVIN R. GOLDFRIED

Behavior therapy has its roots in a tradition that had little to say about the significance of the therapeutic relationship. Far greater emphasis has typically been placed on the development of techniques and the extrapolation of findings from the laboratory setting to the clinical situation. Indeed, early descriptions of behavior therapy depicted the therapist as "a social reinforcement machine" (Krasner, 1962). Taken together with attempts to automate the therapy process by means of tape-recorded instructions for systematic desensitization (Lang, Melamed, & Hart, 1970), conveying the distinct impression that even the presence of a therapist was unimportant, it often comes as somewhat of a surprise to learn that those who function within a behavioral orientation lend any credence whatsoever to the therapeutic alliance.

Despite the emphasis placed on laboratory- and theory-based techniques, cognitive-behavior therapists in clinical practice eventually acknowledged the importance of the therapeutic relationship. As provocatively suggested by Goldfried and Davison (1976):

> Any behavior therapist who maintains that principles of learning and social influence are all one needs to know in order to bring about behavior change is out of contact with clinical reality. We have seen therapists capable of conceptualizing problems along behavioral lines and adept at the implementation of the various behavior therapy techniques, but they have few opportunities to demonstrate their effectiveness; they often have difficulty keeping their clients in therapy, let alone getting them to follow through on behavioral assignments. (p. 55)

---

* The preparation of this chapter was supported in part by NIMH Grant No. 40196 awarded to the second author. The authors would like to thank Louis G. Castonguay and Leslie S. Greenberg for their helpful comments on an earlier version of this chapter.

Although behavior therapists have grown to recognize the important role of the therapeutic relationship, it nonetheless has tended to be viewed as secondary to the specific techniques that are deemed to be central to the change process. More often than not, the relationship between therapist and client has been conceptualized as comprising the "nonspecifics" of the change process.

Professionals interested in the history of psychotherapy will find more than a bit of irony in the fact that efforts made to clarify and operationalize what behavior therapists have viewed as "nonspecific" have come from their psychodynamic and experiential colleagues. For example, Bordin (1979) has suggested that the working alliance between therapist and client, irrespective of the therapist's orientation, comprises a relational bond, agreement on treatment goals, and agreement on therapeutic procedures. Although behavior therapists have written about the therapeutic importance of the three aspects of the alliance (e.g., Goldfried & Davison, 1976), most of the research on behavior therapy has dealt with the "therapeutic relationship" more globally, perhaps referring primarily to the interpersonal bond between therapist and client. Because virtually no work has been carried out on the working alliance in behavior therapy, this chapter will deal with the more general issue of the relationship in behavior therapy, bearing in mind that most of it probably has had to do with the therapeutic bond.

In considering the role that the therapeutic bond and the alliance in general play in bringing about change in cognitive-behavior therapy, there are several questions that should be addressed: What are the basic characteristics of the therapeutic bond within cognitive-behavior therapy? How is the therapeutic bond viewed by clients who have been seen in cognitive-behavior therapy? How does cognitive-behavior therapy compare with other orientations in its use of the alliance? To what extent does a positive therapeutic alliance in cognitive-behavior therapy actually help facilitate change? This chapter addresses each of these questions.

CHARACTERISTICS OF THE THERAPEUTIC BOND

Nature of the Bond

As previously noted, cognitive-behavior therapists typically view the therapeutic bond between themselves and their clients as a necessary prerequisite to the application of specific techniques (e.g., Beck, Rush, Shaw, & Emery, 1979; Goldfried & Davison, 1976; Wilson & Evans, 1977). Warmth, accurate empathy, and genuineness, though not sufficient for change, are acknowledged as important factors that contribute to the strength of the alliance. The therapeutic bond that subsequently develops is then used to encourage and support appropriate behavior.

The therapeutic relationship is said to be collaborative in that the therapist and client work as a team, the client's role being the open exploration of thoughts, feelings, and behavior, and the therapist's role being to guide this exploration. Both participants work together to identify maladaptive beliefs and then evaluate them by providing objective evidence for and against these beliefs, setting up experiments to test them out, and deciding on more appropriate ways of behaving in the future (Beck et al., 1979). From within a cognitive-behavioral framework, therapists behave more actively in the beginning phases of therapy, providing structure, presenting rationales, setting the agenda, and designing homework assignments. Later, therapists encourage clients to become more active and take more of these responsibilities on themselves. This overall approach to intervention is nicely summarized by Wilson and Evans (1977), who suggest, "The therapist becomes more of a consultant than a controller, skillfully directing consciously involved clients in active problem-solving strategies, instead of conditioning passive responders to external forces" (p. 560).

Components of the Relationship

Gelso and Carter (1985) have described the relationship in cognitive-behavior therapy with regard to three components that they assert are, in fact, characteristic of *all* therapeutic relationships, regardless of orientation. These components are (a) the working alliance, (b) the transference relationship, and (c) the real relationship. The first component, the working alliance, involves the attachment between the "reasonable" side of the client and the working side of the therapist. It consists of the therapeutic bond, an agreement on the goals of therapy, and an agreement on the tasks (Bordin, 1979). Moreover, the strength required of the alliance for successful outcome varies according to the difficulty of treatment demands, and its importance is more pronounced at various stages of therapy (e.g., in the beginning; during difficult periods). The second component, the transference relationship, is "a repetition of past conflicts . . . with significant others such that feelings, behavior, and attitudes belonging rightfully in those early relationships are displaced . . . onto the therapist" (Gelso & Carter, 1985, p. 170). These misperceptions become evident within therapy and can provide information on the sources of problematic reactions. The third component, the real relationship, consists of the genuine and nondistorted perceptions and reactions of both participants to each other (evident in casual conversation as well as in personal disclosures). These three types of relationships are all interrelated; the real relationship fosters the alliance, and the alliance creates a safe environment for clients to experience transferential reactions (if, indeed, this is encouraged by the therapist).

According to Gelso and Carter, cognitive-behavior therapists seek to promote a good collaborative working alliance, as well as a real relationship to the extent that it fosters the alliance. Although a transference relationship may exist in cognitive-behavior therapy, it is typically not fostered or recognized. The authors also suggest that the strength of the therapeutic bond may not need to be as deep as it is with other orientations—cognitive-behavior therapists do not typically require clients to engage in extended exploration of threatening aspects of themselves.

Function of the Bond

Unlike psychodynamic or experiential orientations, where the relationship is seen as the central or crucial element of change, the cognitive-behavioral approach has typically viewed the therapeutic bond as a means to facilitate other important aspects of the change process. Drawing on social learning theory, Goldfried and Davison (1976) and Wilson and Evans (1977) describe several ways that the therapeutic relationship serves this function. First, the bond serves to increase the *reinforcement value* of therapists, leading to greater ability to influence the behavior of clients and ensure that they engage in the work of therapy—whether within or outside the session. Second, therapists can influence clients through *modeling* appropriate behavior. For example, therapists model effective responses in assertiveness training, adaptive and nonfearful behavior in participant modeling, how to solve problems by "thinking out loud," and how to deal with various other situations by providing examples of the ways in which others with similar problems (including the therapist) have handled them in the past.

Third, cognitive-behavior therapists seek to *promote positive expectancies* and *prepare clients* for change. They make efforts to instill hope, increase motivation, counteract despair and anxiety, encourage success, and keep clients in treatment. Structuring the sessions is a powerful way to ensure these things. Structuring involves setting an agenda, designing out-of-session activities, describing the social learning conceptualization of clients' problems, presenting a clear and understandable rationale for the various procedures, and specifying how therapy is likely to progress. Getting clients' input on specifying the goals and the ways these goals will be achieved is crucial in obtaining agreement on them and affirming their commitment to what will be taking place in therapy—key components of the working alliance. Another way to prepare clients for change and possible setbacks is to emphasize that change will be gradual; even steady efforts will be expected to result in uneven progress. Faced with the discouraging belief of clients that they are nowhere near their ultimate goal or ideal level of functioning, cognitive-behavior therapists encourage their clients to shift the comparison back to their level of functioning at the beginning of therapy. In this way, small gains may be better appreciated.

A final, and particularly important function of the therapeutic bond—indeed, the working alliance in general—is as a means to prevent or overcome client *resistance*. We define resistance as any attitude or behavior of clients that counters the change process. Thus, it includes the belief that the chosen procedure will prove ineffective; the belief that change is not possible; an unwillingness to express thoughts, feelings, and behavior relevant to their problems; failure to engage in the work of therapy in session (e.g., relaxation, imaginal activities, role play) or out of session (e.g., practice relaxation, expose self to feared situation, make social contacts); being unreceptive to therapist feedback; and an unwillingness to observe themselves or monitor what they think, feel, and do (Goldfried, 1982).

Goldfried (1982) has suggested that instances of resistance often result from certain aspects of the client's functioning, the therapist's formulation and treatment plan, or environmental factors interfering with the change process. In extending this view so that it relates to the therapeutic alliance, we would suggest that from a cognitive-behavioral vantage point, the alliance plays an important role in the change process in much the same way that anesthesia is needed during surgery. The implementation of certain surgical procedures requires an adequate and appropriate level of anesthesia. Great care is taken to ensure that an effective anesthesia is in place before surgery begins. Once surgery is underway, the primary concern is with the effective implementation of the surgical procedures—the primary reason the patient entered the treatment setting. If problems occur with the anesthesia at any point in the operation, however, *it* becomes the central focus, as the surgery cannot go on without it. Successful cognitive-behavioral interventions are unlikely to occur unless there exists a good working alliance—a good therapeutic bond, and a mutual agreement on goals and therapeutic methods. Should client resistance occur during therapy, the cognitive-behavior therapist must seriously consider the possibility that one or more aspects of the working alliance needs attention.

DeVoge and Beck (1978) have described an interesting integration of behaviorism and interpersonal theory to conceptualize the therapeutic interaction and to deal with resistant clients. Drawing on Leary's (1957) circumplex model—in which social interactions may be characterized according to their degree of friendliness and dominance—the authors note that the social reinforcement through praise and approval is most effective when the therapist is "friendly dominant" and the client is "friendly submissive." The task of therapists with clients who are not friendly submissive (and therefore not responsive to praise and approval, at least in the desired direction) is to bring them into this type of stance. To do this, the therapist must first engage the client in a positive therapeutic relationship (e.g., by listening, reflecting, and communicating interest), and then refute the client's expectations about how the therapist should respond (e.g., by directly confronting critical comments). According to DeVoge and Beck, this should create discomfort in the client, which should then lead to friendly submission (e.g., advice seeking, willingness to listen to the therapist, and responsiveness to direction).

The bond that behavior therapists have with their clients can have important implications for adherence. For example, in a research study on the impact of therapist behavior on client resistance, Patterson and Forgatch (1985) found that therapists' attempts to "teach" and "confront" clients undergoing parent training were significantly associated with increases in the probability of the client engaging in noncompliant behavior. In contrast, therapists' attempts to "facilitate" and "support" were associated with increases in compliance. Although it is unknown at this time whether client noncompliance may be what triggers therapist teaching and confronting to begin with, these behaviors nonetheless tend to have potential negative effects (at least in the absence of facilitation and support). Patterson and Forgatch speculate that other possible effects that client noncompliance may have on the therapist would be a failure to teach or confront at all, distance from the client, a negative perception of the client, and a general sense of pessimism about the case.

Taking a different tack to preventing or overcoming resistance, Dolce and Thompson (1989) apply Kelley's (1979) interdependence theory to the therapeutic relationship and present a model that demonstrates how it can be affected by level of goal and task agreement. Dolce and Thompson maintain that resistance is more likely to occur when clients believe that following the treatment plan will not produce more favorable outcomes than some alternative action. Therapy progresses smoothly when clients give up their preferred actions in return for the satisfaction arising from the therapy process (e.g., pleasing the therapist, avoiding confrontation). Clients are unlikely to do this if they interpret the behavior of therapists as being critical, demanding, or insensitive (i.e., not in their best interests). Therapists should thus be attuned to how their behavior affects clients' perceptions of them. Likewise, if therapists believe that clients would not agree to a certain task, they should select a different one, perhaps one that would result in a less rewarding, but more acceptable outcome. This is in line with Goldfried and Davison's (1976) suggestion to focus on a relatively easily attainable goal when the client is resistant, so as to foster a belief that change is possible.

In summary, the collaborative relationship in cognitive-behavior therapy, particularly as it relates to the working alliance, increases the social influence of the therapist, promotes the belief that change is possible, and provides a way to manage resistance.

RETROSPECTIVE CLIENT REPORTS ON THE THERAPEUTIC BOND

Most of the theoretical, clinical, and research literature on the effectiveness of cognitive-behavioral interventions has dealt with the methods themselves. Unfortunately, as noted by Evans and Robinson (1978), this "concern for quantifiable variables gives the outsider a somewhat distorted picture of clinical behavior therapy and no picture at all of behavior therapy as experienced by the client" (p. 336). Retrospective reports from clients in cognitive-behavior therapy, however, point to the importance of the therapeutic bond. Although methodologically limited, these reports nonetheless shed some light on this aspect of the alliance.

An early study by Ryan and Gizynski (1971) first suggested that the client-therapist relationship may contribute even more to the change process than do specific techniques, which may actually have some negative effects. Specifically, the proportion of behavior therapy techniques (e.g., desensitization or aversive conditioning) was found not to be significantly related to outcome assessed from the vantage point of the client, the therapist, or the experimenter. This emphasis on techniques, moreover, was associated with less liking of the therapist, viewing the therapist as less competent, and finding the techniques less pleasant. Because these findings were reported in the early days of behavior therapy, when less emphasis was placed on the therapeutic relationship, it was somewhat surprising that the following variables were significantly related to successful outcome: client liking of the therapist; client's feeling of being liked by the therapist; client perceiving therapist as being confident, persuasive, and satisfied with outcome; client's perception of therapist creating positive expectations; and client holding positive expectations.

The results of a study by Alexander, Barton, Schiavo, and Parsons (1976) led the authors to hypothesize that therapist-structuring behavior and relationship-enhancement factors interact to produce positive outcome, with a high degree of structure either enhancing or bringing about a positive relationship. They found that in the behavioral treatment of delinquents and their families, both supervisor-rated structuring variables (e.g., directiveness) and therapeutic bond variables (e.g., therapist warmth) were independently related to outcome, and together accounted for 60% of the outcome variance. Having previously ruled out the positive effect of relationship variables alone (Parsons & Alexander, 1973), they assigned crucial importance to the interaction of both types of variables.

In another study by Mathews et al. (1976), agoraphobics receiving behavioral treatment all ranked therapist encouragement and sympathy as being particularly helpful aspects of treatment. Although they also perceived practice and learning to cope with panic as being important, the rankings were less high than for the former conditions. Similarly, Rabavilas, Boulougouris, and Perissaki (1979) examined phobic and obsessive-compulsive client ratings of factors contributing to the success of their exposure treatment at 1-year follow-up, and found a positive relationship with therapist attitudes of understanding, interest, and respect, and a negative relationship with gratification of dependency needs by the therapist. In addition, therapists who conducted treatment in an encouraging, challenging, demanding, and explicit manner secured positive outcomes, whereas those who behaved in a permissive, tolerant, and neutral way obtained negative outcomes.

The inferences we can draw from the preceding studies, although suggestive, are limited due to their retrospective design. First, the direction of causality remains unclear, as positive change in the clients may lead them to recall their therapists positively. Further, it would be more accurate to speak of these studies as focusing on the therapist's contribution to the bond as opposed to the bond itself, which is interactional in nature, involving the perceptions and experiences of both participants. Finally, these studies are limited by their use of client self-reports to study the change process. Just as clients are often not necessarily accurate in their formulation of the determinants of their behavior and the behavior of others, they may likewise misperceive or be unaware of the true mechanism of change.

Before moving on to actual process analyses of the therapeutic alliance in cognitive-behavior therapy, and to studies on the predictive validity of the alliance—which attempt to control these alternative explanations more vigorously—we would like to examine two additional studies that we place in the retrospective class. The first study by Persons and Burns (1985) examined the contributions of technique and relationship variables to *in-session* outcome in cognitive therapy. In a group of largely depressed (but some anxious) clients, the authors chose one session from each course of therapy that contained an intervention involving the challenging of a maladaptive automatic thought. Measures of mood and degree of belief in the particular automatic thought were taken at the beginning and end of the targeted session. At the end of the session, the authors found that both the within-session changes in belief and the client's assessment of the quality of the relationship (e.g., therapist warmth, empathy, trustworthiness) made independent and additive contributions to within-session mood changes ($r = .64$ and $.71$ respectively, with $p < .01$). Together, these variables accounted for 66% of the outcome variance. Although intriguing, caution should be exercised when interpreting these results because the authors served as the sole therapists in the study and there may have been a "halo effect" in the client's ratings.

In a larger study of a heterogeneous group of 185 depressed clients with or without anxiety and personality disorders, Burns and Nolen-Hoeksema (1992) employed structural equation modeling to investigate the causal effect of therapist empathy on depression treated with cognitive-behavior therapy. They administered the Empathy Scale used in the preceding study to clients at the end of the course of therapy and found that client perception of empathy had a moderate-to-large effect on recovery, whereas severity of depression had only a very small effect on perception of empathy. In addition, homework compliance led to greater recovery over and above the effect of empathy. Despite some difficulties in interpreting this and the previously noted studies, it seems that clients in cognitive-behavior therapy see the therapeutic bond as important for change, as assessed at the end of a course of therapy as well as at the end of a targeted session.

COMPARATIVE PROCESS ANALYSES
OF THE THERAPEUTIC ALLIANCE

We now turn to comparative process studies of the therapeutic alliance. These studies examined cognitive-behavior therapy and other forms of therapy in an effort to identify some preliminary similarities and differences. We begin by looking at studies involving the client's perceptions of the therapeutic alliance and then consider research based on the perspective of others, including the therapist and outside observers.

Clients' Perception of the Alliance

The first question concerns whether clients involved in differing forms of therapy are similar or different in terms of how important they perceive aspects of the alliance as contributing to change. In the treatment of a mixed group of neurotic (largely anxious) and personality disorder patients, Sloane, Staples, Cristol, Yorkston, and Whipple (1975) found that 1 or 2 years after completion of either psychoanalytically oriented or behavior therapy, the successful patients in both therapies placed the highest ranking on the same variables in accounting for change. In response to a questionnaire, the following factors—some of which reflect the therapeutic bond— were all rated as "extremely" or "very important" by at least 70% of the successful patients in both therapies:

1. Personality of therapist.
2. Being helped by therapist to understand their problems.
3. Encouragement to gradually practice facing the things that bothered them.
4. Being able to talk to an understanding person.
5. Having someone to help them to understand themselves.

The same retrospective questionnaire was used by Cross, Sheehan, and Khan (1982), who investigated short-term insight-oriented and behavior therapy in the treatment of neurotic patients of unspecified diagnosis. As with the Sloane et al. study, insight-oriented patients gave high rankings for being able to talk to an understanding person, the therapist's helping them to understand their problems, and the personality of the therapist. For behavior therapy clients, helping them to understand their problems was similarly ranked highly; other important factors, however, were encouraging them to shoulder their own responsibilities by restoring confidence in themselves, encouraging them to gradually practice facing things that bothered them, learning to act with the therapist in ways that may have been difficult for them, and encouraging them to speak up for themselves. Thus, whereas bond-related variables were of primary importance to insight patients, both bond- and technique-oriented variables seemed important to behavior therapy clients. The authors also suggest that these "common" factors may not necessarily work the same way in all therapies—perhaps they serve different functions or interact differently with different techniques. In addition, they may play different roles depending on the client's clinical problems.

More recent studies have examined differences in ratings of the quality of the alliance between different therapies. Salvio, Beutler, Wood, and Engle (1990) used the Barrett-Lennard Relationship Inventory (BLRI; Barrett-Lennard, 1962) and the Working Alliance Inventory (WAI; Horvath & Greenberg, 1989) to measure the client's perception of the alliance in cognitive, focused expressive (Gestalt), and supportive/self-directed therapies. The BLRI measures the therapist qualities of empathy, positive regard, and congruence. The WAI is based on Bordin's (1979) transtheoretical conceptualization of the working alliance as consisting of three components: the development of a therapeutic *bond,* an agreement between the client and therapist on *tasks,* and an agreement on *goals.* In contrast to previous notions of the alliance, which have looked separately at therapist or client contributions, this conceptualization emphasizes the mutuality of the interaction between the participants. The BLRI and the WAI, however, intercorrelated highly, suggesting that they may be measuring the same construct. Results based on both scales failed to indicate any significant difference between the three therapies. Another study looked at differences in alliance ratings between behavior, cognitive, and brief dynamic therapies for older depressed adults (Marmar, Gaston, Gallagher, & Thompson, 1989). The instrument used to assess the alliance was the California Psychotherapy Alliance Scales (CALPAS; Marmar, Horowitz, Weiss, & Marziali, 1986), which consists of rating scales for patient working capacity, patient commitment, goal disagreement, therapist understanding and involvement, and therapist negative contribution. According to patient ratings on these scales early in treatment, the quality of the alliance was not significantly different across the three therapies. Associations with outcome will be discussed later in this chapter.

Others' Perception of the Alliance

In the previously described Sloane et al. study, outside observers rated behavior therapists as displaying significantly higher levels of empathy, genuineness, and interpersonal contact than psychoanalytic therapists. Both sets of therapists were rated equally on the display of warmth. Although these ratings were not related to outcome in this study, the somewhat surprising findings contradict the image of behavior therapists as applying techniques mechanically and without concern for the client's experience.

Brunink and Schroeder (1979) similarly analyzed the verbal behavior of expert psychoanalytic, Gestalt, and behavior therapists, finding no differences in empathy, rapport, or structure in the therapeutic situation. However, behavior therapists did use more supportive communications than psychoanalytic or Gestalt therapists, such as reassurance, praise, and sympathy—all of which are consistent with behavior therapists' emphasis on positive reinforcement.

The Marmar et al. study (1989) noted earlier also made use of therapist ratings of the alliance and obtained essentially the same findings as those from the client's perspective. Namely, a composite score of the five alliance factors of the CALPAS as measured early in treatment revealed no significant differences in the level of the alliance between behavior, cognitive, and brief dynamic therapy.

A study carried out by our own research group (Raue, Castonguay, & Goldfried, 1993), which we will describe in some detail, compared the quality of the working alliance of cognitive-behavior and psychodynamic-interpersonal therapies. Thirty-one experienced therapists who were nominated by experts of similar orientations participated in the study, 18 of whom identified themselves as primarily cognitive-behavioral and 13 as primarily psychodynamic-interpersonal. The presenting problems of the clients were restricted to anxiety and/or depression, and these problems had to be related in some way to relationships with other people. For each therapist and client pair, the therapist chose a single session from the middle course of therapy (anywhere after the first five and before the last five sessions) on the basis of its significance. To meet the criteria for significance, the issue dealt with must have reflected an interpersonal theme central to the client's problem, and there must have been some observable impact on the client during the session and in the subsequent session or two as noted by the therapist.

We used the observer form of the Working Alliance Inventory (WAI-O) to measure the quality of the alliance. Before reporting the findings of this research, a description of the guidelines for coding the alliance is in order. Our research group developed these guidelines, based on Bordin's thinking, for use in coding by independent observers.[1]

The therapeutic *bond* was defined as the mutual liking, attachment, and trust between the client and therapist. To attain a good bond, the therapeutic interaction must be characterized by therapist understanding, client comfort, and reciprocal respect. Coders assess these characteristics through tone of voice, amount and ease of client talk concerning intimate issues, therapist comfort and nondefensiveness, therapist accurate empathy, and the value each participant places on the other's contributions.

The therapeutic *tasks* consist of those global strategies and associated techniques that the client and therapist engage in during the session. For example, the strategy of exploration includes the techniques of support, reflection, and reformulation; confrontation includes cognitive restructuring

---

[1] These criteria are available on request.

and any type of reality testing; direction includes therapist suggestion/advice, information giving, homework assignments, and role playing. Coders assess agreement according to how responsive the client is to the therapist's focus, and how responsive the therapist is to the client's focus or need. Examples of agreement would be the client exploring childhood and past relationships and the therapist facilitating this exploration, or the therapist giving advice about child management skills and the client seeing this as appropriate (by agreeing to follow through, by seeking further information or advice, etc.). Examples of disagreement would be a client who speaks intellectually about thoughts or behaviors despite the therapist's efforts to promote emotional experiencing, or a therapist who challenges a client's belief that relationship difficulties are due solely to the client's partner and the client reacting with hostility or avoidance.

The therapeutic *goals* are the objectives of the client and therapist, or those areas specifically targeted for change. They include decrease in symptomatology, improvement in interpersonal skills or relationships, awareness of intrapersonal conflicts, and the development of new ways of thinking or behaving. Coders assess agreement according to the extent to which both participants see the goals as important, clear, and capable of being accomplished. Examples of agreement would be a client desiring to develop more friendships and the therapist supporting attempts at increased social activity, or the therapist identifying a client's maladaptive cognitions and the client seeing this as appropriate and attempting to explore and reevaluate them. Examples of disagreement would be a client who desires a decrease in anxiety symptoms and a therapist who focuses instead on the origins of the symptoms, or a therapist who focuses on altering the behavior of the client toward the spouse, and a client who wants the spouse to change.

Three advanced graduate students in clinical psychology independently rated every session, which was presented to them as an audiotape, and as a typed transcript. Using the intraclass correlation coefficient, coders achieved a reliability of .78 for the total alliance score, and .71 for Bond, .81 for Task, and .74 for Goal subscales. The mean total alliance score was 6.39 for the cognitive-behavior group and 5.82 for the psychodynamic-interpersonal group, where 7 is "always," 6 "very often," and 5 "often." Although both these averages are quite high, a t-test comparing them indicated significantly higher scores for the cognitive-behavior group as a whole [$t(29) = 2.31$, $p = .028$]. T-tests conducted using the three subscales indicated comparable findings for Bond and Goal, and marginal significance for Task. Consistent with past research (Horvath & Greenberg, 1989), the subscales were all highly intercorrelated (.81 for Bond and Task, .82 for Bond and Goal, and .93 for Task and Goal). A comparison of the standard deviations for the total scores of the two groups revealed significantly higher variability in the alliance scores for the psychodynamic-interpersonal (.87) than the cognitive-behavior condition (.51).

Further analyses were performed to assess the effects of client symptomatology and overall level of functioning on alliances scores. These were measured by the Symptom Checklist (SCL-90; Derogatis, Lipman, Rickels, Uhlenhuth, & Covi, 1974) as rated by clients soon after the selected session, and the Global Assessment of Functioning Scale (GAF; Endicott, Spitzer, Fleiss, & Cohen, 1976) as rated by therapists soon after the selected session. A negative correlation was obtained between the SCL-90 and total alliance score for all participants ($r = -.46$, $p = .01$) and for patients in the psychodynamic-interpersonal group ($r = -.64$, $p = .02$), but *not* for those in the cognitive-behavior group ($r = -.32$, $p = .20$). The scatterplots for these correlations are shown in Figure 6.1. When the outlier in the psychodynamic-interpersonal condition was removed, the correlation increased to $-.92$.

These findings indicate that the more symptomatic the psychodynamic-interpersonal patients were, the lower the alliance tended to be. A similar relationship that approached significance for the sample as a whole was between GAF and alliance scores ($r - .31$, $p = .09$), suggesting that the higher the client's level of functioning, the higher the alliance score may be.

How do we interpret our main finding, that the cognitive-behavior group had higher alliance scores than the psychodynamic-interpersonal group, a finding that is consistent with those of Sloane et al. (1975) and Brunink and Schroeder (1979)? One possible explanation is that cognitive-behavior therapists provide greater structure within their sessions, which makes the therapeutic tasks and goals explicit and clear to the clients. It might also reflect the emphasis in cognitive-behavior therapy on establishing and maintaining a good, collaborative relationship, the primary purpose of which is to foster and support between-session change. In psychodynamic-interpersonal therapy, where the proposed mechanism of change requires a focus on the transferential aspects of the relationship itself, negative issues within the relationship are likely to be fostered and explored. At times, this not only can strain the working alliance, but also can explain our finding that alliance scores were more variable within this orientation than in cognitive-behavior therapy. Although previous research would suggest that the higher the alliance—at least at the outset of therapy—the greater the client improvement (Gaston, 1990; Orlinsky & Howard, 1986), a lack of outcome measures in our study precludes us from making conclusions on the effectiveness of the alliance in either type of treatment.

How can we account for our other significant finding that more symptomatic psychodynamic-interpersonal patients had lower alliance scores, whereas symptomatology was not significantly related to alliance in cognitive-behavior clients? As there was no difference in SCL-90 scores for clients in the two treatment conditions, this finding cannot be attributed to differences between the two orientations in clients' level of symptomatology. This finding might be explained by the likelihood that psychodynamic-interpersonal therapists, as their theory would suggest, do not focus on

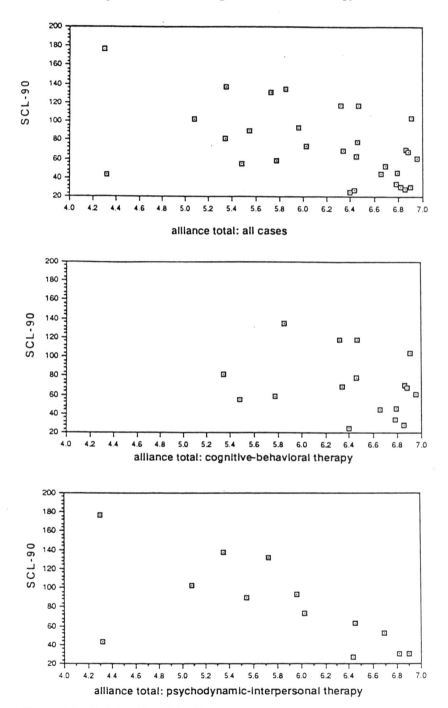

Figure 6.1.   Relationship of SCL-90 score and total alliance score for all cases (n=31), for cognitive-behavioral cases (n=18), and for psychodynamic-interpersonal cases (n=13).

symptoms, and that more symptomatic patients are less willing and able to explore emotional issues underlying their intra- and interpersonal difficulties. In contrast, symptomatology may interfere less with the quality of the alliance in cognitive-behavior therapy, as one of the mutually agreed-on goals in this type of therapy is, in fact, the reduction of symptomatic complaints. Because these measures of symptomatology were taken approximately a week after the targeted session, it cannot be ruled out that something within the session (such as confrontation) could have contributed to an increase in self-reported symptomatology.

Other limitations in interpreting our findings in general include the sole use of outside observers to measure the alliance. Past research indicates low or inconsistent agreement between clients, therapists, and judges (Gurman, 1977; Tichenor & Hill, 1989), suggesting that ratings from different vantage points reflect somewhat distinct aspects of the working alliance. Another limitation is that the coders themselves all came from a cognitive-behavioral background. Although blind to the therapy orientation of the sessions, this may nonetheless have biased their ratings. For example, they were more familiar with cognitive-behavior therapy and may have been more invested in its techniques. Similarly, they were relatively less familiar with psychodynamic-interpersonal therapy, and may have viewed discussion of negative transferential issues more "negatively" than would therapists of this orientation. Future research should look at both issues to determine whether our findings hold up when different perspectives and coders from other orientations are used.

In summary, a number of studies suggest that the quality of the working alliance in cognitive-behavior therapy is at least equal to, or perhaps greater than that in psychodynamically oriented therapy. The key question to be addressed now is how this alliance contributes to outcome.

THE ALLIANCE AND THERAPEUTIC OUTCOME

In a review of the literature on the relation of different aspects of the therapeutic bond to outcome in different kinds of psychotherapy (including cognitive-behavior), Orlinsky and Howard (1986) concluded that the majority of studies have secured positive findings. Some early studies of cognitive-behavior therapy have looked at the effect of warm or cold therapists on the outcome of snake phobics treated with systematic desensitization (Morris & Suckerman, 1974a, 1974b). They have found that clients assigned to warm therapists, whether live or automated, improved significantly more than those assigned to cold therapists. In contrast, observed ratings of bond-relevant conditions in the Sloane et al. study (1975) were found to be unrelated to improvement. However, the small number of experienced therapists within each treatment condition may have been insufficient to generate the variability in ratings required to predict outcome.

Another study (Miller, Taylor, & West, 1980) found that in different treatments of alcohol abusers, supervisory rankings of therapists for accurate empathy accounted for two-thirds of the outcome variance.

Ford (1978) investigated the predictive validity of the client's perception of the therapeutic bond in cognitive-behavioral assertion training with the Relationship Inventory Form (Gurman, 1973). The results showed that the client's perception of the bond after the third session predicted dropouts, and the perceived quality of the bond following the sixth session was predictive of immediate outcome, but not outcome at 2-month follow-up. Ford also looked at the effect of a number of therapist behaviors, and found that a focus on the client (and not significant others), encouragement to engage in some behavior, and a warm and energetic nonverbal style at the third session were associated with higher client ratings of the relationship. At the sixth session, a focus on the client and on the client's cognitive responses to out-of-session events was optimal. At the final session, a focus on the client, reflection, and little direct support were optimal. The author hypothesizes that in the beginning of therapy, a positive nonverbal style is important to the development of a good bond, whereas in the middle and end of therapy, clients' perception of gains made toward goals was most important in influencing their view of the therapeutic bond.

In a previously mentioned study, Marmar et al. (1989) investigated alliance and outcome in a sample of older depressed adults treated with either behavior ($n = 16$), cognitive ($n = 17$), or brief dynamic therapy ($n = 21$). Alliance was rated using the CALPAS early in treatment by both patients and therapists, and outcome was assessed through patient Beck Depression Inventory (Beck, Ward, Mendelson, Mock, & Erbaugh, 1961) scores. Patients and therapists agreed in their alliance ratings for only patient commitment, which consists of the extent to which the patient believed it was important to continue treatment, was hopeful about the future, and was willing to continue despite painful moments. For the sample as a whole, only patient-rated patient commitment was associated with reductions in depression at termination. When looking at treatment condition, however, this association held up only for cognitive therapy, accounting for 53% of the outcome variance. Using hierarchical multiple regression, the authors demonstrated that patient commitment contributed to outcome over and above both initial symptomatology and symptomatic change measured in the middle of therapy. Therefore, satisfaction with positive change occurring during treatment cannot completely account for this alliance variable. It is unclear why commitment was related to cognitive, but not behavior or dynamic therapy. Nonsignificant trends were obtained, however, for therapist-rated total alliance and outcome in dynamic therapy, accounting for 14% of the outcome variance, and for patient-rated working capacity in both dynamic and cognitive therapy, each accounting for about 11% of the outcome variance. A further analysis of this data set (Gaston, Marmar, Gallagher, & Thompson 1991) revealed that alliance ratings may increasingly predict outcome as therapy progresses. Specifically, later alliance ratings accounted for significantly more outcome variance in behavior (32%, 57%, and 55% at the 5th, 10th, and 15th session, respectively) and cognitive therapy (23%, 49%, and 57%, respectively), and nonsignificantly in dynamic therapy (28%, 20%, and 36%, respectively).

A study by DeRubeis and Feeley (1991) looked specifically at cognitive therapy for depressed patients and examined the predictive validity of the alliance (assessed with the Penn Helping Alliance Scale; Morgan, Luborsky, Crits-Christoph, Curtis, & Solomon, 1982), therapist facilitative conditions, concrete symptom-focused methods, and abstract discussions (the latter three assessed with the Collaborative Study Psychotherapy Rating Scale (CSPRS); Hollon et al., 1988). Ratings of these process variables by outside observers as well as the Beck Depression Inventory by patients were obtained at four points throughout the 12-week therapy. Change in depression score was measured not only as the difference between final session and each of the four assessment points, but also as the difference between the assessment points and at initial assessment, thus allowing the researchers to determine the direction of causality. The authors found that use of concrete methods predicted symptom reduction when assessed early in treatment, but not later. Neither abstract methods, facilitative conditions, nor the helping alliance predicted improvement at any point. In the later two quadrants of therapy, however, prior symptom reduction predicted the helping alliance. The authors interpret the findings as being consistent with the thinking that facilitative conditions and the alliance may be important, but in themselves are not sufficient even at high levels for changes in symptomatology. Besides needing replication, however, the study has a few limitations. These include the use of undergraduate coders, who do not possess clinical sophistication, the use of an alliance measure developed from a psychodynamic perspective, and an outcome measure that was restricted to depressive symptomatology.

In a similar study by Castonguay (1992), the predictive validity of the working alliance was shown to be more favorable. One early session in the course of cognitive therapy for depressed clients was chosen. Predictor variables included the alliance (as assessed with the observer form of the WAI) and use of concrete and abstract techniques (as assessed with the CSPRS). Outcome was measured by the Beck Depression Inventory, the Hamilton Rating Scale for Depression (Hamilton, 1960), and the Global Assessment of Functioning Scale. Results showed that the alliance was the only significant predictor of improvement in depressive symptomatology and global functioning at midtreatment, and predicted the former at posttreatment over and above the contributions of the other predictor variables. Thus, in contrast to the DeRubeis and Feeley study, this study supported the primary importance of the working alliance, while failing to provide evidence for the predictive power of the techniques of cognitive-behavior therapy.

In one last study of short-term cognitive therapy with an emphasis on communication about the therapeutic relationship itself (Safran & Segal, 1990), Safran and Wallner (1991) examined the predictive validity of two patient-rated alliance measures, the WAI and CALPAS, both obtained after the third session. A variety of outcome measures were taken before and after therapy, including the Beck Depression Inventory, the SCL-90, the Millon Multiaxial Clinical Inventory (MCMI) as rated by patients, and a global success and target complaints measure, as rated by both patients and therapists. Results showed that both the WAI and CALPAS were positively related to global ratings of success by therapists and clients, as well as to change in severity of target complaints from the therapist's perspective. In addition, CALPAS predicted changes in the Beck Depression Inventory and the Depression scale of the MCMI. The authors propose that the alliance may be a better predictor of global success than specific symptoms, and they note the importance of employing measures that appropriately tap the alliance as is specific to cognitive therapy. Regarding this last point, it is of interest that the CALPAS predicted improvement, despite being based on a psychodynamic model.

In summary, then, most studies of cognitive-behavior therapy conducted to date have found that stronger alliances lead to less dropouts and greater improvement immediately after completion of therapy.

SUMMARY AND CONCLUSIONS

The optimum therapeutic relationship in cognitive-behavior therapy—particularly the bond, which has been studied the most—is collaborative. Such relationships are seen as central to the change process as implemented within this orientation. They increase the reinforcement value of therapists, provide a context for modeling adaptive behavior, promote positive expectations, and provide leverage for overcoming resistance. Regarding this final crucial use of the bond, perhaps the most challenging dilemmas facing cognitive-behavior therapists, as suggested by the work of Patterson and Forgatch (1985) and Goldfried (1985), are (a) how to be active and directive in a manner acceptable to clients, and (b) how to determine those points where it is most appropriate to be active and directive and those points where it is more appropriate to be reflective and nondirective. In other words, how can we guide clients toward adaptive behavior while preserving their sense of autonomy and fostering their decision-making capacity?

The relatively small amount of research that has been conducted on the alliance in cognitive-behavior therapy reveals that clients having undergone cognitive-behavior treatment, although recognizing the importance of particular techniques, place greater weight on the therapeutic bond in accounting for their improvement. In addition, the early development of a strong alliance is a good predictor of treatment dropouts and immediate outcome, at least as measured by global success. Cognitive-behavior therapy is no different from other therapies in this regard (Orlinsky & Howard, 1986). What is less apparent, though, is the unique nature of the therapeutic alliance in this type of therapy, a question that future research must address.

One question is how *technique and alliance interact* in cognitive-behavior therapy. In what ways does a good or poor alliance facilitate or hinder the efficacy of technique? How do choice of technique and its results affect the alliance? Also, how and when can cognitive-behavior therapists use the relationship as a central focus of the therapy itself, and what are the results?

Research also needs to be conducted on the *establishment and maintenance* of the alliance. Which characteristics of clients and therapists (e.g., gender, level of client symptomatology, overall functioning) affect its development, either positively or negatively? Which therapist stances are most appropriate for which client stances? How and why do fluctuations in the therapeutic alliance occur over the course of treatment, and how can threats to the alliance be repaired?

A third area in need of research involves various *methodological concerns*. Different alliance measures should be compared to determine which are appropriate to cognitive-behavior therapy. At present, our preference is for the Working Alliance Inventory, as it seems to be the only measure constructed from a purely transtheoretical perspective, whereas most others have emerged from the psychodynamic tradition. As in all psychotherapy research, the importance of appropriate outcome measures cannot be overemphasized. We need to examine not only specific symptomatology, but also overall functioning, quality of interpersonal relationships, self-esteem, and ratings of overall success, to mention but a few indicators of change. As suggested previously, we need to establish the nature of the differences in client, therapist, and observer perspectives, and to investigate the potential biasing effects of rater orientation.

Finally, we believe that it would be of interest to test out the *assumptions of cognitive-behavior therapists* about the nature and function of the therapeutic alliance. For example, how collaborative are cognitive-behavior therapists with their clients in terms of goal setting and choice of task, and does this vary with phase of therapy? What is the effect of structuring on the alliance? To what extent does all this vary with client problem and personality characteristics? Given the finding that a good working alliance is essential for the change process in cognitive-behavior therapy, answers to these and other questions are needed to enhance our clinical efficacy.

REFERENCES

Alexander, J. F., Barton, C., Schiavo, R. S., & Parsons, B. V. (1976). Systems-behavioral intervention with families of delinquents: Therapist characteristics, family behavior, and outcome. *Journal of Consulting and Clinical Psychology, 44,* 656–664.

Barrett-Lennard, G. T. (1962). Dimensions of therapist response as causal factors in therapeutic change. *Psychological Monographs, 76* (42, Whole No. 562).

Beck, A. T., Rush, A. J., Shaw, B. F., & Emery, G. (1979). *Cognitive therapy of depression.* New York: Guilford Press.

Beck, A. T., Ward, C. H., Mendelson, M., Mock, J., & Erbaugh, J. (1961). An inventory for measuring depression. *Archives of General Psychiatry, 4,* 561–571.

Bordin, E. S. (1979). The generalizability of the psychoanalytic concept of the working alliance. *Psychotherapy: Theory, Research, and Practice, 16,* 252–260.

Brunink, S. A., & Schroeder, H. E. (1979). Verbal therapeutic behavior of expert psychoanalytically oriented, gestalt, and behavior therapists. *Journal of Consulting and Clinical Psychology, 47,* 567–574.

Burns, D. D., & Nolen-Hoeksema, S. (1992). Therapeutic empathy and recovery from depression in cognitive-behavioral therapy: A structural equation model. *Journal of Consulting and Clinical Psychology, 60,* 441–449.

Castonguay, L. G. (1992). *Unique and common factors in cognitive therapy for depression.* Doctoral dissertation. State University of New York at Stony Brook.

Cross, D. G., Sheehan, P. W., & Khan, J. A. (1982). Short- and long-term follow-up of clients receiving insight-oriented therapy and behavior therapy. *Journal of Consulting and Clinical Psychology, 50,* 103–112.

Derogatis, R., Lipman, R. S., Rickels, K., Uhlenhuth, E. R., & Covi, L. (1974). The Hopkins Symptom Checklist (HSCL): A self-report symptom inventory. *Behavioral Science, 19,* 1–15.

DeRubeis, R. J., & Feeley, M. (1991). Determinants of change in cognitive therapy for depression. *Cognitive Therapy and Research, 14,* 469–482.

DeVoge, J. T., & Beck, S. (1978). The therapist-client relationship in behavior therapy. In M. Hersen, R. M. Eisler, & P. M. Miller (Eds.), *Progress in behavior modification* (Vol. 6, pp. 203–248). New York: Academic Press.

Dolce, J. J., & Thompson, J. K. (1989). Interdependence theory and the client-therapist relationship: A model for cognitive psychotherapy. *Journal of Cognitive Psychotherapy: An International Quarterly, 3,* 111–122.

Endicott, J., Spitzer, R. L., Fleiss, J. L., & Cohen, J. (1976). The Global Assessment Scale. *Archives of General Psychiatry, 33,* 766–771.

Evans, I. M., & Robinson, C. H. (1978). Behavior therapy observed: The diary of a client. *Cognitive Therapy and Research, 2,* 335–355.

Ford, J. D. (1978). Therapeutic relationship in behavior therapy: An empirical analysis. *Journal of Consulting and Clinical Psychology, 46,* 1302–1314.

Gaston, L. (1990). The concept of the alliance and its role in psychotherapy: Theoretical and empirical considerations. *Psychotherapy, 27,* 143–153.

Gaston, L., Marmar, C. R., Gallagher, D., & Thompson, L. W. (1991). Alliance prediction of outcome beyond in-treatment symptomatic change as psychotherapy processes. *Psychotherapy Research, 1,* 104–112.

Gelso, C. J., & Carter, J. A. (1985). The relationship in counseling and psychotherapy: Components, consequences, and theoretical antecedents. *The Counseling Psychologist, 13,* 155–241.

Goldfried, M. R. (1982). Resistance and clinical behavior therapy. In P. L. Wachtel (Ed.), *Resistance*. New York: Plenum Press.

Goldfried, M. R. (1985). In-vivo intervention or transference. In W. Dryden (Ed.), *Therapists Dilemmas*. London: Harper & Row.

Goldfried, M. R., & Davison, G. C. (1976). *Clinical behavior therapy*. New York: Holt, Rinehart & Winston.

Gurman, A. S. (1973). Effects of therapist and patient mood on the therapeutic functioning of high- and low-facilitative therapists. *Journal of Consulting and Clinical Psychology, 40,* 48–58.

Gurman, A. S. (1977). The patient's perception of the therapeutic relationship. In A. S. Gurman & A. M. Razin (Eds.), *Effective psychotherapy* (pp. 503–543). New York: Pergamon Press.

Hamilton, M. (1960). A rating scale for depression. *Journal of Neurological and Neurosurgical Psychiatry, 23,* 56–61.

Hollon, S. D., Evans, M. D., Auerbach, A., DeRubeis, R. J., Elkin, I., Lowery, A., Kriss, M. R., Grove, W. M., Tuason, V. B., & Piasecki, J. M. (1988). *Development of a system for rating therapies for depression: Differentiating cognitive therapy, interpersonal psychotherapy and clinical management pharmacotherapy*. Unpublished manuscript, Vanderbilt University, Nashville, TN.

Horvath, A. O., & Greenberg, L. S. (1989). Development and validation of the Working Alliance Inventory. *Journal of Counseling Psychology, 36,* 223–233.

Kelley, H. H. (1979). *Personal relationships: Their structures and processes*. New York: Wiley.

Krasner, L. (1962). The therapist as a social reinforcement machine. In H. H. Strupp & L. Luborsky (Eds.), *Research in psychotherapy* (Vol. II). Washington, DC: American Psychological Association.

Lang, P. J., Melamed, B. G., & Hart, J. (1970). A psychophysiological analysis of fear modification using an automated desensitization procedure. *Journal of Abnormal Psychology, 76,* 220–234.

Leary, T. (1957). *Interpersonal diagnosis of personality*. New York: Ronald Press.

Marmar, C. R., Gaston, L., Gallagher, D., & Thompson, L. W. (1989). Alliance and outcome in late-life depression. *The Journal of Nervous and Mental Disease, 177,* 464–472.

Marmar, C. R., Horowitz, M. J., Weiss, D. S., & Marziali, E. (1986). Development of therapeutic rating system. In L. S. Greenberg & W. M. Pinsof (Eds.), *The psychotherapeutic process: A research handbook* (pp. 367–390). New York: Guilford Press.

Mathews, A. M., Johnston, D. W., Lancashire, M., Munby, M., Shaw, P. M., & Gelder, M. G. (1976). Imaginal flooding and exposure to real phobic situations: Treatment outcome with agoraphobic patients. *British Journal of Psychiatry, 129,* 362–371.

Miller, W. R., Taylor, C. A., & West, J. C. (1980). Focused vs. broad spectrum behavior therapy for problem drinkers. *Journal of Consulting and Clinical Psychology, 48,* 590–601.

Morgan, R., Luborsky, L., Crits-Christoph, P., Curtis, H., & Solomon, J. (1982). Predicting the outcomes of psychotherapy by the Penn Helping Alliance Rating Method. *Archives of General Psychiatry, 39,* 397–402.

Morris, R. C., & Suckerman, K. R. (1974a). Therapist warmth as a factor in automated systematic desensitization. *Journal of Consulting and Clinical Psychology, 42,* 244–250.

Morris, R. C., & Suckerman, K. R. (1974b). The importance of the therapeutic relationship in systematic desensitization. *Journal of Consulting and Clinical Psychology, 42,* 148.

Orlinsky, D., & Howard, K. (1986). The relation of process to outcome in psychotherapy. In S. L. Garfield & A. E. Bergin (Eds.), *Handbook of psychotherapy and behavior change: An empirical analysis* (3rd ed., pp. 311–338). New York: Wiley.

Parsons, B. V., & Alexander, J. F. (1973). Short-term family intervention: A therapy outcome study. *Journal of Consulting and Clinical Psychology, 41,* 195–201.

Patterson, G. R., & Forgatch, M. S. (1985). Therapist behavior as a determinant for client noncompliance: A paradox for the behavior modifier. *Journal of Consulting and Clinical Psychology, 53,* 846–851.

Persons, J. B., & Burns, D. D. (1985). Mechanisms of action of cognitive therapy: The relative contributions of technical and interpersonal interventions. *Cognitive Therapy and Research, 9,* 539–551.

Rabavilas, A. D., Boulougouris, J. C., & Perissaki, C. (1979). Therapist qualities related to outcome with exposure in vivo in neurotic patients. *Journal of Behavior Therapy and Experimental Psychiatry, 10,* 293–294.

Raue, P. J., Castonguay, L. G., & Goldfried, M. R. (1993). The working alliance: A comparison of two therapies. *Psychotherapy Research, 3,* 197–207.

Ryan, V. L., & Gizynski, M. N. (1971). Behavior therapy in retrospect: Patients' feelings about their behavior therapies. *Journal of Consulting and Clinical Psychology, 37,* 1–9.

Safran, J. D., & Segal, Z. V. (1990). *Interpersonal Process in Cognitive Therapy.* New York: Basic Books.

Safran, J. D., & Wallner, L. K. (1991). The relative predictive validity of two therapeutic alliance measures in cognitive therapy. *Psychological Assessment: A Journal of Consulting and Clinical Psychology, 3,* 188–195.

Salvio, M. A., Beutler, L. E., Wood, J. M., & Engle, D. (1990, June). *The strength of therapeutic alliance in three treatments for depression.* Paper presented at the 21st annual meeting of the Society for Psychotherapy Research, Wintergreen, VA.

Sloane, R. B., Staples, F. R., Cristol, A. H., Yorkston, N. J., & Whipple, K. (1975). *Psychotherapy versus behavior therapy.* Cambridge, MA: Harvard University Press.

Tichenor, V., & Hill, C. E. (1989). A comparison of six measures of working alliance. *Psychotherapy, 26,* 195–199.

Wilson, G. T., & Evans, I. M. (1977). The therapist-client relationship in behavior therapy. In A. S. Gurman & A. M. Razin (Eds.), *Effective psychotherapy: A handbook of research* (pp. 544–565). New York: Pergamon Press.

CHAPTER 7

The Alliance in Experiential Therapy: Enacting the Relationship Conditions

J. C. WATSON and LESLIE S. GREENBERG

The therapeutic relationship has long been recognized as an important factor in the change process in experientially oriented therapies (Bozarth, 1990; Elliott, Clark, Kemeny, Wexler, Mack, & Brinkerhoff, 1990; Gendlin, 1974, 1980; Greenberg, Rice, & Elliott, 1993; Greenberg, Elliott, & Lietaer, in press; Lietaer, 1990; Polster & Polster, 1973; Rogers, 1959). Rogers (1959) and his colleagues suggested that the therapist conditions of empathy, positive regard, or prizing and congruence were the necessary and sufficient conditions of therapeutic change. The fundamental importance of a genuine relationship between therapist and client, emphasized in client-centered theory, was echoed by Perls. Although Perls characterized the therapeutic relationship as an "I-Thou" encounter, it was left to others to explicate its role in therapy (Friedman, 1985; Yontef, 1969). Gestalt theorists who acknowledged the healing role of the therapeutic relationship emphasized the qualities of directness, mutuality, and presentness in the therapeutic encounter.

PROCESS-EXPERIENTIAL THERAPY

The process experiential approach to therapy, which synthesizes client-centered, experiential, and Gestalt interventions, emphasizes the importance of the therapeutic relationship (Greenberg, Rice, & Elliott, 1993). However, process-experiential therapy distinguishes between the relationship conditions and the working conditions (Rice, 1983). According to this view, therapy has a collaborative component that includes agreement on tasks and goals and a bonds dimension conceptualized as the affective components of the alliance that result from the client experiencing the therapist as safe, warm, involved, and empathic. A safe working environment is seen as necessary to facilitate the work of therapy. (Elliott et al., 1991; Greenberg, Rice, & Elliott, 1993; Lietaer, 1990; Rennie, 1992).

The distinction between the relationship conditions and the working conditions in experiential therapy echoes Bordin's (1979) conceptualization of the working alliance. Bordin's conceptualization of the working alliance in terms of the degree of agreement and understanding between therapists and clients on the goals and tasks of therapy captures the dictionary definition of the term alliance: ". . . any union for a common purpose . . ." (Webster's Dictionary, 1989). However, in addition to the sharing of a common objective, Bordin emphasized the bonds that form between the participants. Bordin used the term *bonds* to apply to the sentiments of the therapy participants for each other, thereby proposing that clients and therapists need to have a common purpose as well as positive sentiments for a good working alliance. Like Rogers' (1959) earlier conceptualization of the relationship conditions, Bordin (1979) posited that the working alliance established between therapist and client is a common factor across all therapies.

In this chapter, the development and maintenance of the collaborative and affective aspects of the alliance in experiential therapy will be examined. First, the goals and tasks of experiential therapy will be explicated and their impact on clients illuminated by a study which examined clients' subjective experiences of participating in a specific experiential task. It will be argued that the process diagnostic approach that enables therapists to intervene differentially in therapy enacts the relationship conditions in ways which have not yet been articulated. Subsequently, the importance of establishing a safe working environment to foster and maintain collaboration and the affective bonds between the participants will be examined.

THE GOALS AND TASKS OF EXPERIENTIAL THERAPY

An important aspect of experiential therapy is to help clients find their inner voice. By helping clients to actively attend to and represent their inner experience, therapists support clients in realizing more hidden or latent parts of themselves. In voicing hidden aspects of themselves, clients gain understanding and strength as they come to know their needs, desires, values, and experience better and formulate more productive ways of being in the world. To perform these tasks effectively clients need to focus on and accurately symbolize their internal and external experience.

Experiential therapists attempt to facilitate clients' awareness of, and access to their inner experience, by adopting a nonjudgmental stance of acceptance and prizing, rather than a stance of appraisal toward the client. This posture fosters an environment in which clients can explore and concentrate on issues which concern them, free from external threat.

Self-reflection is a fundamental task of experiential therapy (Clarke, 1990; Gendlin, 1982; Greenberg, Rice, & Elliott, 1993; Lietaer, 1990; Phillips, 1985; Rennie, 1992; Rogers, 1965; Watson, 1992) which is facilitated best in the context of a positive therapeutic relationship. Rennie's

(1990, 1992) analysis of clients' subjective experiences of therapy revealed that, if the relationship is negative, then the clients' attention is deflected from themselves to the task of managing the therapy. Clients value therapists' operations, such as paraphrasing and reflection of feeling, which encourage them to pursue a train of thought. However, other operations, that shift clients from nonreflectively pursuing a train of thought to a state of reflexive appraisal, are experienced as discordant. Clients can forgive occasional therapeutic aberrations, if they occur in the context of congruent therapeutic plans and strategies. However, if discordant therapeutic operations occur in the context of contested plans and strategies, then clients are likely to be preoccupied covertly and thematically with the therapeutic relationship (Rennie, 1990, 1992). Clients' preoccupation with the relationship is particularly problematic in experiential therapy, as change is not facilitated by the working through of transference issues or interpersonal cycles, but rather by the representation of experience, particularly inner subjective experience, which is then reflected upon in relation to current values, needs, and goals.

One of the primary tasks in experiential therapy is to help clients access their emotional experiencing associated with problematic issues to symbolize it more fully in awareness. The act of symbolizing experience makes clients aware of the impact of their environment and their responses to it. Thus, while the empathic relationship is curative in and of itself, it also provides an optimal environment for completing specific therapeutic tasks. Experiential therapists assume that different problems require different interventions and, thus, take care to identify clients problematic areas of experiencing prior to implementing the relevant interventions. For example, therapists determine whether clients are working on self-evaluative splits, problematic reactions, or unfinished business and then implement the specific therapeutic procedures designed for these problems (Greenberg et al., 1993). Thus, one of the objectives in developing a good working alliance in experiential therapy is to facilitate clients' engagement in certain therapeutic tasks which are relevant to the attainment of their goals in therapy. Not only is the implementation of specific interventions tailored to the issues that clients wish to explore in therapy, conducive to the formation of a good working alliance, but they foster its maintenance.

The work of Rice and Greenberg (1984) has pioneered our understanding of some of the specific tasks in which clients and therapists engage to effect changes in experiential psychotherapy. More recently Greenberg et al. (1993) have identified seven essential phases to the change process in a task-oriented experiential therapy:

1. The relationship phase.
2. The empathic exploration phase.
3. The task initiation phase.
4. The evocation and arousal phase.

5. The experiential exploration phase.
6. The scheme change phase.
7. The post resolution phase.

Rice and Greenberg (1984) stress the importance of therapists attending to specific questions clients pose about their experience and then intervening differentially at these points to facilitate clients' exploration of their concerns. They suggest that therapists, while empathically exploring issues with their clients, attend to and listen for "markers," or statements indicating that clients are pondering a particular aspect of their experience which is currently salient for them. For example, if clients express a sense of puzzlement or surprise about a reaction they had, it would indicate a problematic reaction (Rice & Saperia, 1984); alternatively, if they expressed a sense of being in conflict, a conflict split would be indicated (Greenberg & Webster, 1982); whereas a sense of a lingering bad feeling about a significant other would indicate unfinished business (Greenberg et al., 1993).

Markers are considered to be direct or indirect requests for help from therapists and indicate clients' readiness to work on particular problems. The help sought may not be in the form of answers but instead may be requests to therapists to assist clients in resolving particular issues (Greenberg et al., 1993). Subsequently, therapists confirm their understanding of their clients' formulation of their problem and establish whether their clients would like to work on it. Once therapists have established their clients' agreement, the relevant task interventions are implemented.

Markers may be conceived as indicators of an affective problem, the resolution of which represents a subgoal of treatment. The explicit identification, clarification, and established salience of the marker for both partners ensures agreement and understanding about the client's desired goal at that point in therapy. It is this process-diagnostic method of intervening differentially at different markers that helps in establishing the task relevance of each intervention.

Once the specific markers have been identified and clients' concerns have been articulated, it is possible to implement interventions that are directly relevant and facilitate clients' process at these points in therapy. If we see psychotherapy as a means of facilitating clients' inquiry into self (Dewey, 1933; Orlinsky & Howard, 1986; Watson, 1992), then by understanding their clients' focus of inquiry, therapists are likely to be perceived as more empathic and to be more effective. As their interventions become more directly relevant to the types of problems presented and the goals their clients are seeking to attain (Greenberg et al., 1993). A marker guided approach enables therapists to be more discriminating in the timing and use of their interventions.

After establishing goal and task collaboration, therapists and clients work to represent clients' experience in the most helpful manner possible in the specific context. The general aim is to reevoke clients' experiences of their inner states and their external environment as strongly as possible so that clients may better apprehend or comprehend the impact of their experience on themselves. This is done in a variety of ways depending on the task. For example, in unfolding a problematic reaction, clients and therapists work to describe vividly the situation in which clients experienced that reaction; in resolving splits in two chairs, therapists ask clients to criticize an aspect of themselves; and in unfinished business, clients are asked to evoke an image of a significant other (Greenberg et al., 1993).

Once clients have evoked the problematic areas of their experience, they are able to engage in the task of differentiating their subjectively felt sense to better understand the impact and significance of those areas. This therapeutic process leads to new insights and realizations that clients deem valuable and helpful (Elliott, 1984; Elliott et al., 1990; Lietaer, 1990, 1992; Watson, 1992).

Once they have differentiated their experience, clients can engage in a reflexive examination of self (Orlinsky & Howard, 1986; Rennie, 1990, 1992; Watson, 1992). During this process, they begin to alter their schemes of themselves, others, and/or their environment. This may involve a new awareness or positive reevaluation of themselves or of another (Greenberg et al., 1993). Thereafter, they are able to devise new plans for action or living that are more congruent with their altered perspective.

Interventions pertinent to specific problem modes in experiential therapy have been criticized by more traditional client-centered therapists (Brodley, 1990) as too directive. Yet, it seems to the present authors that the marker guided interventions demonstrate enhanced attunement to the client being instantiations of empathy that have not heretofore been articulated. Support for the position that positive collaboration on the goals and tasks of therapy represent important components of an empathic relationship was obtained from correlations between the task components of the Working Alliance Inventory and the empathy component on the Barrett-Lennard Scale. Empathy and the working alliance correlated in the region of .69 (Horvath & Greenberg, 1986, 1989). However, although task and empathy correlate highly with each other, the task dimensions of the working alliance are more predictive of outcome than the bond dimensions (Horvath & Greenberg, 1986, 1989; Greenberg & Adler, 1989).

These data imply that clients who perceive the tasks of therapy as relevant to their goals perceive their therapists as empathic and in tune with them. Thus, the clearer specification of the tasks and goals of experiential therapy as demonstrated in the work of Rice and Greenberg (1984) productively operationalize some aspects of client-perceived empathy. Therapists who understand clients' goals and implement relevant tasks demonstrate a high degree of empathic attunement to their clients' experience. The implementation of a relevant task is a way of enacting therapists' empathic understanding of their clients' experience in the session. It is likely that clients' perceptions of their therapists as empathic and agreement on the goals and tasks of therapy contribute to the development of a positive affective bond between the participants in the therapy dialogue. To the extent that clients and therapists agree about the goals and tasks of therapy and develop affective bonds with each other, the client-centered relationship conditions may be judged to have been realized. Data from a study which examined clients' subjective experiences of participating in a specific task will be presented to illuminate further the role of the working alliance in experiential therapy.

CLIENTS' SUBJECTIVE EXPERIENCE DURING A TASK IN EXPERIENTIAL THERAPY

Interpersonal process recall is a method of determining clients' and therapists' subjective experience of the bond and the nature of their collaboration with each other during the session (Elliott, 1984). Recent research on the impact of therapist operations suggests it is productive to focus clients' attention inward to their subjective experience of the therapeutic encounter (Elliott et al., 1990; Lietaer, 1990; Orlinsky & Howard, 1986). It has been recognized that emotions inform people about their environment's impact on them, trigger their action tendencies in response to that impact, and provide a means of communication with others. Thus, emotional responses are a valuable source of information to assess the quality of the relationship and the effect of various therapeutic procedures. The utility of obtaining clients' reports of their experience during therapy to illuminate the results of various therapeutic procedures and the development of a working alliance is demonstrated in a study by Watson (1992).

The study investigated clients' subjective experience of working on a specific task in experiential therapy entitled "Resolution of Problematic Reactions" (Rice & Saperia, 1984). Rice (1986) developed the technique of systematic evocative unfolding to help clients explore reactions that they do not understand or that they find puzzling in some way. After determining exactly what it is about their reaction that clients find problematic, therapists ask clients to vividly evoke the scene in which their reaction occurred using concrete, specific, and imagistic language. Therapists ask clients to slow down and focus on the scene as they work together to bring it alive with as graphic and vivid a description as possible.

There were eight clients in the study; six of them reviewed two therapy sessions in which they had explored a problematic reaction and identified significant moments during the session with a recall consultant using the method of interpersonal process recall (Elliott, 1986; Kagan, 1975). The remaining two clients reviewed only one session. Clients reported on their subjective experience during the three moments they judged as most significant in the session. In addition, if they had not independently identified it as significant, clients were asked to report on their subjective experience after they had vividly evoked the scene in which their problematic reaction occurred.

Clients' reports of their subjective experience during the exploration of a problematic reaction were analyzed qualitatively using the Grounded Theory method (Glaser & Strauss, 1967). Responses were broken down into meaning units consisting of a single idea. Subsequently, descriptive categories were developed for each meaning unit to illuminate the clients' activities during the exploration of their problematic reaction. The analysis highlighted the cognitive and affective processes clients use to effect change in therapy and provided additional information on the role of the therapeutic alliance.

The analysis revealed that while clients were representing and reevaluating their experience, they were also monitoring their alliance with the therapist through a prereflective attention to their feelings and their sense of themselves in the session. Feelings have been observed to have an orienting function; to provide people with a sense of themselves in relationship (Greenberg & Safran 1984, 1987; Orlinsky & Howard, 1986). Thus, flowing beneath clients' attempts to symbolically represent their experience in words is their subjective experience of this process. Clients' accounts of their experience during the session reveal a sense of momentum—the quality of being on a journey or a voyage of discovery.

Initially, clients seem to be concerned about the productivity of the session and worried that it will not lead anywhere (Watson, 1992). However, once clients pose a question clearly and have agreed on a goal or direction with their therapist, they become focused and mobilize their energies to symbolize and represent their experience accurately. It is as if clients map out an area they wish to explore after they articulate a problem and then focus their energies on the task at hand. As one client described it, ". . . I was trying to control my energies and figure out where to put them. I was impatient to explain and understand what was going on . . . ." Another simply said, ". . . I was pretty focused . . . ," while a third commented on her experience in this way: ". . . I became quiet. It wasn't so much what anybody said, it was just that I was trying to think of something that wasn't safe . . ." (Watson, 1992).

Once clients have determined their direction and established a line of thought, it is as if they become unstopped and experience a surge in energy that propels them along. The session assumes momentum as clients eagerly and impatiently follow a lead. Their curiosity is aroused as they begin their exploration. For example, clients said, ". . . I felt like I was really exploring something . . ." and ". . . I was just curious. I wanted to find out more about it. It was positive energy more . . . ." When talking about becoming unstopped, clients said, ". . . I'm just blurting out everything . . ."; ". . . Those different thoughts I didn't let myself think were coming out instead of feeling a big block all the time . . . ." Often the therapist facilitated this process by encouraging the client to speak. Thus, one client commented, ". . . It was clever of her to give me permission to say whatever I needed to say . . . ." Permission to speak their minds seems to catalyze clients' thoughts. As one client explained, ". . . It started everything, and it's something that I never admitted . . . ." Later she commented, ". . . I wasn't sure what I wanted to say, but the way she started got me going. In that sense, we were working really well together . . . ." When this process is going well, a sense of teamwork and camaraderie supports the thesis that the implementation of relevant tasks impacts positively on the working alliance, both in terms of the participants' feelings about one another and the clients' sense of purpose within the session.

At other times, synchrony may be lacking between the participants. This is more likely to occur when clients are asked by their therapists to perform specific actions in therapy. For example, during the unfolding of a problematic reaction, therapists ask their clients to provide concrete and vivid details of the situation in which they experienced their problematic reaction. All clients expressed difficulty with meeting such task demands. Examples of other times when clients expressed difficulty with their therapists' requests were when they were asked to clarify a problematic reaction or to elaborate an insight for their therapists. At these times, clients experienced a sense of frustration and impatience. They felt stalled and sidetracked, as if they had been forced to detour from their planned route. At times, clients would question the therapist's direction and the relevance of the therapeutic procedures to their task. As a result, their attention on themselves would become deflected to the other (Rennie, 1985). Thus, it is apparent that clients monitor their relationship with their therapists while engaging in specific tasks. During periods of synchronicity, clients' attention to their therapists' presence and the specific interventions fades into the background; when the synchrony is broken, however, therapists' interventions and presence becomes more focal.

A client described her experience when asked to recreate the scene, "I had difficulty remembering it. It was difficult at that point to do what I was supposed to do. We weren't doing the same thing. She wanted me to slow down and tell her the story and I wanted to babble about something else . . . . I was frustrated with myself for not being able to explain the situation in complete detail and remember everything as I wanted to . . . ." Another client questioned the relevance of the task to build the scene, "We'd gone over this before. I was wondering why we were doing it again. I couldn't make myself clearer . . . ." Another pondered, "What was its relevance? I wanted to deal with the problem, not the circumstances around it . . . ." A third client said, "We were pondering too much on details, putting too much emphasis on them. I wanted to pursue my story, but I was interrupted and had to go back to bring out little details to clarify . . . ." A number of clients had difficulty remembering. One client recounted feeling ". . . distressed and confused because I couldn't remember what happened one week ago . . . ." Another client recalled feeling ". . . frustrated because I couldn't remember. It seemed so unimportant [to me] but important to (the therapist) . . . ."

Although all clients expressed difficulty with building the scene during their review of their therapy session, they did not express this directly to their therapists. The clients in this study, like those observed by Rennie (1985), tended to defer to their therapists' requests to engage in specific tasks and attempted to strike a balance between that which was being asked of them by their therapists and their own goals and needs at the time. However, the initial turbulence that clients felt when asked to perform a certain task soon dissipated, and in fact, clients retrospectively judged their therapists' interventions to have been valuable and helpful. A client who perceived the requirement to reconstruct the scene in which her problematic reaction occurred as having beneficial consequences commented, "Her questions led me elsewhere, which was good because it got us somewhere . . . ."

Some clients may be more hesitant to defer to their therapists' directions if they anticipate negative consequences as a result of complying. One client who felt resistant to performing the task saw her therapist as ". . . trying to provoke some emotion to illustrate what I was feeling at that moment. That is hard for me to do . . . ." She explained this, saying, ". . . I was reluctant because I don't want to open it up, or else it will all just come flooding out and I will have no control . . . ." Later, this same client reported that she felt ". . . frustrated because I couldn't describe my feeling. If I showed her, I would become agitated and I didn't want to do so . . . ."

These clients' reports highlight the role of clients' agency within the therapeutic encounter. Although it is important to understand and specify potentially effective therapeutic techniques, it may be necessary to enlist clients' support in implementing these techniques to ensure their viability and successful utilization within the therapeutic context. Techniques can be offered to clients as possible methods for solving problems. Metacommunication about the process of therapy and the relevance of particular interventions is a useful way of enlisting clients' cooperation and support for the tasks of therapy.

The benefits of metacommunication in establishing a good working alliance can be illustrated with another example from the same study. One client felt confused and uncertain about what to do to be ". . . a good client and communicate properly . . ." in therapy. He said, "I'm feeling a little bit confused and a little lost because I am not sure how to do it properly. I'm trying to figure out what she wants me to do or what she wants me to say . . . ." This client's concern and desire to be a "good client" seemed to cause him some performance anxiety. Moreover, his anxiety was exacerbated by the therapist's attempts to understand his problematic reaction, providing support for the findings of Elliott, James, Reinschuessel, Cislo, and Sack (1985) and Lietaer (1992) that clients experience their therapists' misunderstanding and misperception of them as negative.

The client felt it took a long time to arrive at a shared understanding with his therapist of what was troubling him and found his therapist's attempts to clarify and reflect his experience as interruptions. He expressed his frustration in these words, "It kind of stops my flow or it stops whatever I was thinking or however I would have described it . . . . She describes and then I have to stop and consider that and then it stops me from continuing on."

In his review of the session, the client commented that he had expected his therapist to be more challenging and confronting and to draw attention to patterns and themes in his behavior and feelings. Moreover, he felt disconcerted by his therapist's attentive listening and attempts to capture his phenomenological perspective as this reminded him of interactions with a caretaker. In his interactions with this caretaker, any information he revealed was used against him punitively. Later in therapy, the client expressed his confusion and asked the therapist to explain her therapeutic modality. Once she did this, the client seemed to relax and was able to explore his phenomenological world more easily. In fact, he elected to continue with additional sessions after he understood the nature of the task in which he was engaged.

This client's experience highlights the need for therapists to be attuned to differences in clients' expectations. It may be necessary at times to explain to clients how and why certain interventions may be helpful to promote greater convergence between therapists' interventions and intentions and clients' reactions. The establishment of convergence between client and therapist has been identified as an important characteristic of successful therapy (Hill, Helvis, Spiegel, & Tichenor, 1988).

At times when clients experience a lack of synchrony with their therapists, the alliance may be strained. Rennie (1990) has identified a number of different ways in which clients respond to discordant therapeutic operations (Rennie, 1990). They may ignore the therapist's response; they may challenge it, or as happens most frequently, they may defer to it. Thus, a delicate balance must be struck between following the clients' lead, the preferred mode in experiential therapy, and introducing more active therapeutic measures to augment and facilitate productive client process. Because clients tend to defer to therapists' demands, clinicians need heightened sensitivity so they do not impose meaning on their clients' experiencing or deflect them from their inner track.

Therapists need to be especially responsive to clients' moment-to-moment goals during the therapy hour. These may not be readily apparent in the exchange but may need be elicited when therapists sense resistance to particular tasks or when tasks are not proceeding as anticipated. When clients do not respond to therapists' requests or seem resistant to engage in particular tasks, it may sometimes be better for therapists to defer to their clients' needs. The interventions can be reintroduced at a later stage once the alliance is more secure and clients more open to exploring other modes of engagement. Some task interventions may be unsuitable with some clients; for example, the detailed description required during the exploration of a problematic reaction may frustrate some clients. One client who had difficulty with the requirement to build the scene during the exploration of a problematic reaction, commented, "We were pondering too much on details, putting too much emphasis on them. I wanted to pursue my story, but I was interrupted and had to go back to bring out little details to clarify . . . ." Yet this same client was able to successfully engage in a two-chair dialogue in a subsequent session. This supports the idea in process-experiential therapy that some tasks are more relevant for some clients than others.

A SAFE WORKING ENVIRONMENT

Recent research supports the thesis that the tasks of experiential therapy are best facilitated in a safe working environment (Elliott et al., 1990; Lietaer, 1990; Rennie, 1992; Watson, 1992). The term "safe working environment" was coined to refer to a particular aspect of a client's subjective experience of being in relationship with a therapist (Elliott et al., 1990, 1985). The idea of a safe working environment reflects the affective components of the relationship, which can be broken down in two ways: (a) the person's subjective experience of being in the relationship, and (b) the person's feelings for the other. The clients' subjective experience reflects the felt impact of the other, for example, whether clients feel safe, content, trapped, or invalidated. Clients' feelings for their therapists also indicate their response to the other, for example, whether they feel warm, cold, trusting, or friendly toward the other. These two components are not independent; they continually interact in a circular fashion as the subjective impact of the other influences one partner's responses, which influences the other's response, which influences the impact in a continuing cycle.

A review of the research on clients' subjective experience of psychotherapy reveals that they value feeling accepted, prized, understood, supported, and affirmed by their therapist. There seems to be a general consensus about how to characterize a helpful, positive relationship. In their analysis of clients' subjective experience of being in therapy, Elliott et al. (1985, 1990) and Lietaer (1990, 1992) isolated some of the factors that provide clients with a safe working environment. Elliott et al. (1985, 1990) identified four interpersonal impacts as important: (a) a feeling of being understood, (b) a sense of being supported or reassured, (c) a sense of the other as involved, and (d) a sense of being close to the therapist. These factors reflect the distinction made earlier between the subjectively felt impact of the other and clients' affective responses to the other. The first three factors can be subsumed under the category *subjective impact,* and the latter factor can be subsumed under the category *clients' affective responses to the other.*

Lietaer (1990, 1992), in his analysis of helpful and hindering processes in client-centered/experiential therapy, observed that clients in good outcome dyads identified the following categories as helpful: therapists' warmth, interest, involvement, empathy, acceptance, respect, and patience. In addition, clients found their therapists' confirmation and valuing of their personhood important. Other qualities that clients identified as helpful were their therapists' inner comfort and authenticity.

In an earlier study, Orlinsky and Howard (1986) investigated the quality of patient-therapist relatedness. Their work differed from that of the previous two authors as they obtained clients' responses using a standardized questionnaire, the items for which were based on the researcher's theoretical assumptions about the clients' experience. The use of a standardized questionnaire can limit the discovery of new and different aspects of the process than might have been possible using more open-ended approaches. Notwithstanding, these authors found that the client's experience of the therapeutic relationship was experienced as "vivid . . . mutually receptive and sensitively collaborative . . . liberal and open, and . . . warm and mutually reaffirming."

BUILDING A SAFE WORKING ENVIRONMENT IN EXPERIENTIAL THERAPY

The client-centered relationship conditions were initial attempts to define a safe working environment that faltered on a number of counts. The relationship conditions conceptualized in client-centered therapy do not capture the interpersonal or transactional nature of the therapeutic encounter. Although conceived as conditions offered by the therapist and supposedly received by the client, the measures, especially those of communicated empathy, measure only what the therapist does independently of the interaction between the two participants. A therapist might accurately reflect the feelings of another, but if the client is attempting to be distant or does not wish to be known or to explore inner feelings, empathic reflections may be experienced as intrusive. Because there are two agents in the therapeutic dialogue, a measure that captures the transactional nature of the alliance is necessary. Subjective reports from each participant will be more likely to capture the interactional aspects of this process.

It is important to explicate the behaviors in experiential therapy that help create a safe working environment. In doing so, we have drawn on our knowledge of relationships in general, client-centered practice and the literature on expressed emotion in families (Kuipers, 1979; Leff & Vaughan, 1980, 1981). Experiential therapists who wish to provide a safe working environment need to, first, perceive the clients' verbal and nonverbal communications accurately; second, communicate and seek confirmation of their understanding; third, negotiate a shared understanding or otherwise readjust their understanding in line with their clients' phenomenological perspective; and fourth, refrain from expressing critical, intrusive, or hostile thoughts during the session. The behaviors that are important in communicating understanding, support, and respect include attentive and active listening, and the vivid representations of clients' feelings. Orlinsky and Howard (1986) identified the first of these as responsiveness. This type of listening is communicated by means of reflections in experiential therapy. Rennie (1990) observed that clients evaluated therapists' operations of paraphrasing and reflection of feelings positively.

In effect, reflections do not merely repeat the client's description of experiences but rather function as a complex way of organizing and constructing meaning with clients. Through the use of metaphors, active listening, and the vivid representation of clients' feelings, reflections serve a number of important functions within the therapeutic dialogue:

1. They communicate understanding and empathy.
2. They help clarify the clients' thoughts and feelings.
3. They help clients articulate fine-grained differentiations of meaning and feeling as the result of using slightly different words and images to convey a person's sense of the situation.
4. They validate the clients' experience as legitimate and valuable.
5. They symbolically represent clients' experience.

In some ways, reflections function like metacommunications in that they enable the participants to negotiate their shared understandings and differences to become more mutually responsive.

Given the thematic and narrative potential of metaphors, care must be taken to ensure a shared understanding of the metaphor for each of the participants as it is developed and explicated during the therapy discourse (Angus & Rennie, 1988, 1989). This is especially important because clients evaluate therapists' misunderstandings as hindering (Elliott et al., 1990).

It is reasonable to assume that the absence of certain behaviors is essential to feeling safe in a relationship. Such behaviors include the expression of criticism, hostile feelings, and impatience, as well as hostile acts, controlling behavior, repetitive behavior, and the attribution of blame (Blaker, Paulson, & Soluberg, 1980; Cole, 1992; Kuipers, 1979; Leff & Vaughan, 1980, 1981; Orlinsky & Howard, 1986). These behaviors represent dysfunctional forms of communication in a variety of contexts and have been associated with the increased likelihood of relapse among schizophrenic patients if prevalent in the family environment (Leff & Vaughan, 1980). Moreover, the presence of negative behaviors in families with a schizophrenic member is a better predictor of relapse than the absence of these behaviors. Thus, it may be as important to assess the presence of negative behaviors in determining the quality of the therapeutic encounter as it is to assess the presence of the facilitative conditions of empathy, prizing, and genuineness.

It appears that a certain level of therapist activity may be optimal for productive client process (Elliott et al., 1990; Orlinsky & Howard, 1986). Too little activity on the part of therapists may be interpreted as lack of responsiveness by clients, whereas too much activity may be interpreted as therapists being overly dominant and controlling and restricting clients' autonomy. A domineering and intrusive therapeutic style might inhibit the development of the latent or hidden self, an important goal of experiential therapy as outlined earlier. Recently researchers have focused on alliance ruptures (Safran, Crocker, McMain, & Murray, 1990) and misunderstanding events (Rhodes, Greenberg, Geller, & Elliott, 1992) to more precisely specify therapist and client behaviors that cause clients to feel misunderstood.

FUTURE RESEARCH

A number of researchers have attempted to define and measure the relationship in client-centered and experiential therapy. These include Truax and Carkhuff (1967) empathy rating scales and Barrett-Lennard's (1959) client-perceived relationship inventory. Barrett-Lennard (1986) devised the Relationship Inventory to measure therapists' levels of empathy, prizing, congruence, and level of regard for the client, which Rogers deemed important to fostering an optimal working relationship. The Relationship Inventory is a paper-and-pencil test that requires clients to evaluate the therapist's level of regard, empathic understanding, and congruence.

Despite research that initially showed promise, relationship conditions posited by Rogers were not found to relate to therapeutic change across all approaches and were only moderately related to outcome in client-centered therapy, with the exception of client-perceived empathy (Grummon, 1965; Lambert, De Julio, & Stein, 1978; Orlinsky & Howard, 1986). The lack of significant findings has been attributed to the complexity of the relationship conditions and ensuing difficulties with operationalizing them. One such problem has been that the relationship conditions reflect both interpersonal and intrapersonal processes; that is, both what is experienced within participants and communicated between them (Greenberg et al., in press; Orlinsky & Howard, 1986). The complexity of the concepts and the interpersonal nature of the therapeutic encounter made it necessary for Barrett-Lennard to distinguish between *therapists'* personal *felt sense* of their clients' experience, *therapists' expressed sense* of their clients' experience and *clients' perceived sense* of their therapists' level of empathy, prizing, and congruence (Barrett-Lennard, 1986; Orlinsky & Howard, 1986). Thus, to more fully understand the therapeutic encounter, we need to obtain information on therapists' inner experience, the observable aspects of the therapeutic environment, and clients' inner experience.

Measures of the therapist conditions of empathy, prizing, and congruence have not adequately separated out these three dimensions. Rather in existing self-report measures, the client is often required to comment on all three. In addition, measures of the client-perceived relationship conditions have focused on clients' *perception* of the therapist, rather than on clients' inner experience of themselves within the relationship. The difficulty in measuring these conditions with this type of inquiry and client reports is that the processes clients are asked to report on are internal to the therapist and not necessarily observable to the client. In effect, many of the items on the Relationship Inventory require clients to evaluate and report on their therapist's intentions, feelings, and motivations. For example, "The therapist *wants* to understand how I see things" as opposed to "I feel understood," or "At times my therapist *feels* contempt for me" as opposed to "I feel belittled."

The difficulty of reading another's mind has been highlighted in numerous studies (Hill, Helvis, Spiegel, & Tichenor, 1988; Horvath & Marx, 1990; Martin, Martin, Meyer, & Slemon, 1986; Orlinsky & Howard, 1986). Martin et al. (1986) investigated the relationship between counselor intention and behavior and client perceptions of counselor intention and behavior and client cognitive processing. It was found that the relationship between intrapersonal cognitive variables and behavioral variables was high as was the relationship between interpersonal cognitive variables. However, the relationship between intrapersonal cognitive variables was low. The authors concluded that it is easier to translate congruently one's own thoughts and behavior and to perceive accurately and act on the observable behavior of others than it is to read someone else's mind.

We can comment more reliably and accurately on our own inner processes than on the internal processes of another, unless these processes are communicated to us verbally or in observable nonverbal ways; even still, they may require clarification and confirmation. These findings highlight the difficulties inherent in operationalizing concepts such as empathy, congruence, and regard. To the extent that those aspects of the alliance refer to the participants' feelings for each other or their subjective experience of the therapeutic encounter, the reliability and validity of the items may be enhanced if clients and therapists are asked about their own feeling states separately.

Currently the authors are developing a questionnaire and conducting interpersonal process recall interviews with clients to examine the relational aspect of the therapeutic process. The questionnaire focuses on clients' feelings during the session, and will be related to outcome to determine whether a measure of clients' subjective experience provides a better prediction of outcome than reports of clients' perception of their therapists' feelings, intentions, and actions. In addition, a task analysis of therapists' performance is being conducted. It is anticipated that this type of intensive analysis will provide a description of therapist behaviors that contribute to clients' feeling understood, respected, and supported in experiential therapy.

CONCLUSION

Consistent with Bordin's conceptualization of the working alliance, experiential therapists distinguish between the working and the relationship conditions in therapy. The working conditions refer to the collaborative aspects of the alliance which reflect common purposes, as in agreement on tasks and goals, between clients and therapists. In contrast, the relationship conditions refer to the bond aspect of the alliance which reflects the sentiments the participants have for each other.

The distinction between the goals and tasks of therapy and the bond dimension of the alliance has permitted a more fine grained analysis of the behaviors and conditions which create a good working alliance in experiential therapy. A number of researchers have specified at a molecular level specific tasks and interventions, for example resolving problematic reactions and conflict splits, which enable therapists to intervene differentially during therapy. These tasks are best facilitated in the context of a safe therapeutic relationship. According to experiential therapists, if clients experience feelings of safety within the therapeutic relationship, then not only is this beneficial in and of itself but optimal conditions exist for clients to accomplish the specific tasks of experiential therapy. Ideally, if clients experience a safe working environment, agree with their therapists on the goals of therapy, and perceive the tasks in which they are engaged as relevant, they are likely to achieve their objectives.

It was argued first, that agreement on goals and on the implementation of relevant marker guided tasks in therapy are concrete enactments of therapists' understanding, respect, and empathy with their clients problems and goals and as such are instantiations of the relationship conditions not heretofore articulated; second, to facilitate further examination of the development and maintenance of the affective components of the working alliance in experiential therapy, it is useful to conceptualize the bond in terms of two factors: (a) the subjectively felt impact of being in a relationship with the therapist and, (b) the feelings the participants have toward each other as a function of their interaction; and, third that the bonds that develop between the participants result from their collaboration toward the achievement of a common purpose and the provision of a safe working environment.

Future research will attempt to separate the multiple dimensions of the alliance by exploring participants' subjective experiences as well as the task environment using interpersonal process recall, questionnaires, and task analysis. This work will increase understanding of the nature, development, and maintenance of the alliance in experiential therapy.

REFERENCES

Angus, L., & Rennie, D. (1988). Therapist participation in metaphor generation: Collaborative and non-collaborative styles, *Psychotherapy, 25,* 552–560.

Angus, L., & Rennie, D. (1989). Envisioning the representationist world: The client's experience of metaphoric expression in psychotherapy. *Psychotherapy, 26,* 371–379.

Barrett-Lennard, G. T. (1986). The relationship inventory now: Issues and advances in theory, method, and use. In L. S. Greenberg & W. M. Pinsof (Eds.), *The psychotherapeutic process: A research handbook.* New York: Guilford Press.

Blakar, R. M., Paulsen, O. G., & Soluberg, H. A. (1980). Schizophrenia and communication efficiency: A modified replication taking ecological variation into consideration. In R. M. Blakar (Ed.), *Familial studies in communication and psychopathology.* Oslo: Universiteitsforlaget.

Bordin, E. S. (1979). The generalizability of the psychoanalytic concept of the working alliance. *Psychotherapy: Theory, Research, and Practice, 16,* 252–260.

Bozarth, E. (1990). The essence of client-centered therapy. In G. Lietaer, J. Rombauts, & R. Van Balen (Eds.), *Client-centered and experiential psychotherapy in the nineties.* Leuven, Belgium: Leuven University Press.

Brodley, B. T. (1990). Client-centered and experiential: Two different therapies. In G. Lietaer, J. Rombauts, & R. Van Balen (Eds.), *Client-centered and experiential psychotherapy in the nineties.* Leuven, Belgium: Leuven University Press.

Cole, J. (1992). *Environmental factors in schizophrenia: A new assessment measure of expressed emotion.* Unpublished doctoral dissertation, York University, North York, Ontario, Canada.

Dewey, J. (1933). *How we think.* New York: Bantam Books.

Elliott, R. (1984). A discovery-oriented approach to significant change events in psychotherapy: Interpersonal process recall and comprehensive process analysis. In L. Rice & L. Greenberg (Eds.), *Patterns of change.* New York: Guilford Press.

Elliott, R. (1986). Interpersonal process recall (IPR) as a psychotherapy process research method. In L. S. Greenberg & W. M. Pinsof (Eds.), *The psychotherapeutic handbook: A research handbook.* New York: The Guilford Press.

Elliott, R., Clark, C., Kemeny, V., Wexler, M., Mack, C., & Brinkerhoff, J. (1990). The impact of experiential therapy on depression: The first ten cases. In G. Lietaer, J. Rombauts & R. Van Balen (Eds.), *Client-centered therapy and experiential psychotherapy in the nineties.* Belgium: Leuven University Press.

Elliott, R., James, E., Reinschuessel, C., Cislo, D., & Sack, N. (1985). Significant events and the analysis of immediate psychotherapeutic impacts. *Psychotherapy, 22,* 620–630.

Friedman, M. (1985). *The healing dialogue in psychotherapy.* New York: Aronson.

Gendlin, E. (1974). Client-centered and experiential psychotherapy. In D. Wexler & L. Rice (Eds.), *Innovations in client-centered therapy.* Toronto: Wiley.

Gendlin, E. (1982). *Focusing.* New York: Bantam Books.

Glaser, B. G., & Strauss, A. (1967). *The discovery of grounded theory: Strategies for qualitative research.* Chicago IL: Aldine.

Greenberg, L. S., & Adler, J. (1989, June). *Clients' perceptions of the working alliance.* Paper presented to the Society for Psychotherapy Research, Toronto, Canada.

Greenberg, L. S., Elliott, R., & Lietaer, G. (in press). Research on humanistic and experiential psychotherapies. In S. Garfield & A. Bergin (Eds.), *Handbook of Psychotherapy and Behavior Change.* New York: Wiley.

Greenberg, L. S., Rice, L., & Elliott, R. (1993). *Process-experiential therapy: Facilitating emotional change.* New York: Guilford Press.

Greenberg, L. S., & Safran, J. D. (1984). Integrating affect and cognition: A perspective on the process of therapeutic change. *Cognitive therapy and Research, 8*(6), 591–598.

Greenberg, L. S., & Safran, J. D. (1987). *Emotion in psychotherapy.* New York: Guilford Press.

Greenberg, L. S., & Webster, M. C. (1982). Resolving decisional conflict by gestalt two-chair dialogue: Relating process to outcome. *Journal of Counselling Psychology, 29*(5), 468–477.

Grummon, D. L. (1965). Client-centered therapy. In B. Steffre (Ed.), *Theories of counselling.* New York: McGraw-Hill.

Hill, C. E., Helvis, J. E., Spiegel, S. B., & Tichenor, V. (1988). Development of a system for categorizing client reactionist therapist interventions. *Journal of Counselling, 35*(1), 27–36.

Horvath, A. O., & Greenberg, L. S. (1986). The development of the Working Alliance Inventory. In L. S. Greenberg & W. M. Pinsof (Eds.), *The psychotherapeutic handbook: A research handbook.* New York: The Guilford Press.

Horvath, A. O., & Greenberg, L. S. (1989). Development and validation of the Working Alliance Inventory. *Journal of Counselling Psychology, 36*(2), 223–233.

Horvath, A. O., & Mary, R. W. (1990). The development and decay of the working alliance during time-linked counseling. *Canadian Journal of Counceling, 24,* 240–259.

Kagan, N. (1975). *Interpersonal process recall: A method of influencing human interaction.* Unpublished manuscript, University of Houston, Houston, Texas.

Kuipers, L. (1979). Expressed emotion: A review. *British Journal of Social and Clinical Psychology, 18*(2), 237–243.

Lambert, N. J., De Julio, S., & Stein, D. M. (1978). Therapist interpersonal skills: Process and outcome. Methodological considerations and recommendations for future research. *Psychological Bulletin, 85*(3), 467–489.

Leff, J. P., & Vaughan, C. E. (1980). The interaction of life events and relative's EE in schizophrenia and depressive neurosis. *British Journal of Psychiatry, 136,* 146–153.

Leff, J. P., & Vaughan, C. E. (1981). The role of maintenance therapy and relatives' expressed emotion in relapse of schizophrenia: A two-year follow up. *British Journal of Psychiatry, 139,* 102–104.

Lietaer, G. (1990). The client-centered approach after the Wisconsin project: A personal view on its evolution. In G. Lietaer & R. Van Baten (Eds.), *Client-centered and experiential therapy in the nineties.* Leuven, Belgium: Leuven University Press.

Lietaer, G. (1992). Helpful and hindering processes in therapy. In S. Toukmanian & D. Rennie (Eds.), *Psychotherapy process research: Paradigmatic and narrative approaches.* Newbury Park, CA: Sage.

Martin, J., Martin, W., Meyer, M., & Sleman, A. (1986). Empirical investigations of the cognitive mediational paradigm for research on counselling. *Journal of Counselling Psychology, 33*(2), 115–123.

Orlinsky, D., & Howard, K. (1986). The psychological interior of psychotherapy: Explorations with the therapy session reports. In L. S. Greenberg & W. M. Pinsof (Eds.), *The psychotherapeutic process: A research handbook.* New York: Guilford Press.

Phillips, J. R. (1985). Influences on personal growth as viewed by former psychotherapy patients. *Dissertation Abstracts International, 44, 441A.*

Polster, E., & Polster M. (1973). *Gestalt therapy integrated.* New York: Bruner/Mazel.

Rennie, D. L. (1985). *An early return from interviews with clients about their therapy interviews: The functions of the narrative.* Paper presented at the 34th annual meeting of the Ontario Psychological Association, Ottawa, Canada.

Rennie, D. L. (1990). Toward a representation of the client's experience of the psychotherapy hour. In G. Leitaer, J. Rombauts, & R. Van Balen (Eds.), *Client centered and experiential therapy in the nineties.* Leuven, Belgium: Leuven University Press.

Rennie, D. L. (1992). Qualitative analysis of the client's experience of psychotherapy: The unfolding of reflexivity. In S. Toukmanian & D. Rennie (Eds.), *Psychotherapy process research: Paradigmatic and narrative approaches.* Newbury Park, CA: Sage.

Rhodes, R., Greenberg, L., Geller, J., & Elliott, R. (1992, June). *A task analysis of misunderstanding events.* Paper presented to the Society for Psychotherapy Research, Berkeley, California.

Rice, L. N. (1983). The relationship in client-centered therapy. In M. J. Lambert (Ed.), *Psychotherapy and patient relationships.* Homewood, IL: Dow Jones-Irwin.

Rice, L. N. (1986). *Therapist Manual for Unfolding Problematic Reactions.* Unpublished manuscript, York University, New York.

Rice, L. N., & Greenberg, L. S. (1984). The new research paradigm. In L. N. Rice & L. S. Greenberg (Eds.), *Patterns of change.* New York: Guilford Press.

Rice, L. N., & Saperia, E. P. (1984). Task analysis and the resolution of problematic reactions. In L. N. Rice & L. S. Greenberg (Eds.), *Patterns of change.* New York: Guilford Press.

Rogers, C. R. (1959). A theory of therapy, personality, and interpersonal relationships, as developed in the client-centered framework. In S. Koch (Ed.), *Psychology: A study of a science: Vol. II. Formulations of the person and the social context.* New York: McGraw-Hill, 184–256.

Rogers, C. R. (1965). *Client-centered therapy: Its current practice, implications and theory.* Boston, MA: Houghton, Mifflin Co.

Safran, J. D., Crocker, P., McMain, S., & Murray, P. (1990). Therapeutic alliance rupture as a therapy event for empirical investigation. *Psychotherapy, 25,* 1–17.

Toukmanian, S. G. (1986). A measure of client perceptual processing. In L. S. Greenberg & W. M. Pinsof (Eds.), *The psychotherapeutic process: A research handbook.* New York: Guilford Press.

Truax, C. B., & Carkhuff, P. R. (1967). *Toward effective counselling and psychotherapy: Training and practice.* Chicago, IL: Aldine.

Watson, J. C. (1992). *The process of change when exploring problematic reactions: An inquiry into self.* Unpublished doctoral dissertation, York University, North York, Ontario, Canada.

Webster's Dictionary. (1989). New York: Windsor Court.

Yontef, A. (1969). *A review of the practice of Gestalt therapy.* Los Angeles, CA: Trident Books.

CHAPTER 8

An Integrative Systems Perspective on the Therapeutic Alliance: Theoretical, Clinical, and Research Implications*

WILLIAM M. PINSOF

In the late 1970s and early 1980s, psychotherapists and psychotherapy researchers focused their emerging interest in the therapeutic alliance almost entirely on the individual. Both theory and research viewed the alliance as occurring between two individuals—a patient and a therapist—engaged in individual psychotherapy (Greenberg & Pinsof, 1986a). The alliance in family and marital therapies was not addressed, and the alliance within individual therapy was viewed from a noncontextual and nonsystemic perspective that ignored the interpersonal context of individual therapy (Greenberg & Pinsof, 1986b).

In a series of articles and chapters (Pinsof, 1988, 1989, in press-b; Pinsof & Catherall, 1986), I attempted to address these deficits. Working from an integrative systems perspective, these publications presented a clinical theory of the therapeutic alliance, a research-based model of the alliance, and a model of psychotherapy process that contains the alliance. This chapter pulls together and organizes these theories and models into a more consistent and cohesive theoretical framework. The first section describes an integrative systems model of therapeutic process that provides the basis for this framework. The clinical model of the alliance that derives from this model is presented subsequently. The chapter concludes with a presentation and critique of the original research-based model of the alliance and an exploration of key issues that lie ahead for systems-oriented alliance researchers.

These models and the full framework derive from Integrative Problem Centered Therapy (IPCT)—my effort over the past two decades to develop a clinical-theoretical model for integrating individual and family therapies (Pinsof, 1983, in press-a). Increasingly, alliance theory has become the

* I would like to thank Mary Halberg, James Wasner, and especially Doug Breunlin, as well as the editors of this book, for their helpful comments on earlier drafts of this chapter.

relationship theory of IPCT. It not only plays a central theoretical role but also functions as a guiding and at times overriding set of principles for the conduct of problem centered therapy.

THE INTEGRATIVE SYSTEMS MODEL OF THERAPEUTIC PROCESS

Therapy is the interaction between therapist and patient systems. The *patient system* consists of "all of the human systems that are or may be involved in the maintenance and/or resolution of the presenting problem" (Pinsof, 1983). It includes anyone who might be part of the presenting problem or the solution to the problem. The patient system is not equivalent to the family system. Blood and/or intentionality define the family system. The presenting problem defines the patient system. Every presenting problem has its own unique patient system. Patient systems can never be definitively identified, but key players are usually apparent. For instance, with Karen, a 6-year-old, school-phobic girl, the patient system includes Karen, her siblings, her parents, her teacher, school personnel with whom she interacts and who can influence her school experience, and possibly, her pediatrician. In contrast, if Karen were not symptomatic and her parents, Bob and Annette, presented with marital problems, the patient system would not include school personnel or her doctor, but would probably include the woman with whom Bob is having an affair, some of his problematic business associates, Annette's intrusive mother, and Annette's best friend, the only person in whom she confides.

The *therapist system* comprises all of the human systems that are or may be involved in providing psychotherapy to the patient system (Pinsof, 1989, 1992). It always involves the therapist and any other people associated with the therapist with whom members of the patient system interact during the course of therapy (receptionists, administrators, etc.). It also includes anyone with whom the therapist consults during that period.

Seldom, if ever, will all members of the patient and therapist systems interact directly with each other. Patient and therapist systems can be divided into direct and indirect subsystems. The *direct patient system* contains the members of the patient system directly engaged in therapy at any particular time. The *indirect patient system* contains the members not engaged in therapy at that time. The *direct therapist system* consists of the members of the therapist system engaged with the direct patient system members at any particular time. Typically, the therapist is the primary member of the direct patient system. The *indirect therapist system* contains the members of the therapist system not directly in therapy at a particular time.

In an interpersonally integrative treatment, the boundary between the direct and indirect patient systems fluctuates. For instance, with Karen's system, the initial session would typically involve Karen, her parents, and her siblings. The second session might involve Karen alone, the third might be with her parents, and the fourth might bring the whole nuclear family back together. If Bob and Annette presented for marital therapy, most sessions would involve both of them. At some point in the middle of therapy, however, Annette and/or Bob's parents might be invited in for a therapeutic episode of two or three sessions.

It is not unusual in marital and family therapy training programs for members of the indirect therapist system to move temporarily into the direct system. In live supervision, the therapist's supervisor observes a session through a one-way mirror, telephones suggestions in, and/or directly enters the session. In consultation, the consultant may join the therapy for a complete session or two and then reenter the indirect therapist system.

Together, the therapist and patient systems constitute the therapy system (see Figure 8.1). The therapy system and its constituent subsystems (patient, therapist, direct/indirect) are characterized by certain systemic principles, two of which are particularly relevant to alliance theory. The first, the concept of hierarchical integration, or *inclusive organization,* asserts that systems are hierarchically organized. Systems contain subsystems and are themselves subsystems of larger systems. In terms of alliance theory, the lowest or smallest relevant system is the individual (and/or the self) and the largest or most inclusive system is the therapy system—the interacting patient and therapist systems.

The second systemic principle—*mutual causality*—asserts that every subsystem within a system influences every other subsystem bidirectionally or recursively. This applies to both horizontally and vertically related systems. Within Karen's family, Karen is very upset by her mother's recent depression and Annette is upset and further depressed by Karen's school phobia. Bob is upset by his wife's depression but pulls away from her and criticizes Karen for depressing her mother even more by being school phobic. Karen is angry at her father for being so withdrawn and critical but expresses her feelings by becoming more symptomatic and babyish. Mutual

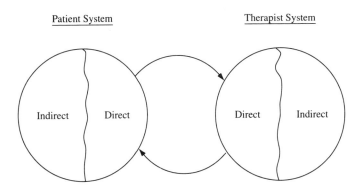

Figure 8.1.   The therapy system.

causality recognizes that although all subsystems within a system influence each other, some subsystems are more powerful and contribute more to certain systemic processes, such as physical and sexual abuse.

Another tenet of this integrative systems model is that *therapy is process.* Therapy is the interaction between systems. This interaction is continuous and dynamic outside as well as within sessions. The distinction between process and outcome is arbitrary and primarily a function of the goals of the observer. Anything that happens within and between the therapist and patient systems during the course of therapy is part of the therapeutic process.

The key assertions of the integrative systemic model are that therapy is the interaction of patient and therapist systems, which each contain direct and indirect subsystems. Together, they form the therapy system, which is characterized by inclusive organization and mutual causality. Lastly, therapy is a dynamic process that goes on outside as well as within the office.

TOWARD A GENERIC SYSTEMS MODEL OF PSYCHOTHERAPY

This integrative systems model of therapy process provides a new way of thinking about the distinction between family and individual therapy. The only difference between them becomes the locus of the boundary between the direct and indirect patient systems. Individual therapy uses the smallest possible direct patient system—one person. In marital or family therapy, the direct system is larger—it includes more than one member of the patient system. The critical point is that the conception of therapy as the interaction between patient and therapist systems, each of which includes direct and indirect systems, encompasses both individual and family therapies. Within this integrative systems perspective, individual and family therapy do not differ fundamentally. The difference is contextual—which members of the patient system are in the office and which are not.

A CLINICAL/THEORETICAL MODEL OF THE INTEGRATIVE SYSTEMS ALLIANCE

The integrative systems model of therapeutic process provides the theoretical ground for an integrative and systemic model of the therapeutic alliance. The alliance can no longer just be viewed as an alliance between individuals—regardless of who is in the therapy room. The alliance exists within the therapy system, between and within therapist and patient systems. Building on prior definitions (Pinsof & Catherall, 1986), the therapeutic alliance consists of those aspects of the relationships between and within the therapist and patient systems that pertain to their capacity to mutually invest in and collaborate on the tasks and goals of the therapy.

The therapeutic alliance from an integrative systems perspective consists of two dimensions:

1. The *Interpersonal System Dimension* addresses the different levels and loci of the alliance in regard to the patient and therapist systems and derives directly from the integrative systems model.
2. The *Content Dimension* deals with the content or specific qualities of the alliance in regard to the different subsystem levels.

The four subdimensions of the Interpersonal System Dimension and the three subdimensions of the Content Dimension are illustrated in Figure 8.2.

THE INTERPERSONAL SYSTEM DIMENSION: LEVELS OF THE ALLIANCE

The concept of inclusive organization facilitates thinking about the therapeutic alliance on different levels within the therapy system. In Figure 8.2, the first three interpersonal dimensions, the three top rows, deal with three

INTERPERSONAL SYSTEM	CONTENT		
	Tasks	Goals	Bonds
Individual			
Interpersonal Subsystem			
Whole System			
Within-System			

Figure 8.2. A clinical/theoretical model of the integrative systems alliance.

distinct levels of the alliance between the therapist and patient systems. In contrast, the fourth interpersonal dimension, the bottom row, does not deal with another level of the alliance, but with another locus. It addresses the alliance between the members of the patient system, rather than between the therapist and patient systems. The three levels and two loci of the alliance constitute the four subdimensions of the Interpersonal System Dimension.

The lowest level and most molecular alliances, the *Individual* alliances (Pinsof, 1988, in press-a), pertain to the alliances between individual members of the patient and therapist systems. This level taps the alliances between individual patients, in family, couple, or individual therapy, and the therapist. With Karen's family, there are Individual alliances between each member of the patient system and the therapist. However, it could also include the alliance between the therapist and a member of the indirect patient system who is not directly involved in therapy, such as Karen's maternal grandmother, who babysits for Karen and provides occasional financial support to Bob and Annette; or between a patient directly engaged in treatment and the supervisor of the therapist—a key member of the indirect therapist system.

At the next more inclusive level, the *Interpersonal Subsystem* alliances target alliances between interpersonal subsystems of the patient and therapist systems. To qualify as a subsystemic alliance, the alliance must include at least a group (more than one person) from either the patient or therapist system. For instance, in family therapy, it would include the alliance between the parental subsystem (e.g., Bob and Annette in the therapy focusing on Karen's school phobia) and the therapist. The Interpersonal Subsystem alliances also include alliances involving subsystems of the patient and therapist systems, such as the alliance between the sibling subsystem and the members of the therapist's supervision team not directly involved in the therapy. This type of alliance is reflected in the following statement by a teenage daughter to the therapist in a family session: "We (me and my sister) don't think you ever do anything without your team's approval. Do you?" Within the integrative systems framework, the direct and indirect systems are subsystems of the patient and therapist systems. As such, the alliances they form with members of the opposite system are viewed as subsystemic alliances.

The next most macroscopic level of the alliance, the *Whole System* alliance, targets the alliance between the whole patient system and the whole therapist system. It is the most inclusive level of the alliance. Although this level does not have to include both the whole patient and the whole therapist systems, it must include at least one or the other system in its entirety. Typically, the Whole System alliance from a family therapy perspective would be the alliance between the family (including direct and indirect system members) and the therapist. From an individual therapy perspective, it could be viewed as the alliance between the individual patient and the therapist system (including direct and indirect subsystems). Of course, the Whole System alliance also includes the alliances between the whole patient system and subsystems within the therapist system and vice versa. The three levels of the alliance are illustrated in Figure 8.3.

Within-System Alliances

Typically, alliance theory addresses alliances between the patient and therapist systems, but alliances also exist within the patient system and within the therapist system. *Within-System* alliances, depicted as the fourth row in Figure 8.2, logically pertain to the individual and interpersonal subsystem alliances, as opposed to the whole system alliances. They address the alliances between individuals and/or subsystems within the patient system or the therapist system. For instance, Bob and Annette can be in agreement or disagreement about the tasks and goals of therapy. They can support and facilitate each other, or conversely discourage and undermine each other. In marital therapy, when Bob begins to get in touch with his grief about the death of his father 3 years ago, Annette may reach out and nonintrusively support him, or she may pull away and unempathically change the subject. Similarly, a young therapist and her supervisor may agree or disagree about the way a case should be handled or they may trust or distrust each other. Their alliance is likely to impact the therapy for better or worse.

The *Within-System* alliance is not another (fourth) level of the alliance. Rather, it defines a different locus of the individual and interpersonal subsystem alliances. The model of the Within-System alliance is illustrated in Figure 8.4. As illustrated, Within-System alliances can exist between individuals, between interpersonal subsystems, and/or between individuals and interpersonal subsystems.

The Interpersonal Determinants of the Total Alliance

The Individual, Interpersonal Subsystem, Whole System, and Within-System alliances together constitute the total therapeutic alliance. Consistent with the principle of mutual causality, each of the four interpersonal

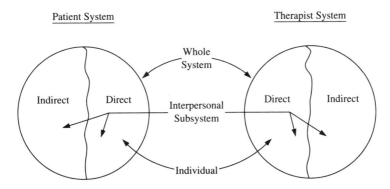

Figure 8.3. The three levels of the therapeutic alliance.

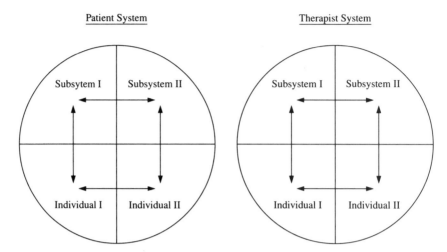

Figure 8.4.   The Within-System alliances.

subdimensions contributes to the total alliance. Typically, the direct system (patient-therapist) alliance plays the most critical role, but each of the four makes some contribution. The four types of alliances need to be sufficiently strong to create a viable total alliance and ultimately, a viable therapy. However, they do not all need to be equally strong.

In a particular therapy system, the Interpersonal Subsystem alliance may be the most powerful, whereas in another system, an Individual alliance may be the primary determinant of the total alliance. For instance, with a single-parent family, if the single parent has a positive alliance with the therapist, it may be sufficient to overcome a negative alliance between the therapist and the children. In a conventional individual therapy situation with an adult patient who controls the financial and logistical resources necessary to maintain involvement in therapy, the members of the indirect system may hate the therapist, but the alliance and therapy can still be viable. A very strong Within-System alliance between Bob and Annette regarding Karen's problems can overcome a weak between-system alliance with the therapist.

Split Alliances

Defining the alliance as pertaining to the patient and therapist systems, as opposed to just the therapist and the patient, creates the possibility of a split alliance. The most common and problematic form of the split alliance occurs when one subsystem (an Individual or Interpersonal Subsystem) of the patient system has a positive alliance with the therapist system and another patient subsystem has a negative alliance.

Depending on two factors, split alliances can be extremely pernicious or merely bothersome. The first is the strength of the split. How negative in intensity is the negative alliance relative to the intensity of the positive alliance? For instance, if Annette hates and distrusts the therapist and Bob is just neutral, the alliance is not viable. However, if she just feels some uneasiness with the therapist and Bob feels positive, the alliance may work.

The second factor is the relative strength or power of the subsystem with the positive alliance. Different patient subsystems possess different degrees of power in regard to keeping the patient system in therapy. This power distribution does not necessarily reflect the absolute power of a patient subsystem. For instance, a father may have the power to pull a family out of therapy by virtue of his economic power and control, but the mother in the same family may possess the power to change the relationship system. Father can cut off the therapy, but the mother can stymie it.

In the face of a split alliance, the therapist should make sure that the positive alliance is with the more powerful patient subsystem. Positively allying with the weaker subsystem is always perilous, and has probably accounted for many unexplained clinical failures. Many unsuccessful cases of conventional child therapy may well be a result of the therapist's failure to build a positive alliance with the child's parents. The best alliance in the world with a young, preadolescent child cannot overcome a strong negative alliance with the parental subsystem. Similarly, a strong individual alliance with a wife/mother in individual therapy may not be sufficient to overcome her husband's and her children's negative feelings toward the therapy and the therapist.

This principle is not an argument justifying a lack of concern about the therapeutic alliance with relatively weak subsystems. The ideal is a positive alliance with all subsystems and on all levels. However, the therapist system should always attempt to analyze the patient system sufficiently to assess the relative power of the different subsystems in determining the total alliance and then prioritize the maintenance of a positive alliance with the most powerful systems.

THE CONTENT DIMENSION: TASK, GOAL, AND BOND

The three subdimensions of the Content Dimension—Tasks, Goals, and Bonds—derive originally from Bordin's (1979) formulation of the key dimensions of the therapeutic alliance in individual psychotherapy. They have been adapted and elaborated subsequently (Pinsof & Catherall, 1986; Pinsof, in press-b). *Tasks* pertains to the major activities that the therapist and patient systems engage in during therapy. It deals specifically with two aspects of tasks: (a) the extent to which the systems and subsystems expect and agree about their respective tasks; and (b) the degree of comfort or anxiety that the systems and their members experience when they engage in their respective tasks.

If key members of the patient and therapist systems disagree about the tasks that they expect to engage in during therapy, the Tasks component's contribution to the overall alliance will be low. For instance, if the patients expect the therapist to be active and to give them guidance early in therapy and the therapist refuses to do so, the therapeutic alliance is going to be in trouble. Similarly, if the therapist relies heavily on action techniques such as enactment or sculpting and key patients expect to sit passively and talk to the therapist rather than interact verbally and motorically with each other, the therapy will be jeopardized.

The second Task aspect—*comfort/anxiety*—deals with the extent to which key members of the therapist and patient systems, especially the latter, are comfortable or fearful in the face of the expected (and/or unexpected) tasks. For instance, a young woman who was sexually abused by her father in childhood may know that she needs to talk about what happened with her father, but she may be deathly afraid to do so. If the therapist pushes the issue prematurely, even though the patient expects and understands the appropriateness of the task, it may rupture the alliance and destroy the therapy.

Goals refers to the extent to which the therapist and patient systems agree about and invest in the goals or outcomes of the therapy. In terms of agreement, do the patients and therapist think and feel that they are working as allies toward mutually accepted goals? For instance, if the key members of the patient system are primarily interested in symptomatic change in a child, but the therapist is primarily interested in changing the family system to be more open, democratic, and less gender biased, the contribution of the Goals component to the alliance will be very low.

The extent to which key members of both systems invest in and commit to their goals is crucial. For instance, if the therapist gives lip service to symptom change as a goal with Karen's family but is really invested in changing the marriage, Bob and Annette may feel threatened by the relative attention the therapist pays to their concerns about Karen versus their marriage, particularly if they are ambivalent about exploring their marital issues. To be high on Goals, the therapist system not only needs to understand and accept the patient system's goals but also to understand their goal hierarchy and degree of relative commitment to the different goals in the hierarchy.

The Goals subdimension is particularly important for Within-System alliances. For instance, if a husband in a couple comes to therapy to separate from his wife, whereas the wife is coming to save the marriage, a viable therapeutic alliance is problematic. It may be possible to establish a Goals alliance if the therapist can forge an alliance between the husband and the wife around the metaproblem—that they cannot agree about the future of their relationship. Thus, pursuing a mutually defined goal becomes a goal of therapy. Significantly discrepant goal hierarchies for key members of the therapist system also weaken the alliance.

Bonds addresses the affective and psychodynamic aspects of the relationships between and within the therapist and patient systems. In terms of affective components, it deals most commonly with the extent to which the key patient system members trust, respect, care about, and feel cared about by the therapist and the therapist system. Psychodynamically, the Bonds component of the alliance also includes the transferences.

Over the years, I have argued with myself and colleagues as to whether transference should be included within the Bond aspect of the alliance, or even more fundamentally, whether transference should be included within the concept of the alliance at all. After considerable vacillation, I have concluded that it should be part of the Bonds component of the alliance. The argument for inclusion understands transference, particularly as conceptualized by Kohut and his successors within self psychology, as a set of categories for describing qualitative aspects of the therapeutic bond or relationship.

Historically, within psychoanalytic theory, transference referred to the neurotic distortion of the patient-therapist relationship based on the patient "transferring" conflicts and issues from prior, particularly early, parental relationships to the current therapeutic relationship. More recently, the concept of transference has been modified by various psychoanalytic theorists. The reconceptualization of transference by Kohut and his colleagues is particularly relevant to alliance theory.

Kohut viewed transference as a natural and not necessarily pathological phenomenon that characterizes all psychologically meaningful relationships over the life cycle. People become self-objects for each other once a transference is established. These self-object relationships create the foundation for the person's experience of the self—the essential and most fundamental component of psychological identity. Without self-objects and the transferences that link them to the self, there is no self. Although the transferences characterize all psychologically meaningful relationships (parent-child, intimate partners, friends, etc.), I will focus primarily on transferences within the therapeutic relationship.

Kohut described three transferences—mirroring, idealizing, and twinship (1971, 1978, 1984; Wolf, 1988). Mirroring deals with patients' desires to be positively and empathically viewed by the therapist and therapist system. Idealizing transferences refer to patients' desires to idealize the therapist and therapist system. Twinship transferences deal with patients' desires to identify with the therapist and therapist system and through that identification to develop particular skills and talents.

These transferences describe the particular quality of the bond between the therapist system and the patient system at various points during the course of therapy. They all assume that the therapist and/or the therapist system has become a meaningful, cathected psychological object for the key members of the patient system. By including the transferences within Bonds, my primary intent is to focus on the meaning of the relationship with the therapist system to the key members of the patient system. Undoubtedly, there are more than three types of transferences or meaning clusters that patient systems can establish with therapist systems. The specific number or types of transferences are not particularly important. What is critical is the idea that Bonds reflects the meaning of the therapist system to the patient system as well as the more general affective components of intersystem and intrasystem relationships.

Beyond meaning, the self psychological perspective on transference also introduces the concept of intensity. The stronger the bond between the patient and therapist systems, the more the patients use the therapists to strengthen and enlarge the self. Thus, the bond can function to reduce narcissistic vulnerability, the vulnerability of the self system to destabilization and fragmentation in the face of self-object failures. The more positive and intense the transference, the stronger the self.

Before leaving Bonds and the notion of transference, it is important to note that the bond between the therapist and patient systems is not unidirectional—from the patient system to the therapist system. The patient system also has meaning for the therapist system. The bond is bidirectional. The meaning of the patient system for the therapist system can be thought of as *countertransference.*

I do not mean countertransference in the classical psychoanalytic sense as a distortion of the patient-therapist relationship due to the therapist's intrusion of psychologically archaic residues. In keeping with a self psychological perspective, I mean countertransference as a normal process in which the therapist attributes meaning to and psychologically cathects key members of the patient system. In fact, this process may best be thought of as transference—not just a counter or responsive transference, but as an active process in which members of the therapist system idealize patients, feel a sense of twinship with them, and desire some degree of empathic responsiveness or mirroring from them. In fact, failure to develop these positive therapist transferences or countertransferences probably bodes poorly for the future of a therapy system.

Alliance Profiles

The Content subdimensions provide a framework for profiling the alliance at the various levels and loci delineated by the Interpersonal System subdimensions. For instance, a young male therapist in an outpatient clinic who is assigned a patient system that does not know him, starts therapy with a relatively low Bond. Therefore, he will have to build the alliance initially through being high on Tasks and Goals. This might be characterized as a *Task/Goal* alliance.

As therapy progresses and the therapist becomes known by and takes on particular meanings for the patient system, the Bonds component contributes increasingly to the overall alliance. As this happens, the therapist can take advantage of the strengthened bond by being more adventurous and taking more risks. The therapist may encourage the patient system to engage in tasks that may be unexpected or anxiety provoking. Increased Bonds may act as an anxiety-reducing or "holding" environment that permits patients to address feared issues with greater equanimity and strength.

Similarly, increased Bonds may permit the therapist to address or introduce goals that the system needs to focus on, but finds threatening. For instance, Karen's parents, Bob and Annette, may have felt most comfortable beginning therapy with the goal of helping Karen. They may have known that they had marital problems but felt too frightened to address them. As they felt more comfortable with the therapist—as trust, respect, and idealization emerged—they could permit the therapist to address their marital problems, defining their amelioration as goals of therapy. In this *Task/Goal/ Bond* alliance, all three dimensions contribute substantially and equivalently to the alliance.

In contrast, a patient system that has waited 2 months to see a therapist they consider the "best in town" may begin therapy with a *Bond* alliance. In this situation, or in a situation later in therapy in which patients have come to deeply trust and respect their therapist, they may be willing to engage in frightening or unexpected therapeutic tasks. The therapist can take advantage of the intense Bonds and "push" the patient system into tasks or toward goals that key members would not be ready to consider with another therapist or at an earlier point in therapy.

The preceding discussion presumes that a strong Bond alliance quells or contains patient system anxiety sufficiently to permit patients to engage in tasks or to pursue goals that stimulate anxiety. How does this work? Self psychology offers a possible explanation. Frequently, patients are threatened by particular tasks that might be helpful or goals that might be useful to pursue, because they constitute a narcissistic threat. They threaten patients' self esteem and cohesion. The strong Bond with self-object or narcissistic transferences to the therapist strengthens patients' selves and decreases narcissistic vulnerability. The appropriate narcissistic transferences buttress patients' selves sufficiently to handle the potential narcissistic injury and anxiety involved in confronting threatening tasks and goals.

To illustrate, at the beginning of therapy, Frank was unwilling to talk to his homosexual son, Frank Jr., who recently confessed his homosexuality to Frank's wife, Arlene. Frank could not accept his son's homosexuality. Arlene insisted that she and Frank get into therapy. Over time, Frank increasingly felt understood and accepted by their therapist, a man Frank respected and admired. After 3 months, Frank expressed a willingness to talk to Frank Jr. Subsequently, Frank and Arlene invited Frank Jr. in for several sessions to discuss his homosexuality and their feelings. This step was linked to Frank's emerging sense of connectedness to the therapist.

There are at least two key points in regard to alliance profiles. First, at the beginning of treatment, different therapy systems have different Task, Goal, and Bond profiles, depending on their prior knowledge of each other and their initial experience with each other. Second, Content profiles of the alliance change during therapy and can facilitate therapeutic progress. The alliance is a process—a dynamic phenomenon that continually evolves throughout therapy.

ALLIANCE TEARS AND REPAIRS

An inevitable event in all but the most short-term therapies, is the tearing and repairing of the therapeutic alliance. At some point, the therapist system will fail the patient system. Such failures may derive from some type of gross clinical error or more often from an alliance profile discrepancy in which anxiety-provoking changes in Tasks and/or Goals outstrips the capacity of Bonds to contain or neutralize the anxiety. For instance, in working individually with a married depressed woman who complains continually about her verbally abusive husband, the therapist may eventually insist that the wife bring her husband into therapy or that they get into marital therapy with another therapist. In this situation, the therapist is introducing a new task—bringing the husband into therapy. If the wife is not sufficiently bonded to the therapist to feel strong enough to bring her husband in, the therapy will be in jeopardy. The most common alliance tear experience for the therapist is the feeling, at the end of the tear session, that the patient(s) may not return. Premature termination anxiety is the key indicator that the alliance has been torn.

More often than not, alliance tears based on alliance profile discrepancies, as opposed to clinical errors, can be repaired. The repair process has been conceptualized by self psychologists in regard to inevitable therapist failures to perform self-object or self-regulating functions for the patient—mirroring, permitting idealization, and twinning. In the face of such failures, which patients experience as narcissistic injuries, the therapist system must respond with empathic understanding and a clear acknowledgment of its role in the tear process.

Kohut asserts that this empathic response results in an expansion and strengthening of the patient's self (1984). Similarly, such responses to inevitable tears in the alliance expand and strengthen Bonds, creating a stronger and more durable overall alliance. When confronted with the patient system's anger during an alliance tear episode, the therapist system needs to respond with empathy and acknowledgment. In the preceding example, after insisting that the wife engage her husband in therapy, the therapist should respond to the wife by empathically understanding her fear and anger, as well as by acknowledging the therapist's role in precipitating a frightening crisis in her life and therapy. The therapist may even relent and slow down the process of engaging the husband, so long as it does not compromise the integrity and viability of the treatment.

Bordin (1980) hypothesized that the tearing and repairing of the therapeutic alliance is perhaps the most potent and beneficial experience in the therapeutic process. Kohut's position also views manageable transferential failures, which are in fact alliance tears, as the yeast of the therapeutic process. Within the process of individual and family therapy, inevitable and genuine disruptions in the alliance and the repair of those disruptions, constitute significant and powerful events.

CLINICAL/THEORETICAL MODEL SUMMARY

The preceding section presented a theoretical and clinically relevant model of the therapeutic alliance with two primary and orthogonal dimensions—Interpersonal System and Content. The Interpersonal System dimension consists of four subdimensions that address the locus and level of the alliance. The first three Interpersonal System subdimensions delineate three levels of the alliance between the patient and therapist systems—Individual, Interpersonal Subsystem, and Whole System. The fourth subdimension—Within-System—focuses on alliances within the patient system and the therapist system.

The Content dimension contains three subdimensions: (a) Tasks targets the extent to which the therapist and patient subsystems expect and are comfortable with their tasks; (b) Goals concerns the extent to which the patient and therapist systems agree about and commit to particular outcomes for the therapy; (c) Bonds addresses the emotional and semantic quality of the alliance between and within patient and therapist systems. Not only dealing with the "real" aspects of the relationship such as trust, caring, and respect, Bonds contains the transferences, particularly as conceptualized within Self Psychology.

Viewing the alliance as a dynamic process, three different alliance profiles were delineated to demonstrate the alliance within different therapy systems at the beginning and over the course of therapy. Lastly, the critical importance of fluctuations in the alliance, particularly tear and repair episodes, was highlighted, with special emphasis on the therapeutic and self-strengthening role of these fluctuations.

RESEARCH IMPLICATIONS

Research on the therapeutic alliance from an integrative systems perspective is much more complicated than research from an individual or nonsystemic perspective because it conceptualizes the alliance as pertaining to two multiperson systems, regardless of who is in the office. Alliance research from an integrative systems perspective should reflect and test the integrative systems model of the therapeutic alliance. Thus, as minimal criteria, research on the alliance should focus on the *interaction between both patient and therapist systems* as well as the *interaction between the key subsystems within each major system.* Furthermore, the alliance should be targeted on *multiple levels.*

A comprehensive exploration of research on the alliance from an integrative systems perspective exceeds the scope of this chapter. The following limited exploration of integrative systems alliance research focuses on the research Don Catherall and I conducted on the alliance. I present that research with particular emphasis on our conceptualization of the alliance for research purposes and the instruments we developed to measure that concept of the alliance. I then criticize that conceptualization and those instruments in light of the fully developed integrative systems model presented above. This presentation and critique of the original model and research highlight key conceptual and methodological issues and point the way for subsequent scientific investigations from an integrative systems perspective.

THE INTEGRATIVE PSYCHOTHERAPY ALLIANCE MODEL AND SCALES

Our effort to address the alliance in marital and family therapy from a systemic perspective produced the Integrative Psychotherapy Alliance Model (Pinsof & Catherall, 1986). This model delineated an interpersonal systemic perspective on the alliance in individual, couple, and family therapy. Our theory, linked to an earlier version of the integrative systems model involved the two dimensions that constitute the core of that model—Content and Interpersonal System.

The matrix formed by these two dimensions in Figure 8.5 led to the creation of three self-report instruments to measure the alliance in individual (Individual Therapy Alliance Scale—ITAS), couple (Couple Therapy Alliance Scale—CTAS) and family (Family Therapy Alliance Scale—FTAS) therapy. Although derived from the same theoretical structure, three distinct instruments were created to accommodate the pragmatic realities (who is in the direct system) of measuring the alliance in three different therapy contexts. Each instrument is filled out by each patient directly involved in therapy (except young children). The perspective on the alliance in these instruments was the "reporting" patient's. The instruments contain approximately 25 statements about the alliance that the patient rates on a 7-point scale ranging from Completely Agree to Completely Disagree. Methodological aspects of the instruments, such as administration and scoring procedures are delineated in our original publication (Pinsof & Catherall, 1986).

The theoretical structure of the Integrative Psychotherapy Alliance Model, depicted in Figure 8.5, used Bordin's Tasks, Goals, and Bonds dimensions as the *Content* subdimensions of the alliance. Although similarly named, the three Content subdimensions in the original alliance model (Pinsof & Catherall, 1986) were defined somewhat differently than they are now within the integrative systems model. The original definition of Tasks

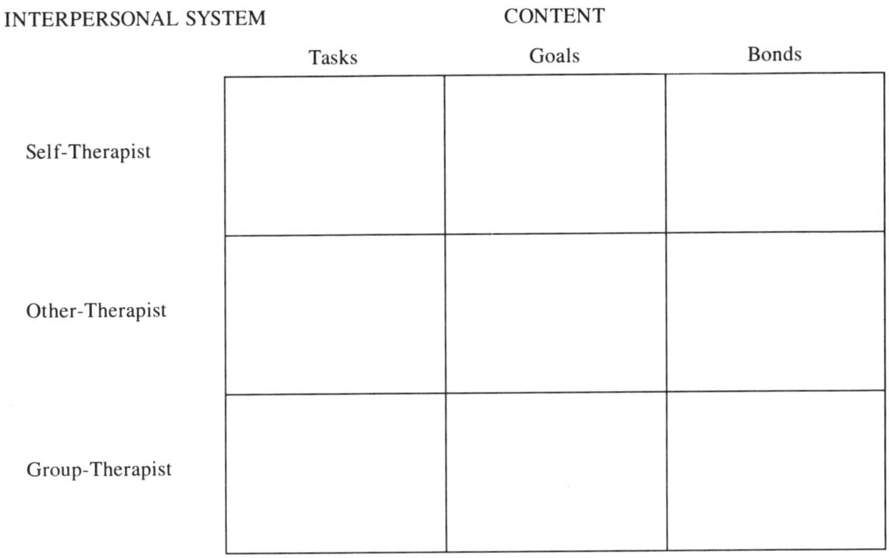

INTERPERSONAL SYSTEM   CONTENT

	Tasks	Goals	Bonds
Self-Therapist			
Other-Therapist			
Group-Therapist			

Figure 8.5.   The theoretical structure of the integrative psychotherapy alliance.

resembled the current one in regard to agreement about the suitability of tasks, but did not address the comfort/anxiety component. The original presentation of Goals focused on mutual agreement between the therapist and patient system, but did not address goal hierarchy or relative commitment. Lastly, Bonds did not address transference.

We operationalized the *Interpersonal System* dimension with three subdimensions instead of the four in the integrative systems model. Proceeding from the molecular to the molar, we labeled the first subdimension *Self-Therapist*. It targeted tasks, goals, and bonds between an individual patient and the therapist. "I am in agreement with the way in which the therapist is conducting the therapy," typifies Task/Self-Therapist items. "I trust the therapist" taps Bonds/Self-Therapist. Because Self-Therapist addressed the relationship between the reporting patient and the therapist, which is pragmatically identical in individual, couple, and family therapy, it was the only Interpersonal System subdimension that had identical items on all three scales. The Self-Therapist subdimension taps the Individual subdimension of the Integrative Systems Alliance Model.

The second subdimension, *Other-Therapist,* addressed tasks, goals, and bonds between the "other" members of the patient system and the therapist. "My partner and the therapist are in agreement about the goals of the therapy," typifies Goals/Other Therapist items on the CTAS. "The therapist cares about the people who are important to me," derives from the Bonds/Other-Therapist cell on the ITAS. The Other-Therapist subdimension links to both the Individual and Interpersonal Subsystem subdimensions of the

Integrative Systems Alliance Model. As we operationalized the Other-Therapist subdimension on the CTAS (where the other is one person—"my partner"), it taps the Individual subdimension. As we operationalized the Other-Therapist subdimension on the ITAS (where the other is "the people who are important to me") FTAS (where the other is "the other people in my family"), it relates to the Interpersonal Subsystem subdimension.

The third interpersonal subdimension, *Group-Therapist,* focused on tasks, goals, and bonds between all the members of the patient system, including the reporting patient, and the therapist. "We agree with the therapist about the goals of this therapy" taps the Goals/Group-Therapist cell of the FTAS, whereas "The therapist cares about my important relationships" pertains to the Bonds/Group-Therapist cell of the ITAS. By targeting the whole patient system ("We/Us"), The Group-Therapist subdimension attempts to operationalize the Whole System subdimension of the Integrative Systems Alliance Model.

The original formulation and presentation of the Integrative Psychotherapeutic Alliance Model was the product of two desires: to create a systemic model of the alliance and a series of research instruments to operationalize that model in three different intervention contexts—family, couple, and individual therapy. As such, it embodied various shortcomings that limited both its theoretical clarity and consistency as well as its clinical relevance.

Most of the problems concerned the original formulation of the Interpersonal System dimension. Our formulation hypothesized the Self-Therapist, Other-Therapist, and Group-Therapist subdimensions. These labels did not reflect our theoretical understanding of the integrative alliance, but rather the way in which we decided to formulate our research instruments. Because we were formulating a set of self-report measures, we had to administer the instrument to individual patients in all three contexts. Our labels of the Interpersonal subdimensions reflected that individual perspective. From the perspective of the individual patient, Self-Therapist reflects "my experience of the alliance with the therapist"; Other-Therapist reflects "my perception of the alliance between the therapist and other members of my family or social network"; and Group-Therapist reflects "my experience of the alliance between my family as a group (including me) and the therapist."

Our theoretical thinking was too skewed by our desire to create a set of research instruments that could accommodate the pragmatics of measuring the alliance in three contexts from the perspective of the individual patient. It failed to view the therapist as part of a system and did not consider the Within-System alliances. Additionally, our original model only addressed the indirect patient system in the Individual Therapy Alliance Scale ("the people who are important to me" for the Other-Therapist subdimension and the "my important relationships" for the Group-Therapist subdimension). The other two scales, the Couple Therapy and Family Therapy Alliance

Scales, dealt with the reporting patient and that patient's perception of the alliance between the therapist and the other people in the family who were directly involved in treatment.

Research Results

To date, the studies that have investigated the predictive validity of the alliance measures, particularly the extent to which the family (FTAS) and couples (CTAS) measures predict outcome, have found a generally positive relationship between alliance scores and various outcome or impact measures (Bourgeois, Sabourin, & Wright, 1990; Catherall, 1984; Heatherington & Friedlander, 1990; Johnson & Greenberg, 1985). Generally, the reliability of the measures in these as well as Pinsof and Catherall's (1986) original investigation has been adequate. Questions about the construct validity of the measures, in particular the extent to which the factors (Content and Interpersonal Structure) are measuring distinct underlying dimensions, have emerged in several studies.

RECOMMENDATIONS AND ISSUES FOR INTEGRATIVE SYSTEMS ALLIANCE RESEARCH

The following recommendations are offered to facilitate research that is as consistent as possible with the integrative systems model of the alliance.

System versus Scale

Rather than a single instrument to measure the alliance in any particular direct system context (individual, couple or family), a system of instruments should be developed. This recommendation derives from several concerns. First, it is methodologically impossible to cover the patient and therapist systems and their interaction with one instrument. There should be at least one instrument to measure the alliance from the perspective of the therapist system and one, like the current measures, to tap the alliance from the patient system perspective. For instance, a Family Therapy Alliance Measurement System might include a set of instruments. One, like the current FTAS, might tap the alliance from the perspective of the patient system (FTAS-P), whereas another might tap the alliance from the therapist's perspective (FTAS-T). The Couple System and the Individual System would also include therapist- and patient-perspective instruments.

The second concern is that in our research with the alliance instruments, as well as in the research that others have conducted with the measures, particularly the Couple Therapy Alliance Scale (Bourgouis, Sabourin, & Wright, 1990), the subdimensions tend to be highly correlated. There is little empirical evidence to support the independence of the Content or Interpersonal System subdimensions as conceptualized and operationalized in the Integrative Psychotherapy Alliance Scales.

One of the problems may be a response bias as patients fill out the items on the self-report questionnaire. For patients to differentiate their individual experience of the alliance from their perception of the alliance between the therapist system and the other people in the patient system (direct and indirect), there need to be gross differences. For instance, the mother in family therapy would have to perceive her alliance with the therapist as distinctly unlike the alliance between the therapist and someone else in her family for it to become sufficiently noticeable to rate it differently on her alliance scale.

In regard to this response bias, which also tends to be associated with uniformly positive ratings (at best, patients damn with faint praise), separate instruments with separate instructions focusing the reporting patient on the locus or level of the alliance being rated, might aid in overcoming the bias and making the ratings more independent. Instructing the patient to "Focus now on the people who are important to you who are not directly involved in this therapy," and then proceeding to ask the patient about them without questioning other systems or loci in the same question set, may help to experientially separate the ratings. Thus, the FTAS-P may include one scale that asks only about the indirect system and another scale, like the current one, that targets the direct system.

Within-System Rating

The Integrative Psychotherapy Alliance Scales focused solely on the between-system alliances. Our theory at that time did not encompass within-system alliances. Any system for studying and measuring the alliance must focus on the within-system alliances as well. To do so without overwhelming the patient, a separate instrument or set of instruments should be developed. Consistent with the Within-System theory articulated earlier, these instruments might respectively address the reporting patient's (or the therapist's in the therapist system measures) experience of the alliance (Tasks, Goals, and Bonds) with other individuals in the patient system (Individual subdimension) or with other multiperson subsystems within the patient system (Interpersonal Subsystem subdimension).

Self-Report and Observational Measures

As well as self-report instruments, which solely characterized the Integrative Psychotherapy Alliance Scales, a comprehensive research system for measuring the alliance from an integrative systems perspective, might well include some observational measures that target the alliance from a nonparticipant perspective. Like other researchers measuring the alliance in individual therapy (see other chapters in this book), a set of observational rating measures could be created. The particular advantage of such measures is that they provide an alternative to the individual perspective of the reporting patient or the reporting therapist. Like all observational measures, they still rely on an individual perspective—that of the observer—but because such measures offer a nonparticipant perspective that targets the therapy system from outside, they are probably less subject to positive response bias.

Expanded Content Dimensions

As mentioned in the critique of the Content subdimensions of the initial research formulation and scales, the original definitions did not include some key components of the recently expanded integrative systems model of the alliance. Any new measurement system should include the additional components in its formulation. Specifically, a new system should include the comfort/anxiety component of Tasks, the hierarchy and relative commitment components of Goals, and the transference or meaning aspect of Bonds.

The Institutional Alliance

The community programs of The Family Institute have increasingly impressed us with the importance of what we have come to talk about as the Institutional Alliance (IA). The Institutional Alliance is that aspect of the patient system's experience of the therapist system that concerns the institution in which treatment occurs. For instance, we have seen highly troubled and treatment resistant African-American families create strong and effective therapeutic alliances with Caucasian female therapists, when they worked with their therapists in a trusted and comfortable community center run by African-American staff. The patients' alliance with the host institution seemed to greatly enhance their ability to create a therapeutic alliance with the therapist.

We have begun to explore strategies for measuring the IA. We alternatively think about the IA as part of the patients' experience of the therapist system or as a distinct and independent alliance in its own right. We believe that the IA may play a crucial role in determining engagement and outcome in therapy, particularly when the therapist and patient systems are culturally, racially, and/or socioeconomically distinct.

RESEARCH SUMMARY

This section presented and critiqued our original effort to conceptualize and measure the alliance from an integrative systems perspective. This critique of the Integrative Psychotherapy Alliance Model and Scales highlighted key criteria and critical issues for subsequent integrative and systemic research on the alliance. Particular recommendations were made, with special emphasis on the need for a more comprehensive and multiscale measurement system to do justice to the breadth and complexity of the integrative systems model of the therapeutic alliance.

CONCLUSION

This chapter delineated a model of the therapeutic alliance that reflects key principles of integrative systems thinking. The model, which views all forms of psychotherapy as occurring within an integrative systems framework, provides concepts and potentially suggests methods for enhancing the alliance. The research implications of this model were explored, and recommendations were made for the conduct of the scientific study of the alliance from an integrative systems perspective. The central thesis of this chapter is that regardless of the type of psychotherapy, a systemic and integrative perspective enhances our theories, our practice, and our research.

REFERENCES

Bordin, E. S. (1979). The generalizeability of the psychoanalytic concept of the working alliance. *Psychotherapy: Theory, Research and Practice, 16*, 252–260.

Bordin, E. S. (1980). *New developments in psychotherapy research.* Unpublished presidential address, Society for Psychotherapy Research Annual Conference, Asilomar, CA.

Bourgeois, L., Sabourin, S., & Wright, J. (1990). Predictive validity of therapeutic alliance in group marital therapy. *Journal of Consulting and Clinical Psychology, 58* (5), 608–613.

Catherall, D. (1984). *The therapeutic alliance in individual, couple and family therapy.* Unpublished doctoral dissertation, Northwestern University, Evanston, IL.

Greenberg, L. S., & Pinsof, W. M. (Eds.). (1986a). *The psychotherapeutic process: A research handbook.* New York: Guilford Press.

Greenberg, L. S., & Pinsof, W. M. (1986b). Process research: Current trends and future perspectives. In L. S. Greenberg & W. M. Pinsof (Eds.), *The psychotherapeutic process: A research handbook* (pp. 3–21). New York: Guilford Press.

Heatherington, L., & Friedlander, M. (1990). Couple and family therapy alliance scales: Empirical considerations. *Journal of Marital and Family Therapy, 16* (3), 299–306.

Johnson, S., & Greenberg, L. (1985). Emotionally focused couples therapy: An outcome study. *Journal of Marital and Family Therapy, 11* (3), 313–317.

Kohut, H. (1971). *The analysis of the self.* New York: International Universities Press.

Kohut, H. (1978). *The restoration of the self.* New York: International Universities Press.

Kohut, H. (1984). *How does analysis cure?* Chicago, IL: University of Chicago Press.

Pinsof, W. (1983). Integrative problem centered therapy: Toward the synthesis of individual and family therapies. *Journal of Marital and Family Therapy, 9,* 19–35.

Pinsof, W. (1988). The therapist-client relationship: An integrative systems perspective. *Journal of Integrative and Eclectic Psychotherapy, 7,* 303–313.

Pinsof, W. (1989). A conceptual framework and methodological criteria for family therapy research. *Journal of Consulting and Clinical Psychology, 57,* 53–59.

Pinsof, W. (1992). Toward a scientific paradigm for family psychology: The integrative process systems perspective. *Journal of Family Psychology, 5,* 432–447.

Pinsof, W. (in press-a). *Integrative problem centered therapy: The synthesis of individual and family psychotherapies.* New York: Basic Books.

Pinsof, W. (in press-b). The Integrative Systems Alliance. Chapter 3. In W. Pinsof, *Integrative problem centered therapy: The synthesis of individual and family psychotherapies.* New York: Basic Books.

Pinsof, W., & Catherall, D. (1986). The integrative psychotherapy alliance: Family, couple and individual therapy scales. *Journal of Marital and Family Therapy, 12,* 137–151.

Wolf, E. (1988). *Treating the self: Elements of clinical self psychology.* New York: Guilford.

PART THREE

The Alliance as Process

.

CHAPTER 9

The Role of the Therapeutic Alliance in Psychoanalytic Therapy with Borderline Patients

SIEBOLT H. FRIESWYK, GLEN O. GABBARD, LEONARD HORWITZ, JON G. ALLEN, DONALD B. COLSON, GAVIN E. NEWSOM, and LOLAYFAYE COYNE

OVERVIEW

Instability remains the key identifying descriptive characteristic of the borderline state (Gunderson, 1984). Life events that would prove uneventful for most individuals destabilize the borderline, and the heart of these events is often an experience of loss or separation. Such a happening evokes a remarkable transformation. It is as though the borderline patient becomes a bewildered child overcome with panic, rage, and despair, beyond containment or soothing and at grave risk for self-harm. Grotstein, Solomon, and Lang (1987) have argued that this core vulnerability resides in a neurobiological substrate that impairs the borderline patient's capacity to engage in self-regulation and results in adaptive and integrative failure as well as dyscontrol. By way of contrast, Adler (1985) and Adler and Buie (1979) have contended that environmental factors (parental neglect, abuse, or empathic failure) undermine the borderline patient's capacity to tolerate separateness, leaving the patient vulnerable to painful experiences of aloneness and despair. Adler views the borderline's dysfunctional behavior as a restitutive effort designed to extract from the environment a response to those internal states of distress. Even more so, he believes that such behavior is designed to reestablish a lost relatedness.

Nearly 20 years ago, Horwitz (1974) addressed this core deficiency from a research perspective. He proposed that lasting therapeutic results in the supportive treatment of borderline patients was a product of the internalization of the therapeutic alliance. This observation was consistent with the point Bordin (1979) later made that the establishment of a sustained collaboration with a therapist and its resurrection and repair contribute to the evolving capacity of the patient to experience the therapist's interventions and intentions as benevolent. Within the context of the borderline's dilemma, the increasing capacity to recall a benign memory of the therapist serves to counteract the patient's catastrophic reactions to separation and the attendant behavioral disturbances, depression, and lowered self-esteem.

In keeping with the emphasis on the importance of the alliance in the change process with borderline patients, there is a developing consensus regarding the specific activity of the therapist essential to promoting the alliance. Noting this broad agreement, Waldinger and Gunderson (1987) underscore several interrelated requirements for the therapist. Specifically, the therapist must provide:

1. A stable framework for treatment.
2. A level of activity sufficient to underscore the therapist's presence to define his or her reality and counteract patient distortions.
3. A containing relationship to withstand and endure the patient's destructive hostility.
4. A focus on clarifying the meaning of the patient's actions.
5. Appropriate limit setting to prevent the destruction of the treatment framework.

Despite this broad agreement on the basic framework for the treatment process, a consensus has not yet developed regarding the timing, place, focus, and therapeutic action of interpretation in the psychotherapeutic process with the borderline. There are fundamentally two questions. First, should interpretive approaches be attempted at all? Some will argue against such a strategy, noting the borderline patient's narcissistic fragility, affective instability, action proneness, self-destructiveness, and potential for paranoid distortions. The second question is really an array of related issues. Are there types of patients, phases of treatment, and styles of interventions that promote a stable therapeutic alliance, and if so, what is their impact on treatment outcome? To address these issues, we will first review the perspectives of clinical theorists and then selectively examine salient research contributions regarding the most suitable approaches to alliance formation with the borderline patient.

CLINICAL THEORY

Over the past 30 years, the broadening scope of psychoanalysis has witnessed a revolution in the treatment of borderline patients. Whereas early recommendations for the treatment of those patients emphasized infrequent and supportive contacts (Knight, 1953; Zetzel, 1971), recent contributions have been more ambitious. Drawing on developments in ego psychology, object relations theory, self psychology, and developmental theory and research (Pine, 1985, 1990), these contributions have spelled out modified analytic approaches to address specific transference-countertransference issues (Adler, 1985; Gabbard, 1991; Gunderson, 1984; Masterson, 1976, 1978; Masterson & Klein, 1989; Meissner, 1984, 1991; Rinsley, 1982; Searles, 1986). Kernberg, Selzer, Koenigsberg, Carr, and Appelbaum (1989), for example, have espoused an interpretive approach in which the structure of the treatment permits the constant reestablishment of therapeutic neutrality. The focus of the interpretive efforts is to bring together fragments of the self that become manifest in fluctuating and chaotic transference and countertransference configurations. The treatment begins with the establishment of a therapeutic contract in which both the therapist and the patient review their mutual limits and responsibilities. The therapist, in particular, attends to those behaviors that signal a potential disturbance or destruction of the treatment setting. This preparatory phase of the treatment—structuring the relationship between patient and therapist—is designed to foster a setting that will promote an increasingly exploratory piece of work. The cornerstone of that effort is the therapist's consistent attention to the negative transference. Specifically, the therapist must monitor the patient's acting out and violations of the treatment contract. In doing so, the therapist must directly confront those blatant resistances to the treatment process and seek to integrate those behaviors into the treatment relationship, focusing on the negative aspects of the transference. Throughout, the therapist seeks to restore therapeutic neutrality. Although not emphasized by Kernberg, the inevitable thrust of this work is to develop an increasingly collaborative and trusting relationship.

Masterson (1976, 1978; Masterson & Klein, 1989) also focuses on developing the therapeutic alliance, but he does so primarily through supportive measures. For example, he seeks to demonstrate his consistency, commitment, and trustworthiness. He acknowledges that some borderline patients do not tolerate moving beyond the alliance-building stage. Nonetheless, for those who can manage, he develops a special interpretive focus on interactions between the patient and therapist that reflect core relational dynamics involving the patient's maternal attachment to the therapist. Masterson points out that therapists must consistently address their patients' fears (a) that growth and development will bring abandonment, and (b) that relatedness can be secured only through remaining regressively attached to the therapist. To foster separation and the adaptive steps necessary to achieve that goal, Masterson seeks to develop a relationship with patients characterized by what he calls communicative matching through which he can convey his unabashed enthusiasm and support for the steps that patients take to improve their lives. Thus, whereas Kernberg et al. (1989) adopt a modified expressive approach, seeking to maintain therapeutic neutrality and to reestablish it when it is lost, Masterson abandons neutrality in favor of consistent, overt support for patients' adaptive behavior. Thus, his therapeutic approach can be characterized as supportive-expressive, or a mixed approach.

Gunderson (1984; Gunderson et al., 1989) also espouses an intensive approach but cautions against premature exposure to exploration of the negative transference. Rather, he seeks to foster the patient's sense of relatedness through a variety of supportive means. In fact, he is in agreement with Masterson that the therapist should foster adaptive behavior and provide a corrective emotional experience for the patient. Thus, while Kernberg seeks to establish a treatment setting that permits a focus on the transference through interpretation in the context of therapeutic neutrality, Masterson emphasizes the development of the alliance and the fostering of adaptive behavior through the enthusiastic support of the therapist. Gunderson weaves a course midway between these approaches, seeking on the one hand to employ interpretive strategies when the alliance permits it, but also providing a supportive relationship much in Masterson's style. Gunderson further adds that only an experienced therapist should conduct such work.

Clinical theorists who emphasize environmental failure (neglect, abuse, unempathic parenting) as a key factor in the borderline patient's vulnerability also see the therapeutic relationship as an opportunity for a new experience that will redress the impact of early environmental failure. For example, Adler (1985), much influenced by self psychology, notes that the borderline patient's inability to call up the memory of a soothing and meaningful experience with others leaves the patient sensitive to frustration, loss, and aloneness. This vulnerability, in turn, exposes the borderline to fragmentation that becomes evident, for example, in disorganization and chaotic behavior. To counteract the lack of internal stabilizing experience and memory, Adler vigorously emphasizes the reality of his continuing care and presence for the patient, drawing the contrast between the patient's expectation of frustration and abandonment and the reality of his continuing tolerance and presence. His view of the patient's rage is also compassionate. He sees it as an expression of the patient's disillusionment and disappointment with the frustrations of childhood, relived as they are in the patient's current relationships.

Chessick (1982) and Meissner (1984, 1991) recognize with Adler that impediments to the establishment of a trusting relationship with the therapist are rooted in paranoid and erotic transferences, which must be confronted and interpretively resolved. Such work, however, must be done cautiously and slowly, underscoring the reality of the therapeutic relationship while maintaining the therapeutic alliance.

A most useful perspective on the timing and style of therapist interventions and interpretations is that of Pine (1985). He notes that the therapist should "strike when the iron is cold." He underscores, as do Adler, Gunderson, and Masterson, that he will not abandon the patient and that he will persevere, no matter how provocative the patient may become. He recommends offering interpretations within the context of support. Thus, he, like

Masterson, is less concerned with the maintenance of therapeutic neutrality. Finally, Schafer (1983) recommends what he calls "the affirmative interpretation" in which he emphasizes the adaptive value of the patient's behavior, the patient's search for a relationship, and a compassionate view of the patient's struggle, tolerating maladaptive behavior as an effort to find relatedness.

THERAPEUTIC ALLIANCE RESEARCH

Following the pioneering work of Bordin (1979) and Horwitz (1974), investigators in the Penn, Vanderbilt, and Center for the Study of Neuroses projects, evaluated the role of the therapeutic alliance as a vehicle for treatment change in psychotherapy on a broad scale (Crits-Christoph, Cooper, & Luborsky, 1988; Hartley & Strupp, 1983; Horowitz, Marmar, Weiss, DeWitt, & Rosenbaum, 1984; Luborsky, 1976; Luborsky, Crits-Christoph, Alexander, Margolis, & Cohen, 1983; Luborsky et al., 1980; Marmar, Marziali, Horowitz, & Weiss, 1986; Marziali, 1984b; Marziali, Marmar, & Krupnick, 1981; Mintz, Luborsky, & Crits-Christoph, 1979). The convergent finding from these studies was that the initial level of the alliance was positively associated with treatment outcome. These studies antedated the emergence of manual-guided therapies and were also large-scale group comparison designs; thus, the details of therapeutic strategy were left unspecified. Moreover, these projects were not specifically addressed to the evaluation of contrasting treatment strategies with specific types of borderline patients. Nevertheless, perspectives regarding the most effective therapeutic strategies with particular types of borderline patients were beginning to emerge in research studies employing single-case methodology.

SINGLE-CASE STUDIES

Two studies reporting the results of the application of specific therapeutic strategies to the treatment of borderline patients have recently emerged utilizing single-case methodology. The first, reported by Abend, Porder, and Willick (1983), was the study of the application of a relatively unmodified psychoanalytic approach to borderline psychopathology. Detailed process notes were used to evaluate process and outcome with four high-level borderline patients who were seen in psychoanalysis by psychoanalytic candidates in training. Although these were challenging patients, none required hospitalization, nor did their impulsivity and projective thinking make the analytic regression and exploration an intolerable experience; in fact, there was some therapeutic benefit. Subsequently, Waldinger and Gunderson (1987) reported a study where five borderline patients were seen in an extended psychoanalytically informed psychotherapy with experienced therapists. A key finding of the study was that good outcome appeared to have resulted from the strong commitment by each therapist in the study to carry on the therapeutic work until substantial clinical progress had been made. For the most part, noninterpretive strategies were employed. Following an initial period of alliance building, confrontation and limit setting were employed in the latter phases of treatment. Of special importance was the therapist's encouragement to the patients to express their rage without fear of retaliation. This strategy appears to have contributed to the development of a strong alliance. Interpretive resolution of conflict within the therapeutic process was attempted on a limited basis and in a selective fashion, respecting the tolerance of the patients and building on the alliance.

In a related study, Stone (1987) followed up 500 previously hospitalized patients, many of whom were diagnosed as borderline. He focused, in particular, on a subsample of borderline patients who had achieved successful outcomes. He concluded that approximately a third of his sample benefited from an exposure to exploratory psychotherapy. Given the retrospective nature of the study, a more specific evaluation of therapeutic strategies was impossible. Nonetheless, an exploratory comparison was attempted with inexperienced therapists. Seeking to determine the impact of supportive-expressive techniques, the study yielded no compelling differences between those approaches.

TREATMENT INTERVENTIONS PROJECT

The Treatment Interventions Project (Horwitz et al., 1991) was initiated more than a decade ago to explore a research finding that emerged from the Menninger Foundation Psychotherapy Research Project. That project's quantitative study (Kernberg et al., 1972) reported that borderline patients who were seen in a psychotherapy process characterized by "high focus on the transference" achieved greater therapeutic gains than those borderline patients who were seen in a psychotherapy process characterized by "low focus on the transference." When those findings were reviewed from a predominantly qualitative perspective (Horwitz, 1974), it was noted that some borderline patients, when treated in a primarily supportive process, showed surprisingly stable gains unanticipated by the study's prediction team. A later retrospective review of the Psychotherapy Research Project findings (Wallerstein, 1986) also confirmed that borderline patients made stable therapeutic gains in supportive psychotherapy processes. The issue at stake was whether interpretive approaches, modified or not along the lines recommended by Kernberg, would yield greater therapeutic benefits for borderline patients than supportive measures.

In devising a research strategy to explore these contrasting perspectives, Horwitz et al. (1991) became disenchanted with group comparison techniques that appeared to yield little information regarding the specifics of the change process. Although large-scale studies might prove useful in segregating and identifying major dimensions of the change process, single-case methodology (Rice & Greenberg, 1984) appeared to hold greater promise of allowing a microscopic examination of the moment-to-moment impact of therapeutic interventions. In such a framework, the change process could be examined from both a micro- and macroscopic perspective looking at the relationship between moment-to-moment changes and long-term treatment outcome. It also appeared to hold out a greater promise for the discovery of unanticipated effects likely to be obscured by the inevitable collapsing of data in large-group comparison designs.

To develop an explanatory framework within which the impact of supportive psychotherapy with borderline patients could be understood, Horwitz (1974) proposed that internalization of the therapeutic alliance was the principal agent of change. The mode of action of that internalization, however, was not clear. Thus, efforts were undertaken to evolve suitable research methods and measures. The first step was to specify and operationalize the therapeutic alliance. Given the controversial, nonspecific, and difficult-to-measure character of the therapeutic alliance as discussed in the psychoanalytic literature (Brenner, 1979; Greenson, 1965, 1967; Zetzel, 1956, 1966) and the equally broad definition in the psychotherapy research literature (e.g., Bordin, 1979), we chose to narrow our focus to the patient's collaboration with the therapist around the tasks of the psychotherapy (Frieswyk, Colson, & Allen, 1984; Frieswyk et al., 1986). We sought in doing so to distinguish the patient's collaboration from the activity of the therapist. Unfortunately, the research and theoretical literature had often combined both therapist and patient contributions to the alliance. Thus, it was not possible to discern what therapeutic strategies enhanced the alliance in a research context. In separating out the patient's collaboration as a dependent variable, we hoped to evaluate independently the therapist's contributions to increases or decreases in collaboration.

As part of our scale development, we first constructed a 7-point example-anchored scale of global collaboration (Allen, Gabbard, Newsom, & Coyne, 1990; Allen, Newsom, Gabbard, & Coyne, 1984; Colson et al., 1988) which was later modified to evaluate shifts in collaboration for relatively small segments of verbatim transcripts of a psychotherapy process (50 lines). The purpose of that measure was to evaluate the extent to which the patient (a) raised significant issues, and (b) made use of the therapist's interventions. We also developed a manual to categorize therapist interventions (Colson, Horwitz, Frieswyk, & Coyne, 1989).

To summarize our strategy, we sought to develop a research method that would enable us to assess changes in the therapeutic alliance resulting from specific therapeutic interventions. In doing so, we narrowly constructed the alliance as the patient's collaboration in the therapy process, seeing this as the best observable marker of the more broadly conceived therapeutic alliance with the therapist. Our research aim has been to link shifts in collaboration within sessions to specific interventions by the therapist. This research paradigm requires that the therapy process be divided into clinically meaningful and recurrent episodes or events. Furthermore, the strategy requires that the focus be on changes in the patient rather than in the therapist. The recurrent event that we examine is the shift in the patient's collaboration with the therapist. Our intent is to determine the relationship between the shift, that is, either an increase or decrease in collaboration, with the preceding therapist interventions. Through the study of a series of cases, we hope to begin to address the questions: Which borderline patients are likely to respond well to interpretation, and which to supportive interventions? Furthermore, what mix of specific interpretive interventions/strategies with supportive measures is required at what point in the treatment to foster the alliance?

METHODOLOGY

Our research group included six experienced psychotherapists and psychoanalysts. All members of the research team have had considerable experience in the treatment of borderline patients. The case to be reported here was conducted by one of the research team members on a twice-weekly basis for two years. All sessions were audiotaped. Three consecutive sessions were randomly selected from six evenly divided intervals throughout the psychotherapy process and were typed verbatim, leaving us with 18 typescripts for intensive review. Two subgroups from the research team worked independently—one to rate the changes in the collaboration, the other to classify therapist interventions.

THERAPEUTIC ALLIANCE RATINGS

The therapeutic alliance subgroup comprised three research team members as raters. They evaluated collaboration as measured by the degree to which the patient (a) brought in significant issues and (b) made use of the therapist's efforts. Dividing the sessions into 50-line segments, the raters were asked to assess whether an increase in collaboration had occurred at any point (+) or if there had been a decline in collaboration (−). Raters were asked to rate only one shift for each segment, with no attempt to assess its magnitude. Nonetheless, a distinction was drawn between "possible" shifts and "definite" shifts. This resulted in four categories: (S−) definite negative shift; (PS−) possible negative shift; (PS+) possible positive shift; and (S+) definite positive shift. Since the transcripts were often several hundred lines in length, the potential existed for several shifts in collaboration for each session.

THERAPIST INTERVENTION CODING

Three members of the research team, working independently as the intervention rating subgroup, were instructed to categorize therapist interventions for the same set of sessions rated for changes in the alliance. Our scheme was a modification of Gill's Process Coding Categories (Gill & Hoffman, 1982). In our system, an intervention was assigned two scores, the first indicating whether the intervention was one of seven types: an interpretation (I), confrontation (C), clarification (CL), encouragement to elaborate (E), affirmation (A), empathy (EM), and advice and/or praise (AP). The second category indicated whether the therapist had addressed the relationship (R) or other matters not regarding the relationship with the therapist (X). This second category was applied to I, C, CL, E, and AP but not A or EM. Thus, for example, an interpretation addressed to the relationship was given the composite score IR. Similarly, a confrontation concerning matters not directly concerning the relationship was scored CX. Our system thereby provided a more detailed description of therapeutic activity than Marziali's (1984a), which predicted outcome in brief psychotherapy as a product of therapist interventions. For both the therapeutic alliance rating subgroup and the intervention rating subgroup, shifts and interventions were first scored independently and then a consensus was achieved for those scores prior to the final step, which was to examine the link between the therapist intervention and the shift in collaboration.

LINKING INTERVENTIONS AND COLLABORATION SHIFTS

Once the subgroups completed the work for each session, the results of those ratings were circulated to members of the research team, who were then requested to infer the link or links between the therapist intervention and changes in collaboration. The raters were free to consider the immediately preceding interventions as well as events external to the sessions and changes in the patient that might have contributed to the shift in collaboration. These independent assessments were then shared, and a consensus was developed regarding the link between the collaboration shift and the events preceding it.

THE PATIENT UNDER STUDY

The patient whose psychotherapy process was evaluated and reported here is the third in a series first reported by Gabbard et al. (1988) and Horwitz and Frieswyk (1980). She was a young married woman, the mother of several children. She was seen in consultation prior to beginning the psychotherapy.

The consultant noted that she was acutely depressed, finding herself apathetic and puzzled that despite a good marriage and good job, and reasonable achievements in her education and career, she was miserable. In fact, she had become frightened that she would commit suicide and had entertained the idea of slitting her wrists but did not believe that she would do so.

She was the eldest child in a family with many children, born to a couple who, for most of her childhood, had been engaged in chronic marital discord. Life at home was chaotic. She was recruited as a caretaker at an early age and became a parentified child. She had little privacy and had other difficulties in establishing appropriate boundaries.

Her siblings appeared to be equally if not more troubled. In fact, one of them had been depressed and self-destructive, and had been seen in numerous psychiatric consultations for many years. Even more problematic was another sibling, who had committed suicide sometime prior to the patient's seeking consultation. That suicide had destroyed the family's belief that they were close and warmly connected. As the eldest child, she felt overwhelmed with guilt, feeling herself to be responsible but a failure.

The sister's suicide had only exacerbated a chronic state of depression. At her worst, she became barely able to function and had lost her appetite and interest in life. Antidepressant medication, while initially helpful, could not resolve her fears, the constant family upheaval, the lifelong depressive symptomatology, and her bulimia. Despite the family turmoil, chronic depressive state, and episodic crises in the lives of her siblings, she had nonetheless been able to achieve a remarkable degree of professional development and was already well on her way to significant additional achievements.

Prior to the inception of the psychotherapy, the patient was seen for psychological testing, where the findings were consistent with the diagnosis of borderline personality organization. The psychologist noted in particular that under the pressure of her angry feelings she could become highly projective and illogical. He also noted evidence of an identity disturbance, as well as compliant and masochistic trends. She was seen to be vulnerable to emotional flooding and dyscontrol, as well as self-destructive action. He noted a variety of characterological difficulties, most notably narcissistic and compulsive features, with a tendency to disengage from others while investing excessively in work. She had great difficulty in regulating distance. Although she might feel in distress and express a need for help and nurturing, she might distance herself for fear of attacking whoever sought to help. Thus, she was left feeling deprived, frustrated, and even more in need. Finally, he underscored that, given her vulnerability to these emotional disturbances and her loss of impulse control with impaired reality testing, she might require considerable support to maintain a reflective stance in the psychotherapy. The diagnosis of borderline personality disorder was further substantiated by a Gunderson Diagnostic Interview for Borderlines (Gunderson, Kolb, & Austin, 1981) conducted by a member of the research team. This videotaped interview was independently rated by the members of the research group, with the overall scores averaging 5.4 (a score of 5 representing probable borderline and a score of 7 representing definite borderline).

After obtaining informed consent, the research team member who conducted the psychotherapy began taping the sessions for this twice-weekly process. The sessions selected for study were chosen at random, except for being spaced approximately 25 sessions apart.

Summary of Methodology

To summarize our methodological approach, the following steps were taken:

1. Eighteen audiotaped and transcribed psychotherapy sessions were divided into 50-line segments.
2. The three members of the therapeutic alliance subgroup rated increases or decreases in patient collaboration.
3. The three members of the intervention subgroup, working independently of the therapeutic alliance subgroup, coded therapist interventions for the same sessions.
4. Prior to a consensus meeting for all six researchers, ratings of the collaboration for each session were circulated to each member to develop a narrative account of the raters' clinical inferences regarding the link between therapist interventions and shifts in collaborations for each segment.
5. All six investigators arrived at a consensus regarding the factors contributing to each shift.

RESULTS

To focus our discussion, we will limit the reporting of our results in this communication to the relationship of the therapist's interventions to shifts in collaboration. Of the 18 sessions under study, 26 shifts in collaboration were identified. The number of shifts in each session ranged from none to 2, with an average of 1.4. Twenty-one of those shifts were judged to be related to the therapist's interventions. Although occasional key interventions immediately preceded a shift, more often than not, those pivotal interventions took place in the context of a series of interventions that the judges felt cumulatively facilitated the therapeutic process. The therapist's attunement to the patient's emotional state appeared to be important in providing a context that fostered the therapeutic work. However, on several occasions shifts in the alliance appeared to have occurred spontaneously, that is, without any link to therapist interventions. Table 9.1 summarizes our findings for each of the 26 shifts. The therapist's interventions were linked to 21 shifts. Of the 16 shifts that were in the direction of an increase in collaboration, 12

TABLE 9.1.   Contribution of Therapist's Interventions to Shifts in Collaboration

	Direction of Shift[a]	Therapist Intervention Viewed as Contributory?	Coding of Contributory Interventions[b]	Comments
Session 6				
Shift 1 (L.101)	S+	Yes	ER (L.83), EX (L.100)	
Shift 2 (L.273)	S+	Yes	IR (L.269)	
Session 7				
Shift 1 (L.157)	S+	Yes	CX (L.140), EX (L.142)	
Shift 2 (L.203)	S+	Yes	CR (L.188)	The shift was influenced by a cumulative effect of interventions
Session 8				
Shift 1 (L.115)	PS+	Yes	IR (L.112–114)	Series of other interventions also contributed to the shift
Shift 2 (L.219)	PS−	Yes	IR (L.205–214)	
Session 30				
Shift 1 (L.278)	PS+	Yes	CR (L.273)	The shift was influenced by a cumulative effect of interventions
Session 31—No Shifts				
Session 32				
Shift 1 (L.102)	S+	Yes	EX (L.82)	Series of other interventions also contributed to the shift
Session 55				
Shift 1 (L.77)	PS−	Yes	CR (L.37), CR (L.56)	
Shift 2 (L.148)	S+	Yes	IR (L.128)	The shift was influenced by a cumulative effect of interventions
Session 56				
Shift 1 (L.123)	S+	Yes	IR (L.98–115)	
Shift 2 (L.220)	PS−	Unclear	Unclear	Therapist interventions may have influenced the shift, but more likely it was spontaneous due to patient's anger
Session 57				
Shift 1 (L.141)	PS−	No	—	Spontaneous due to anger over interruptions of therapy
Shift 2 (L.207)	PS+	Yes	IR (L.166–206)	
Session 89				
Shift 1 (L. 136)	PS−	Yes	IR (L.125)	

TABLE 9.1.   *(Continued)*

	Direction of Shift[a]	Therapist Intervention Viewed as Contributory?	Coding of Contributory Interventions[b]	Comments
Session 90				
Shift 1 (L.147)	S+	Yes	APR (L.130), APR (L.138) APR (L.143)	A series of other interventions also influenced the shift
Session 91				
Shift 1 (L.87)	PS−	Yes	IX (L.61), IX (L.83)	
Shift 2 (L.226)	PS+	Yes	EMR (L.209), IR (L.222)	A series of other interventions also influenced the shift
Session 121				
Shift 1 (L.146)	S+	Yes	EX (L.97)	
Session 122				
Shift 1 (L.95)	S−	No	—	The shift was spontaneous with the patient beginning the session wanting to flee therapy
Session 123				
Shift 1 (L.114)	PS+	Unclear	—	The shift appeared to be spontaneous
Shift 2 (L.248)	S+	Yes	IR (L.236)	
Session 142				
Shift 1 (L.90)	PS−	Yes	CR (L.86)	
Shift 143				
Shift 1 (L.89)	PS+	No	—	The patient reflected on her emotional response to the therapist spontaneously
Shift 2 (L.161)	S+	Yes	ER (L.150), ER (L.152)	
Session 144				
Shift 1 (L.212)	S+	Yes	ER (L.208)	

[a] Shift designations: S = Judges' consensus of a definite shift; PS = Judges' consensus of a probable shift; "+" = Positive shift; "−" = Negative shift.

[b] Coding categories:
Coding of contributory interventions were comprised of two subsets of scores, Intervention Categories and Nontransference (X) vs Transference (R) designations. The Intervention Categories are: Interpretation (I); Confrontation (C); Clarification (CL); Encouragement to Elaborate (E); Affirmation (A); Empathy (EM); Advice and Praise (AP). For example, an interpretation directed toward the transference is thus scored IR.

were judged to be definite shifts and 4 were probable shifts. In addition, 13 positive shifts were linked to interventions that focused on the transference. Of the 5 negative shifts in the alliance, 4 were also linked to transference-related interventions. These negative shifts appeared to reflect either a lack of attunement with the patient's emotional state or the fostering of more intense emotion than the patient could tolerate at the moment. In this table, therapist interventions are reported with the combination score (type plus relationship direction). Out of the 21 shifts linked to interventions, only 4 were not transference-related, indicating that the therapist's focus had a notable impact on the relationship.

To illustrate our methodology, we will examine two vignettes taken from transcripts of sessions. The first example occurs early in the process, where the therapist is attempting to evaluate the impact of his efforts to explore the transference in the here and now. At the beginning of this session (Session 8), the patient has responded reasonably well to transference explorations, expressing with increasing intensity her despair, confusion, discomfort, embarrassment, and resentment that she carries on with these distressing emotions while the therapist appears to her to look calm and controlled. She is initially able to address her negative view of the therapist, finding him to be bored. She begins to elaborate some of the experiences with her father that are evoked at this moment in the process and continues:

P: (lines 158–169) 'Cause he didn't, he doesn't know how to love. He didn't know how to behave. He never knew. He never did anything on purpose to hurt us. He just . . . was a poor soul that wasn't loved in his life and (sniff) had a tough life, you know, and . . . everyone makes mistakes. I stopped crying. When I . . . when you started asking me about Dad (sniff) I got to straighten up my thoughts. I guess it turned the subject away from me. I just resent . . . being like I am. I haven't really looked at . . . why I'm that way. Like I say, you know, you have certain things in your past but . . . you can bring out the old environmental versus genetic . . . argument. A little of both.

T: (lines 170–174) Do you feel reluctant to be . . . annoyed with me because I seem to have been busy with other things to do . . . and that if you told me . . . how irritated you might feel that I was attending to something else . . . that it would somehow seem inappropriate to you, it would burden me . . . in some way?

P: (lines 174–176) No. No, I don't think about, I think about like when you move around in your chair . . . it seemed to, you know, I wonder if you're los-, if I'm just talking, you're not listening maybe (small laugh).

T: (lines 177–178) Why would I not? Or what have I missed that you've been saying?

P: (line 179) Because this has got to be boring.

T: (line 180) Why does it have to be?

P: (lines 181–204) To *you*. And we talked about that last time. You know, I said . . . I say it's boring to me but I think what I mean is . . . I don't like seeing myself like this. I . . . I've been (sniff) trying to see your position, you know, 'cause I think, I think about this (sniff) . . . me being boring to you. And I think, well, uh (sniff) that's his (sniff) job so . . . I kind of thought of it like (sniff) me taking care of people and (sniff) how much *I* care when I'm doing that and how import-, seriously I take that. (sniff) Maybe I am trying to work on . . . (sniff) the fact that, um . . . you really care about what I'm saying. But as I said before, that's going to be very difficult. (Patient crying) Well, I just think it's impossible. That's when I feel like giving up. Just . . . (sniff) . . . it's like I've realized how miserable I really am. I've realized . . . I've, you know . . . broken down some defense . . . defenses and looked at myself a little bit more closely . . . and I just see more confusion and . . . mix up, lack of order. And then when I get a glimpse of . . . I get, you know, how much . . . change there needs to be or how much . . . work there needs to be done, I feel like it just can't happen. And I thought of it particularly when I thought, you know, I can't even (sniff) trust *you* enough . . . to think that you're not bored listening to me.

T: (lines 205–214) Well, I think that may be a clue. That you . . . just punished yourself for having, uh, an angry thought about me. (T elaborates.)

P: (lines 215–216) It's easy not to, it's easy to say bad things about myself though. It doesn't . . . take much.

T: (line 217) You pay the price though . . . protecting me.

P: (lines 218–226) I sure do. (small laugh) It's . . . something, I, uh, that's when I start . . . it's just not worth living sometimes with . . . (sniff) . . . the feelings . . . (trails off—several lengthy pauses) I was thinking . . . like when I leave here I was thinking I want to look at my watch but I think I'll let him watch the time today. And then I thought about when I leave and . . . you know, I always have red eyes and carry my kleenex and . . . you're perfectly fine.

The possible downward shift in collaboration (PS− at line 219) occurs as the patient backs away from dealing with the transference and becomes deeply immersed in her depressive experience and resentment. The therapist appears to have pushed his luck by trying too much to confront and explore her experiences in the here and now, exposing too directly her transference-anger and criticism, making it difficult for the patient to assimilate his comments and her experience. He becomes especially forceful in the lengthy and premature interpretation at line 205, and thereby contributes to the difficulty the patient has in owning her feelings. She gives only superficial agreement. She ends masochistically, experiencing the therapist as someone who is distant, uncaring, all-knowing, and in control, feeling also that he can coldly cause her trouble and pain. The therapist appears to be interested in reconstructing the patient's disguised resentment as an expression of her long-standing feelings about her busy father. She prefers to protect herself, her therapist, and her father, paying the price through her masochistic resolution. The emergence of this configuration (forceful therapist versus masochistically submissive, resentful patient) appears to be an example of the inevitable transference-countertransference binds that occur in every therapy (Tansey & Burke, 1989) and whose resolution can lead to therapeutic change for both (Mitchell, 1988).

In the sessions that follow, the therapist appears to have shifted strategy (see Table 9.2). In Table 9.2, to simplify reporting of the data, composite scores are not used, as in Table 9.1. Here the *type* of intervention is enumerated separately from its *direction,* that is, whether focused on the relationship with the therapist or not. Note that Sessions 30, 31, and 32 are devoid of transference interpretations. There is also an overall reduction in references to the relationship and a preponderance of references to outside relationships. It may well be that the therapist changed course in response to the patient's reactions to his interpretive activity.

We next pick up the process with Session 121, which begins with the patient's protest that it was not fair "that I should go through this and feel so

TABLE 9.2.   Intervention Consensus Ratings Profiles

Session	I	C	CL	E	A	EM	AP	Nontransference (X) vs. Transference (R) X	R
6	3	2	2	11	12	1	6	7	18
7	2	4	2	16	1	0	2	14	12
8	8	3	1	15	2	0	1	14	14
30	0	8	0	14	8	0	0	6	16
31	0	6	0	11	2	0	0	10	7
32	0	4	0	14	4	0	0	13	5
55	4	8	1	4	1	0	0	1	16
56	2	3	1	21	8	0	0	5	22
57	6	6	0	14	9	1	1	3	25
89	6	4	0	6	0	0	0	5	11
90	3	5	0	2	1	0	10	10	10
91	8	5	1	23	8	1	7	26	19
121	1	2	2	21	15	0	0	12	14
122	5	6	0	8	5	0	0	9	10
123	1	3	4	12	2	0	0	14	6
142	5	6	0	7	5	0	0	8	10
143	0	7	0	14	4	0	0	13	8
144	5	10	1	12	8	0	1	15	14

[a] Intervention categories:
   I = Interpretation; C = Confrontation; CL = Clarification; E = Encouragement to Elaborate; A = Affirmation; EM = Empathy; AP = Advice and Praise.

uncomfortable." At first jokingly, and then with bitterness and tears, she said that she wished that her husband could make her bad feelings go away, and thought that he was really useless and that she was feeling lonely and bitter, not feeling close to anyone, while noting an increased investment in her work. The therapist then asked her what made her feel that her husband was useless:

P: (lines 89–96) Hmm, useless. Like all I really wanted him for was to make me feel better. I guess it goes back to what we used to talk about . . . regarding my demanding a lot from people and not having much to give them. And I just noticed that I just felt . . . cold and hard. I really don't know what else to say about it. I just feel real confused about it.

T: (line 97) What was the dream?

P: (lines 98–101) Just me at work, working really hard and giving a lot of myself and . . . then being rejected, I guess, by a group of people, the people I was giving to. And feeling very, very bad about that . . . like the world had come to an end.

T: (line 102) What was the basis for their rejecting you?

P: (lines 103–111) Not really wanting my services, I think. It was like a misinterpretation . . . me thinking it was something they wanted and them saying, "We don't need you to do that." Just a total misunderstanding on my part of what they wanted. What comes to mind in reality is the experience I had with the one person that . . . um, I made a comment about some way she could help with the work . . . and, uh, her saying, "I don't need you to tell me what to do." It was like I was trying to help the situation . . . and her saying, "I don't need you to do that." I was very hurt 'cause I didn't . . . mean it that way.

T: (line 112) What occurs to you, what comes to mind?

P: (lines 113–142) [Here the patient elaborates her feeling unpopular, in the minority, sensitive to others questioning her motives, and insecure.]

P: (lines 143–147) I was just wondering if I wasn't feeling some of that stress in the dream. That's the most direct thing that comes to mind. The other thing that came to mind was that I was feeling like, um . . . I wanted, I was working really hard in psychotherapy and I wanted, uh, more recognition maybe . . . from you.

T: (line 148) When did this thought occur to you?

P: (lines 149–155) I'm trying to think if it came . . . before or after the other thought about work. The direct idea was, you know, work related. The more indirect idea and it was shortly after I woke up and then thought about the dream. I think it might have been the first thought I had about it. Why, you know, tha-that feeling of, uh . . . thinking I'm working pretty hard in therapy and . . . maybe wanting more, a pat on the back maybe or . . .

T: (line 156) Hmm?

P: (lines 157–161) But, you know, the feeling I got was that of . . . of total rejection in the dream. It hurt so bad. Maybe kind of like, uh, I had talked about what it feels like walking out of here every day after I get to the certain point at about 15 or 10 till, when it's that far from time to go and, you know, I've started talking and, uh . . .

The judges noted an increase in the alliance at line 146 (S+) since the patient was being reflective and demonstrated insight about the transference and the meaning of her dream. After examining this segment of the therapy, the research group reached a consensus that the therapist stayed with the patient, tracking her reactions to the dream. The therapist was empathic, failed to be provoked, and did not pick up other hints of the transference. Instead, at line 97 the therapist brought the patient back to the dream. This intervention was well timed and helped to focus and organize the patient, who had been skipping around as well as expressing a great deal of resistance. Then, in a series of interventions, the therapist encouraged and promoted the patient's reflectiveness. She subsequently arrived at her insight spontaneously. It appeared that the safe climate of the therapy, the intensity of the patient's transference struggles, and the series of interventions contributed to the shift. The therapist's timing of his interventions, as well as his not pursuing transference issues directly, may have left the patient feeling more in control and safe to become conscious of and discuss her transference feelings.

DISCUSSION

Case Example

As previously noted, the literature on the treatment of borderline patients in an expressive exploratory mode has increasingly emphasized the role of supportive measures to structure and contain the emotional turbulence activated by the mobilization of more primitive transference experiences. Interestingly, in the middle phase of the treatment reported here, there was an upward shift in the ratings of supportive activity of the therapist in response to a deteriorating alliance (see, e.g., in Table 9.1, the use of advice and praise (APR) in Session 90). In addition to the within-session increase in therapist-supportive interventions, he also referred the patient for pharmacotherapy (antidepressants) and marital therapy, and at one point offered brief inpatient psychiatric hospitalization. This reflected a shift in therapeutic strategy occasioned by the therapist's efforts to respond to regressive shifts in the transference and the activation of turbulent, difficult-to-contain emotional states. Despite the increase in supportive measures, the therapist's exploratory, transference-focused efforts did not decline. In fact, the therapist engaged in a markedly increased effort to explore the patient's experience of the therapeutic relationship, as noted, for example, by the preponderance of relationship-focused interventions (R) and encouragements to elaborate (E), concurrent with an increased frequency of transference interpretations (I) (see Table 9.2, Session 91 on). Thus, a mixed supportive-expressive strategy was employed by the therapist to address emotional crisis. The broader shifts in strategy discussed here across sessions parallel the within-session shifts.

This mixed strategy appears to have paid off. Following the turbulence in the middle phase of the therapy, the therapist was able once again to employ an interpretive focus on the transference, as can be seen in Session 123 (see Table 9.1) where an interpretation of the transference led to a definite increase in collaboration. By referring to Table 9.1, it is possible to see that in the concluding sessions the patient appears to have been able to increasingly take on the work of the therapy, spontaneously addressing her experience of the therapeutic relationship in Session 143. She further elaborates that experience with a notable increase in collaboration, following the therapist's simple encouragement for her to elaborate (ER). A similar shift occurs as well in the last session where a definite increase in collaboration occurs following another encouragement by the therapist for the patient to elaborate her experience of the therapeutic relationship (ER). The solid alliance that has been established with the patient permits her to participate in the therapeutic process, working in tandem with the therapist.

Application of Methodology

We believe our methodology provides a useful bridge between clinical theory, psychotherapy research, and clinical practice:

1. It allows facets of clinical theory to be evaluated in their application to a psychotherapeutic process and to observe the moment-to-moment impact of that strategy as it is concretely applied through the therapist's interventions.
2. It is also a move in the direction of a manualized therapy insofar as profiles of therapist activity can be generated to determine a therapist's compliance with the guidelines of a manual. These profiles of therapist interventions permit a detailed examination of the application of the strategies specified by a research-based psychotherapy manual.
3. Furthermore, this methodology allows the psychotherapy researcher to integrate such a strategy within a group comparison design. There it becomes possible to systematically move from the macroscopic perspective of group comparisons to the microscopic view to determine the manner in which the broadly identified factors accounting for

treatment change impact on the therapeutic process. Spontaneous variations, of course, occur naturally in every therapeutic encounter, providing the opportunity for the discovery of new interrelationships between patient characteristics and therapist activity. Such spontaneous variations are not lost in such an approach and do not get treated as error variance, as might be the case in a group comparison design.

Relevance for Psychotherapy Training

The decline of psychoanalytically informed psychotherapy in the training of psychiatrists has recently been decried (Lewis, 1991; Wallerstein, 1992). In part, the decline can be attributed to the reemerging link between neurology and psychiatry and the proliferation of somatic and biological therapies. Another factor in the decline of teaching psychoanalytic psychotherapy, however, may be the absence of the application of psychotherapy research findings to (a) demonstrate efficacy or (b) provide training models. The methodology illustrated in this study has been applied to the teaching of psychotherapy at the Karl Menninger School of Psychiatry in the Menninger Clinic and has shown promise in specifying therapeutic interventions and evaluating their moment-to-moment impact. It has been possible to observe videotaped research-based psychotherapy sessions and make direct application of such strategies in role playing supervised by therapists grounded in this approach. The link between clinical theory, psychotherapy research, and clinical practice can be observed and integrated by the psychiatric resident, significantly impacting his or her emergent skills and identification as a psychotherapist. The monitoring and evaluation of psychotherapists in training perhaps could be modeled along these lines. The focus would be on the assessment of the skillful application of specific interventions while evaluating their appropriate utilization for specific therapeutic challenges. Research comparison with other emergent therapies for the treatment of patients falling within the borderline spectrum—for example, brief therapy (Horowitz et al., 1984) and cognitive—behavioral therapy (Beck et al., 1990)—would be facilitated with such a methodology. It would allow direct assessment of the relative effectiveness of particular classes of interventions on targeted patient characteristics, phases of treatment, and treatment outcome. Certainly, the prevalence rates for borderline personality disorder and the enormous personal and social costs of that psychopathology warrant intensive research to discover the most suitable and effective approaches.

Research Implications

An unexpected finding that emerged in our assessment of the patient's collaboration over the course of the psychotherapy was that it remained constant from beginning to end. We have come to consider this surprising result in a number of ways. Perhaps collaboration as we initially defined it (the degree to which the patient brings in significant issues and makes use of the therapist's efforts) may not be sufficiently specific to capture the multiple forms that emerge during a psychotherapy. Collaboration may, in fact, encompass a broad array of qualitatively different activities, and thus lack a unitary mode. Specifically, for this patient in the initial stages of the psychotherapy, her collaboration consisted primarily of her bringing in emotionally significant material. Later in the process, she identified with the activity of the therapist and joined him in observing her emotional responses and fantasies, often spontaneously linking these to developmentally significant interactions. There was, in effect, a qualitative shift in her collaboration that the quantitative ratings did not capture. For future research, it may be crucial to track the emergence and sequence of these specific collaborative activities.

We also wondered whether collaboration should be viewed as an agent of change rather than the result of other shifts that occurred during the psychotherapy process. Could it be that collaboration is the final common pathway for other change processes that we did not measure? As we began our research efforts, we had, with many others, conceptualized the therapeutic alliance rather broadly. It included collaboration, but it also encompassed a variety of facilitating factors in the patient—trust, acceptance, optimism, as well as tolerance for the emotions stirred by the therapeutic relationship. From the difficult-to-specify and broadly conceived character of the therapeutic alliance, we selected collaboration as a marker variable that could be more easily operationalized and measured. Nevertheless, in our qualitative review of the psychotherapy reported here, we became aware that the patient shifted significantly in her perception of the therapist over the course of the process. The shifts permitted her to be more trusting and open in her therapeutic engagement. We were left with a question of how to conceptualize those shifts and how to understand their relationship to the qualitative changes in her collaborative activity.

Furthermore, it remained unclear how to account for the effectiveness of the therapeutic interventions. Informal reporting of the therapist's responses to the patient revealed substantial and at times intense countertransference responses, yet assessments of the psychotherapist's level of competence remained high throughout the process, with only occasional dips that were ascribed to countertransference intrusions. Clinical theory (Gabbard, 1993; Mitchell, 1988; Searles, 1986; Tansey & Burke, 1989) would suggest that the therapist's capacity to process the patient's provocative behavior is essential to therapeutic success. From this perspective, the therapeutic moment in which change occurs is an internal process for the therapist. Specifically, the therapist must resist the intense pressure applied by the patient to repeat earlier trauma through frustrating, rejecting, or retaliating. By focusing on the acceptance of the patient's affect, fantasy, and behavior for the purpose of understanding, the therapist sets in motion a benign cycle that leads the patient to anticipate understanding. Thus, the patient has the opportunity to experience a containing/soothing response rather than retaliation. This perspective is in keeping with Bordin (1979), who pointed out that repairing breaches in the alliance leads to treatment change. It is also consistent with Horwitz's (1974) observation that the patient internalizes a new experience with the therapist that permits the development of trust and makes further collaboration possible. These "microepisodes," consisting of a breakdown or rupture of the alliance or the transference/countertransference relationship, are thus the beginnings of the change process. The repair of these ruptures, whether done through interpretation or some other combination of interventions, contributes to the curative process. The cumulative impact of favorable microepisodes ultimately results in a positive outcome. Does this then mean that the therapeutic alliance is only an enabling variable and not an outcome variable? It may be that the strengthening or enhancement of the therapeutic alliance in itself is capable of producing an effective outcome with borderline patients. We would propose that the change in the alliance eventually produces a favorable outcome because the repair process gradually builds up a new view of self in relationship to other. This new view becomes internalized and eventually leads to structural change.

At this juncture, we must explore the range of collaborative activities in which the patient engages, and track the emergence, development, and changes in those collaborative activities over the course of a therapeutic process. In doing so, we must clarify the relationship of collaboration to the broader construct, the therapeutic alliance. We must also evaluate the contributions of what we have previously termed mediating factors in the patient (trust, acceptance, optimism, and tolerance) to shifts in collaboration. Our theoretical perspective requires us to explore the processing of countertransference responses and their relationship to the patient's new internalizations, and to track the shifts in the patient's perception of the therapist while exploring the impact of these new perceptions on the patient's collaboration in the therapeutic process. Ultimately, we seek to evaluate the relationship of these mini-outcomes to overall treatment outcome. We hope that these conceptual developments and strategic shifts in research activity will enhance our understanding of the relationship between therapist interventions, shifts in the alliance, and treatment outcome with the borderline patient.

REFERENCES

Abend, S. M., Porder, M. S., & Willick, M. S. (1983). *Borderline patients: Psychoanalytic perspectives* (Monograph No. 7, The Kris Study Group of the New York Psychoanalytic Institute). New York: International Universities Press.

Adler, G. (1985). *Borderline psychopathology and its treatment.* New York: Aronson.

Adler, G., & Buie, D. (1979). Aloneness and borderline psychopathology: The possible relevance of child development issues. *International Journal of Psychoanalysis, 60,* 83–96.

Allen, J. G., Gabbard, G. O., Newsom, G. E., & Coyne, L. (1990). Detecting patterns of change in patients' collaboration within individual psychotherapy sessions. *Psychotherapy, 27*(4), 522–530.

Allen, J., Newsom, G., Gabbard, G., & Coyne, L. (1984). Scales to assess the therapeutic alliance from a psychoanalytic perspective. *Bulletin of the Menninger Clinic, 48,* 383–400.

Beck, A. T., Freeman, A., Pretzer, J., Davis, D. D., Fleming, B., Ottaviani, R., Beck, J., Simon, K. M., Padesky, C., Meyer, J., & Trexler, L. (1990). *Cognitive therapy of personality disorders.* New York: Guilford Press.

Bordin, E. S. (1979). The generalizability of the psychoanalytic concept of the working alliance. *Psychotherapy: Theory, Research, and Practice, 16,* 252–260.

Brenner, C. (1979). Working alliance, therapeutic alliance, and transference. *Journal of the American Psychoanalytic Association, 27,* 137–158.

Chessick, R. D. (1982). Intensive psychotherapy of a borderline patient. *Archives of General Psychiatry, 39,* 413–419.

Colson, D. B., Horwitz, L., Allen, J. G., Frieswyk, S. H., Gabbard, G. O., Newsom, G. E., & Coyne, L. (1988). Patient collaboration as criterion for the therapeutic alliance. *Psychoanalytic Psychology, 5,* 259–268.

Colson, D. B., Horwitz, L., Frieswyk, S. H., & Coyne, L. (1989). *A system for categorizing therapist interventions: Interrater reliability.* Manuscript submitted for publication.

Crits-Christoph, P., Cooper, A., & Luborsky, L. (1988). The accuracy of therapists' interpretations and the outcome of dynamic psychotherapy. *Journal of Consulting and Clinical Psychology, 56,* 490–495.

Frieswyk, S. H., Colson, D. B., & Allen, J. G. (1984). Conceptualizing the alliance from a psychoanalytic perspective. *Psychotherapy, 27,* 460–464.

Frieswyk, S. H., Colson, D., Coyne, L., Gabbard, G., Horwitz, L., & Newsom, G. (1986). The therapeutic alliance: Its place as a process and outcome variable in psychotherapy research. *Journal of Consulting and Clinical Psychology, 54,* 32–38.

Gabbard, G. O. (1991). Technical approaches to transference hate in the analysis of borderline patients. *International Journal of Psychoanalysis, 72*(4), 625–637.

Gabbard, G. O. (1993). An overview of countertransferences with borderline patients. *Journal of Psychotherapy, Practice and Research, 2,* 7–18.

Gabbard, G. O., Horwitz, L., Frieswyk, S., Allen, J. G., Colson, D. B., Newsom, G., & Coyne, L. (1988). The effect of therapist interventions on the therapeutic alliance with borderline patients. *Journal of the American Psychoanalytic Association, 36,* 697–727.

Gill, M., & Hoffman, I. (1982). A method for studying the analysis of aspects of the patient's experience of the relationship in psychoanalysis and psychotherapy. *Journal of the American Psychoanalytic Association, 30,* 137–167.

Greenson, R. R. (1965). The working alliance and the transference neurosis. In *Explorations in psychoanalysis* (pp. 199–264). New York: International Universities Press.

Greenson, R. R. (1967). *The technique and practice of psychoanalysis.* New York: International Universities Press.

Grotstein, J. S., Solomon, M., & Lang, J. (Eds). (1987). *The borderline patient: Emerging concepts in diagnosis, psychodynamics, and treatment.* Hillsdale, NJ: Analytic Press.

Gunderson, J. G. (1984). *Borderline personality disorder.* Washington, DC: American Psychiatric Press.

Gunderson, J. G., Frank, A. F., Ronningstam, E. F., Wachter, S., Lynch, V. J., & Wolf, P. J. (1989). Early discontinuance of borderline patients from psychotherapy. *Journal of Nervous Mental Disorders, 177,* 38–42.

Gunderson, J. G., Kolb, J. E., & Austin, V. (1981). The diagnostic interview for borderline patients. *American Journal of Psychiatry, 138,* 896–903.

Hartley, D. E., & Strupp, H. H. (1983). The therapeutic alliance: Its relationship to outcome in brief psychotherapy. In M. Masling (Ed.), *Empirical studies of psychoanalytic theories* (pp. 1–27). Hillsdale, NJ: Analytic Press.

Horowitz, M. J., Marmar, C., Krupnick, J., Wilner, N., Kaltreider, N., & Wallerstein, R. (1984). *Personality styles and brief psychotherapy.* New York: Basic Books.

Horowitz, M. J., Marmar, C., Weiss, D., DeWitt, K. N., & Rosenbaum, R. (1984). Brief psychotherapy of bereavement reactions: The relationship of process to outcome. *Archives of General Psychiatry, 41,* 438–448.

Horwitz, L. (1974). *Clinical prediction in psychotherapy.* New York: Aronson.

Horwitz, L., Allen, J. G., Colson, D. B., Frieswyk, S. H., Gabbard, G. O., Coyne, L., & Newsom, G. E. (1991). Psychotherapy of borderline patients at the Menninger Foundation: Expressive compared with supportive interventions and the therapeutic alliance. In L. E. Beutler & M. Crago (Eds.), *Psychotherapy research: An international review of programmatic studies* (pp. 48–55). Washington, DC: American Psychological Association.

Horwitz, L., & Frieswyk, S. H. (1980, December). *The impact of interpretation on therapeutic alliance in borderline patients.* Paper presented at the meeting of the American Psychoanalytic Association, New York, NY.

Kernberg, O., Burstein, E. D., Coyne, L., Appelbaum, A., Horwitz, L., & Voth, H. (1972). Psychotherapy and psychoanalysis: Final report of the Menninger Foundation's psychotherapy research project. *Bulletin of the Menninger Clinic, 36,* 3–275.

Kernberg, O. F., Selzer, M. A., Koenigsberg, H. W., Carr, A. C., & Appelbaum, A. H. (1989). *Psychodynamic psychotherapy of borderline patients.* New York: Basic Books.

Knight, R. (1953). Borderline states. *Bulletin of the Menninger Clinic, 17,* 1–12.

Lewis, J. M. (1991). Thirty years of teaching psychotherapy skills. *International Journal of Group Psychotherapy, 41* (4), 419–432.

Luborsky, L. (1976). Helping alliances in psychotherapy. In J. L. Claghorn (Ed.), *Successful psychotherapy* (pp. 92–116). New York: Brunner/Mazel.

Luborsky, L., Crits-Christoph, P., Alexander, L., Margolis, M., & Cohen, M. (1983). Two helping alliance methods for predicting outcomes of psychotherapy: A counting signs vs. a global rating method. *Journal of Nervous and Mental Disease, 171,* 480–491.

Luborsky, L., Mintz, J., Auerbach, A., Crits-Christoph, P., Bachrach, H., Todd, T., Johnson, M., Cohen, M., & O'Brien, C. P. (1980). Predicting the outcome of psychotherapy: Findings of the Penn Psychotherapy Project. *Archives of General Psychiatry, 37,* 471–481.

Marmar, C. R., Marziali, E., Horowitz, M. J., & Weiss, D. S. (1986). Development of the Therapeutic Alliance Rating System. In L. Greenberg & W. Pinsof (Eds.), *The psychotherapeutic process: A research handbook.* New York: Guilford Press.

Marziali, E. (1984a). Prediction of outcome of brief psychotherapy from therapist interpretive interventions. *Archives of General Psychiatry, 41,* 301–304.

Marziali, E. (1984b). Three viewpoints on the therapeutic alliance: Similarities, differences, and associations with psychotherapy outcome. *Journal of Nervous and Mental Disease, 172,* 417–423.

Marziali, E., Marmar, C., & Krupnick, J. (1981). Therapeutic Alliance Scales: Development and relationship to therapeutic outcome. *American Journal of Psychiatry, 138,* 361–364.

Masterson, J. F. (1976). *Psychotherapy of the borderline adult: A developmental approach.* New York: Brunner/Mazel.

Masterson, J. F. (1978). The borderline adult: Therapeutic alliance and transference. *American Journal of Psychiatry, 135,* 437–442.

Masterson, J. F., & Klein, R. (Eds.). (1989). *Psychotherapy of the disorders of the self: The Masterson approach.* New York: Brunner/Mazel.

Meissner, W. W. (1984). *The borderline spectrum: Differential diagnosis and developmental issues.* Northvale, NJ: Aronson.

Meissner, W. W. (1991). *What is effective in psychoanalytic therapy: The move from interpretation to relation.* Northvale, NJ: Aronson.

Mintz, J., Luborsky, L., & Crits-Christoph, P. (1979). Measuring the outcome of psychotherapy: Findings of the Penn Psychotherapy Project. *Journal of Consulting and Clinical Psychology, 47,* 319–334.

Mitchell, S. A. (1988). *Relational concepts in psychoanalysis.* Cambridge, MA: Harvard University Press.

Pine, F. (1985). *Developmental theory and clinical process.* New Haven, CT: Yale University Press.

Pine, F. (1990). *Drive, ego, object and self.* New York: Basic Books.

Rice, L. M., & Greenberg, L. S. (Eds.). (1984). *Patterns of change: Intensive analysis of psychotherapy process.* New York: Guilford Press.

Rinsley, D. B. (1982). *Borderline and other self disorders.* New York: Aronson.

Schafer, R. (1983). *The analytic attitude.* New York: Basic Books.

Searles, H. F. (1986). *My work with borderline patients.* Northvale, NJ: Aronson.

Stone, M. H. (1987). Psychotherapy of borderline patients in light of long-term follow-up. *Bulletin of the Menninger Clinic, 51,* 231–247.

Tansey, M. J., & Burke, W. F. (1989). *Understanding countertransference: From projective identification to empathy.* Hillsdale, NJ: Analytic Press.

Waldinger, R. J., & Gunderson, J. G. (1987). *Effective psychotherapy with borderline patients: Case studies.* New York: Macmillan.

Wallerstein, R. S. (1986). *Forty-two lives in treatment: A study of psychoanalysis and psychotherapy.* New York: Guilford Press.

Wallerstein, R. S. (1992). The future of psychotherapy. *Bulletin of the Menninger Clinic, 55,* 421–443.

Zetzel, E. R. (1956). Current concepts of transference. *International Journal of Psychoanalysis, 37,* 369–378.

Zetzel, E. R. (1966). The analytic situation. In R. E. Litman (Ed.), *Psychoanalysis in the Americas* (pp. 86–106). New York: International Universities Press.

Zetzel, E. R. (1971). A developmental approach to the borderline patient. *American Journal of Psychiatry, 127,* 867–871.

CHAPTER 10

*Resolving Therapeutic Alliance Ruptures: A Task Analytic Investigation**

JEREMY D. SAFRAN, J. CHRISTOPHER MURAN, and LISA WALLNER SAMSTAG

The concept of the therapeutic alliance originated in early psychoanalytic literature (e.g., Sterba, 1934; Zetzel, 1956). In the past 10 years, however, it has become a topic of growing theoretical and empirical interest among psychotherapy theorists and researchers in general (e.g., Gaston, 1990). One important impetus for this development has been Bordin's (1979) transtheoretical conceptualization of the therapeutic alliance. Bordin suggested that the development of an adequate therapeutic alliance is essential in all forms of psychotherapy, but that the particular nature of the therapeutic alliance essential for effective therapy varies from approach to approach. Accordingly, the strength of the alliance is a function of the degree of agreement between patient and therapist about the tasks and goals of psychotherapy and the quality of the relationship bond between them. These three components (i.e., bond, task, and goal) are interdependent. Thus, the quality of the bond mediates the extent to which the patient and therapist are able to negotiate an agreement about the tasks and goals of therapy, and the ability to negotiate an agreement about the tasks and goals in therapy in turn mediates the quality of the bond.

There has now been a considerable amount of research evidence indicating that the quality of the therapeutic alliance as measured from different perspectives (therapist, patient, and third-party observers) and in a number of different ways is a good predictor of therapy outcome in different forms of psychotherapy (e.g., Greenberg & Pinsof, 1986; Hartley, 1985; Horvath & Symonds, 1991; Luborsky & Auerbach, 1985). The research presented here is predicated on the assumption that it is important to move beyond predictive validity studies toward clarifying the factors that mediate the establishment of good therapeutic alliances as well as those factors involved in repairing strains or ruptures in the therapeutic alliance (Foreman & Marmar, 1985; Safran, Crocker, McMain, & Murray, 1990).

* We gratefully acknowledge the contributions of Naomi Stein, Rhonda Love, Mirek Lojkasek, and Ed Cook to the research presented in this chapter.

There are both practical and conceptual reasons for moving in this direction. From a practical perspective, the evidence regarding the importance of establishing and maintaining an adequate therapeutic alliance suggests that improving problematic alliances should be an important therapeutic focus. At a more conceptual level, the growing evidence of the importance of the therapeutic alliance combined with the consistent failure to find differences in the efficacy of different forms of therapy has led a number of theorists to conclude that the traditional distinction between therapy specific and non-specific factors is conceptually problematic (e.g., Butler & Strupp, 1986; Henry, Schacht, & Strupp, 1986, 1990; Strupp, 1989). As Bordin's (1979) conceptualization of the alliance makes clear, therapy specific and non-specific factors are completely interdependent. What we think of as the alliance consists of both the quality of the bond between therapist and patient, and the degree of agreement between therapist and patient about tasks and goals of therapy. The quality of the bond mediates agreement about tasks and goals, and vice versa. It thus becomes particularly interesting to ask what it means when there is a disagreement between therapist and patient about the tasks or goals of therapy, such that the patient construes them as unhelpful or destructive. In other words, what is the meaning of a particular therapeutic task or intervention for a patient? Or what is the meaning of a particular therapeutic goal?

For example, a therapist asks a patient to engage in a behavioral assignment between sessions; the patient construes this therapeutic task as condescending or manipulative, and a rupture in the therapeutic alliance ensues. Or, a therapist asks a patient what he or she is experiencing at a particular point in time; the patient construes this intervention as invasive and a strain in the alliance takes place. Or again, a patient comes to therapy and requests that the therapist help him eliminate his phobic symptoms. The therapist responds by suggesting that the elimination of the symptoms is of secondary importance and that a more valuable goal of therapy would be to help the patient develop greater self-awareness. The patient construes the therapist's response as invalidating, and as a result, they cannot establish an adequate therapeutic alliance. In all the preceding cases, the disagreement about the tasks or goals of therapy that impairs the therapeutic alliance also provides potentially valuable information about the patient's construal processes, which can in turn lead to a better understanding of some of the patient's fundamental beliefs about self and others.

The resolution of such alliance ruptures can also provide an important corrective emotional experience for the patient—an experiential disconfirmation of core maladaptive beliefs. For example, when a patient experiences a therapist's interpretation as condescending and a rupture in the therapeutic alliance ensues, she withdraws from the therapist instead of expressing her anger. Exploration of her experience at this point reveals her feeling that she is being condescended to, as well as her fear that expressing anger is dangerous. Further exploration reveals that this is a common pattern for her. By exploring and empathizing with the patient's experience and tolerating her resentment, the therapist can provide a new, constructive interpersonal experience for her. Subsequently, the therapist can help the patient to challenge her belief that expressing anger is dangerous and that the most adaptive response is withdrawal. This emphasis on the importance of focusing on alliance ruptures is very much consistent with Kohut's (1984) assertion that working through empathic failures is an important vehicle of change. Moreover, the Mount Zion Group's (Weiss et al., 1987) research provides empirical support regarding the central role that disconfirming the patient's pathogenic beliefs through the therapeutic relationship can play in the change process.

In this chapter, we will present the results of the first phase of a task analysis of the process involved in resolving ruptures in the therapeutic alliance. We will build on the preliminary model of rupture resolution initially articulated by Safran et al. (1990). Ultimately, an empirically refined model will be presented, along with some preliminary verification data supporting its validity. It is our hope that this chapter will serve as a manual of sorts in task analytic methodology.

A TASK ANALYSIS

The approach we have been employing to clarify the processes involved in resolving therapeutic alliance ruptures is adapted from Rice and Greenberg's (1984) task analytic model. Task analysis consists of a combination of discovery and verification-oriented strategies. The overarching principle is one of ongoing oscillation between theory building and empirical analysis. It employs a combination of intensive and extensive analytic procedures to develop a model of the change process for a particular psychotherapy event. The task is to identify recurring patterns of change that take place across cases. The model of the resolution process is initially developed and refined through the intensive observation of single cases. At different stages of development the model is tested using group data. Our task analytic methodology is represented in Figure 10.1, which identifies the steps taken to refine and verify our model of rupture resolution.

Development of a Preliminary Model

The first step in a task analysis involves the articulation of a preliminary model that can subsequently be used to guide the observation of the resolution process in a number of single cases. This model, which is derived from available psychotherapy theory as well as any intuitions the investigators have about the resolution process, is employed as a preliminary map that is

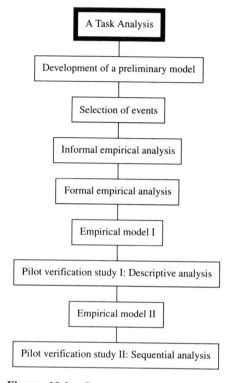

Figure 10.1.   Rupture research paradigm.

successively refined in response to careful observations of the resolution process in specific individual cases (Greenberg, 1984; Safran, Greenberg, & Rice, 1988).

The preliminary model we began with was derived from psychodynamic and contemporary interpersonal theory, and can be described as follows: In the first stage, the patient enacts a maladaptive cognitive-interpersonal cycle that is characteristic of him or her. For example, the patient anticipates that others will be hostile and thus puts up a hostile defense. In the second stage, the therapist becomes hooked by the patient's behavior and responds in a complementary fashion. In this example, the therapist responds to the patient's hostility with complementary hostility. In the third stage, the therapist becomes aware of his or her role in the dysfunctional cognitive-interpersonal cycle and thus begins an unhooking process. In the fourth stage, the therapist begins to metacommunicate with the patient about their current interaction by exploring with the patient the nature of their current interaction and the patient's experience of it, rather than simply participating in it automatically. In the fifth and final stage, the therapist accepts responsibility for contributing to the interaction. For example, the therapist who becomes aware of having responded to the patient's hostility with counterhostility acknowledges this to the patient.

Selection of Events

The next step of our research program involved selecting alliance rupture events for investigation. A rupture can be identified from three perspectives (therapist, patient, and third-party observer). In the early phases of the research, we selected rupture events from therapist and patient perspectives; in the later phases, we employed third-party perspectives as well.

To select rupture events from patient and therapist perspectives, we extracted six questions from the Working Alliance Inventory (WAI) (Horvath & Greenberg, 1986): two corresponding to each of the three dimensions of the therapeutic alliance (task, goal, and bond). The six questions that were selected were chosen on the basis of demonstrated ability, in a previous data set (Safran & Wallner, 1991), to predict outcome in short-tern therapy with an integrated cognitive-interpersonal focus (Safran, 1984a, 1984b, 1990a, 1990b; Safran & Segal, 1990) across a range of different dependent measures (see Table 10.1). These questions represent an important intermediate link between more molecular in-session change and ultimate outcome. Their

TABLE 10.1.   Mean Pearson Correlations of Six WAI Items with Outcome Measures from a Previous Data Set (Safran & Wallner, 1991)

WAI Item	Pearson Mean	Correlations Range[a]
Bond Factor		
17. I believe _____ is genuinely concerned for my welfare.	.48	.47–.48
29. I have the feeling that if I say or do the wrong things, _____ will stop working with me.	.55	.50–.60
Task Factor		
13. I am clear on what my responsibilities are in therapy.	.50	.44–.55
15. I find what _____ and I are doing in therapy is unrelated to my concerns.	.43	.42–.44
Goal Factor		
22. _____ and I are working toward mutually agreed upon goals.	.51	.44–.62
25. As a result of these sessions, I am clearer as to how I might be able to change.	.52	.43–.67

[a] All statistics are first order correlations and are significant at $p < .05$.

validity as indexes of intermediate outcome was further corroborated in a study by Muran and Safran (1990).

These six alliance questions were then administered independently to patients and therapists after every session. Both therapists and patients were instructed to think of the therapy session as consisting of three parts—a beginning, a middle, and an end—and to rate each portion of the session separately on each question. In this fashion, we obtained perceptions independently from both therapists and patients regarding fluctuations in the quality of the therapeutic alliance over the course of each session. For example, a particular patient and/or therapist may rate the first portion of the session relatively high on the therapeutic alliance questions, the second portion as low, and the third portion as high. This pattern of ratings would suggest that a deterioration in the therapeutic alliance had taken place toward the middle of the session but that the quality of the alliance had improved once again toward the end of the session.

We reasoned that sessions in which both therapists and patients rated the quality of the alliance as significantly poorer in the middle phase than in both the beginning and end phases would have a reasonably high likelihood of providing events in which an alliance rupture had occurred during the session and then subsequently had been resolved. A fluctuation of at least 20 points[1] was chosen as the criterion. In contrast, we reasoned that questionnaires on which both therapist and patient rated the middle portion of the session as being at least 20 points lower on the therapeutic alliance items than the first portion and did not show substantial improvement in the final portion, indicated sessions in which alliance ruptures had occurred and had not been resolved by the end of the session. In this way, we were able to select a sample of resolution and nonresolution sessions.

Informal Empirical Analysis

Once a procedure had been developed for selecting alliance rupture events, we began the process of refining the model of the resolution process by carefully reviewing audiotapes and transcripts of ruptures that had been successfully resolved (as indicated by therapist and patient reports on the WAI items) and by successively revising the preliminary model in response to observed discrepancies between the model and actual sessions. These sessions were drawn from a pool of 29 patients being treated in 20-session, time-limited therapy with an integrated cognitive-interpersonal approach (Safran, 1990a, 1990b; Safran & Segal, 1990). Eight therapists were involved in the study.

Through a careful step-by-step comparison with actual resolution events, the preliminary model was gradually refined. In this step of the research,

---

[1] The 7-point Likert scale of the WAI was changed to a 100-point scale to increase variance.

the model was refined in response to actual observations of psychotherapy sessions, rather than a purely conceptual or armchair analysis. At this point, however, the empirical analysis took place at an informal level, in that no procedures were employed for ensuring the reliability and the validity of the observations.

Through this process, it became apparent that there are a number of different alliance rupture types, each following unique resolution patterns. The seven different rupture types that were distinguished were described in Safran et al. (1990). Ultimately, we grouped these seven rupture categories into two major alliance rupture types corresponding to rupture types similarly described by Harper (1989a, 1989b): (a) confrontation ruptures, and (b) withdrawal ruptures.

A confrontation rupture is characterized by an aggressive and accusatory statement of dissatisfaction by the patient regarding the therapist, the therapy, or some aspect of the therapeutic process. This is exemplified by such statements from the patient as "You're not helping me" or "This is a stupid exercise." A withdrawal rupture is characterized by a patient statement or behavior that distances the patient from the therapist or the therapeutic task, and/or their own internal experience. Examples would be intellectualization, shifting the topic, justification, compliance, or immediate agreement with the therapist's statement without exploration or elaboration. To date, our research has focused more intensively on the analysis of the resolution process for withdrawal ruptures, and the rest of the chapter will thus focus on this rupture type.

Formal Empirical Analysis

As regularities in patterns of rupture resolution emerged, we began to operationalize the different components of the proposed model, using a battery of process measures chosen to capture different aspects of the relevant phenomena. The use of converging measurement procedures, in this context, is important since no one measure can comprehensively capture the important features of any given aspect of clinical process. Operationalizing the model's components in this fashion serves a number of functions (Rice & Saperia, 1984; Safran et al., 1988). First, it forces the user to articulate the hypothesized constructs more precisely. Second, using reliable coding categories ensures that the observations will be rigorous and that there is ultimately some interrater reliability to the observations. This is a prerequisite if the model is going to have any validity and generalizability. Third, specifying operational criteria allows for subsequent verification studies to test the validity of the proposed model. In other words, it allows for testing the proposed model empirically using more conventional aggregate data studies that evaluate the hypothesis that resolution and nonresolution events differ in the presence or absence of the proposed model components. Finally, the operationalization of model components with converging process measures provides specific markers that can be useful to the practitioner in identifying the presence or absence of processes relevant to the resolution of alliance ruptures.

Process Measures

Four measures were employed in the operationalization of the rupture resolution model components:

1. The Structural Analysis of Social Behavior (SASB; Benjamin, 1974, 1979, 1982, 1984).
2. The Patient Experiencing Scale (P-EXP; Klein, Mathieu, Gendlin, & Kiesler, 1969; Klein, Mathieu-Coughlan, & Kiesler, 1986).
3. The Therapist Experiencing Scale (T-EXP; Klein et al., 1986).
4. The Client Vocal Quality Scale (CVQ; Rice & Kerr, 1986; Rice & Wagstaff, 1967).

In our research, which emphasizes the interpersonal aspects of therapy, the cluster version of SASB analysis was used to code process, rather than content, on Surface 1 (focus on other) and Surface 2 (focus on self) of the SASB model. Readers not familiar with these scales are directed to the references cited for detailed descriptions of them.

Procedure

A number of withdrawal ruptures were coded using the preceding process measures. This helped us discern regularities in patterns of change that occurred across cases. By tracking recurring patterns of transition between recurring configurations of process measure codings, we were able to further revise the model in an iterative fashion. The process was facilitated by charting these patterns in graphlike form (Greenberg, 1984).

Operationalizing the model components is a complex and subtle procedure in which provisional criteria are set on the different process measures in an attempt to capture clinical intuitions about what different resolution components should look like. The criteria are adjusted in an iterative fashion as we apply them to new clinical material and gauge how well they actually capture the model components as currently conceptualized.

The conceptualization of the relevant constructs and their operationalization takes place over time in a mutually influencing bootstrapping process, in response to new observations of clinical material (Rice & Saperia, 1984). The operationalization of the components of the model thus sharpened our observations and facilitated a rigorous interplay between empirical observation and conceptualization. Through this iterative, bootstrapping process, a revised model was ultimately developed in which each component was operationalized with specific criteria on multiple process measures. Where it was felt that the process measures would not completely capture the important aspects of a component, additional semantic criteria were stipulated as well.

Empirical Model I

The first empirical model consisted of four components. Each of the first three components consisted of two subcomponents: a therapist subcomponent and a patient subcomponent. This arrangement allowed us to capture important patient-therapist sequences or interaction patterns that were observed to be characteristic of resolution sessions. For example, the significance of a patient withdrawal marker that is followed by a therapist response of drawing the patient's attention to the rupture will be different from one that is followed by a therapist response of withdrawal. The final resolution component in this model consisted exclusively of a patient process. It was felt that this component was sufficiently rare, and far enough along in the resolution process to be a significant marker of resolution, regardless of the particular therapist response that either precedes or follows it.

The first empirical model, along with the operational criteria for the resolution components, is diagrammed in Figure 10.2. Although an actual resolution process tends to be complex, with many repetitions and loops, the model captures the essence of the resolution process.

Component 1. Attending to the Rupture Marker

The first component in the model consists of Subcomponent 1A: Patient Withdrawal Marker; it is followed by Subcomponent 1B: Therapist Focuses Attention on Rupture Experience in the Here and Now.

Subcomponent 1A. Patient Withdrawal Marker. The presence of a withdrawal marker is indicated by a behavior on the patient's part suggesting that he or she is in some way avoiding the exploration of certain feelings. As the operational criteria on the SASB (Figure 10.2) indicate, typical indications of this marker involve Deferring and Submitting (2-5), Sulking and Appeasing (2-6), or Walling Off and Avoiding (2-8) on the part of the patient. At least two patient statement "units" receiving this constellation of codes would have to occur in sequence (either within one speech turn or across two speech turns) to be classified as a subcomponent 1A.

In one session, for example, the therapist asked the patient to participate in the two-chair exercise from Gestalt therapy. The patient began to do so, but the therapist, sensing an odd quality in her voice, began to explore whether or not she was doing so wholeheartedly or out of deference. The patient's compliant behavior receives a code of Deferring and Submitting (2-5) on the SASB. As indicated on Figure 10.2, this process is also marked by codings of Externalized or Limited on the CVQ Scale and a coding of no more than 2 on the P-EXP Scale. These codings reflect the low level of self-exploration that is characteristic here.

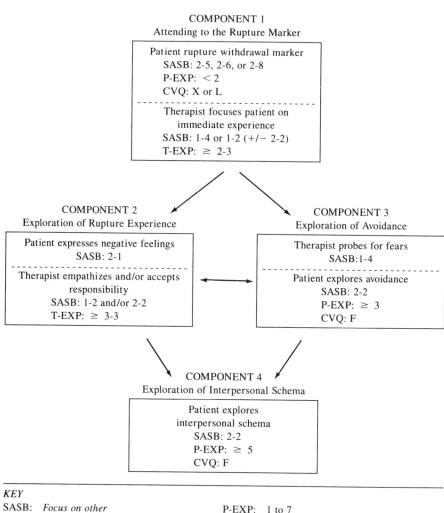

COMPONENT 1
Attending to the Rupture Marker

Patient rupture withdrawal marker
SASB: 2-5, 2-6, or 2-8
P-EXP: < 2
CVQ: X or L
- -
Therapist focuses patient on
immediate experience
SASB: 1-4 or 1-2 (+/− 2-2)
T-EXP: ≥ 2-3

COMPONENT 2
Exploration of Rupture Experience

Patient expresses negative feelings
SASB: 2-1
- -
Therapist empathizes and/or accepts
responsibility
SASB: 1-2 and/or 2-2
T-EXP: ≥ 3-3

COMPONENT 3
Exploration of Avoidance

Therapist probes for fears
SASB:1-4
- -
Patient explores avoidance
SASB: 2-2
P-EXP: ≥ 3
CVQ: F

COMPONENT 4
Exploration of Interpersonal Schema

Patient explores
interpersonal schema
SASB: 2-2
P-EXP: ≥ 5
CVQ: F

KEY

SASB: *Focus on other*
   1-2 Affirming and Understanding
   1-4 Helping and Protecting
   1-5 Watching and Managing
   1-6 Blaming and Belittling

   Focus on self
   2-1 Asserting and Separating
   2-2 Disclosing and Expressing
   2-5 Deferring and Submitting
   2-6 Sulking and Appeasing
   2-8 Walling Off and Avoiding

P-EXP: 1 to 7
T-EXP: Manner-Referent (1 to 7)

CVQ: L = Limited
   X = Externalizing
   E = Emotional
   F = Focused

N. B. Each subcomponent includes a semantic definition as part of the operational criteria.

Figure 10.2.   Empirical model I.

Subcomponent 1B. Therapist Focuses Attention on Rupture Experience in the Here and Now.   It appears to be critical at this point for the therapist to draw attention to the rupture and to maintain a focus on the here and now of the therapeutic relationship. Often, the therapist needs to consistently return the focus to the here and now in the therapeutic relationship, as the patient tends to retreat into generalities or speaks about other situations. For example, a patient, who had left the previous session apparently upset about what he saw as being the therapist's unresponsiveness, came to the current session focusing on his frustration with his supervisor's nonresponsiveness rather than on the therapist's. At this point, the therapist drew the patient's attention to the similarity between the two situations and asked if he felt there were any similarities.

The therapist can do this in a number of ways. A common intervention is for the therapist simply to probe for the patient's current experience with statements such as, "What are you experiencing right now?" This type of intervention would be coded as Helping and Protecting (1-4) on the SASB. Another intervention consists of a therapist empathizing with any negative feelings that the patient may be expressing. For example, a patient begins to express some frustration with the therapy and then withdraws. The therapist empathizes with the frustration that the patient has expressed. This would receive an Affirming and Understanding (1-2) code on the SASB. Another common intervention is for the therapist to provide feedback about his or her subjective perception of negative sentiments that the patient is directly or indirectly expressing. For example, the therapist says: "You seem kind of irritated to me. My sense is that you seem kind of frustrated." This would receive a double code of Helping and Protecting (1-4) and Disclosing and Expressing (2-2) on the SASB. Therapist responses at this point must have a minimum of a 4-3 coding on the T-EXP Scale, indicating that the therapist is attuning to the patient's experiences in the moment and elaborating on them in an empathically involved manner. We defined these three types of therapist interventions as a Subcomponent 1B if they occurred within a minimum of three speech turns of the patient's rupture marker.

Component 2. Exploration of Rupture Experience

This component consists of Subcomponent 2A: Patient Expression of Negative Sentiments; and Subcomponent 2B: Therapist Empathy and/or Acceptance of Responsibility.

Subcomponent 2A. Patient Expression of Negative Sentiments.   At this point, in response to a therapist intervention focusing attention on rupture experience in the here and now, the patient may begin to express negative sentiments more directly. This type of response receives a coding of Asserting and Separating (2-1) on the SASB. At least one speech unit coded as Asserting and Separating (2-1), which immediately follows a Component 1, is defined as Subcomponent 2A. For example, a patient who has been responding to the therapist's intervention in a defensive way begins to acknowledge that he is feeling hurt by the therapist's statement or that he is feeling angry.

A noteworthy point here is that neither the P-EXP Scale nor the CVQ Scale were found to provide reliable guidelines as to the presence of this process. Comparing resolution to nonresolution sessions, it emerged that the acts of self-assertion and individuation seemed to be more important in this context than any type of deeper self-exploration. In fact, a number of nonresolution sessions emerged where patients engaged in a self-exploratory process, as indicated by high ratings on the P-EXP Scale or CVQ codings of Focused, in what appeared to be a compliant fashion. This observation underscores the importance of clarifying precisely what type of process is therapeutic in what context (Rice & Greenberg, 1984).

Subcomponent 2B. Therapist Empathy and/or Acceptance of Responsibility. It is important for the therapist to respond to any expression of negative sentiments by either empathizing (SASB: Affirming & Understanding [1-2]), or by accepting responsibility for his or her contribution to the interaction (SASB: Disclosing & Expressing [2-2]). In one session, for example, the patient asked the therapist whether he felt critical toward him. At first, the therapist indicated that the patient's subjective experience was more important than whether indeed he really was being critical. When, however, the therapist acknowledged that indeed he was being critical, this broke through the impasse.

Component 3. Exploration of Avoidance

This component consists of Subcomponent 3A: Therapist Probe for Patient's Block; and Subcomponent 3B: Patient Exploration of the Block.

Subcomponent 3A. Therapist Probe for Block. Here, typically in response to difficulties that the patient is having in expressing negative sentiments, the therapist begins to probe directly for any fears that may be blocking their expression. For example, the patient begins to express some anger at the therapist, but then appears to withdraw. In response to the therapist's probing, she indicates that she is experiencing some anxiety. The therapist then begins to explore the nature of the patient's anxiety by asking her what her concerns are. This type of direct question receives a Helping and Protecting (1-4) code on the SASB and is operationally defined as a Subcomponent 3A if it occurs anytime after a Component 1.

Subcomponent 3B. Patient Exploration of the Block. In response to the therapist's probing, the patient explores the fears that block the expression of negative sentiments. For example, the patient explores his or her fear of being abandoned if he or she expresses any negative sentiments. This type of response receives a Disclosing and Expressing (2-2) code on the SASB.

There must be some indication in the process coding systems that exploration is experientially real (either Focused on the CVQ Scale or a minimum of 3 on the P-EXP Scale). This seems to be important in helping the patient gain a tangible experience of the way he or she is blocking self-assertion. We defined Component 3 as this type of patient exploration (Subcomponent 3B) following within at least two speech turns of the therapist's probes (Subcomponent 3A).

Typically, there is an oscillation between Component 2 (Exploration of Rupture Experience) and Component 3 (Exploration of Avoidance). The Exploration of Avoidance helps the patient become increasingly free to express the avoided experience in an assertive fashion. Conversely, as the patient increasingly comes to express his or her avoided experience, he or she often contacts anxiety, which leads to the exploration of the avoidance.

Component 4. Exploration of Interpersonal Schema

The fourth component consists of only a patient process. The exploration of both the rupture experience and the fears that are blocking the acknowledgment and the expression of the rupture experience ultimately may lead to the clarification of a patient's interpersonal schema, or working model of self-other interactions. This is coded as Disclosing and Expressing (2-2) on the SASB. It is important that this exploration take place in an experientially real fashion, as indicated by a CVQ coding of Focused Voice Quality and a coding of at least 5 on the P-EXP Scale. Operationally, we defined this type of exploration of interpersonal schema as a Component 4 if it was preceded by a Component 1 and either a Component 2 or 3 sometime in the same session. For example, the previously discussed patient, who was reluctant to explore his frustration about the earlier session with the therapist, gradually came to see the way in which his belief that the exploration of his frustrations would be useless played a central role in terms of his feeling of powerlessness in his interactions with people in general.

Our conceptualization of this component emerged out of the observation that in some cases, patient responses that initially looked very much like Component 3B (Patient Exploration of Block), were distinguished from other instances of this component by a combination of higher P-EXP ratings (≥ 5) *and* CVQ ratings of Focused (F). (The criteria for Component 3B are P-EXP ≥ 3 *or* CVQ = F). This combination of codings suggests that there is a more advanced stage of exploration taking place in these instances.

Pilot Verification Study I: Descriptive Analysis

In the next phase of the research program, four rupture resolution sessions were compared with three nonresolution sessions. The operational criteria for model components were used to evaluate the extent to which resolution sessions contained a higher frequency of model components than nonresolution sessions. This is not a formal test of the hypothesis since the sample is too small to allow the use of inferential statistics. It does, however, provide a preliminary indication of the potential usefulness of the model. The four resolved rupture events can be conceptualized as a series of single-case studies. Each successful replication increases confidence about the generalizability of the model. The unresolved rupture events, while not serving as a formal control group, do facilitate the development of preliminary impressions about the extent to which various model components are found exclusively in resolved rupture events or appear to varying degrees in unresolved rupture events. Furthermore, the comparison of resolved rupture events with unresolved rupture events permits us to glean preliminary impressions about various ways in which the rupture resolution process breaks down in unresolved ruptures.

Procedure

Four resolution sessions and three nonresolution sessions were selected on the basis of converging therapist and patient responses on the postsession alliance questions (as described earlier). In addition, two independent raters, naive to the nature of the study, were asked to rate all sessions on a 5-point scale, indicating the degree to which they perceived the rupture as resolved. Both raters were PhD clinical psychology students with four years' experience as psychotherapists. They participated in a 2-hour training session that focused on the concept of therapeutic alliance ruptures and examined a number of examples of resolved and unresolved alliance rupture events. The intraclass correlation of the two raters was .88. Their ratings were then averaged, and the sessions were rank ordered on the basis of this average. The four highest ranked sessions were found to correspond to the sessions that had been identified as rupture resolution sessions on the basis of patient and therapist ratings.

All four resolution sessions (101a, 103a, 103b, 106) came from one therapist (the senior author), with two of them coming from the same patient (103). In addition, one of the nonresolution sessions (101b) came from a patient who had also provided one resolution session. The two remaining resolution sessions (1701, 1904) came from two different therapists (one woman, aged 44, with a PhD degree, and one woman, aged 38, with an MA degree).

The five patients included in the formal analysis of the rupture resolution model were two women and three men with a mean age of 37.5 years; two of the patients were married, one was single, and one was divorced (marital status information was not available for one patient). The Axis I diagnoses were as follows: Three cases presented with depression symptoms, one case with both depression and anxiety symptoms, and one case with interpersonal problems. None of the patients received an Axis II diagnosis. Four patients completed all 20 sessions of the treatment protocol, and one terminated treatment after Session 15 (this patient was in the nonresolution sample).

Reliability of Process Coding

First, transcripts of the seven sessions selected for analysis were broken into speech units according to instructions in the SASB manual (Grawe-Gerber & Benjamin, 1989). A speech unit is defined as "a complete thought or a psychologically meaningful interaction" within a speech turn (Grawe-Gerber & Benjamin, 1989, p. 6). All sessions were then coded on the SASB, P-EXP, and T-EXP Scales, and CVQ Scale. Given the labor-intensive, time-consuming nature of this coding, individual raters coded the seven sessions after adequate reliability had been established. All coded sessions were then reviewed by the research team, and any disagreements were resolved by group consensus. A similar coding and group consensus procedure was used for all instruments. The model components were then identified, using the previously described criteria, after the sessions had been coded with all the process measures.

Training for all instruments was done using sessions drawn from the general patient pool at the clinic, but these sessions were not included in the analyses. Interrater agreement of SASB coding was established between two independent raters on one therapy session. Raters were blind to session number, patient, and therapist in all training cases. A weighted kappa coefficient of .69 was obtained. This result is within the range of interrater agreement estimates reported by Benjamin (1974). After training on the P-EXP Scale was completed, interrater reliability was assessed using 34 randomly selected 2-minute segments. Two independent raters achieved adequate intraclass correlation coefficients of .83 for mode and .95 for peak ratings (see Klein et al., 1986, for a review). Interrater reliability on T-EXP ratings was calculated on a sample of 31, 2-minute segments of sessions drawn from the sample. For the two independent raters, the intraclass correlation coefficients were .72 for manner and .79 for referent ratings, suggesting adequate reliability. Interrater agreement of CVQ ratings was also calculated between two independent raters, using one 50-minute therapy session drawn from the sample. The estimate of overall rater agreement (kappa) was .55, which is consistent with previously reported indexes (Rice & Kerr, 1986).

Comparison of Resolution and Nonresolution Sessions

Table 10.2 compares resolution and nonresolution events in terms of the frequency with which each of the four model components was found. The mean number of components found in resolution versus nonresolution sessions suggests the presence of differences that are consistent with the hypothesis.

The pattern that emerges when component frequencies for each of the individual cases is examined is further illuminating. The first observation is that each of the four resolution sessions had at least one occurrence of Components 1 (Attending to the Rupture Marker), 2 (Exploration of the Rupture Experience), and 3 (Exploration of Avoidance). Component 4 (Exploration of Interpersonal Schema), however, was only found in two of the

TABLE 10.2.   Component Frequency of Resolution versus Nonresolution Cases

	Component			
	1 (Attending to Rupture)	2 (Exploration of Rupture)	3 (Exploration of Avoidance)	4 (Exploration of Interpersonal Schema)
Session				
Resolution				
101a	4	9	4	1
103b	5	5	3	1
103a	2	4	1	0
106	8	3	1	0
M	4.75	5.3	2.2	0.5
Nonresolution				
101b	0	0	0	0
1904	0	0	0	0
1701	2	3	0	0
M	0.67	1	0	0

four resolution cases, and none of the resolution cases was found to have more than one occurrence of this component. Inspection of component frequencies in nonresolution sessions indicates that two of the three nonresolution events contained one of the model components. The third nonresolution session (1701) contained two instances of Component 1 (Attending to Rupture) and three instances of Component 2 (Exploration of Rupture Experience). However, no instances of either Component 3 (Exploration of Avoidance) or Component 4 (Exploration of Interpersonal Schema) were found.

The results of the pilot verification study were generally encouraging. Since all four resolution sessions came from the same therapist, it seems likely that differences emerging between resolution and nonresolution sessions are attributable at least in part to a therapist effect. To provide some evaluation as to whether differences are attributable to pretreatment differences in the patients, we compared the resolution and nonresolution subjects on a battery of symptom severity measures administered prior to treatment (see Table 10.3). Although the sample size is too small to permit the use of inferential statistics, inspection of the group means reveals a consistent pattern in which subjects who provided the resolution sessions actually reported more severe symptomatology prior to treatment. This suggests that any theory-consistent differences between the two groups emerging in the resolution patterns cannot be attributed to pretreatment symptom severity.

Empirical Model II

The results of the Pilot Verification Study I, while not definitive, provided encouraging support for the four-component resolution model. Having

TABLE 10.3. Means and Standard Deviations of Outcome Measures at Pretreatment

Outcome Measures	Resolution Sample ($N = 3$)		Nonresolution Sample ($N = 2$)	
	M	SD	M	SD
ATQ				
Frequency	76.00	13.89	66.00	21.21
Degree of belief	79.67	14.98	71.00	29.70
SCL-90 (GSI)	47.33	8.14	43.50	4.95
BDI	14.50	8.24	12.75	2.48
MCMI Sum	123.33	12.42	115.00	15.56
Mean patient target				
complaint ratings	83.33	7.18	66.67	14.40

Note: ATQ = Automatic Thoughts Questionnaire; SCL-90 (GSI) = Symptom Checklist-90 (Global Severity Index) (Derogatis, 1977); BDI = Beck Depression Inventory (Beck, Ward, Mendelson, Mock, & Erbaugh, 1961); MCMI = Million Multiaxial Clinical Inventory (Millon, 1983).

formally coded seven alliance rupture events on our battery of process measures, we were now in a position to go through the next phase of refining the model. By looking for regularities in transitions between specific configurations of process measures that had been identified, we were able to further clarify certain aspects of the resolution process.

The following provides a simple example of these procedures. A repeated observation was that a number of transcript segments that had previously been identified as examples of Subcomponent 2A (Patient Expression of Negative Sentiments) were actually receiving double codings on that SASB of Asserting and Separating (2-1) and either Belittling and Blaming (1-6) or Deferring and Submitting (2-5) or Walling Off and Avoiding (2-8). An example of a 2-1 and 1-6 double code would be "You're not helping me," rather than "I'm not finding this useful," "I'm angry at you," or "I would like more structure." The client is in some sense individuating from the therapist, but stops short of taking full responsibility for his or her position by blaming the therapist, rather than stating his or her position or making more of an "I-statement." An example of a 2-1 and 2-5 double code is as follows: The patient says, "Do you think it could be useful if we worked out some kind of agenda?" rather than "I'd like a clearer idea of where we're going." Here the patient appears to be making a move toward individuation, but the form of the statement still implies a dependency on the therapist for approval or guidance, rather than a pure act of self-assertion.

These transcript segments stood in contrast to segments that had received a pure code of Asserting and Separating (2-1). Furthermore, it appeared that the pure 2-1 codings were often preceded by one or more transcript segments that had received double codings of the type described earlier. A distinction thus began to emerge in our thinking between unambiguous acts of self-assertion on the patient's part, which tended to occur later on in the resolution process, versus partial acts of self-assertion that were adulterated either by a simultaneous compliance with the therapist or by an other-directed blaming stance, rather than showing the patient's assumption of full responsibility for his or her feelings or needs.

Another common pattern observed was that acts of partial assertion often appeared to be followed by one of three therapist responses. In one response type, the therapist asks the patient to make a direct statement. For example, the patient says, "Do you think it could be useful if we worked out some kind of agenda?" and the therapist says, "Are you willing to tell me directly what you want, rather than ask a question?" This type of response would receive a SASB code of Helping and Protecting (1-4), which suggests that the therapist is attempting to teach or stimulate the patient in a kind or positive manner.

In the second response type, the therapist provides either accurate empathy or subjective feedback about the way in which he or she perceives or experiences the patient's statement. An example of the first subtype is as follows: "You seem dissatisfied with the way we are proceeding," which would receive a SASB code of Affirming and Understanding (1-2) and a T-EXP code reflecting a modest level of therapist contribution and involvement (at least 2-3). The second subtype is exemplified by the response: "I sense you as kind of letting me know what you want, but in a very cautious way." This would receive a double code on the SASB of Helping and Protecting (1-4) and Disclosing and Expressing (2-2), and a T-EXP code reflecting a modest level of empathic involvement (at least 3-3).

The third and final type of therapist behavior involves an acknowledgment of responsibility for his or her contribution to the interaction. For example, in response to the patient's statement, "I feel like you're being critical of me," the therapist responds, "I think you're right. I was being critical of you." This behavior receives a SASB code of Disclosing and Expressing (2-2), and a P-EXP code reflecting a higher level of therapist contribution and involvement than the other types (at least 4-3).

Another significant refinement of the rupture resolution model involved Component 3 (Exploration of Avoidance). In its original conceptualization, the component included two subcomponents; however, repeated observations showed that it was important to recognize the patient's acknowledgment of a block prior to the therapist's probe and subsequent exploration by the patient. For example, in response to the therapist's probe for immediate experience, the patient says, "I'm feeling anxious." This component, therefore, came to include three subcomponents with the first identified as Patient Disclosure of a Block, which receives a SASB code of Disclosing and Expressing (2-2) and an EXP code reflecting the patient's ability to react emotionally and acknowledge such a reaction (≥ 3).

A final refinement of the model involved Component 4 (Exploration of Interpersonal Schema). Since we had only found two instances of this component, we reasoned that it may not be an *essential* part of the resolution process as currently defined. At this point in our research, we speculate that either the exploration of the interpersonal schema is embedded in the entire resolution process or that it is unreasonable to expect many clear-cut instances of it early in treatment, considering that our data set only includes events occurring within the first third of a 20-session protocol. This will need to be clarified in future research.

The refined model is presented in Figure 10.3. This consists of four components, including five patient operations and three therapist behaviors, or eight subcomponents taken altogether. Each of the subcomponents was operationalized using criteria on multiple process measures, in the same way as before.

To evaluate raters' ability to reliably identify these components on the basis of the operational criteria, an interrater reliability study was conducted using eight 6-minute segments drawn from the four resolution sessions. For two raters blind to session number, patient, and therapist, the estimate (kappa) was .67.

Pilot Verification Study II: Sequential Analysis

As a way of more rigorously mapping out the sequence of transitions among the model components, we conducted confirmatory sequential analyses on the four rupture resolution events. To test important hypothesized sequences, both within the components (between subcomponent therapist and patient operations), and between components, lag one sequential analyses were conducted using the program ELAG (Bakeman & Gottman, 1986) on the level of the subcomponents or the eight specific patient and therapist behaviors.[2]

Because the four rupture resolution events included only 183 coded behaviors, the analyses proceeded in a stepwise progression, confirming first the sequences within the components and then the sequences between each component and the following subcomponent. A general model representing the overall structure of rupture resolution (from component to component) was subsequently abstracted from the results of these analyses. The study-wise alpha levels were divided by the number of sequences for which tests were performed (Bonferroni correction).

The first step in the analysis of resolution events evaluated the hypothesized sequences within each of the four components (see Figure 10.4). This involved a sequential analysis of the 183 coded behaviors for which seven sequences were tested. What we found was a significant forward ($z = 7.46$, $p < .001$) and backward ($z = 3.01$, $p < .05$) sequence between the rupture withdrawal marker (P1) and the therapist focusing the patient on his or her immediate experience (T1), which confirms Component 1 (C1). In terms of

---

[2] The confirmation process entailed establishing the significance of sequences hypothesized to exist and the nonsignificance of sequences hypothesized to not exist.

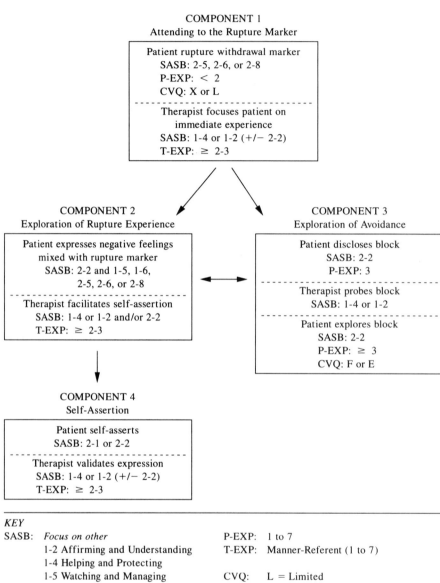

COMPONENT 1
Attending to the Rupture Marker

Patient rupture withdrawal marker
SASB: 2-5, 2-6, or 2-8
P-EXP: < 2
CVQ: X or L
- -
Therapist focuses patient on
immediate experience
SASB: 1-4 or 1-2 (+/− 2-2)
T-EXP: ≥ 2-3

COMPONENT 2
Exploration of Rupture Experience

Patient expresses negative feelings
mixed with rupture marker
SASB: 2-2 and 1-5, 1-6,
2-5, 2-6, or 2-8
- -
Therapist facilitates self-assertion
SASB: 1-4 or 1-2 and/or 2-2
T-EXP: ≥ 2-3

COMPONENT 3
Exploration of Avoidance

Patient discloses block
SASB: 2-2
P-EXP: 3
- -
Therapist probes block
SASB: 1-4 or 1-2
- -
Patient explores block
SASB: 2-2
P-EXP: ≥ 3
CVQ: F or E

COMPONENT 4
Self-Assertion

Patient self-asserts
SASB: 2-1 or 2-2
- -
Therapist validates expression
SASB: 1-4 or 1-2 (+/− 2-2)
T-EXP: ≥ 2-3

KEY

SASB: *Focus on other*
         1-2 Affirming and Understanding
         1-4 Helping and Protecting
         1-5 Watching and Managing
         1-6 Blaming and Belittling

         Focus on self
         2-1 Asserting and Separating
         2-2 Disclosing and Expressing
         2-5 Deferring and Submitting
         2-6 Sulking and Appeasing
         2-8 Walling Off and Avoiding

P-EXP: 1 to 7
T-EXP: Manner-Referent (1 to 7)

CVQ: L = Limited
         X = Externalizing
         E = Emotional
         F = Focused

N. B. Each subcomponent includes a semantic definition as part of the operational criteria.

Figure 10.3.   Empirical model II.

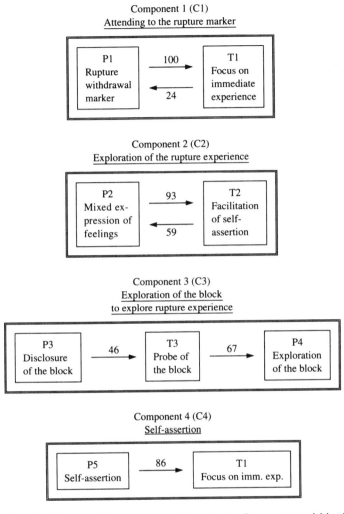

Figure 10.4. Confirmatory lag one sequential analysis of sequences within the components ($N=183$).

Component 2 (C2), there was a similar forward ($z = 10.06$, $p < .001$) and backward ($z = 5.04$, $p < .001$) sequence between a patient partial assertion (P2) and a therapist facilitation of self-assertion (T2). The bidirectionality evidenced with regard to both these components is consistent with our observation that the exploratory process in both contexts often has a circular or repetitive quality that deepens as it progresses.

As for Component 3 (C3), a patient disclosure of block to exploring a rupture experience (P3) was significantly followed by a therapist probe of the block (T3) ($z = 5.26$, $p < .001$), which in turn was significantly followed by a patient exploration of avoidance (P4) ($z = 5.56$, $p < .001$). Finally, there was a significant sequence from a patient expression of self-assertion (P5) to a therapist focus on immediate experience (T1) ($z = 3.46$, $p < .01$), which confirms Component 4 and supports the hypothesis that it is important for the therapist to respond to the patient's self-assertion in a validating fashion.

The second step of the analysis involved confirming the sequences following the first three components. Because the overall number of coded behaviors was small, three separate sequential analyses were conducted, one for each of the components. For example, the first analysis only analyzed the sequences following Component 1 (C1). This involved recoding our original data set of 183 coded behaviors so that, where P1 was followed by T1, we inserted instead a single code identified as C1. The first analysis was conducted on 154 coded events (see Figure 10.5). It tested the hypothesis that Component 1 (Attending to the Rupture) would be followed by either of two patient behaviors: Patient Mixed Expression (P2) or Patient Disclosure of Block (P3). Therefore, two sequences were tested. Both sequences were significantly evidenced ($z = 2.33$, $p < .05$ and $z = 4.24$, $p < .001$, respectively). This confirms the hypothesis that the resolution process tends to follow the two pathways of Exploration of Rupture Experience and Exploration of Avoidance.

The second analysis involved only the sequences following Component 2. It was conducted on 142 coded behaviors, which included the insertion of the code C2 where P2 was followed by T2 in the original data set (see Figure 10.6). It was found that the Exploration of Rupture Experience (C2) was significantly followed by Component 4 (Self-Assertion) ($z = 2.82$, $p < .01$), thus confirming the hypothesized sequence between Components 2 and 4 in the resolution process. Exploration of Rupture Experience does appear to

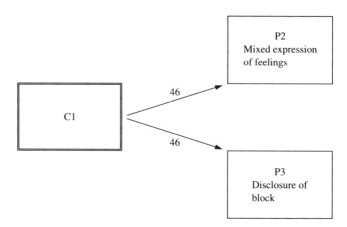

Figure 10.5.   Confirmatory lag one sequential analysis of sequences following the first component ($N = 154$).

Figure 10.6. Confirmatory lag one sequential analysis of the sequence following the second component ($N = 142$).

facilitate direct self-assertion and individuation, suggested by the patient's movement toward the independence pole of the SASB control dimension.

The third analysis analyzed only the sequences following Component 3. It was conducted on 175 coded behaviors, which included the insertion of C3 where the sequence of P3 to T3 to P4 occurred (see Figure 10.7). The exploration of Avoidance (C3) was significantly followed by the therapist focusing the patient on his or her immediate experience (P1) ($z = 2.77$, $p < .01$). This result confirms the hypothesis that there is an interplay between Components 2 and 3 where the therapist behavior of focusing the patient on immediate experience is the link. This suggests a sequence in which the patient's exploration of his or her avoidance becomes progressively deepened, as the therapist attends to any indications of this avoidance, probes for the patient's subjective experience, and maintains a focus on the here and now, both through redirection of attention (e.g., "What are you experiencing now?"), and empathic reflection.

Although it was impossible to unequivocably confirm the overall structure of the rupture resolution model from these stepwise analyses because of the small size of the data set, it is possible to infer such a structure, working back and forth from the hypothesized model and the separate analyses. Such an inference can only be made with the realization that the model is particularly susceptible to Type I error. Therefore, we present the following overall structure as strictly preliminary in nature, but with the intent of conveying a gestalt of the entire resolution process.

In Figure 10.8, following the occurrence of attending to a rupture withdrawal marker (C1), two different directions seem to emerge: one involving Exploration of Rupture Experience and then Self-Assertion (C2 to C4); the other involving Exploration of Avoidance (C3). Both these pathways appear to be followed by therapist responses that are validating,

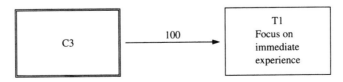

Figure 10.7. Confirmatory lag one sequential analysis of sequence following the third component ($N = 175$).

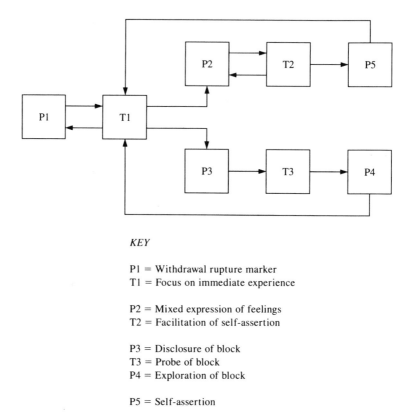

KEY

P1 = Withdrawal rupture marker
T1 = Focus on immediate experience

P2 = Mixed expression of feelings
T2 = Facilitation of self-assertion

P3 = Disclosure of block
T3 = Probe of block
P4 = Exploration of block

P5 = Self-assertion

Figure 10.8.   Overall structure of the rupture resolution model inferred from all confirmatory sequential analyses.

empathic, or exploratory in nature. Although the link between the exploration of the patient's avoidance and his or her self-assertion is not a direct one, the fact that this pathway is as probablistically likely as the exploration of the avoided experience suggests that it plays a role in the resolution process.

A Clinical Illustration of Empirical Model II

The following session, from which transcript material will be excerpted for illustrative purposes, followed on the heels of a previous session in which there had been a clear rupture in the therapeutic alliance. It had focused on the patient's concern about being observed through a one-way mirror. He reported that between sessions he had met one of the observers (Bill), who failed to say hello upon meeting him. He was thus distressed about the interaction, viewing the observer's behavior as inappropriately unfriendly. During the session, he had discussed this with the therapist and had left feeling frustrated, perceiving the therapist to be unresponsive.

P1: Patient Withdrawal Marker

In this clinical illustration of the rupture resolution process, the patient began the next session without making any reference to the previous session. Instead, he talks about his frustration with his supervisor at work:

P: Had a little talk with the boss yesterday about things. I don't feel terribly satisfied. I suppose I got some things said that I've been waiting to say for a long time, but I never got much back from her, you know, so it leaves me feeling basically unsatisfied.

T1: Focus on Immediate Experience

The therapist responds to the patient withdrawal marker by empathizing with his feelings about the boss and attempting to establish a focus on the here and now of the therapeutic relationship:

T: So. You tried to bring things out in the open with your boss. You brought out a number of things you had been reluctant to, and you were left feeling sort of confused and unsatisfied. You know, as you're talking right now, I can't help, I guess in my own mind thinking back to our last session. That seemed to me to be the kind of situation in which you were unhappy and frustrated, and you were kind of confronting me, and I'm wondering how that resolved for you?

By establishing and maintaining a focus on the patient's immediate experience and on the here and now of the therapeutic relationship, the therapist facilitates the exploration of two parallel paths. One path involves the exploration of the rupture experience (e.g., negative sentiments toward the therapist), while the other path involves the exploration of fears, beliefs, and expectations that inhibit the exploration of the first path. There appears to be a shuttling back and forth between these two paths, with the exploration of inhibiting beliefs or expectations subsequently facilitating the exploration of avoided experience, and the exploration of avoided experience helping the patient to contact fears and beliefs that inhibit this exploration.

P3: Disclosure of Block

In this stage of the process, the patient begins to disclose his or her hesitation about exploring the avoided experience, either in anticipation of this prospect or as a result of having begun to explore and express the experience. In the current session, in response to the therapist's inquiry about any unresolved feelings from the previous week's session, the patient responds:

P: Well, I guess I sort of was putting that issue on the back burner. I mean, it was on my mind. It was there for me this morning. You know, "Well, am I going to follow through or not, or are we going to follow through on that?" You know—"Am I going to bring it up again—will I make an issue of it?"

T3: Therapist Probes Block

This disclosure leads to an attempt on the therapist's part to clarify the nature of the patient's avoidance, or the nature of the fears, beliefs, and/or expectations inhibiting the exploration and/or expression of avoided experience. In the current session, the therapist asks the patient to elaborate on his reservations about bringing it up again or "making an issues of it." The therapist responds to the patient's statement that "We never followed that through" with the question: "What stopped you from pushing things further last week?" At a later phase of the session, the therapist asks him, "What would be the risk of asking Bill in now?"

P4: Exploration of Block

This consists of an exploration of the fears that block the expression of negative sentiments. In the current session, the patient responds, "I guess I'm afraid that if we did ask Bill in and talk about it, I wouldn't really feel any better about it anyways." In response to further probes he indicates:

P: Part of the risk is that there's nothing we can really do of any substantial nature, that I will be left with my negative feelings—and whatever we can do in the context of this thing is not really going to—resolve any negative feelings about it, and I will be left with negative feelings.

P2: Mixed Expression of Feelings

The following excerpt illustrates the process of beginning to express negative sentiments and then withdrawing:

P: When we started out, you indicated that Bill [the observer] wasn't there at the time, but that he might show up sometime during the session. It's not a big deal, though.

Here, the patient begins to express dissatisfaction with the way in which things were handled during the previous session. His use of the term "we," however, indicates his reluctance to express anger at the therapist for being unresponsive and also precludes the exploration of his own possible role in not pushing things further. He also minimizes the importance of the issue by qualifying, "It's not a big deal, though."

In a somewhat later section of this session, after the patient has spoken about his dissatisfaction with the preceding session, the therapist asks him if he is currently dissatisfied. In response to this probe, the patient responds:

P: I guess I do feel dissatisfied. I'm not sure—I don't know—maybe, maybe I'm looking to you to spoon-feed me or something. You know, tell me what is reasonable to do in this situation.

Here, the patient begins to acknowledge his dissatisfaction but, rather than taking the risk of articulating the nature of his dissatisfaction fully and making it clear what he wants, he turns to the therapist for some cue as to how he should handle the situation or what kind of demand on his part would be acceptable. There is thus some expression of negative sentiments mixed again with a withdrawal.

T2: Facilitation of Self-Assertion

In some instances, the therapist helps to sharpen the exploration of the rupture experience by directly asking the patient what he or she wants in the present moment. For example, in this illustration, he asks the patient:

T: What would satisfy you with me right now? Do you have any sense of what you want, and whether you are getting what you want right now?

In other instances, the therapist may facilitate a more direct, self-assertive response, by suggesting that the patient try an experiment of directly expressing sentiments or asking the therapist for something he or she wants. For example, a patient suggests tentatively that she may be a little irritated with the therapist, but that it's not very important (P2: Mixed Expression of Feelings), and the therapist suggests that the patient try the experiment of saying directly to the therapist "I'm angry at you" without qualifying it. This may help the patient access underlying feelings of self-assertion or alternatively may help the patient contact fears and beliefs, which may interfere with such feelings.

P5: Self-Assertion

Through a combination of exploring the avoidance to expressing the rupture experience and mixed expressions of the negative feelings that are responded to empathically by the therapist prompts designed to facilitate self-assertion, the patient eventually moves to a position of being able to express his or her feelings in a more direct, self-assertive fashion.

In the current case, the patient gradually moves increasingly toward this assertive position.

P: Is one of the options for me to say "I don't want Bill behind there"?
T: Yes.
P: Is one of the options for me to say, "I don't want anybody behind there"?

T: Yes.

P: Actually one of the thoughts that occurred to me last week was, well, OK, I suppose one of the reasons the observers are behind the mirror is because it's supposedly a nonobtrusive observation. Except that there is a lot of noise going on back there, which you know, now that it's becoming an issue, I'm very conscious of it. So in that sense it's not really unobtrusive. What would be wrong with having them in the room, so that there could be more of an ongoing relationship?

This is still one step short of directly stating what he wants, but it nevertheless constitutes a considerable risk that will test his belief that his demands are excessive and that articulating them will be futile or dangerous. The therapist's response is a direct and unequivocal "Yes." A more ambiguous response might be experienced by the patient as hedging and might be less likely to challenge his dysfunctional belief that it is futile to self-assert. The energetic and enthusiastic style with which the patient makes a suggestion at the end of the transcript contrasts with his caution and tentativeness earlier in the session, suggesting that the interaction with the therapist has begun to disconfirm his dysfunctional interpersonal schema.

CONCLUSION

Our findings to this point are preliminary. The pilot verification studies, while encouraging, need to be extended with a larger samples. For this purpose, it would be ideal to select one resolution and one nonresolution event or session from the same subject. In this manner, each subject can serve as his or her own control, thereby ruling out the possibility that differences between rupture resolution and nonresolution events are attributable to patient characteristics, rather than dynamic and potentially malleable features of the patient-therapist interaction. The sequential analyses provide a more rigorous way of capturing patterns of transition between resolution components than would a purely descriptive analysis, and the results are encouraging in that they are theoretically coherent and intelligible. To constitute a true test of the hypothesized model, this type of analysis will have to be replicated on new samples of patients and therapists.

There is an old story about two Talmudic sages, Shamai and Hillel. Shamai was renowned for his sharp intelligence and for his detailed grasp of the finer points of Talmudic law. He was also known for his stern and exacting disposition, and his short temper. Hillel was known for his emphasis on the spirit of the law, rather than the letter of the law. One day a Roman citizen visited Shamai and said to him that he would convert to Judaism if Shamai could teach him the entire Torah while he stood on one foot. Shamai, in inimitable Shamai style, chased him away, incensed by his ludicrous request. When the Roman addressed the same request to Hillel, he was asked to stand on one foot. The citizen responded by doing so, whereupon Hillel instructed him as follows, "Repeat after me, 'One should treat one's fellow man as one would wish to be treated oneself.'" The Roman repeated the adage, and Hillel told him he could now put his foot down. "That," he said, "is the essence of the Torah. The rest is commentary. Now go and study."

Both theoretical trends and empirical evidence are increasingly implicating the therapeutic relationship as the essence of psychotherapy. In the past few years, we have been attempting to elaborate a commentary on this basic truth by teasing out some of the subtleties of the processes through which tears in the relationship fabric of psychotherapy are mended and contribute to change. Although we have made a start in this direction, in many ways we are still very much at the beginning.

REFERENCES

Bakeman, R., & Gottman, J. M. (1986). *Observing interaction: An introduction to sequential analysis.* Cambridge: Cambridge University Press.

Beck, A. T., Ward, C. H., Mendelson, M., Mock, J., & Erbaugh, J. (1961). An inventory for measuring depression. *Archives of General Psychiatry, 4,* 561–571.

Benjamin, L. S. (1974). Structural analysis of social behavior. *Psychological Review, 81,* 392–425.

Benjamin, L. S. (1979). Use of structural analysis of social behavior (SASB) and Markov chains to study dyadic interactions. *Journal of Abnormal Psychology, 88,* 303–319.

Benjamin, L. S. (1982). Use of structural analysis of social behavior (SASB) to guide intervention in psychotherapy. In J. C. Anchin & D. J. Kiesler (Eds.), *Handbook of interpersonal psychotherapy* (pp. 190–212). New York: Pergamon Press.

Benjamin, L. S. (1984). Principles of prediction using structural analysis of social behavior (SASB). In R. A. Zucker, J. Aronoff, & A. J. Rabin (Eds.), *Personality and the prediction of behavior.* New York: Academic Press.

Bordin, E. (1979). The generalizability of the psychoanalytic concept of the working alliance. *Psychotherapy: Theory, Research, and Practice, 16,* 252–260.

Butler, S. F., & Strupp, H. H. (1986). Specific and non-specific factors in psychotherapy: A problematic paradigm for psychotherapy research. *Psychotherapy, 23,* 30–40.

Foreman, S., & Marmar, C. R. (1985). Therapist actions that address initially poor therapeutic alliances in psychotherapy. *American Journal of Psychiatry, 142,* 922–926.

Gaston, L. (1990). The concept of the alliance and its role in psychotherapy: Theoretical and research considerations. *Psychotherapy, 27,* 143–153.

Grawe-Gerber, M., & Benjamin, L. S. (1989). Structural analysis of social behavior (SASB): Coding manual for psychotherapy research. Unpublished manuscript, University of Bern, Switzerland.

Greenberg, L. S. (1984). A task analysis of intrapersonal conflict resolution. In L. N. Rice & L. S. Greenberg (Eds.), *Patterns of change: Intensive analysis of psychotherapy process* (pp. 67–123). New York: Guilford Press.

Greenberg, L. S., & Pinsof, W. M. (1986). *The psychotherapeutic process: A research handbook*. New York: Guilford Press.

Harper, H. (1989a). Coding guide I: Identification of confrontation challenges in exploratory therapy. Unpublished manuscript, University of Sheffield, England.

Harper, H. (1989b). Coding guide II: Identification and classification of therapist markers and withdrawal challenges. Unpublished manuscript, University of Sheffield, England.

Hartley, D. E. (1985). Research on the therapeutic alliance in psychotherapy. In R. Hales & A. Frances (Eds.), *Psychiatry Update* (pp. 532–549). American Psychiatric Association Annual Review, Vol. 4.

Henry, W. P., Schacht, T. E., & Strupp, H. H. (1986). Structural analysis of social behavior: Application to a study of interpersonal process in differential psychotherapeutic outcome. *Journal of Consulting and Clinical Psychology, 54*, 27–31.

Henry, W. P., Schacht, T. E., & Strupp, H. H. (1990). Patient and therapist introject, interpersonal process, and differential psychotherapy outcome. *Journal of Consulting and Clinical Psychology, 58*(6), 768–774.

Horvath, A. O., & Greenberg, L. S. (1986). The development of the Working Alliance Inventory. In L. S. Greenberg & W. M. Pinsof (Eds.), *The psychotherapeutic process: A research handbook* (pp. 529–556). New York: Guilford Press.

Horvath, A. O., & Symonds, B. D. (1991). Relation between working alliance and outcome in psychotherapy: A meta-analysis. *Journal of Counseling Psychology, 38*, 139–149.

Klein, M. H., Mathieu, P. L., Gendlin, E. T., & Kiesler, D. J. (1969). *The experiencing scale: A research and training manual* (Vol. 1). Madison, WI: University of Wisconsin Extension Bureau of Audiovisual Instruction.

Klein, M. H., Mathieu-Coughlan, P. L., & Kiesler, D. J. (1986). The experiencing scales. In L. S. Greenberg & W. M. Pinsof (Eds.), *The psychotherapeutic process: A research handbook* (pp. 21–71). New York: Guilford Press.

Kohut, H. (1984). *How does analysis cure?* Chicago, IL: University of Chicago Press.

Luborsky, L., & Auerbach, A. (1985). The therapeutic relationship in psychodynamic psychotherapy: The research evidence and its meaning for practice. In R. Hales & A. Frances (Eds.), *Psychiatry Update*. American Psychiatric Association Annual Review, Vol. 4.

Millon, T. (1983). *Millon Clinical Multiaxial Inventory Manual* (3rd ed.). Minneapolis, MN: National Computer Systems.

Muran, J. C., & Safran, J. D. (1990). The relationship between in-session change and ultimate outcome in cognitive therapy. A poster presented at the annual convention of AABT, San Francisco, CA.

Rice, L. N., & Greenberg, L. S. (1984). *Patterns of change: Intensive analysis of psychotherapy process*. New York: Guilford Press.

Rice, L. N., & Kerr, G. P. (1986). Measures of client and therapist voice quality. In L. S. Greenberg & W. M. Pinsof (Eds.), *The psychotherapeutic process: A research handbook* (pp. 73–105). New York: Guilford Press.

Rice, L. N., & Saperia, E. P. (1984). Task analysis of the resolution of problematic reactions. In L. N. Rice & L. S. Greenberg (Eds.), *Patterns of change: Intensive analysis of psychotherapy process.* New York: Guilford Press.

Rice, L. N., & Wagstaff, A. K. (1967). Client voice quality and expressive style as indexes of productive psychotherapy. *Journal of Consulting Psychology, 31,* 557–563.

Safran, J. D. (1984a). Assessing the cognitive-interpersonal circle. *Cognitive Therapy and Research, 8,* 333–348.

Safran, J. D. (1984b). Some implications of Sullivan's interpersonal theory for cognitive therapy. In M. A. Reda & M. J. Mahoney (Eds.), *Cognitive psychotherapies: Recent developments in theory, research, and practice* (pp. 251–272). Cambridge, MA: Ballinger.

Safran, J. D. (1990a). Towards a refinement of cognitive therapy in light of interpersonal theory: I. Theory. *Clinical Psychology Review, 10,* 87–105.

Safran, J. D. (1990b). Towards a refinement of cognitive therapy in light of interpersonal theory: 2. Practice. *Clinical Psychology Review, 10,* 107–122.

Safran, J. D., Crocker, P., McMain, S., & Murray, P. (1990). Therapeutic alliance rupture as a therapy event for empirical investigation. *Psychotherapy, 27,* 154–165.

Safran, J. D., Greenberg, L. S., & Rice, L. N. (1988). Integrating psychotherapy research and practice: Modeling the change process. *Psychotherapy, 25,* 1–17.

Safran, J. D., & Segal, Z. V. (1990). *Interpersonal process in cognitive therapy.* New York: Basic Books.

Safran, J. D., & Wallner, L. K. (1991). The relative predictive validity of two therapeutic alliance measures in cognitive therapy. *Psychological Assessment: A Journal of Clinical and Consulting Psychology, 3,* 188–195.

Sterba, R. (1934). The fate of the ego in psychoanalytic therapy. *International Journal of Psychoanalysis, 15,* 117–126.

Strupp, H. H. (1989). The nonspecific hypothesis of therapeutic effectiveness: A current assessment. *American Journal of Orthopsychiatry, 37,* 947–954.

Sullivan, H. S. (1953). *The interpersonal theory of psychiatry.* New York: Norton & Co.

Weiss, J., Sampson, H., & The Mount Zion Psychotherapy Research Group (1987). *The psychoanalytic process: Theory, clinical observation and empirical research.* New York: Guilford Press.

Zetzel, E. R. (1956). Current concepts of transference. *International Journal of Psychotherapy, 37,* 369–376.

PART FOUR
Empirical Findings

CHAPTER 11

Research on the Alliance

ADAM O. HORVATH

THE HISTORICAL CONTEXT

Although alliance, as a clinical construct, has been in use since 1912 (Freud), empirical research on the role and function of the alliance did not exist prior to 1976. Several factors seem to have contributed to this lag between conceptual formulation and systematic investigation, perhaps the most of which was the general lack of research interest in the psychotherapeutic process. The process of change was much debated in psychodynamic circles, but until the mid-1970s, investigation of the "inner workings" of psychotherapy appeared beyond the scope of empirical investigation. Most psychotherapy researchers, instead of studying the microcosm of the therapeutic hour directly, tried to infer the mechanisms of change indirectly. The focus of the majority of investigations was the efficacy of specific interventions because it was assumed that evidence of treatment efficacy would confirm the theoretical assumptions (including the hypothesized change mechanisms) undergirding the treatment being studied.

Another probable cause for the delay in investigating the role of the alliance was lack of familiarity with the concept by clinicians and researchers outside the psychodynamic framework. Moreover, the lack of reliable measurement techniques further impeded research efforts to investigate the status of the alliance.

Recently, interest in the investigation of therapy process was rekindled by reexamining the theoretical assumptions underlying research practices (Kiesler, 1973; Rice & Greenberg, 1984) and by overcoming some of the technical barriers to the intensive exploration of the content of therapy through the help of audio and videotape recording technologies. Interest in the alliance specifically was bolstered in the mid-1970s when Bordin (1975) recast the alliance construct in broader, pantheoretical terms.

A significant impetus behind the development of the body of research on the alliance was the emerging interest in the *nonspecific*[1] factors (Frank,

---

[1] The term *nonspecific* was used historically to refer to factors not uniquely associated with a specific form of intervention. The use of this word was unfortunate since it initially

1961) in therapy. The importance of these generic variables was also strongly emphasized by Rogers (1951, 1957), who believed that the therapist's ability to provide the client with three basic interpersonal conditions (empathy, unconditional positive regard, and congruence) was necessary *and sufficient* to produce therapeutic improvements. Rogers' insistence on empirical validation of these claims was an important factor in the development of research on the therapeutic relationship. Investigation of the impact of the client-centered facilitative conditions combined with the availability of affordable and portable audio recording technology encouraged the emergence of a new genre of research: the detailed qualitative/ quantitative examination of the relationship in therapy and attempts to link this variable with outcome. Although research on the client-centered facilitative conditions did not fully corroborate Rogers' original hypotheses (e.g., Mitchell, Bozart, & Krauft, 1977; Watson, 1992), it demonstrated the feasibility of reliably quantifying the relationship in therapy.

The last important factor in the growth of research on the alliance was the finding that, overall, different therapies (i.e., therapies based on diverse theoretical premises using a variety of different interventions) produce comparable client improvements (Luborsky, Singer, & Luborsky, 1975; Smith & Glass, 1977). Although some of these research syntheses have been criticized on both methodological (Shadish & Sweeney, 1992) and conceptual (Stiles, Shapiro, & Elliot, 1986) grounds, the general conclusions are seldom questioned: Most researchers interpret these findings as an indication that variables common to all forms of therapies are likely responsible for significant portions of therapeutic gains. One of the most likely common denominators among these different approaches is the relationship between the therapist and the client (Orlinsky & Howard, 1986).

In this chapter, I will attempt to sum up the alliance research from approximately 1975 to the present. The material is introduced under the following topic headings:

1. Measurement Issues.
2. The Relation between Alliance and Outcome.
3. Predispositional Factors.
4. The Alliance across Time.
5. Therapist Actions Influencing the Alliance.
6. Future Directions.

---

led to some confusion between nontherapy-related variables, such as expectations and attention, and factors specific to therapy but available to some degree in all therapies. The word *generic* will be used in this chapter to refer to the latter.

MEASUREMENT ISSUES

By the mid-1970s, the "Zeitgeist" was favorable to the investigation of the interpersonal process between the therapist and client, and its relation to outcome. Between the late 1970s and early 1980s, a number of instruments were developed independently and more or less simultaneously to measure the alliance. Although additional measures have been constructed subsequently and instrument development continues, the five original instrument "families" and their derivatives have been used by the overwhelming majority of the researchers.[2] These instrument clusters are:

1. The California Psychotherapy Alliance Scales (CALPAS/CALTRAS; Gaston, Chapter 4, this volume; Marmar, Horowitz, Weiss, & Marziali, 1986).
2. Penn Helping Alliance Scales (PEN/HAQ/HAcs/HAr; Alexander & Luborsky, 1987).
3. Therapeutic Alliance Scale (TAS; Marziali, 1984a).
4. Vanderbilt Psychotherapy Process Scale of Vanderbilt Therapeutic Alliance Scale (VPPS/VTAS; Hartley & Strupp, 1983).
5. Working Alliance Inventory (WAI; Horvath, 1981, 1982).

The development and successive refinements of many of these instruments are described in other chapters in this volume.

All the preceding measures assess the status of the alliance over the time span of a single session or longer. More recently, there has been a growing interest in observing the growth and decay of the alliance within a therapy session (see section "The Alliance across Time," later in this chapter). The research group at the Menninger Institute has developed a method of assessing such fluctuations (Frieswyk et al., 1986). In addition, Watson and Greenberg (see Chapter 7, this volume) have taken the first steps in investigating the phenomenology of the moment-to-moment relational experience of the client.

Perspectives in Alliance Assessment

The very first attempt to measure the alliance was based on raters' judgments (Luborsky, 1976); subsequently, however, self-report scales (based on

---

[2] In fact, at least 12 distinct alliance assessment methods are currently available. Most of these fall into two broad categories: (a) subsets of instruments or questionnaires originally developed to measure a different, usually broader, construct, and from which researchers have extracted data thought to be relevant to the alliance (e.g., Frank & Gunderson, 1990; Kolden, 1990, June; Saunders et al., 1989); (b) new scales developed specifically to measure the alliance (e.g., Agnew & Shapiro, 1988; Barends, 1992). Some of these measures are of potential interest; however, insufficient data was available to review them at this time.

both therapists' and clients' impressions) were also developed. Currently, most instruments are available both as an observer's rating scale and as a self-report measure.

These different perspectives (client's, therapist's, and observer's views) on the alliance, however, do not necessarily coincide. For example, Tichenor and Hill (1989) compared the ratings of observers, clients, and therapists across six instruments and found, "Clients, therapists and observers clearly did not agree or come to a consensus on what working alliance was, indicating that measures from different perspectives are not interchangeable" (p. 198). More recently, Bachelor (1992) documented significant differences between clients' and therapists' ratings across several instruments. There is some indication, however, that the ratings are most discrepant early in treatment and therapists' and clients' alliance scores converge during the later stages of therapy (Mallinckrodt, 1993).

Alliance Components

Over the years, a number of alliance components have been proposed. Psychodynamic theorists (e.g., Sterba, 1934; Zetzel, 1956) suggested constituent elements such as "therapeutic alliance"—the client's attachment and identification with the therapist; "ego alliance"—the connection between the reasonable aspects of both the therapist and the client; "working alliance"—the client's identification with the therapist's style. Bordin (1975, 1976, 1980) extended the range of relationships in which the alliance plays a role and suggested that the alliance has three basic components: bonds (personal liking, valuing), goals (agreement on the purpose of the therapy), and tasks (the collaborative endorsement of the within-therapy activities).

The alliance scales tend to mirror the diversity of these theoretical positions. Most scales purport to measure a number of constituent elements (subscales) as well as the overall strength of the alliance. Some of the scales try to capture the participants' *capacity* or *motivation* to form a useful therapeutic alliance and the actual collaborative component separately (e.g., CALPAS, VTAS); whereas other scale developers apparently do not feel that capacity and performance can be disentangled once therapy has actually started (e.g., WAI, HAQ). The TAS subscales endeavor not only to separate the therapist's and the client's components but also to deal with positive and negative contributions separately; while other measures combine positive and negative elements in the same scale but score the items differentially depending on the valence (i.e., whether the item impacts positively or negatively on the alliance). Moreover, although there are no clear theoretical guidelines as to the relative importance of these components, all the scales tacitly assume that the components are of equal import (i.e., weighted equally) and are additive. Thus, an alliance score that is the unweighted sum of all the scale scores is generated by each instrument.

Consequently, each measure, in practice, defines the alliance as well as its inner structure somewhat uniquely.

As a result of this diversity among the measures, the researcher has the choice of a number of instruments, each implementing a related but not identical vision of the alliance, in terms of both overall definition and structure (components). Although a number of these conceptualizations can be seen as complementary or hierarchical in the sense that some alliance components subsume other proposed constituents, currently there is only partial theoretical consensus in the field (Gaston, 1990; Horvath & Symonds, 1991).

Instrumentation

A number of these instruments are discussed in detail in this volume. So the following brief descriptions are provided only to develop a context for presenting the research results:

- *The Penn scales* grew out of Luborsky and his colleagues' large-scale investigation of psychodynamic therapies (the Penn Psychotherapy Project). They identified "Type 1 alliance" and "Type 2 alliance" as major categories. Type 1 was described as "A therapeutic alliance based on the patients experiencing the therapist as supportive and helpful with himself as a recipient" (Luborsky, 1976, p. 94); Type 2 alliance is ". . . based on a sense of working together in a joint struggle against what is impending the patient. . . . on shared responsibility for working out treatment goals. . . . a sense of 'we-ness'" (p. 94). The PENN measures were initially based on raters counting alliance signs (client statements indicating alliance); however, later versions of the scale used the simpler, global rating method.

- *The VPPS/VTAS alliance scales* were derived from a larger instrument designed to measure differences between trained and untrained therapists' activities (Gomes-Schwartz, 1978). The alliance components in these measures include Patient's Participation, Patient's Exploration, Patient Motivation, Patient's Acceptance of Responsibilities, Therapist Warmth and Friendliness, and Negative Collaboration.

- *The TAS* was designed to assess both positive and negative alliance factors, though subsequent investigations indicated that the latter is probably not related to outcome (Marziali, 1984b). The alliance components measured were Patient's Positive Contribution, Therapist's Positive Contribution, Patient's Negative Contribution, Therapist's Negative Contribution.

- *The CALPAS/CALTRAS scales* originated with the same group of California researchers as did the TAS, however the former has been further refined based on subsequent factor analytic studies (Gaston, 1991; Gaston & Ring, in press; Marmar, Horowitz, Weiss, & Marziali, 1986; Saburin, Hansell, Gutfreund, Gaston, & Marmar, 1990). The most current version of the instrument yields four scales: Patient Commitment, Patient Working Capacity, Therapist Understanding and Involvement, and Working Strategy Consensus.

- *The WAI* was developed expressly to measure Bordin's three alliance components: Goals, Tasks, and Bonds. Scores on these scales (particularly Task) obtained early in therapy were found to be strongly predictive of outcome and differentiate between those who terminate prematurely and those who remain in therapy (Kokotovic & Tracey, 1990; Plotnicov, 1990). The distinctiveness of the subscales, however, is unclear. On one hand, there is evidence of moderate-to-strong correlation between the measures (Adler, 1988; Cummings, Martin, Hallberg, & Slemon, 1992; Horvath & Greenberg, 1987; Salvio, Beutler, Wood, & Engle, 1992); on the other hand, the three-part structure has received preliminary support in at least one factor analytic study (Tracey, Glidden, & Kokotovic, 1988). Although a number of refinements were made to the original scale and several different versions (e.g., Observers', Short Forms, Couple's Version) were developed, the original theory-based structure remains unaltered.

Two of the scales (PENN, WAI) are theoretically homogeneous, and attempt to capture a specific theoretical perspective on the alliance. Some of the other instruments were developed using the latent trait (factor analytic) model to derive their subscales and thus represent a more eclectic theoretical position. The homogeneous scales tend to have higher interscale correlations, whereas blended scales (particularly the CALPAS/CALTRAS) appear to have more independent subscales (Horvath, Gaston, & Luborsky, 1993).

The state of the art in alliance measurement offers a potential compromise: On one hand, the link between the theoretical definitions and the factor analytically derived subscales is not fully documented. On the other hand, instruments that are based on a priori explicit theoretical model have not been able to confirm the distinctive alliance structure predicted by the theory (Salvio et al., 1992).

The Relation among Instruments

In view of the preceding discussion, the question arises: If these instruments with their diverse underlying conceptualizations empirically define different "alliances," do we know the extent of the overlap between the constructs thus defined?

We can approach this issue in three different ways:

1. The theoretical approach to this question involves an analysis of the extent to which the definitions undergirding each of these instruments are equivalent.
2. A more empirical perspective involves the estimation of the covariance among the measures.

3. Researchers could investigate whether all these instruments predict outcome equivalently.

Looking at the implicit and explicit definitions undergirding the instruments, Horvath and colleagues (1993) found, "Two aspects of the alliance: (a) personal attachments or bonds, and (b) collaboration or willingness to invest in the therapy process, are common elements among each of the instruments." Moreover, they noted that a number of related concepts were common to two or more instruments: participants' positive and/or negative contributions to the therapy (CALPAS, TAS), shared or mutually determined goals for the sessions (CALTRAS, WAI, PEN), the client's capability to form a relationship with the therapist (PEN, VTAS, CALTRAS), a positive attitude toward and belief in the efficacy of the in-therapy tasks (CALTRAS, WAI), and the willingness to participate actively in therapy (PEN, CALTRAS, VTAS). It should be noted, however, that the weight or emphasis given to these components varies among measures.

The ideal method to assess the actual overlap (correlation) among these measures is to use parallel instrumentation on the same subjects. Administering multiple instruments purportedly measuring the same construct is seldom justified in clinical research, so it is not surprising that only four studies report covariance among alliance measures. Tichenor and Hill (1989) compared three observer-rated instruments plus the client and therapist versions of the WAI. They found a 12% to 71% overlap among three observer-rated (PENN, VTAS, and WAI_0) scales. Safran and Wallner (1991) contrasted two self-report scales (WAI, CALPAS). The overall shared variance was 76%. Adler (1988) reported 34% variance overlap between the clients' ratings and 9% overlap between the therapists' ratings of the WAI and the HAQ.

At the subscale level, the relation between scales are different: covariances range from 0% to 67% with an average value of 37%. When Bachelor (1990) examined the subscale level correlations of three self-report measures (PEN, VPPS[3], TAS), she found a wide range of commonalities (0%–69%), with an average overlap of approximately 21% for the clients and 18% for the therapists' scales.

Although no instrument has emerged as the "best predictor of therapy outcome," there is evidence that not all outcomes are equally well predicted by each (Adler, 1988; Bachelor, 1991; Greenberg & Adler, 1989; Safran & Wallner, 1991). There are also indications that some therapy-outcome combinations are better prognosticated by some instruments than others (DeRubeis & Feely, 1990). What is still unclear, however, is whether these differences are mostly due to the different demands of each therapeutic approach or to differential sensitivity of the measures.

---

[3] The VPPS was translated into French and adapted for use as a self-report instrument in this study.

In summary, the extensive overlap across measures at the global level supports the notion that each is assessing a related underlying construct. Using the same logic, it can be argued that the generally lower between-subscale (across instruments) correlations are to be expected, since there appears to be little consensus as to the constituent elements of the alliance. Thus, the current state of instrumentation appears to mirror the developmental process characterizing the field: There is evidence of a basic consensus at the most coarse level of analysis (defining the alliance in global terms). As progressively finer distinctions are made within the overall alliance framework, however, there are indications of diminishing consensus.

Reliability

These alliance measures appear to be reasonably reliable. Horvath and Symonds (1991) reviewed the literature and estimated that across 34 studies using different instruments, the average reliability of alliance measures was .86. Although there may be minor differences between instruments, the five measures reviewed earlier each met generally accepted criteria of stability. Overall, the measures rated by therapists were the most reliable ($r = .93$, based on five studies), but the client's scales were likewise stable (.88, based on the results of 13 investigations). The reliability of the observers' scales was usually reported in terms of interclass correlation; across 16 studies reporting such indexes, the average correlation was .82.

Therapists' Scales

One of the current problems in measuring the alliance is that therapists' scores appear to be independent of or, in at least one case, negatively correlated with alliance data obtained from clients (Adler, 1988; Bachelor, 1992; Tichenor & Hill, 1989). Moreover, therapist's alliance scales appear to yield significantly poorer predictions of all types of therapy outcomes than client's and observer's alliance assessments (Horvath & Symonds, 1991). This seems to be true whether therapy outcome assessment is based on therapists' rating or data from other sources. For example, Horvath and Symonds (1991) found that the effect size representing the relation between therapists' alliance score and outcome[4] was .13, −.04, −.17 for clients', therapists', and observers' reported outcome, respectively.

A possible reason for this anomaly is that the therapists' scales are essentially direct rewordings of client instruments. This approach is based on two assumptions: The first is that the therapy relationship is essentially symmetrical—the qualities of a positive environment are the same for the client as for the therapist. The second assumption has to do with the therapist's ability to judge the client's inner experience. Specifically, while almost all

---

[4] The effect sizes reported are based on the correlation coefficient between alliance and outcome weighted by sample size (Rosenthal, 1991).

the client's items reference his or her experience directly, the therapist's questionnaire often asks the respondent to infer the beliefs or feelings of the client.

The preceding assumptions, though they have some prima facie appeal, may not be sound: The relationship in therapy is not symmetrical, nor is it likely that the absence or presence of some of the relationship elements have equivalent impact on the therapist and the client. Also, the therapists' view of therapy process is likely less immediate than that of clients: They perceive therapy events through a lens colored by expectations (both for self and client) and intentional states influenced by their specific theoretical perspective. Thus, the response to an item such as "the [client] trusts me" may depend on how the therapist evaluates the observed client behavior in light of the class of events that theoretically would be evidence of trust rather than transference. While clients' perceptions are also subjective, they are more directly referencing their immediate and felt experience and are less likely to preprocess these impressions. Interestingly, so far no direct effort has been made to identify how any of the mediator variables previously discussed may influence the therapist's rating of the alliance.

Another conceivable reason for the poor predictive power of therapists' alliance scores is the possibility that many therapists significantly misjudge their client's sense of the relationship due to their own relational predispositions (e.g., attachment style, countertransference). Based on such distorted perception of the relationship, the therapist might persist with interventions that would have been abandoned if the alliance had been correctly assessed as poor or under stress. There appears to be an obvious need to examine how therapists form opinions about the alliance, and under what conditions these perceptions are most likely to differ from the client's.

Finally, another clue may be the finding that early client-rated alliance, though not strongly correlated to the therapist's rating, is highly predictive of outcome, whereas therapist and client alliance scores obtained later in therapy are more related but less predictive (Mallinckrodt, in press). Conceivably, clients form a judgment based on "Type 1" alliance data almost immediately after treatment begins, and this judgment may exert a strong influence on their commitment to and willingness to follow the demands of treatment. This early alliance, however, may be quite opaque to the therapist, who does not have access to information as to the degree of commitment and collaboration until the therapeutic situation offers an opportunity to test these qualities.

THE RELATION BETWEEN ALLIANCE AND OUTCOME

The Overall Alliance-Outcome Relation

A number of reviews have been published recently on the relationship between the strength of the alliance and a variety of treatment outcomes (see

Gaston, Marmar, Gallagher, & Thompson, 1990; Horvath & Symonds, 1991; Luborsky, 1990). Each has concluded that a moderate-to-strong relation appears to link positive alliance with good therapy outcome. Horvath and Symonds' (1991) meta-analytic review included 24 clinical studies published between 1975 and 1991; these are listed in Table 11.1.

These studies, on the average, had 49 participants, approximately 70% of whom were female. The treatments averaged just over 20 sessions, and most of the therapists involved had more than 8 years' experience. Across this sample, the overall effect size was .26. This value is likely conservative due to the large number of dependent variables measured but not reported by a number of these studies.[5] This effect size, however, is significantly different from zero ($p < .001$) and roughly comparable to the magnitude of the effects reported in meta-analytic syntheses of gains associated with diverse forms of psychotherapy (Smith & Glass, 1977). A 95% confidence interval can be computed to estimate the region of the true value of the average ES (Rosenthal, 1987). This range is .2–.32. Since the original figure is most probably overly conservative, it is likely that the true value is closer to the top of the range (i.e., .32).

The magnitude of the relation between alliance and outcome was not related to sample size, length of treatment, or whether the study was published. These findings indicate that, in general, there are important links between the quality of the alliance and the degree of success in therapy. However, the variance among the reported results was greater than expected by chance alone; thus, the results are also consistent with the possibility that several factors such as the time the alliance was assessed and the type of outcome indexes collected may influence the magnitude of such association. The impact of these variables will be discussed next.

Different Treatments

The emphasis on the relationship in therapy varies across theories, ranging from Rogers' claim that the proper therapeutic ambience is both necessary and sufficient for therapeutic gains to the classic behavioral position that assigns little importance to it (Skinner, 1974). Moreover, it has been anticipated that therapies based on divergent theoretical premises will have unique alliances associated with them (Bordin, 1976; Gelso & Fretz, 1992). Horvath (1991) investigated the alliance outcome relations across different treatments: Of these investigations, 8 used psychodynamic, 3 used cognitive, and 10 used eclectic therapies. The average correlation between outcome and alliance (weighted by sample size) was .17 for psychodynamic and .27 for eclectic and cognitive therapies. Each of these

---

[5] To minimize the probability of Type 1 error, these missing values were set to $r = .0$ which is, in light of the range and distribution of the reported values, most likely, an overly pessimistic assumption.

TABLE 11.1. Meta-Analysis of Alliance Outcome Relations

Data Set	Study	Rater[a]	Alliance Measure	Time	Outcome Measure	Rater	Treatment Sessions	Treatment Type	Study ES(r)	Set ES(r)	N
1	Adler, J. (1988)	C,T	WAI HAQ CIS	E,L	Target Complaints Symptom Checklist-90 Self-Esteem Index Inventory of Interpersonal Problems Client's Post-Therapy Questionnaire Therapist's Post-Therapy Questionnaire	C,T	12	Various	.28		44
2	Hartley & Strupp (1983)	O	VTAS	A	Composite Gain Score	O	25[b]	Various	.2		22
3	Horowitz, Marmar, Weiss, DeWitt, & Rosenbaum (1984)	O	TAS	A	Impact of Event Scale Stress Response Rating Symptom Checklist-90 Brief Psychiatric Rating Scale Patterns of Individual Change Scales	O,C	12	Dynamic	.05		52
3	Marmar, Weiss, & Gaston (1989)	O	CALTRAS	A	Patterns of Individual Change Scales Symptom Checklist-90	O,C	12	Dynamic	.07	.06	52
4	Horvath (1981)	C,T	WAI	E	Client's Post-Therapy Questionnaire Therapist's Post-Therapy Questionnaire	C,T	10	Various	.47		29
5	Kokotovic & Tracey (1990)	C,T	WAI	E	Premature Termination	C	4[c]	Various	.09		144
6	Luborsky, Crits-Christoph, Alexander, Margolis, & Cohen, (1983)	O	HAr HAcs	E,L	Rated Benefits Residual Gain "Success, Satisfaction, and Improvement"	C,T,O	52	Dynamic	.44		20
6	Morgan, Luborsky, Crits-Christoph, Curtis, & Solomon (1982)	O	HAr	E	Rated Benefits Residual Gain "Success, Satisfaction, and Improvement"	C,T,O	52	Dynamic	.56	.46	20
7	Luborsky, McLellan, Woody, O'Brien, & Auerbach (1985)	C	HAQ	E	Drug Use Employment Legal Status Psychological Function	C,O	14	Various	.64		77

TABLE 11.1. (*Continued*)

Data Set	Study	Alliance Rater[a]	Alliance Measure	Time	Outcome Measure	Rater	Treatment Sessions	Treatment Type	Study ES(r)	Set ES(r)	N
8	Moseley (1983)	C	WAI	E	Client's Post-Therapy Questionnaire Therapist's Post-Therapy Questionnaire	C	14	Various	.24		25
9	Gomes-Schwartz (1978)	O	VPPS	A	Overall Ratings MMPI Target Complaints	C,T,O	17	Various	.36		35
9	O'Malley, Suh, & Strupp (1983)	O	VPPS	E	Overall Ratings Target Complaints	C,T,O	25	Various	.39	.36	38
10	Marziali, Marmar, & Krupnick (1981)	O	TAS	A	Dynamic Change Stress Dynamic Outcome Impact of Event Scale Symptom Checklist-90	C	12	Dynamic	.5		10
11	Gaston, Marmar, Gallagher, & Thompson (1990)	C,T	CALPAS	E,L	Beck Depression Inventory	C	18	Various	.25		54
11	Marmar, Gaston, Gallagher, & Thompson (1989)	C,T	CALPAS	E	Beck Depression Inventory Hamilton Rating Scale for Depression	C,O	18	Various	.19	.22	54
12	Tichenor (1989)	C,T,O	CALPAS VTAS PEN WAI	A	Symptom Checklist-90 Target Complaints Hamilton Rating Scale for Depression Hamilton Rating Scale for Anxiety Tennessee Self Concept Scale	C,T,O	16	Various	.18		8
13	Greenberg & Webster (1982)	C	WAI	E	State-Trait Anxiety Inventory Target Complaints Scale of Indecision	C,T	6	Gestalt	.62		31
14	Marziali (1984)	C,T,O	TAS	A	Behavior Symptom Index Mood Scale Wisman Social Adjustment Scale Therapy Evaluation Questionnaire Global Outcome Patterns of Individual Change Scales	C,T,O	20	Dynamic	.19		42

No.	Study	Raters	Alliance Measures	Time	Outcome Measures	Raters	n	Orientation	r	N
15	Windholtz & Silberschatz (1988)	O	VPPS	A	Symptom Checklist-90 Target Complaint Global Assessment Scale Overall Change	C,T,O	16	Dynamic	.05	38
16	Rounsaville, Chevron, Prusof, Elkin, Imber, Sotsky, & Watkins (1987)	O	VPPS	E	Social Adjustment Scale Schedule for Affective Disorder Patient Self-Assessment	C,O	14	Cognitive[d]	.19	35
17	Saunders, Howard, & Orlinsky (1989)	C	TBS[c]	E	Session Quality Termination Outcome	C,O	26	Dynamic	.23	113
18	Eaton, Abeles, & Gutfreund (1988)	C,T	TARS	A	Symptom Checklist-90 Client's Post-Therapy Questionnaire Therapist's Post-Therapy Questionnaire	C,T	29	Dynamic	.04	40
19	Frank & Gunderson (1990)	T	AE	E	Premature Termination Compliance with Medication Recidivism Composite Outcome "Broad Index of Outcome"	C,T,O	52	Various	.28	143[f]
20	Safran & Wallner (1991)	C	WAI CALPAS	E	Symptom Checklist-90 Global Success Target Complaint Millon Multiaxial Clinical Inventory Beck Depression Inventory	C,T	20	Cognitive	.4	22

Key to abbreviations:

Raters: C = Client, T = Therapist, O = Observer.

Alliance Measures: WAI = Working Alliance Inventory, HAQ = Helping Alliance Questionnaire, HAr = Helping Alliance Rating, HAcs = Helping Alliance Counting Signs, CIS = Client Involvement Scale, VTAS = Vanderbilt Therapeutic Alliance Scale, TAS = Therapeutic Alliance Scale, VPPS = Vanderbilt Psychotherapy Process Scale, CALTRAS = California Therapeutic Alliance Rating System, CALPAS = California Psychotherapy Alliance Scales, PEN = Penn Helping Alliance Rating Scale, TBS = Therapeutic Bond Scale, AE = Active Engagement.

Time of Assessment: E = Early alliance, L = Late alliance, A = Averaged or midphase alliance.

[b] Up to 25 sessions.

[c] Four or more sessions.

[d] Short-term interpersonal psychotherapy (Klerman, 1984).

[e] The Working Alliance subscale of the Therapeutic Bond Scale.

[f] Some of the results are based on fewer subjects.

271

relations was significantly different from zero, but the differences between these values were not statistically reliable.

Recently, alliance-outcome relationship strengths across three different, manualized psychotherapies (behavioral, cognitive-behavioral, and interpersonal) and drug therapy were contrasted directly. This study was part of a multisite research project investigating the efficacy of different methods (including psychoactive pharmaceutical agents) of treating depression. It was discovered that alliance and outcome were correlated ($p < .01$) for each treatment but the differences between the various treatments were not statistically reliable (Krupnick, Stotsky, Simmens, & Moyer, 1992). This finding is of particular note because it suggests that even the impact of a psychoactive drug may be enhanced by a positive patient-doctor alliance.

Different Outcomes

A related question is whether the alliance predicts certain types of outcomes better (or exclusively) and is less prognasticative of other therapy results. Horvath and Symonds (1991) investigated a number of such possible biases: They compared therapist-, client-, and observer-reported outcome and alliance relations across 24 studies. The outcome-alliance correlations were the strongest for client-reported outcome data ($r = .21$) followed by therapists' assessment of the results of therapy ($r = .17$), with observers' outcome data, on the average, having only a weak relation ($r = .10$) to alliance. These relations change significantly if the data are disaggregated using the *source* of alliance report as a sorting variable: Clients' alliance score predicts their own outcome assessment best ($r = .31$), closely followed by observers' outcome ($r = .29$); therapists' rated outcome was the least predictable ($r = .22$). Observers' alliance evaluation was most positively linked to therapists' outcome ($r=.31$), followed by the relation with client's outcome ($r = .20$); and their own (observers') outcome ratings were least predictable. As previously noted, therapist's alliance scores are the least related to any of the outcome indexes: Across the same group of studies, the correlations were .13 (client-rated outcome), $-.04$ (therapist's outcome), and $-.17$ (observer-rated outcome).

Horvath and Symonds explored another possible bias: whether a "self-fulfilling prophecy" factor was inflating the alliance outcome relations. Would basing the alliance and outcome data on the same source lead to a positive method bias (Campbell & Fiske, 1959)? In fact, such contamination does not seem to be an important factor: They disaggregated the data in their meta-analysis according to whether the alliance/outcome relation was based on *homogeneous* (same rater providing relationship and outcome data) or *heterogeneous* (outcome and alliance score provided by different raters) sources. It was discovered that the 22 alliance/outcome correlations based on the homogeneous studies had an average value of $r = .21$[6] whereas the 32

---

[6] Effect size based on correlation weighted by sample size.

results based on heterogeneous designs yielded $r = .18$. While that later coefficient is of lesser magnitude, the difference between these results is not statistically significant.

Lastly, certain aspects of outcome may be more dependent on the alliance than others (Gelso & Carter, 1985). A review of the available data indicates that researchers have investigated a broad cross section of improvement criteria including hard data such as drug use and recidivism (Luborsky, McLellan, Woody, O'Brien, & Auerbach, 1985), social adjustment (Rounsaville et al., 1987), psychodiagnostic evaluations (Krupnick et al., 1992; Windholtz & Silbershatz, 1988), as well as client's and therapist's subjective ratings of global improvement (Eaton, Abeles, & Gutfreund, 1988). In general, the alliance seems to predict outcomes better if the evaluation is tailored to the individual client such as the Target Complaint measure (TC; Battle et al., 1966) than to assessments of symptomatic change such as the SCL-90 (Derogatis, Rickels, & Rock, 1976). A reanalysis of Horvath's (1991) data suggests that the eight studies that used the TC as an outcome measure had an average correlation with alliance of .30; the same correlation for the SCL-90 was .15 (N of seven studies). At first glance, it may appear that the self-rated outcome might be a less reliable index of improvement and thus easier to forecast than the psychometrically more rigorous rating scales. This is not always the case, however; one of the most successful predictions of therapeutic gain was documented by Luborsky and his colleagues. In this study, the correlation of alliance and behavioral indexes such as drug use, employment, and legal status was .65 (Luborsky, McLellan, Woody, O'Brien, & Auerbach, 1985), one of the highest relationships documented. Moreover, the relatively lower correlation between symptom-based outcome indicators (such as the SCL-90) and the alliance may be due to the rather uniform response of these indexes in the early phases of treatment regardless of the ultimate results of the therapy (Orlinsky & Howard, 1986).

PREDISPOSITIONAL FACTORS

From the clinician's perspective, one of the most crucial questions about the alliance is the extent to which the client's or the therapist's prior characteristics influence the quality of the relationship that eventually develops between them. As noted in the preceding chapters, historically the alliance was linked to positive transference (Freud, 1912; Gelso & Fretz, 1992) and was thought to be based on the unconscious projection of the client's early relationships. Later conceptualizations emphasized the influence of the conscious in-therapy transactions on the alliance (see Bordin, Chapter 1, this volume); however, the client's response to the therapist's attempt to forge a bond and establish mutually endorsed goals may still be tinted by dispositions stemming from prior relationships (Hatcher, 1990; Mallinckrodt, 1992; Henry & Strupp, Chapter 3, this volume). This suggestion is not incompatible with the pantheoretical formulations of the alliance: If we acknowledge the potential impact of these predispositions, it becomes clear that the therapist's awareness of these factors and her skill in dealing with them may be important variables in determining the success of therapy. Likewise, it has been suggested that therapists may also bring to the relationship important relational bias that can block or forestall the development of an optimal therapeutic relationship (see Henry & Strupp, Chapter 3; Safran, Muran, & Wallner Samstag, Chapter 10, this volume). Techniques aimed at the initial development and subsequent repair of the alliance would depend on the degree of influence of these predispositions in determining the quality of the alliance. Although the data are limited, some empirical research has been done to examine the relation of some of these predispositional factors and the alliance.

Client's Predisposing Characteristics

In an earlier report (Horvath, 1990), I summarized the results of 11 studies that dealt with the impact of client pretreatment characteristics on the alliance. A broad assortment of client characteristics was investigated; to make the interpretation of the data easier, these factors were grouped into three categories: (a) interpersonal capacities or skills, (b) intrapersonal dynamics, and (c) diagnostic features. The interpersonal category included measures of quality of the clients' social relationships (e.g., Wallner Samstag, Muran, Zindel, Segal, & Schuman, 1992), quality of family relations (e.g., Kokotovic & Tracey, 1990), and indexes of stressful life events (e.g., Luborsky et al., 1983). The intrapersonal category subsumes measures of clients' motivation (e.g., Marmar, Weiss, & Gaston, 1989), psychological status (e.g., Ryan & Cicchetti, 1985), quality of object relations (e.g., Piper et al., 1991), and attitudes (e.g., Kokotovic & Tracey, 1990). Diagnostic feature refers to the severity of the client's problem in the beginning of treatment (e.g., Luborsky, Crits-Christoph, Alexander, Margolis, & Cohen, 1983) or to prognostic indexes (e.g., Klee, Abeles, & Muller, 1990).

A meta-analysis of these investigations indicates that both intrapersonal and interpersonal client pretreatment characteristics have similar impact on the alliance. The average correlation coefficient (weighted by sample size) between these variables and alliance was $r = .3$ and $r = .32$, respectively. Both these values are statistically significant at the $p < .05$ level. Thus, clients who have difficulty maintaining social relationships or have poor family relationships prior to the commencement of therapy are less likely to develop strong alliances. Similarly, patients with a pretherapy pattern of negative expectation for success or poor object relations, who score high on measures of defensiveness, hostility, dominance, are more likely to end up with poor alliance in therapy. Severity of symptoms, on the other hand, appears to have little impact on the ability to develop a good therapeutic relationship.

In a study typical of these investigations, Piper and colleagues (Piper et al., 1991) examined the relation between clients' quality of object relations, six aspects of current interpersonal functioning, the level of the alliance, and three posttreatment and follow-up outcome indicators. Their results indicate a link between clients' early object relations and their subsequent ability to develop a positive alliance: Both the quality of object relations and the alliance were correlated significantly with outcome ($r = .23$). However, the relation between the quality of the client's *current* relationships was not predictive of the alliance. Overall, the alliance was a superior predictor of outcome compared with the quality of early object relations, suggesting that the alliance may be influenced but not determined by early relationship experiences. The data are also consistent with the notion that the impact of the quality of early object relations is strongest in the beginning of therapy and likely waning in the later phases.

A number of important unanswered questions remain with respect to the impact of client pretreatment factors: Do these variables affect the alliance only at the beginning phase of treatment or throughout therapy? This question has crucial practical implications: Therapists' strategies would depend on whether the deleterious effects of poor object relations impact only the initial building of the alliance or also its subsequent maintenance. Another puzzle waiting for an answer is the degree of specificity of these factors: Do poor object relations, for example, damage the alliance most when specific topics or core relational issues are dealt with, or are the influences of these pretherapy variables pervasive in all aspects of the therapeutic work? I will return to these questions later in this chapter.

Therapist's Predisposing Characteristics

Historically, in the psychodynamic literature, there was a great deal of emphasis on the characterological development of the therapist and its influence on therapy process. Subsequently, these factors received less attention, particularly from researchers; energy has been focused on the precise definition of specific intervention modalities, the development of manuals facilitating the implementation of a circumscribed set of techniques, and the development of more sophisticated research designs. The major thrust of this research is the quest to better understand the differential efficacy of treatments within a variety of contexts.

More recently, therapy processes, including the influence and function of the relationship variables such as the alliance, have been examined by researchers but predominantly from the client's perspective. Perhaps because early attempts to link therapist characteristics with outcome were less successful than studies using clients' data (Mitchell, Bozart, & Krauft, 1977), the impact of a variety of therapist characteristics, including relational capacity have been comparatively ignored. Research on the impact of therapists' pretreatment characteristics on the alliance is only beginning to appear in the literature: Henry and Strupp (Chapter 3, this volume) discuss their analysis of therapist-client transactions using a circumplex model (SASB). They define alliance in terms of transactions that are affiliating, autonomy granting, and low on the hostile control dimension of the SASB. After the SASB profiles of therapists with good and poor alliances were analyzed, they concluded that therapists' internal representation of past relationships (introjects) has a strong influence on the quality of alliance developed with at least some of their clients. Their research suggests that a tendency to recreate the original interpersonal patterns in current relationships may be a factor not only for clients but for therapists as well.

Although specific pretherapy qualities were not monitored, the investigation by Safran and his colleagues indirectly supports the preceding hypothesis (Safran, Muran, & Wallner Samstag, 1992). Their results indicate that the therapist's ability to accept responsibility for his or her own relational struggles in therapy is a precursor of alliance improvement in the session. In another study currently in progress, the relation between therapist attachment styles and the ability to develop the bond aspect of the alliance is being directly assessed for the first time (G. M. McKee, personal communication, 1993).

An important gap in our current knowledge is whether these client and therapist predispositions are independent or interactive. Researchers thus far have monitored client and therapist factors independently, and the possibility that either specific relational issues or particular client personality structures trigger negative therapist response has not been directly investigated. There is, however, no lack of a theoretical framework for the generation of such hypotheses (e.g., Bowen, 1978). The results of such investigations might reveal possible interactions among specific therapist-client variable combinations and therapy tasks that prognosticate progress or deterioration in therapy. Task analytic studies of these transactions (Greenberg, 1984) would also permit an examination of client-therapist configurations that result in the therapist's midjudging the true status of the alliance. We might also be able to identify combinations of factors making early disengagement from therapy more likely. Most importantly, the ability to predict these relational failures might provide us with important clues about the change process itself; we would be able to generate and evaluate hypotheses probing the parameters of psychotherapy as corrective relational experience.

THE ALLIANCE ACROSS TIME

The variability of the alliance along the time dimension has been investigated across two somewhat independent dimensions: the *qualities* of the relationship that indicate positive alliance at different phases of therapy, and the changes in the *strength* of the alliance over time. Although both these issues are important theoretically and clinically, each speaks to a distinct aspect of the therapy process and there has been some confusion in the literature as to which aspect is being investigated. In the review that follows, I will attempt to identify these components distinctly and integrate the findings available to date.

Luborsky examined the *distinct qualities* of the therapist-client relationship that predicted positive outcome at different points in therapy (Luborsky, 1976). As noted earlier, he described two clusters of relationship attributes—Type 1 and Type 2 alliances—corresponding to different phases in therapy. The earlier phase is ". . . based on the patient's experiencing the therapist as supportive and helpful with himself [the client] as a recipient," whereas alliance in the latter part of therapy is "[the client having] a sense of working together in a joint struggle against what is impeding the patient. . . . on shared responsibility for working out treatment goals. . . . a sense of 'we-ness'" (p. 94).

The variations in the *strength* of the alliance over time has been investigated using two different paradigms:

1. Group studies (e.g., Bachelor, 1992; Gaston & Ring, 1992; Greenberg & Horvath, 1991; Horvath, 1991). These investigations, in essence, ask the question: Are there predictable, systematic shifts in the alliance strength corresponding to different time-phases in therapy?
2. Longitudinal studies (e.g., Horvath & Marx, 1991; Safran et al., 1992). These investigations have pursued two questions: Are there fluctuations in alliance over time (within or across sessions)? And, do these changes in the alliance represent a pattern stereotypic of a particular therapy, or do they signal a reaction to specific therapy events?

The results of the group studies are equivocal: Gaston and Marmar (in press) and Krupnick et al. (1992) did not find strong evidence of systematic shifts in the strength of the alliance over time; two investigations, however (Bachelor, 1992; Greenberg & Horvath, 1991), did note such differences. In addition, Horvath and Symonds (1991) found early alliance to be a slightly more powerful prognosticator of outcome ($r = .3$) than alliance measures averaged across sessions or taken toward the middle of treatment ($r = .2$). Although the differences between these values are small, subsequent investigations (DeRubeis & Feeley, 1991; Piper et al., 1991; Piper, Azim, Joyce, & McCallum, 1991) appear to confirm this trend. Horvath et al. suggested that the apparent anomaly of early alliance being a better predictor of success than later assessments may be due to more individual variability (i.e., session-to-session fluctuations) in alliance strength during this phase.

Longitudinal within-case analyses of the levels of the alliance in more and less successful therapy (e.g., Horvath & Marx, 1991; Safran, Crocker, McMain, & Murray, 1990) support the hypothesis that the alliance is labile, particularly in the middle phase of therapy. There is likely an early, developmental alliance-building phase possibly followed by rupture-repair cycles in successful therapies predicted by Zetzel (1956) and Bordin (1989). There are also some preliminary indications that we may be able to identify and describe some specific types of transaction that lead to positive alliance development. Some of these studies and the findings are described in the following sections.

THERAPIST ACTIONS INFLUENCING THE ALLIANCE

It is widely accepted that a good relationship between client and therapist enhances the effectiveness of therapy (Freud, 1912; Goldfried, 1980; Rogers, 1957). Success has been much more limited, however, in demonstrating links between specific therapist's actions, improvement in the relationship, and better outcome in psychotherapy. Throughout this volume, it has been suggested that the concept of the alliance is a theoretical improvement over previous conceptualizations of the active ingredient of the relationship. In this chapter, furthermore, I have reviewed the growing body of evidence supporting the links between positive alliance and good outcome (the second part of the previously proposed chain). However, the study of the relationship must ultimately focus on the specification of actions that promote and maintain the alliance to enable the therapist to use this knowledge for the benefit of the client.

The road leading from identification of broad generalizations, such as the therapist must show "serious interest" and "sympathetic understanding" (Freud, 1912), or even more experientially defined constructs, such as "empathy" or "positive regard" (Rogers, 1957), to the narrow specification behaviors or transactional sequences is a long and difficult one in psychotherapy research. Therapy is highly idiosyncratic even when implemented according to rigorous, manualized specifications; clients' understanding of therapists' behaviors can be reconstructed only if we take into account the contexts in which they occur (Horvath, Marx, & Kamann, 1990). Nonetheless, progress has been made in linking therapist activities to changes in alliance.

Safran and his colleagues proposed a model specifying a sequence of therapist behaviors that will heal ruptures in the alliance (see Chapter 3, this volume). The essence of this model is the direct focus on the relationship in therapy. The benefit of focusing on the client-therapist relation rather than outside-of-therapy events was observed by several other investigators as well (Coady, 1988; Foreman & Marmar, 1985; Marziali, 1984a).

Henry and Strupp (see Chapter 3, this volume) investigated the quality rather than the content of therapist-initiated transactions. They identified three dimensions on the SASB scales (affiliative, autonomy granting, not hostile or controlling) that were associated with client improvement. Interestingly they also report that efforts to train therapists to produce more of these responses appear to have had limited success.

The effect of interpretations on the alliance has also been investigated. The general consensus appears to be that neither the frequency nor the accuracy of interpretations bears a direct relation to the status of the alliance (Crits-Christoph, Cooper, & Luborsky, 1988; Gaston & Ring, 1992). In a recent study, however (Crits-Christoph et al., 1988), links were discovered between a specific type of accurate interpretations (those dealing with wish and response from others) and alliance improvement.

FUTURE DIRECTIONS

I noted earlier that the development of psychometrically sound measures to assess the alliance has played an important role in facilitating research. These assessment tools, in practice, define the construct under investigation. Researchers need to search for a more thorough consensus on the precise identity of this construct and delineate more clearly the alliance from related concepts. Specifically, it is important that investigators not confuse the alliance with the broader term "relationship." If such distinctions are not observed, the value of the research will be much reduced by its lack of specificity. It may well be that under the broad umbrella of the therapeutic relationship, several important relational constructs will have to be accommodated. Gelso and Carter (1985) have proposed one such model using the alliance, transference, and the real relationship as constituent components. Although this model needs refinement in the light of the research results, it seems to represent a desirable trend. The complete or full model of therapeutic relation needs to accommodate (a) the impact of prior relationships, (b) the alliance, (c) compatibilities and similarity of expectations based on the sociocultural background of the participants.

It was also noted previously that alliance based on clients', therapists', and observers' reports do not overlap fully. If these perspectives do in fact differ, which point of view speaks for the "real alliance"? Alternatively, if each of these points of view reflects a different aspect of the alliance, how do these components fit or complement one another? There is evidence supporting the construct validity of the client- and observer-based instruments (Horvath & Symonds, 1991); however, most of the data available link alliance score with outcome only. While this relation is a necessary element to claim validity, it alone may not be sufficient to link these instruments to the theoretical construct they wish to measure. More research is needed to demonstrate directly that the content (items) of these measures adequately and unbiasedly represent the theoretical construct (the alliance) they purport to measure.

Another issue currently confronting researchers is the determination of the most appropriate time lens for investigating the alliance: Is the construct more usefully and accurately encapsulated by moment-to-moment micro-evaluations (e.g., see Chapter 9, this volume). Alternatively, it can be argued that the natural framework of a session is the logical time window on the alliance. This latter perspective is utilized by most observer-rated alliance research, though in some instances, these ratings are summed over or averaged over a number of sessions (e.g., Krupnick et al., 1992). However, even when clients and therapists are asked to evaluate a single session, it is reasonable to assume that their responses may be significantly contaminated by impressions retained from previous sessions. What is the meaning of such summative ratings spanning a number of sessions or a retrospective evaluation of the alliance in a treatment as a whole? These questions raise both theoretical and empirical issues. Whether the alliance is construed as a traitlike phenomenon (as one extreme) or as a process variable influencing the moment-by-moment response of the client to the therapy situation matters a great deal in terms of the role of the alliance in clinical work. If the alliance is construed as a *prerequisite* to the client's engagement in therapeutic tasks that are, in turn, directly responsible for change, it may be most appropriate to see the ideal alliance as steady state, thus traitlike. On the other hand, if the work on the stresses and ruptures of the alliance is endemic and central to the therapeutic work itself, then the ebb and flow of the alliance is the most important phenomenon and the process perspective is more accurate and useful.

Past research has been less than clear on these issues and some of the divergence in findings may result from this lack of clarity. It seems desirable that research on the alliance should follow two distinct but complementary paths: The first one is the intensive microanalytic exploration of events that impact on the alliance. There is evidence to suggest that clients process and interpret transactions very selectively (Horvath, Marx, & Kamann, 1990); we need to identify markers of the events that influence the alliance and explore the contextual significance of these transactions. We need to ask questions about how the content of these transactions relates to both the client's and therapist's past relational experiences and how these factors interact in therapy. Second, the qualitative shifts in more and less successful therapies need to be examined within particular therapy modalities. In examining this issue, researchers may need to use a wider lens and incorporate other possible components of the therapeutic relationship to ascertain whether the alliance is particularly important in certain phase(s) and less important (or perhaps plays a different role) in other phases of the change process.

REFERENCES

Adler, J. V. (1988). *A study of the working alliance in psychotherapy.* Unpublished doctoral dissertation, University of British Columbia, Vancouver, Canada.

Agnew, R. M., & Shapiro, D. A. (1988). *Therapist-client relationships: Development of a measure* (SAPU Memo No. 765). University of Sheffield, England.

Alexander, L. B., & Luborsky, L. (1987). The Penn Helping Alliance Scales. In L. S. Greenberg & W. M. Pinsof (Eds.), *The psychotherapeutic process: A research handbook* (pp. 325–356). New York: Guilford.

Bachelor, A. (1991). Comparison and relationship to outcome of diverse dimensions of the helping alliance as seen by client and therapist. *Psychotherapy: Theory, Research, and Practice, 28,* 534–539.

Bachelor, A. (1992, June). *Variability of dimensions of the therapeutic alliance and alliance predictors of improvement.* Paper presented at the annual meeting of the Society for Psychotherapy Research, Berkeley, CA.

Barends, A. (1992). *Development and validation of patients' and therapists' measures of working alliance in psychotherapy.* Paper presented at the annual meeting of the Society for Psychotherapy Research, Berkeley, CA.

Battle, L. C., Imber, S. D., Hoen-Saric, R., Stone, A. R., Nash, E. H., & Frank, J. D. (1966). Target complaints as criteria of improvement. *American Journal of Psychiatry, 20,* 184–192.

Bordin, E. S. (1975). *The working alliance: Basis for a general theory of psychotherapy.* Paper presented at the annual meeting of the Society for Psychotherapy Research, Washington, DC.

Bordin, E. S. (1976). The generalizability of the psychoanalytic concept of the working alliance. *Psychotherapy: Theory, Research, and Practice, 16,* 252–260.

Bordin, E. S. (1980). *Of human bonds that bind or free.* Paper presented at the annual meeting of the Society for Psychotherapy Research, Pacific Grove, CA.

Bordin, E. S. (1989, June). *Building therapeutic alliances: The base for integration.* Paper presented at the annual meeting of the Society for Psychotherapy Research, Berkeley, CA.

Bowen, M. (1978). *Family therapy in clinical practice.* New York: Aronson.

Campbell, D. T., & Fiske, D. W. (1959). Convergent and discriminant validation by the multitrait-multimethod matrix. *Psychological Bulletin, 56,* 81–105.

Coady, N. (1988). *Prediction of outcome from interpersonal process: A study of the worker-client relationship.* Paper presented at the annual meeting of the Society for Psychotherapy Research, Santa Fe, NM.

Crits-Christoph, P., Cooper, A., & Luborsky, L. (1988). The accuracy of therapists' interpretations and the outcome of dynamic psychotherapy. *Archives of General Psychiatry, 56,* 490–495.

Cummings, A. L., Martin, J., Hallberg, E., & Slemon, A. (1992). Memory for therapeutic events, session effectiveness, and working alliance in short-term counseling. *Journal of Counseling Psychology, 39,* 306–312.

Derogatis, L. R., Rickels, K., & Rock, A. F. (1976). The SCL-90 and the MMPI: A step in the validation of a new self-report scale. *British Journal of Psychiatry, 128,* 280–289.

DeRubeis, R. J., & Feely, M. (1991). Determinants of change in cognitive therapy for depression. *Cognitive Therapy and Research, 14,* 469–482.

Eaton, T. T., Abeles, N., & Gutfreund, M. J. (1988). Therapeutic alliance and outcome: Impact of treatment length and pretreatment symptomology. *Psychotherapy: Theory, Research, and Practice, 25,* 536–542.

Foreman, S., & Marmar, R. C. (1985). Therapist actions that address initially poor therapeutic alliances in psychotherapy. *American Journal of Psychiatry, 142:8,* 922–926.

Frank, J. D. (1961). *Persuasion and healing.* Baltimore, MD: Johns Hopkins Press.

Frank, A. F., & Gunderson, J. G. (1990). The role of the therapeutic alliance in the treatment of schizophrenia. *Archives of General Psychiatry, 47,* 228–236.

Freud, S. (1912). The dynamics of transference. In J. Starchey (Ed.), *The standard edition of the complete psychological works of Sigmund Freud* (pp. 99–108). London, England: Hogarth Press.

Frieswyk, S. H., Allen, J. G., Colson, D. B., Coyne, L., Gabbard, G. O., Horwitz, L., & Newsom, G. (1986). Therapeutic alliance: Its place as process and outcome variable in dynamic psychotherapy research. *Journal of Consulting and Clinical Psychology, 1,* 32–39.

Gaston, L. (1990). The concept of the alliance and its role in psychotherapy: Theoretical and empirical considerations. *Psychotherapy: Theory, Research, and Practice, 27,* 143–153.

Gaston, L. (1991). Reliability and criterion-related validity of the California Psychotherapy Alliance Scales—patient version. *Psychological Assessment, 3,* 68–74.

Gaston, L., Marmar, C., Gallagher, D., & Thompson, L. W. (1990). *Alliance prediction of outcome: Beyond initial symptomology and symptomatic change.* Paper presented at the annual meeting of the Society for Psychotherapy Research, Philadelphia, PA.

Gaston, L., & Ring, J. M. (1992). Preliminary results on the Inventory of Therapeutic Strategies. *Journal of Psychotherapy Research and Practice, 1,* 1–13.

Gaston, L., & Ring, J. M. (In press). Preliminary results on the Inventory of Therapeutic Strategies. *Journal of Psychotherapy.*

Gelso, C. J., & Carter, J. A. (1985). The relationship in counseling and psychotherapy: Components, consequences, and theoretical antecedents. *The Counseling Psychologist, 2,* 155–243.

Gelso, C. J., & Fretz, B. R. (1992). *Counseling psychology.* New York: Harcourt Brace Jovanovich.

Goldfried, M. R. (1980). Toward the delineation of therapeutic change principles. *American Psychologist, 35,* 991–999.

Gomes-Schwartz, B. (1978). Effective ingredients in psychotherapy: Prediction of outcome from process variables. *Journal of Consulting and Clinical Psychology, 46,* 1023–1035.

Greenberg, L. S. (1984). Task analysis: The general approach. In L. N. Rice & L. S. Greenberg (Eds.), *Patterns of change.* New York: Guilford Press.

Greenberg, L. S., & Adler, J. (1989, June). *The working alliance and outcome: A client report study.* Paper presented at the annual meeting of the Society for Psychotherapy Research.

Greenberg, L. S., & Horvath, A. O. (1991, June). *The role of the therapeutic alliance in psychotherapy research.* Paper presented at the annual meeting of the Society for Psychotherapy Research, Lyon, France.

Greenberg, L. S., & Webster, M. C. (1982). Resolving decisional conflict by Gestalt two-chair dialogue: Relating process to outcome. *Journal of Counseling Psychology, 29,* 468–477.

Hartley, D. E., & Strupp, H. H. (1983). The therapeutic alliance: Its relationship to outcome in brief psychotherapy. In J. Masling (Ed.), *Empirical studies in analytic theories* (pp. 1–37). Hillside, NJ: Erlbaum.

Hatcher, R. (1990). *Transference and the therapeutic alliance.* Paper presented at the annual meeting of the Society for Psychotherapy Research, Wintergreen, VA.

Horowitz, M. J., Marmar, C., Weiss, D. S., DeWitt, K. N., & Rosenbaum, R. (1984). Brief psychotherapy of bereavement reactions: The relationship of process to outcome. *Archives of General Psychiatry, 41,* 438–448.

Horvath, A. O. (1981). *An exploratory study of the working alliance: Its measurement and relationship to outcome.* Unpublished doctoral dissertation, University of British Columbia, Vancouver, Canada.

Horvath, A. O. (1982). *Working Alliance Inventory (Revised).* Unpublished manuscript No. 82.1 Simon Fraser University.

Horvath, A. O. (1991, June). *What do we know about the alliance and what do we still have to find out?* Paper presented at the annual meeting of the Society for Psychotherapy Research, Lyon, France.

Horvath, A. O., Gaston, L., & Luborsky, L. (in press). The role of alliance in psychotherapy. In L. Luborsky, N. Miller, & J. Barber (Eds.), *Psychotherapy: Research and practice.* Basic Books. New York.

Horvath, A. O., & Greenberg, L. S. (1987). Development of the Working Alliance Inventory. In L. S. Greenberg & W. M. Pinsof (Eds.), *The psychotherapeutic process: A research handbook.* New York: Guilford Press.

Horvath, A. O., & Luborsky, L. (1993). The role of the therapeutic alliance in psychotherapy. *Journal of Consulting and Clinical Psychology, 61,* 561–573.

Horvath, A. O., & Marx, R. W. (1991). The development and decay of the working alliance during time-limited counselling. *Canadian Journal of Counselling, 24,* 240–259.

Horvath, A. O., Marx, R. W., & Kamann, A. M. (1990). Thinking about thinking in therapy: An examination of clients' understanding of their therapists' intentions. *Journal of Consulting and Clinical Psychology, 58,* 614–621.

Horvath, A. O., & Symonds, B. D. (1990, June). *Relation Among Counsellor and Client Variables, Working Alliance, and Outcome in Counselling and Psychotherapy: An Empirical Review.* Paper presented at the annual meeting of the Society for Psychotherapy Research, Wintergreen, VA.

Horvath, A. O., & Symonds, B. D. (1991). Relation between working alliance and outcome in psychotherapy: A meta-analysis. *Journal of Counseling Psychology, Journal of Counseling Psychology, 38,* 139–149.

Kiesler, D. (1973). *The process of psychotherapy: Empirical foundations and systems of analysis.* Hawthorne, NY: Aldine.

Klee, M. R., Abeles, N., & Muller, R. T. (1990). Therapeutic Alliance: Early indicators, course, and outcome. *Psychotherapy: Theory, Research, and Practice, 27,* 166–174.

Kokotovic, A. M., & Tracey, T. J. (1990). Working alliance in the early phase of counseling. *Journal of Counseling Psychology, 37,* 16–21.

Kolden, G. G. (1990, June). *Further explorations with the generic model: Cross validation studies.* Paper presented at the annual meeting of the Society for Psychotherapy Research, Wintergreen, VA.

Krupnick, J., Stotsky, S., Simmens, S., & Moyer, J. (1992, June). *The role of therapeutic alliance in psychotherapy and pharmacotherapy outcome: Findings in the NIMH Treatment of Depression Collaborative Research Program.* Paper presented at the annual meeting of the Society for Psychotherapy Research, Berkeley, CA.

Luborsky, L. (1976). Helping alliances in psychotherapy. In J. L. Cleghorn (Ed.), *Successful psychotherapy* (pp. 92–116). New York: Brunner/Mazel.

Luborsky, L. (1990). *Therapeutic alliance measures as predictors of future benefits of psychotherapy.* Paper presented at the annual meeting of the Society for Psychotherapy Research, Wintergreen, VA.

Luborsky, L., Crits-Christoph, P., Alexander, L., Margolis, M., & Cohen, M. (1983). Two helping alliance methods for predicting outcomes of psychotherapy: A counting signs vs. a global rating method. *Journal of Nervous and Mental Disease, 171,* 480–491.

Luborsky, L., McLellan, A. T., Woody, G. E., O'Brien, C. P., & Auerbach, A. (1985). Therapist success and its determinants. *Archives of General Psychiatry, 42,* 602–611.

Luborsky, L., Singer, B., & Luborsky, L. (1975). Comparative studies of psychotherapies: "Is it true that everybody has won and all must have prizes"? *Archives of General Psychiatry, 32,* 995–1008.

Mallinckrodt, B. (1992). Client's representations of childhood emotional bonds with parents social support, and formation of the working alliance. *Journal of Counseling Psychology, 38,* 401–409.

Mallinckrodt, B. (1993). Session impact, working alliance, and treatment outcome in brief counseling. *Journal of Counseling Psychology, 40,* 25–32.

Marmar, C. R., Gaston, L., Gallager, D., & Thompson, L. W. (1989). Therapeutic alliance and outcome in behavioral, cognitive, and brief dynamic psychotherapy in late-life depression. *Journal of Nervous and Mental Disease, 177,* 464–472.

Marmar, C. R., Horowitz, M. J., Weiss, D. S., & Marziali, E. (1986). The development of the Therapeutic Alliance Rating System. In L. S. Greenberg & W. M. Pinsof (Eds.), *The psychotherapeutic process: A research handbook* (pp. 367–390). New York: Guilford Press.

Marmar, C., Weiss, D. S., & Gaston, L. (1989). Toward the validation of the California Therapeutic Alliance Rating System. *Psychological Assessment: A Journal of Consulting and Clinical Psychology, 1,* 46–52.

Marziali, E. (1984a). Prediction of outcome of brief psychotherapy from therapist interpretive interventions. *Archives of General Psychiatry, 41,* 301–305.

Marziali, E. (1984b). Three viewpoints on the Therapeutic Alliance Scales similarities, differences and associations with psychotherapy outcome. *Journal of Nervous and Mental Disease, 172,* 417–423.

Marziali, E., Marmar, C., & Krupnick, J. (1981). Therapeutic Alliance Scales: Development and relationship to psychotherapy outcome. *American Journal of Psychiatry, 138,* 361–364.

Mitchell, K. M., Bozart, J. D., & Krauft, C. C. (1977). *Reappraisal of the therapeutic effectiveness of accurate empathy, non-possessive warmth, and genuineness.* In A. S. Gurman & A. M. Razin (Eds.), Effective psychotherapy. New York: Pergamon Press.

Morgan, R., Luborsky, L., Crits-Christoph, P., Curtis, H., & Solomon, J. (1982). Predicting the outcomes of psychotherapy by the Penn Helping Alliance Rating Method. *Archives of General Psychiatry, 39,* 397–402.

Moseley, D. (1983). *The therapeutic relationship and its association with outcome.* Unpublished master's thesis, University of British Columbia, Vancouver, Canada.

O'Malley, S. S., Suh, C. S., & Strupp, H. H. (1983). The Vanderbilt Psychotherapy Process Scale: A report on the scale development and a process-outcome study. *Journal of Consulting and Clinical Psychology, 51,* 581–586.

Orlinsky, D. E., & Howard, K. I. (1986). The psychological interior of psychotherapy: Explorations with the Therapy Session Report Questionnaires. In L. S. Greenberg & W. M. Pinsof (Eds.), *The psychotherapeutic process: A research handbook.* New York: Guilford Press.

Piper, W. E., Azim, H. F. A., Joyce, A. S., & McCallum, M. (1991). Transference interpretations, therapeutic alliance and outcome in short-term individual therapy. *Archives of General Psychiatry, 48,* 946–953.

Piper, W. E., Azim, H. F. A., Joyce, A. S., McCallum, M., Nixon, G. W. H., & Segal, P. S. (1991). Quality of object relations vs. interpersonal functioning as predictor of therapeutic alliance and psychotherapy outcome. *Journal of Nervous and Mental Disease, 179,* 432–438.

Plotnicov, K. H. (1990). *Early termination from Counseling: The client's perspective.* Unpublished doctoral dissertation, University of Pittsburgh, PA.

Rice, L. N., & Greenberg, L. S. (1984). *Patterns of change: Intensive analysis of psychotherapy process.* New York: Guilford Press.

Rogers, C. R. (1951). *Client centered therapy.* Cambridge, Mass.: Riverside Press.

Rogers, C. R. (1957). The necessary and sufficient conditions of therapeutic personality change. *Journal of Consulting and Clinical Psychology, 22,* 95–103.

Rosenthal, R. (1987). *Judgment studies: Design, analysis, and meta-analysis.* Cambridge: Cambridge University Press.

Rosenthal, R. (1991). *Meta-Analytic procedures for social research* (rev. ed.). Beverly Hills, CA: Sage.

Rounsaville, B. J., Chevron, E. S., Prusof, B. A., Elkin, I., Imber, S., Sotsky, S., & Watkins, J. (1987). The relation between specific and general dimensions of the psychotherapy process in interpersonal psychotherapy of depression. *Journal of Consulting and Clinical Psychology, 55,* 379–384.

Ryan, E. R., & Cicchetti, D. V. (1985). Predicting quality of alliance in the initial psychotherapy interview. *Journal of Nervous and Mental Disease, 173,* 717–725.

Saburin, S., Hansell, J., Gutfreund, J., Gaston, L., & Marmar, C. R. (1990). *Reliability and validity of the three versions of the California Psychotherapy Alliance Scales (CALPAS).* Paper presented at the annual meeting of the Society for Psychotherapy Research, Wintergreen, VA.

Safran, J. D., Crocker, P., McMain, S., & Murray, P. (1990). The therapeutic alliance rupture as a therapy event for empirical investigation. *Psychotherapy: Theory, Research, and Practice, 27,* 154–165.

Safran, J. D., Muran, C. J., & Wallner Samstag, L. (1992, June). *A comparison of therapeutic alliance rupture resolution and nonresolution events.* Paper presented at the annual meeting of the Society for Psychotherapy Research, Berkeley, CA.

Safran, J. D., & Wallner, L. K. (1991). The relative predictive validity of two therapeutic alliance measures in cognitive therapy. *Psychological Assessment: A Journal of Consulting and Clinical Psychology, 3,* 188–195.

Salvio, M. A., Beutler, L. E., Wood, J. M., & Engle, D. (1992). The strength of the therapeutic alliance in three treatments for depression. *Psychotherapy Research, 2,* 31–36.

Saunders, S. M., Howard, K. I., & Orlinsky, D. E. (1989). The Therapeutic Bond Scales: Psychometric characteristics and relationship to treatment effectiveness. *Psychological Assessment: A Journal of Consulting and Clinical Psychology, 1,* 323–330.

Shadish, W. R., & Sweeney, R. B. (1992). Mediators and moderators in meta-analysis: There is a reason we don't let the dodo bird tell us which psychotherapies should have prizes. *Journal of Consulting and Clinical Psychology, 59,* 883–893.

Skinner, B. F. (1974). *About behaviorism.* New York: Knopf.

Smith, M. L., & Glass, G. V. (1977). Meta-analysis of psychotherapy outcome studies. *American Psychologist, 32,* 752–760.

Sterba, R. F. (1934). The fate of the ego in analytic therapy. *International Journal of Psychoanalysis, 115,* 117–126.

Stiles, W. B., Shapiro, D., & Elliot, R. (1986). Are all psychotherapies equivalent? *American Psychologist, 41,* 165–180.

Tichenor, V. (1989). *Working alliance: A measure comparison.* University of Maryland Unpublished doctoral dissertation Maryland, VA.

Tichenor, V., & Hill, C. E. (1989). A comparison of six measures of working alliance. *Psychotherapy: Theory, Research, and Practice, 26,* 195–199.

Tracey, T. J., Glidden, C. E., & Kokotovic, A. M. (1988). Factor structure of the Counselor Rating Form—Short. *Journal of Counseling Psychology, 35,* 330–335.

Wallner Samstag, L., Muran, C., Zindel, V., Segal, Z., & Schuman, C. (1992, June). *Patient pretreatment interpersonal problems and therapeutic alliance in short-term cognitive therapy.* Paper presented at the annual meeting of the Society for Psychotherapy Research, Berkeley, CA.

Watson, N. (1992, August). *The current empirical status of Rogers' theory.* Paper presented at the annual meeting of the American Psychological Association, Washington, DC.

Windholtz, M. J., & Silbershatz, G. (1988). Vanderbilt psychotherapy process scale: A replication with adult outpatient. *Journal of Clinical and Consulting Psychology, 56,* 56–60.

Zetzel, E. R. (1956). Current concepts of transference. *International Journal of Psychoanalysis, 37,* 369–376.

Author Index

Subject Index

Acceptance, 164
Active listening, 165
Affiliative autonomy granting, 65
Affiliative complementarity, 70–71
Affiliative control, 65
Affirming and understanding subscale, 235–236, 242
Agoraphobics, 137
Agreement, assessment of, 142
Alliance, generally:
  outcome and, *see* Alliance-outcome
  stages of, 3
  as technique, 61–63
  types of, *see specific types of alliance*
Alliance-outcome:
  generally, 5, 7
  measurement of, *see specific measurement scales*
  research:
    different outcomes, 272–273
    different treatments and, 268–272
    overall, 267–268
    trends, 45–46
Asserting and separating subscale, 235, 241
Associative tasks, 34
Attachment and separation, 17
Attributions, 35
Audiotapes, use of, 5, 230, 259

Barrett-Lennard Relationship Inventory (BLRI), 41, 140, 157
Basic science research:
  formal statement of assumption, 28
  task-oriented program
    implementation of, 28–30
    roots of, 31–35

Beck Depression Inventory (BDI):
  outcome assessment and, 146–147
  predictive success and, 41, 43, 94
  predictive validity of, 148
Behavior therapy:
  outcome studies, 96
  predictive success of, 41
  research regarding, 103
  tasks in, 16
Belittling and blaming subscale, 241
Bias:
  observation and, 6, 145
  positive method and, 272
  psychotherapy and, 52
  self-report questionnaires, 192
Bond(s), *see* Bonding
  client's sense of, 118
  defined, 111, 182
  integrative systems and, 182–184, 189
  tears and repairs, 186
  Working Alliance Inventory and, 115
Bonding:
  change goals and, 21–23
  theories regarding, 16–18
Borderline patients:
  clinical theory regarding, 200–203
  overview of, 199–200
  research regarding, 203
  ruptures and, 27
  single-case studies, 203–204
  strain and, 19, 27
  therapist role with, 200
  treatment interventions project:
    case example, 216–217
    generally, 204–206
    intervention and, collaboration shifts, 207

295